ALEXANDER POPE
AS CRITIC AND HUMANIST

ALEXANDER POPE
AS CRITIC AND HUMANIST

BY

AUSTIN WARREN

ASSISTANT PROFESSOR OF ENGLISH IN BOSTON UNIVERSITY

Princeton Studies in English
Number I

GLOUCESTER, MASS.
PETER SMITH
1963

To

M. L, W. D. and P. F. V.

Scripturus, neque te ut miretur turba labores,
Contentus paucis lectoribus . . . .

FOREWORD TO THE 1963 REPRINT

The only previous edition of *Pope as Critic* was published in 1929 and was exhausted within a year. I have repeatedly been asked to have it reissued 'photographically'; but, since I wanted to produce a revised edition in the hope of which I had made additions, subtractions, and stylistic 'improvements,' I refused.

Yet, since the book, despite its faults, is (along with being still useful) a modest landmark in Pope criticism,—chronologically the first of our century to treat the great poet neither as an enemy to Keats nor as a literary period-piece,—I now consent to its reissue on the granted condition of making it clear that the book is *reprinted* without opportunity to use the rich scholarship and criticism published since 1929 and to revise the method and style of my own early, uneven, yet (I think) still, in the main, sound monograph.

Austin Warren

The University of Michigan
January, 1963.

PREFACE

IN the twentieth-century return to eighteenth-century literature it cannot be said that the poets have fared as well as the writers of prose. The revival has attended Swift and Fielding and Smollett and Sterne, Johnson and Boswell and Goldsmith, rather than Pope and Prior and Thomson and Young. Arnold's dictum that Pope and Dryden were not really poets at all, but only the classics of an age of prose, is still an article of general subscription. Even to some of its advocates, eighteenth-century poetry appeals because of what is felt to be quaint and archaic rather than what is universal.

This book attempts to take the eighteenth century somewhat more at its own valuation, to apprehend more sympathetically its aims and standards. The neo-classicists have been found wanting both by the 'new humanists,' who charge them with being pseudo-classical, and by the practitioners of the historical method,, whose tacit assumptions are commonly romantic. We might defend the Augustans either by maintaining that they were genuinely humanistic or by asserting, from the fashionable vantage ground of historical scepticism, that neo-classicism will seem to future historians at least as dignified and satisfactory a reading of life as the substitutes the nineteenth century and our own have offered in its stead.

It is surprising but true that this is the first book to deal with Pope's criticism in its entirety. The *Essay on Criticism* has, of course, received much attention, and so have the Prefaces to Homer and Shakespeare. But there is much else in Pope which belongs to a definitive discussion of his taste and judgment as arbiter of literature—the pronouncements to Spence and to his correspondents, passages in the poems, and the *Observations on the Iliad*. This last-named collection of criticisms, much the most extensive work of Pope in the *genre*, has not been reprinted in its entirety since the eighteenth century, and appears not to be known by many scholars today. Nor has anyone been at the pains to study Pope's choice of the 'beauties' in Shakespeare's plays. Without adding from unpublished sources to the *corpus* of Pope, the discussion which follows will, I hope, make it apparent that Pope's critical work is more considerable in extent than has been supposed, as well as richer and more liberal in content.

A word should be said about the title of this essay. The scope proposed by my original study was that of Pope's literary criticism, —his critical theories and his opinions of the authors who formed his reading. But as the work went on, it was difficult to exclude other aspects of Pope's intellectual life which would hardly receive adequate treatment in connection with his poetry. The present title indicates the augmented scope: the work undertakes to deal, however inadequately, with Pope as humanist and scholar—Pope the editor of Shakespeare and the translator of Homer—as well as with Pope the critic; also, though far less amply, with Pope the man of general culture,—with his views upon the arts and philosophy.

For their kind assistance at various stages of my work, I am indebted to Professor Parrott of Princeton, Professor White of Boston University, and Mr. Bernard Wagner of Cambridge. The librarians of Princeton and Harvard have been most helpful. To Professor Croll of Princeton, who read the book in its original form, I am indebted for many helpful criticisms of substance and style. Finally, to Professor Robert ,K. Root, under whose direction the work was undertaken, I owe debts too numerous to cite, too heavy to pay. To his experience, his painstaking care, and his judgment, constant appeal has been made, and never in vain. I am especially indebted to him for assistance with the reading of proof.

A. W.

Boston, December 10, 1928

CONTENTS

CHAPTER I

THE ESSAY ON CRITICISM

'THE mental disease of the present generation,' wrote Dr. Johnson, 'is impatience of study, contempt of the great masters of ancient wisdom, and a disposition to rely wholly upon unassisted genius and natural sagacity.'[1] These were the words of a classicist living on into the period of transition which succeeded the Augustan Age. By Dr. Johnson's day, revolt was in the air; orthodoxy on the defensive. Poets were beginning to think and talk of 'inspiration' and 'natural' genius and originality.[2] The tradition of the 'learned poet,' a part of the mental stock of critics and practitioners since the Renaissance, was obsolescent.

In Pope's time the 'laws of poetry'[3] were still in one sense or another articles of belief, one's knowledge of the classics and the 'best critics' objects of justifiable pride. The necessity for talent or native ability was not denied: the critics in the 'great tradition' repeated after Horace the futility for poetic purposes of '*studium sine divite vena.*' But they added with Horace '*Nec rude quid prosit video ingenium*';[4] they emphasized the necessity for '*poetarum limae labor et mora.*'[5]

Pope's *Essay on Criticism* has been frequently misunderstood because not sufficiently studied against its proper background. It is distinctly and confessedly not a new system, not an exposition of a hitherto unthought of view of poetry, not the intuition of a young man who feels he has a 'message' for his elders. Such a venture at such an age would have seemed to Pope, as it perhaps should to us, an impertinence. The humanistic conception of culture, which Pope most decidedly held, is that it constitutes a continuum: each generation does not begin all over again; it carries on the thoughts

---

[1] *Rambler*, no. 154.
[2] See the illuminating study of the rise of these terms in Mr. Pearsall Smith's S.P.E. Tract XVII, *Four Words*.
[3] Charles Gildon wrote a book, *The Laws of Poetry*, 1721.
[4] *Ars Poetica*, 409-10.
[5] *ibid.*, 291.

and art of the past generations. 'The daily food and nourishment of the mind of an artist,' as Sir Joshua Reynolds said, 'is found in the great works of his predecessors.'[6] It is surely at a tremendous risk that one breaks from the tutelage of a great cultural tradition to see what, in his own individual wisdom, he can accomplish. What is produced is, not infrequently, a novelty barren and futile. True, this sort of counsel is now generally disregarded or derided; but one cannot hope to understand the literature of Augustan Rome, seventeenth century France, and eighteenth century England unless he is able, in imagination at least, to assume its validity.

Pope's *Essay* is the last of a long and honorable line of critical manuals, beginning, in the looser sense, with Aristotle's *Poetics*; in the stricter, with the *Ars* of Horace. The latter, in its 'purely didactic part, seems to be a *résumé* of Greek criticism on the drama, ultimately, perhaps, based on the doctrines of Aristotle, but, according to Porphyrion, really made up of selections from an Alexandrian critic, Neoptolemus of Parium.'[7] Even in Augustan Rome, classical doctrine on the composition and criticism of poetry had assumed a canonical form: a host of critics, of which only a few remain to us, filled the interval between Aristotle and Horace, drew from Greek literature the 'rules' for the *genres*, and classified the styles. Horace himself entered in upon an inheritance: 'in the general principles which he lays down he seems to be a mere exponent of the canons of Greek criticism.'[8]

After Horace came Quintillian; the Renaissance had its Vida and Scaliger, its Vossius and Heinsius and a host of others; the French of the 'classical age' had their Boileau and Le Bossu and Rapin and Bouhours and Dacier; in Restoration England Dryden praised and followed the Latin tradition even though he was unable to reconcile it with his equally sincere devotion to the English poets. Dryden wrote no *Ars*, but several of his contemporaries— titled amateurs at poetry—made essays in that direction which enjoyed a vast praise, partly because they expressed the ideas of

---

[6] *Discourses*, 211.

[7] Sellar, 110.

[8] *ibid.*, xx. Similarly Professor Baldwin says: Horace's *sententiae* 'may safely be taken as generally current in Graeco-Roman literary circles. Thus they have the more significance; for Horace's originality is hardly in conception. His contribution to criticism, like Cicero's, is in finality of phrase' (p. 243). I may seem to labor this point, but I am not sure that it is universally familiar, and it is important for the study of classical criticism and of Pope in particular.

contemporary criticism, partly, as was inevitable, on account of the rank of their authors.

In his youth Pope read all the 'best critics,' and the *Essay*, which was written at the end of this period,[9] was no doubt in part a test-piece—a proof to the world of his having mastered the technical studies of the poet, having received the standard training. 'He named among other books he then read the criticisms of Rapin and Bossu; and these,' suggests Spence, 'might be what led him to write his *Essay on Criticism.*'[10] There was no attempt to conceal obligation. Pope was not so naïve as to suppose that his literary contemporaries, who, like him, were read in Horace, Boileau, and the French 'authorities,' would fail to recognize the sources of his doctrine, or the copious incorporation into the texture of his verse of lines and phrases—slightly altered—from the poets. Addison and Johnson, both admirers of the *Essay*, praised it, not for its 'originality,' but for the happiness with which it expressed and 'illustrated' the wisdom of tradition. Those observations which are 'the most known and the most received,' says Addison, 'are placed in so beautiful a light, and illustrated with such apt allusions, that they have in them all the graces of novelty, and make the reader, who was before acquainted with them, still more convinced of their truth and solidity.' 'It is impossible for us who live in the later ages of the world to make observations in criticism, morality, or in any art or science, which have not been touched upon by others.[11] We have little else left us, but to represent the common sense of mankind in more strong, more beautiful, or more uncommon lights.' And having made this defense of the classical point of view and the *Essay* as an illustration of it, he goes on to point out that even the writer of the first *Ars* was no inventor: 'If a reader examines Horace's *Art of Poetry*, he will find but very few precepts in it which he may not meet with in Aristotle, and which were not commonly known by all the poets of the Augustan age. His way of expressing and applying them is what we are chiefly to admire.'[12]

Similarly, Johnson praises the *Essay* for the knowledge shown

[9] The *Essay* appeared in 1711 (for bibliographical details, see Griffith, I, 9-10). It was probably composed in 1709, though Pope later attempted to fix an earlier date. Its author can scarcely, in any case, be denied precocity.

[10] Spence, 193-4.

[11] Of the 'metaphysical poets,' Dr. Johnson, says, 'Those writers who lay on the watch for novelty could have little hope of greatness; for great things cannot have escaped former observation.' *Lives of the Poets*, I, 21.

[12] *Spectator*, no. 253.

'both of ancient and modern learning';[13] it exhibits, he says, 'every mode of excellence that can embellish or dignify didactic composition,—selection of matter,[14] novelty of arrangement, justness of precept, splendor of illustration, and propriety of digression.'[15]

Pope and his friends, then, would admit in advance the charge of indebtedness to past critics which his enemies brought against the *Essay*.[16] Nowadays it is customary to see its relation to Horace and Boileau: Professor Saintsbury, for example, alleges that 'all Pope seems to have done is to take the *Arts* of Horace, Vida, and Boileau, [and] to adopt as many of their principles as he understood.'[17] In Pope's own day, the taunt was rather that he had stolen from the 'noble lords' and other critics of the 'last age.' Dennis, for example, says that the 'young author' 'hath done in this essay what school-boys do by their exercises: he hath borrowed from living and dead, and particularly from the authors of the two famous Essays upon Poetry and Translated Verse.'[18] And Oldmixon, in his amplification of Bouhour's *Manière de Bien Penser*,[19] declares, 'What Father Bouhours teaches us of just thought and expression has been imperfectly hinted by others; there is a good deal of it in the Earl of Roscommon and the last Duke of Buckingham's Essays and in the Lord Lansdowne's *Essay on Unnatural Flights in Poetry*, the hints of which seem to be taken from our French critic; they are all excellent, especially the latter, which, in a very few fine verses, contains more nice remarks than are found in the translator of Homer's long rhyming essay,[20] where there is hardly an observation which is not borrowed from the above mentioned Essays or from Dryden's Prefaces and his *Essay on Dramatic Poesy. . . .*'[21]

But of course it is absurd to suppose that 'all' Pope has done is to borrow from Horace and Boileau, or that he has simply taken

---

[13] *Lives of the Poets*, III, 94.

[14] Rather than 'invention.'

[15] *Lives of the Poets*, III, 228-9.

[16] Frye pertinently remarks of the classicists: 'It must not be forgotten that they borrowed on principle. Only in this way can the extent and barefacedness of their pilferings be understood' (p. 147).

[17] *History of Criticism*, II, 453.

[18] *Reflections upon a Late Rhapsody*, Durham, 221. The *Essays* are by the Earl of Mulgrave and Lord Roscommon.

[19] *The Arts of Logic and Rhetoric*, xix-xx.

[20] i.e., the *Essay on Criticism*.

[21] Better known than the remarks of Dennis and Oldmixon is that of Lady Mary Wortley Montagu: 'I admired Mr. Pope's *Essay on Criticism* at first very much, because I had not then read any of the ancient critics and did not know that it was all stolen.' Spence, 176.

over his 'observations' from the sensible but both brief and casual *Essays* of the 'noble lords.' A careful study of the copious annotations in the Elwin edition will show that Pope's indebtedness to preceding critics is very largely confined to the first of the three sections, while the discussion of the faults of the bad critic, the 'character' of the good, and the brief history of criticism which composed the last two sections are drawn from his own observation and 'good sense.'

Nor was the plan of the *Essay on Criticism* a copy of earlier works. Pope, unlike all his predecessors, is confessedly writing, not for poets, but for critics. We may make of wider application what has been said of his relation to Boileau: 'The general scheme of the work has no resemblance to that of the *Art Poétique*; for Pope's work, on the whole, lives up to its title, which states that it is an essay (that is, a tentative effort) at outlining the principles a good *critic* ought to follow, *not* a Poetic Art for the *poet*.'[22] There is surely some distinctiveness here, even though we remember that, since critics derive their 'rules' from the practice of the poets and 'read each work of wit with the same spirit that its author writ,'[23] the distinction is not ultimate. Pope forgoes the detailed directions for writing correctly in the various *genres* which Horace, Boileau,[24] and Mulgrave had given—which constituted the body of their Arts—and substitutes, after the general observations in which all indulge, an equally detailed study of good and bad critics and criticism.

To sum up the preceding sketch of the historical background of the *Essay*, those contemporaries who praised and those who attacked Pope's criticism both did so understanding that it was an interpretation of the best canons of Latin, French, and English criticism. Those who attacked were pleased, no doubt for reasons of personal prejudice, to misunderstand the conception of art with which Pope was working; Johnson and Addison, on the other hand, were ready to test the *Essay* by the traditional standard of the classical tradition. Their position would have been very much that held by the ancients: 'Imitation of a model, or borrowing from any source whatsoever, was, therefore, never the subject of blame in antiquity, provided the imitator showed independence in the treatment of his material, and aimed at improvement in form or content. Thus Quintillian . . . describes the perfect orator as one: *qui etiam propria adiecerit ut suppleat quae deerunt; circumci-*

---

[22] Clark, 193.
[23] *Essay on Criticism*, II, 33-4.
[24] See Bobertag, 65, on the difference in plan of Boileau and Pope.

dat, si quid redundabit. Of course an unsuccessful effort at improvement was properly subject to critical censure.'[25] Similarly, Pope gives it as his opinion to Walsh that 'writers in the case of borrowing from others are like trees which of themselves would produce only one sort of fruit, but by being grafted upon others may yield variety. A mutual commerce makes poetry flourish; but then poets, like merchants, should repay with something of their own that they take from others, not, like pirates, make prize of all they meet.'[26] Let those who judge the *Essay* recall these remarks and read the poem 'with the same spirit that its author writ'; let them study the *Essay* in the light of its sources, compare the 'imitations' of passages in Horace, Boileau and others with their originals, and consider whether the poet does not 'repay with something of his own' all that he borrows in the 'terseness, conciseness, and elegance' of his verses.

I wish now to discuss in detail Pope's relations to preceding critics: what he took from them; what he thought of them.

There is reason for doubt whether Pope had read the *Poetics* of Aristotle before writing his *Essay*: the characterization of the 'Stagyrite' which opens the 'roll of the critics' is general as well as confused. As Aristotle had 'conquered Nature'[27] so it was fitting that he should 'preside o'er Wit.' Earlier in the *Essay*, we have been given to understand that Aristotle's rules were simply the reduction to method of the practice of the Greek poets;[28] here, Aristotle is described as giving *a priori* laws to 'a race long unconfined and free Still fond and proud of savage liberty,' and poetry, as 'Fancy's wild regions yet unvanquished.'[29] There is surely, as Elwin has noted, a considerable discrepancy here. We, like Warburton, shall find a good many more—and I have no intention of attempting to 'rationalize' them. In this instance, perhaps, Pope has been told that Aristotle drew his rules from the practice of Homer and Sophocles, the most 'regular' of the Greek poets, and may have conjectured that, without rules, most of the others must, like the Elizabethans in English literature, have cherished the right to follow their fancy.

The appreciation of Horace, 'so justly famed,' emphasizes the combination in him of soundness of judgment and ease of manner. Nowadays it is generally recognized that the *Ars* is simply 'the

[25] Fiske, 43-4.
[26] E-C, VI, 52.
[27] *Essay on Criticism*, III, 93.
[28] *ibid.*, I, 98-9.
[29] The last phrase is from the earlier draft, reprinted in E-C, II, 74.

unsystematic epistolary reflections of a Latin poet on poetry';[30] a collection of *sententiae*. But during the long reign of classical criticism it used frequently to be taken as a manual with 'a logical progress' from thought to thought. A critic as late as Bishop Hurd[31] contended for this view. Pope did not make the mistake: it is 'without method' that Horace 'talks us into sense'; he 'charms with graceful negligence.'

Horace was both critic and poet. It may be useful in this connection to refer to Bobertag's theory that the whole *Essay* is to be read in the light of the lines:

> Let such teach others who themselves excel,
> And censure freely who have written well.[32]

'Die Überzeugung steht für Pope so fest,' he says, 'dass man von ihm sagen kann, er behaupte die völlige Identität des Dichters und des Kritikers; der Kritiker sei ihm soviel Kritiker wie er Dichter ist . . .'[33] I cannot think that the *Essay* owes its unity to this conception, or that Pope had it consistently in mind. Indeed, as Bobertag himself sees, the theory is noticeably at variance with Pope's selection of Aristotle as the first and greatest of critics. Still, most of the critics cited in his list were 'creative writers' as well, and so have been many of the greatest critics since, such as—to mention only Englishmen—Hazlitt, Coleridge, Arnold, and Pater. Certainly Horace successfully exemplifies Pope's doctrine, for he was 'supreme in judgment as in wit'—i.e., both critic and poet; he indeed 'might boldly censure' because 'his precepts teach but what his works inspire.'[34]

Miss Goad, who has made a special study of *Horace in the English Literature of the Eighteenth Century*, thinks that though Pope refers frequently to the Roman critics, Horace and Quintillian, his ideas are really 'those of such French critics as Rapin, Bossu, Boileau, and of his English predecessors in literary criti-

[30] Baldwin, 242.

[31] Also Bishop Warburton, in his commentary on the *Essay on Criticism*. Elwin amusingly points out that in the original draft Warburton contrasted the 'regularity' and 'method' of Pope's poem with the 'looseness and inconnection' of Horace's; but just at that juncture his friend Hurd brought out an edition of Horace proving that he 'had the same attention to method' (E-C, II, 86 and n). Of course not everyone agreed with Warburton that the *Essay on Criticism* was 'regular.' Addison, in the *Spectator* (no. 235), declared that 'the observations follow one another like those in Horace's *Art of Poetry*, without that methodical regularity which would have been requisite in a prose writer.'

[32] *Essay*, I, 15-16.

[33] *Englische Studien*, III, 85.

[34] *Essay*, III, 98-101.

cism.[35] So that, whereas there are many thoughts in the poem that are apparently from Horace, and particularly from the *Ars Poetica*, there is always a question as to whether they are directly Horatian, or have been transmitted to Pope through several of the many channels by means of which the precepts of Horace were made familiar to the eighteenth century.'[36] This is all very sensible, and in great part true. The principles and precepts of Horace himself are, as we have seen, not original, but the distillation of current Graeco-Roman criticism. They were endlessly reiterated by Renaissance critics, particularly Vida; and Boileau's *Art Poétique* was confessedly based on Horace. Miss Goad can point to the line in which Pope asserts that 'Boileau still in right of Horace sways,'[37] in particular proof of her contention.

Nevertheless, Pope had read his Horace with attention, and there are at least four passages where he seems definitely to have the original and not simply the general tradition in mind.

> Be sure yourself and your own reach to know,
> How far your genius, taste, and learning go;
> Launch not beyond your depth. . . .[38]

seemed to Wakefield[39] a 'palpable imitation' of Horace's

> Sumite materiam vestris, qui scribitis, aequam
> Viribus, et versate diu, quid ferre recusent,
> Quid valeant umeri.[40]

Miss Goad admits that

> Be Homer's works your study and delight,
> Read them by day and meditate by night;[41]

'seems to come directly from' Horace's

> vos exemplaria Graeca
> Nocturna versate manu, versate diurna.[42]

---

[35] i.e., the 'noble lords,' Sheffield, Roscommon, Lansdowne.
[36] Goad, 136.
[37] *Essay*, III, 155.
[38] *ibid.*, I, 48-50.
[39] E-C, II, 36, n.
[40] *Ars Poetica*, 38-40. The passage in Horace was, to be sure, reinforced by Boileau's 'consultez longtemps votre esprit et vos forces' (*Art*, I, v. 12), and Vida's 'Atque tuis prudens genus elige viribus aptum.' *Ars*, I, 40.
[41] *Essay*, I, 124-5.
[42] *Ars*, 268-9. This is certainly the closest. Horace's 'turn' was, however, echoed by Vida and Boileau. The former extols those who 'veterum explorant opera inclyta vatum noctes atque dies' (*Ars*, I, 72-3) and exhorts:
> Nulla dies tamen interea tibi, nulla abeat nox,
> Quin aliquid vatum sacrorum e fontibus almis
> Hauseris . . . (I, 409-11).

The caution, in behalf of 'freer beauties,' that

> Some figures monstrous and misshaped appear,
> Considered singly or beheld too near,
> Which, but proportioned to their light or place,
> Due distance reconciles to form and grace[43]

comes definitely from Horace's celebrated 'ut pictura, poesis' passage:

> Ut pictura, poesis: erit quae si propius stes
> Te capiat magis, et quaedam si longius abstes.
> Haec amat obscurum, volet haec sub luce videri.[44]

And, finally, Horace's personal confession of tolerance,

> Verum ubi plura nitent in carmine non ego paucis
> Offendar maculis. . . .[45]

finds, it is clear, an adaptation in Pope's impersonal

> And if the means be just, the conduct true,
> Applause, in spite of trivial faults, is due.[46]

Pope 'used to mention Quintillian too as an old favorite author with him.'[47] To this partiality is perhaps to be attributed the curious fact that in Pope's own published notes on the *Essay*, citations from this rhetorician are appended as sources for eight passages, while not one of the borrowings from Horace is so identified. Nor is it that the originals in Quintillian are more closely copied: some of these seem rather remote. For example, Pope gives 'Plus sine doctrina prudentia, quam sine prudentia valet doctrina' as authority (it was hardly needed) for his 'So by

Boileau's injunction is narrowed to the reading of the pastoral poets, Theocritus and Virgil:

> Que leurs tendres écrits, par les Grâces dictés,
> Ne quittent point vos mains, jours et nuit feuilletés.
> *(Art,* II, 27-8.)

The ecstatic praise of Homer's all-sufficiency found a model in the Earl of Mulgrave's lines:

> Read Homer once, and you can read no more,
> For all things else will seem so dull and poor,
> You'll wish't unread; but oft upon him look,
> And you will hardly need another book.
> (Spingarn, II, 295.)

[43] *Essay,* I, 171-4.
[44] *Ars,* 361-3.
[45] *ibid.,* 351-2.
[46] *Essay,* II, 257-8.
[47] Spence, 194.

false learning is good sense defaced.'[48] It is certainly doubtful if 'True wit is nature'[49] was suggested by Quintillian's general injunction to 'follow Nature': 'Naturam intueamur, hanc sequamur.' His nearest parallel to Quintillian was not cited by Pope at all: 'For not to know some trifles is a praise'[50] is an excellent variation on 'Ex quo mihi inter virtutes grammatici habebitur, aliqua nescire.' Though very dissimilar in expression, it is quite possible that from this Latin original Pope borrowed, as he alleged, the thoughts that the Greek critics drew their 'just precepts' 'from great examples given';[51] that one should speak 'modeste, et circumspecto judicio' of great writers, 'lest, as generally happens, we condemn what we do not understand';[52] that one ought to 'survey the whole'[53] of a book ('nec per partes modo scrutanda sunt omnia, sed perlectus liber utique ex integro resumendus')[54] before judging it; that it is an offensive affectation to make pretence to fame by the use of archaic diction;[55] that 'oft the ear the open vowels [i.e., hiatus] tire.'[56] I leave for the last the most important passage from Quintillian. The conception that 'rules were made but to promote their end,' that they were simply tried and approved means of attaining the object of poetry, the pleasure and instruction of the reader, that they could be set aside when the end could better be attained another way, was, as we shall see later, generally held by the neo-classicists; but it is first clearly stated in Quintillian's 'Necque enim rogationibus plebisve scitis sancta sunt ista praecepta, sed hoc, quicquid est, utilitas excogitavit. Non negabo autem sic utile esse plerumque; verum si

[48] *Essay*, I, 25.

[49] *ibid.*, I, 297.

[50] *ibid.*, II, 262.

[51] *ibid.*, I, 98.

[52] Quoted, E-C, II, 44. Appended by Pope to 'Nor is it Homer nods but we that dream' (I, 180).

[53] *Essay*, II, 235.

[54] E-C, II, 48.

[55] II, 324. The apposite passage from Quintillian is quoted, E-C, II, 53. In Quintillian's time there was a reversion from the taste for Seneca and his contemporaries back to Cicero (this our critic fostered) which ended in rejecting Augustan literature as well and returning, decadently, to the archaic writers such as the elder Cato, Gracchus, Naevius, Ennius, Accius, and Pacuvius:— an interesting parallel to the taste of eighteenth century *virtuosi*. See Friedländer's brilliant *Roman Life and Manners* (III, 5-11, in the English translation).

[56] *Essay*, II, 345. Pope quoted Quintillian on 'hiatus' again in his remarks on versification; (E-C, VI, 59) also Turnebus, the sixteenth century French critic, 'on Quintillian.'

eadem illa nobis aliud suadebit utilitas, hanc, relictis magistrorum auctoritatibus, sequemur.'[57]

The 'character' of Quintillian[58] emphasizes the fullness of his exposition, the clarity of his method, and the justness of his 'rules.' Warton felt[59] that insufficient justice was done to the critic's 'elegance' of style and 'beautiful metaphors.' Pope does speak of the materials as 'disposed with grace'; but he felt, rightly, that Quintillian was first the instructor and only secondarily the stylist. He was not to be compared merely from the point of view of literary distinction with such other critics in his roll as Horace and Longinus.

Longinus 'On the Sublime' (as it used to be translated) was favorite reading in the late seventeenth and the eighteenth centuries. In 1674 Boileau published a free version of it in French, accompanied by 'Reflections'; and it was in Boileau's translation, or one of the general English translations made largely from Boileau's French, with occasional collation of the original Greek or the Latin, that Englishmen came to be familiar with the treatise.[60] For example, three years after the appearance of Boileau's Longinus, Dryden, who had never before even named the great Greek, mentions him four times—once, as, 'after Aristotle, the greatest critic among the Greeks.'[61] All the men of letters read him: Addison and Shaftesbury show his influence; Pope's enemy, Leonard Welsted, translated him; another enemy, John Dennis, was so manifest in his devotion that his contemporaries dubbed him 'Sir Longinus.' *On the Sublime* was an enlarging influence on eighteenth century criticism. Longinus was not in the 'Latin tradition.' He considers in an orderly way the means by which elevation of style may be attained, but his emphasis is all along on passion and intensity. From him may be traced the ancestry of the 'school of taste' which emphasized the 'beauties' of a work of literature rather than its defects. Longinus was particularly qualified to bring a liberalizing impulse to neo-classicists themselves, since he was at once a Greek, a devoted student of Homer and Pindar, and at the same time was so remote in point of view from such criticism as, say, that of Horace.

Such an influence he did exercise upon Boileau, whose neo-classicism is notably relaxed in the *Réflexions sur Longin*; and such, I

[57] Quoted, E-C, II, 42. Pope's own identifications will be found given in E-C, II, on pages 34, 39, 44, 47, 48, 51, 53, 54.
[58] *Essay*, III, 669-74.
[59] *Genius of Pope*, I, 169.
[60] Clark, 364-71, gives a very useful account of 'Longinus in England.'
[61] *ibid.*, 369.

think it safe to say, he exercised upon Pope, especially in the
Preface to Homer, but also, to a lesser degree, in the *Essay*, where
so many strains of influence meet. In the case of Pope, however,
there were other influences which would bear in the same direction. While Boileau repudiated French literature before Malherbe,
Pope had, as we shall see, extensive knowledge and very considerable appreciation of all the great English poets, Chaucer, Spenser,
Shakespeare, and Milton. Like Dryden, Pope was confronted with
the necessity of reconciling two kinds of literary genius, the
Latin-French and the English. Accordingly, one cannot attribute
his literary liberalism to Longinus as clearly as one can that of
Boileau.

Between Longinus and Horace there is certainly disparity of
spirit, if no direct verbal contradiction. Pope, who, like Dryden,
felt in turn the justness of both positions, never really saw his way
to unifying them. He had a fondness for Creech's dictum (in paraphrase of Horace) that 'only fools admire,' and often repeated
it.[62] Aaron Hill, one of the 'dunces,' but later Pope's friend and
correspondent, 'abhorred the sentiment' and 'once asked him if he
still adhered to the opinion of Longinus that the true sublime
thrilled and transported the reader. On Pope's replying in the
affirmative, his interrogator pressed him with the contradiction';
and the poet took refuge in an unintelligible answer.[63] There was a
real inconsistency here which was based on Pope's genuine enjoyment of two different types of art without full consciousness of
their difference. We 'approve' Addison; we 'admire' (i.e., wonder
at) Shakespeare; and so did Pope. Elwin points out that even in
the *Essay*, there is mention of '*rapture* warming the mind' and of
'the generous pleasure to be *charmed* with wit.'[64] From the *Preface
to Homer* I can collect much stronger expressions. 'It is to the
strength of this *amazing* invention,' he says, 'we are to attribute
that unequalled fire and rapture which is so forcible in Homer
that *no man of a true poetical spirit is master of himself while he
reads him.*' We find 'this poetic fire, this *vivida vis animi*, in a very
few. Even in works where all those ['exact disposition, just
thought, correct elocution, polished numbers'] are imperfect or
neglected, this can *overpower criticism, and make us admire even
while we disapprove.*'[65]

[62] *Essay on Criticism* has it, 'For fools admire, but men of sense approve'
(II, 391).

[63] E-C, II, 58, n.

[64] *loc. cit.*, 58, n.

[65] Durham, 324-5 (The Preface to Homer is not included in E-C).

There is evidence of understanding and sincere appreciation in the celebrated characterization of Longinus in the *Essay on Criticism*:

> Thee, bold Longinus, all the Nine inspire,
> And bless their critic with a poet's fire.
> An ardent judge, who, zealous in his trust,
> With warmth gives sentence, yet is always just;
> Whose own example strengthens all his laws;
> And is himself that great sublime he draws.[66]

The epithets 'bold' and 'ardent' are felicitous; the combination of 'warmth' and 'justice' in the verdicts of Longinus marks truly his 'character.' The last verse is taken from a sentence in Boileau's Preface 'Souvent il fait la figure qu'il enseigne; et, en parlant du sublime, il est lui-même très sublime':[67] it was probably in Boileau's translation that Pope read Longinus.

The couplet on Dionysius of Halicarnassus[68] first appeared in the second edition of the *Essay*. In a letter published as addressed to Addison in 1714, but probably written later, Pope calls attention to 'an observation upon Homer's verses of Sisyphus' Stone,' which, he says, 'I happened to find . . . in Dionysius of Halicarnassus' treatise, περὶ συνθέσεως ὀνομάτων, who treats very largely upon these verses.'[69] It is more than doubtful if Pope had looked into Dionysius when he wrote the *Essay*, for he gives, as he had evidently received, the impression that the Halicarnassian was an Homeric commentator. Warton and Wakefield justly censure[70] the injustice done this excellent critic, who, like Longinus, was conspicuously an appreciator of poetic style. But what Pope hit upon was rather inadequate than untrue. Indeed, Professor Rhys Roberts[71] calls it 'a happy instinct that leads Pope to find in Dionysius a gifted interpreter of Homeric poetry, who can "call new beauties forth from every line." In his entire attitude, not only towards Homer but towards Sappho and Simonides, Herodotus and Demosthenes, Dionysius has proved that he can rise above the debased standards of the ages immediately preceding his own, and can discern and proclaim a classic excellence.'

It was certainly singular that Pope should omit from his roll of

[66] III, 675-80.
[67] As first noted by Wakefield.
[68] *Essay*, III, 665-6.
[69] E-C, VI, 410. The so-called letters to Addison were not published until 1735, and Elwin considers them all fabrications.
[70] E-C, II, 75, n.
[71] In the Preface to his excellent edition of the *De Compositione Verborum* (London, 1910).

critics Cicero, whom he twice cites in his annotations,[72] and yet include Petronius,[73] in whose work 'there are not above two or three pages containing critical remarks.' Perhaps from the celebrated 'curiosa felicitas' and a few more quotable phrases,[74] he conjectured a more considerable critic than exists.

Of the Renaissance critics in Latin only Erasmus[75] and Vida[76] are mentioned in the *Essay on Criticism*, though Pope seems to have known, either at that time or later, some of the others: 'Scaliger's *Poetics*,' he told Spence, 'is an exceeding useful book in its kind, and extremely well collected.'[77] Erasmus was hardly a literary critic, in spite of his *Ciceronianismus*; and indeed he is not introduced as such, but, in far more impressive capacity, as the man who put an end to the Middle Ages and drove the monks ('those holy Vandals') off the stage. It is evident that the period of transition from the Middle Ages to the Renaissance was not very well known when Pope could write in that vein, and Warton say of Erasmus that 'to him was the restoration of literature principally owing.'[78]

'The merits of Vida seem not to have been particularly attended to in England till Pope had bestowed this commendation [i.e., in the *Essay*] upon him, although the *Poetics* had been correctly published at Oxford some time before.'[79] From Vida, Pope derived two important doctrines: the importance of adapting sound to sense in one's versification,[80] and the propriety and advantage of 'borrowing' from the ancients. The latter doctrine is not preached in the *Essay*; but we have already had sufficient evidence that it was there practised with industry and taste. There were many other things in Vida which must have appealed to Pope. I am particularly struck with a general consonancy in mood between these two poets. Both, though emphasizing with Horace and Boileau the

[72] E-C, II, 34 (*De Oratoribus*); *ibid.*, II, 54 (the pseudo-Ciceronian *Rhetorica ad Herennium*, favorite text-book in the Middle Ages).

[73] *Essay*, III, 677-8.

[74] The phrase 'curious, not knowing' (*Essay*, II, 286) comes from Petronius; and on the margin of his manuscript Pope was found to have copied the original: 'Est et alter, non quidem doctus, sed curiosus, qui plus docet quam scit' (E-C, II, 50, n).

[75] *Essay*, III, 693-6.

[76] *ibid.*, III, 705-8.

[77] Spence, 199.

[78] *Genius of Pope*, I, 179, n.

[79] *ibid.*, I, 185; Pope included Vida's poems in his *Selecta Poemata Italorum*, for which see Chapter VII. In 1726, he read Christopher Pitt's translation 'with eagerness' and commended it in a letter to the translator as 'both a correct and spirited translation.' E-C, X, 129.

[80] *Essay*, II, 365.

necessity for the labor of the file, for method and reason, and for imitation of the classics, do so not with the prudent good sense of the pedagogue but with—particularly in Vida's case—a fire and enthusiasm which seem wholly genuine. I wonder that even Professor Saintsbury, who is eager to discover good things everywhere, does not feel in Vida the intensity of the Renaissance devotion to the classics. If he is the most narrowly Latin of the celebrated writers of *Arts Poetic* he is also the most fervent and the farthest from prose in expression. In particular, each of the three books of his *Ars* concludes with a burst of eloquence which adds a heightening of emotion rather than an advancement of the thought. Pope has, in his *Essay*, several passages I should similarly characterize: for example, the lines on 'unerring nature.'[81] In particular, I see a very considerable resemblance between the conclusion of Vida's *Ars*[82] and that of the first book of the *Essay*,[83] in which Pope pauses in his argument to contemplate the ever venerable altars of the 'ancients,' to call every voice to join 'in praise so just' and 'fill the general chorus of mankind.' Pope's apostrophe,

> Hail, bards triumphant! born in happier days,
> Immortal heirs of universal praise!

is an echo of Vida's apostrophe to Virgil, too long to be quoted in full

> omnia cedant
> Secla, nec invideant primos tibi laudis honores.
> Fortunate operum! tua praestans gloria famae,
> Quo quenquam aspirare nefas, sese extulit alis.

Contemplating the genius of the great poets, Vida depicts himself as a mere giver of rules who is forbidden by the Fates to mount up 'auf Flügeln Gesanges':

> Ipse viam tantum potui docuisse repertam
> Aonas ad montes, longeque ostendere Musas,
> Plaudentes celsae choreas in vertice rupis,
> Quo me haud ire sinunt unquam fata invida, et usque
> Absterrentque, arcentque procul, nec summa jugi unquam
> Fas prensare manu fastigia . . .

Pope, with equal modesty but with the consciousness that he is, though not of the greatest, a true poet, invokes the ancients in some of the most beautiful and moving lines he ever wrote:

---

[81] *Essay*, I, 70-3.
[82] *Ars*, III, 527-91.
[83] *Essay*, I, 181-200.

O may some spark of your celestial fire
The last, the meanest of your sons inspire,
(That on weak wings, from far, pursues your flights,
Glows while he reads, but trembles as he writes). . . .

With Vida and Pope, classicism was not a convention but a devotion.

One significant difference between the doctrines of the two men remains to be noted, though the parallel passages may have suggested it. The place of primacy which Virgil holds in the *Ars*[84] is Homer's in the *Essay*. Of course the contrast must not be taken as wholly representative of personal choice on the part of the critics. Vida and Pope were also the spokesmen of their ages: Scaliger, too, was a Maronolatrist; and, before Pope, Boileau,[85] Mulgrave, Madame Dacier, and many another had praised Homer above Virgil. Still, the contrast is significant for the change within the neo-classical ranks. A new theory of poetry is implicit in the preference of the poet of Nature over the poet of Art, and of this Pope did not remain unconscious.

To Boileau, the greatest of his immediate predecessors, the debt of the *Essay on Criticism* is decidedly important, both in phrasing and in ideas. The *Art Poétique* was available to Pope in a brilliant paraphrase by Soame and Dryden as well as in the original; and sometimes Pope's 'imitations' have in mind one and sometimes the other version. For example, the line in which we are told that Nature 'Life, force, and beauty must to all impart' is very clearly from Soame's injunction that whatever one writes should borrow from reason 'its beauty, force, and light.'[86] Pope's description of 'coldly correct' poetry, 'such lays as neither ebb nor flow,' borrows its figure not from the original line in Boileau but from Soame's 'A frozen style that neither ebbs nor flows.'[87] The phrase 'brave disorder' (Boileau's *beau désordre*) in Soame's translation,

Her generous style at random oft will part,
And by a brave disorder shows her art,

crosses over with the general idea into Pope's

From vulgar bounds with brave disorder part,
And snatch a grace beyond the reach of art.[88]

---

[84] Accounts of Vida usually misrepresent him by implying that this is the chief subject in his poem. In reality, there is not much space allotted to it.

[85] *Art Poétique*, III, 295-308.

[86] E-C, I, 37, n.

[87] Clark, 195.

[88] E-C, I, 43, n.

Other passages come directly from the original, such as the episode of the poet whose passion for reciting his verses respects neither church nor altar: who rushes in 'where angels fear to tread.'[89] The lines satirizing the conventional rhymes and phrases such as amateurs are wont to use in their love poetry seem to derive from Boileau's *Second Satire*, though the particular rhymes and phrases are not the same.[90] Perhaps the most important single passage derivative from Boileau is the celebrated definition of 'true wit.' Pope contributed 'Nature to advantage dressed'; but he found 'what oft was thought but ne'er so well expressed' in some phrases from Boileau's Preface to his Works: 'Qu'est-ce qu'une pensée neuve, brillante, extraordinaire? *Ce n'est point*, comme se le persuadent les ignorants, *une pensée que personne n'a jamais eue, ni dû avoir*: c'est au contraire une pensée qui a dû venir à tout le monde, et que quelqu'un s'avise le premier d'exprimer. *Un bon mot n'est bon mot qu'en ce qu'il dit une chose que chacun pensait, et qu'il la dit d'une manière vive, fine, et nouvelle.*'[91]

More important than this indebtedness for phrase and detached thought is the relation of temper and philosophy. Boileau, like Pope, has long furnished ill-informed and romantically-minded critics with that phantom, the neo-classicist, who tests everything by a pedantic rule of thumb. Even the usually generous Professor Saintsbury is disposed to take this view of Boileau.[92] But, as an American professor clearly sees and emphatically asserts, 'no one was the kind of classicist or rationalist that is to be found in some popular books and essays dealing with eighteenth century literature. The only appearance of this imaginary creature is among the straw figures which writers put together for purposes of demolition. That there was in this period any critic of importance who actually believed that one could make a poet by teaching rules, or that art could replace genius, or any such silly stuff, I emphatically deny.'[93]

Certainly, if the neo-classicist as popularly conceived really existed, Boileau was not such. He was a sensible, moderate, and cultivated man, the friend of great men of letters such as Racine and Molière, responsive to all the currents of thought of his time. He was a classicist to be sure, but his classicism was tempered, was supported by his rationalism. 'Rien n'est beau que le vrai: le vrai

[89] *ibid.*, 73, n.
[90] *ibid.*, 55.
[91] Preface to the edition of 1701. *Oeuvres*, I, 18. (Italics mine.) Clark points out (196) that this borrowing was well recognized in the eighteenth century.
[92] *History of Criticism*, II, 280-300.
[93] Durham, xvi.

seul est aimable' ;[94] the classics please us because they are true. The
writer is instructed to love, not the classics, but reason.[95] Boileau
does not suppose that *all* the 'ancients' are admirable: 'Je n'admets
dans ce haut rang que ce petit nombre d'écrivains merveilleux dont
le nom seul fait l'éloge, comme Homère, Platon, Cicero, Virgile,
etc.'[96] The 'ancients' are to be admired not because they are the
ancients, but because they have stood the test of time—that is to
say, the test of reason.[97]

His rationalism tempered his classicism: the converse is also
true. A purely rationalistic aesthetic, like that of Descartes, would
dry up the springs of poetry entirely: as a matter of fact, this is
just what it did in the French eighteenth century.[98] But in the
seventeenth century, classicism tempered rationalism: 'C'est l'imitation des ancients qui maintient contre l'esprit cartésien, et je
dirais presque contre l'esprit du siècle, la beauté poétique ou ora-
toire, la forme artistique.'[99] So Boileau preached the supremacy of
the understanding in literature, and at the same time was a sincere admirer of the 'irrational and incredible narrations' of
Homer; he preached verisimilitude, but continued to be a firm ad-
herent of the 'pagan marvels.' His love of the classics made it
impossible for him to strip art of imagination.

Boileau also had his connections with the 'school of taste,' so-
called. His translation and prefatory study of Longinus emphasized
the importance of studying the 'beauties' rather than the defects of
a poem. Of course, as we shall see, taste, or more accurately, 'good
taste,' may itself stiffen into a code. But it need not. Boileau, like
Pope, recognized that the 'rules' were means to an end, and that at
times taste might find a more direct road to the heart: 'though the
rules should be respected, if possible, an interesting and effective
work produced in spite of the rules is more estimable than a cold
work which obeys all the dictates of the Aristotelian formalities.'[100]

Boileau, then—to summarize—occupies, in anticipation of Pope,
a central and mediating position between the various schools of
critical thought in his time. A word remains to be said of a sug-

[94] *Epître IX*, 43.

[95] *Art Poétique*, I, 37.

[96] 'Réflexions sur Longin,' *Oeuvres*, III, 215.

[97] . . . 'l'antique et constante admiration qu'on a toujours eue pour ses
ouvrages est une preuve sûre et infallible qu'on les doit admirer.'

[98] See Lanson's excellent study of Descartes and classicism in *La Revue
de Métaphysique et de Morale*, IV (1896), 517-50.

[99] Lanson, 535.

[100] Clark, 197. See *ibid.*, 390-97, for full discussion of 'Boileau and the
School of Taste.'

gested divergence. Bobertag[101] is disposed to make much of the fact that in contexts where Boileau uses 'reason' or 'good sense' Pope frequently substitutes 'Nature'; it seems to me that he overstresses his point. In actual practice, as we shall presently see, the conceptions tended to become synonymous: the laws of Nature were the laws of reason both in the physical universe and in the 'mind of man.' But in potentiality it is quite true that Nature was a significant choice: hold fast to the word, and without being conscious of it, you will discover its meaning developing with the development of philosophic thought. The conception of reason has not been materially altered in all its history: but Nature, which is another name for reality, changes with the conceptions of life as a whole which man successively evolves. Reason is a still current definition of reality; but it is the reality of the study and the laboratory: poetry anticipated a more humanistic philosophy in moving on, or reverting, to a conception of reality which should embrace the other elements in man, such as the will, the emotions, the imagination. The word Nature certainly had the seeds of the future in it to an extent which reason did not: let the most confirmed neo-classicist hold resolutely to this revered term and scrutinize it carefully, and he will find himself insensibly led to a more liberal interpretation of life and literature.

The great Rapin, who, according to Dryden, 'is alone sufficient, were all other critics lost, to teach anew the rules of writing,'[102] was a favorite critic with Pope in his early years. This cultured Jesuit shared with Boileau the chief influence over English criticism. He was not a pedant or a precisian;[103] but, like Boileau, 'combined a general orthodoxy with a saving sense of the 'grace beyond the reach of art.'[104] His respect for the rules was based on his belief in their utility; he never supposed them to be all sufficient, never suggested that one could be taught to become a great writer: 'no man can be a poet without a genius; the want of which no art or industry is capable to repair.'[105] The rules are 'founded upon good sense and sound reason rather than on authority or example.'[106] Moreover, poetry has its secret charms which the rules have not discovered: 'There is a certain *I know not what*[107] in the numbers which is understood by few, and notwithstanding gives

[101] *Englische Studien*, III, 70-2.
[102] Ker, I, 181.
[103] Professor Saintsbury to the contrary.
[104] Clark, 275.
[105] *Works*, II, 139.
[106] *ibid*., II, 146.
[107] The phrase *Je ne sais quoi* was almost the symbol of the 'school of taste': it expresses by a French gesture the beauty that evades analysis.

great delight in poetry.'[108] Rapin has an eloquent essay on Homer
and Virgil; it is not mere analysis; there is appreciation, as we call
it. He emphasized the necessity for appeal to the emotions, for the
vivida vis animi in poetry[109]: 'true poetry is not perceived,' he says,
'but by the impression it makes on the soul; it is not as it should
be unless it go to the heart. Hence it is that Homer animates me,
Virgil heats me, and all the rest freeze me, so cold and flat they
are.'[110]

Perhaps this little collection of passages is sufficient to indicate
that Rapin, like most of us, tried to see his subject as judicially and
comprehensively as possible. His point of view attempts, like
Boileau's, to synthesize the doctrines of all the 'schools'—rationalism, classicism, and the cult of 'taste.' For this reason, it is difficult to disentangle the influence of Rapin from that of Boileau.
For our purposes, it is not necessary; Pope read both, and from
both inferred the possibility of what was, in his time, a central
position.

A few important passages in the *Essay on Criticism* may be
directly traced to Rapin. The notion that

> Those rules of old, discovered, not devised,
> Are Nature still, but Nature methodized;[111]

is clearly expressed in the Jesuit's 'I affirm that, these rules well
considered, one shall find them made only to reduce Nature into
method, to trace it step by step, and not suffer the least mark of it
to escape us.'[112] The liberating conception that the rules are not
all-sufficient, that the main end of poetry is to reach the heart, and
that the end is more important than the means; that there are
'nameless graces which no methods teach,' and a 'lucky license'[113]
comes from Rapin's 'Yet is there in poetry as in other arts certain
things that cannot be expressed which are (as it were) mysteries.
There are no precepts to teach the hidden graces, the insensible
charms, and all that secret power of poetry which passes to the

[108] *Works*, II, 176.
[109] cf. Pope's Preface to Homer.
[110] *Works*, II, 182. This is surely not the emphasis on 'correctness' commonly regarded as the prime characteristic of neo-classicism.
[111] I, 88-9.
[112] *Works*, II, 146. E-C (I, 39, n.) attributes the passage in the *Essay* to
Dryden's 'If the rules be well considered, we shall find them to be made
only to reduce nature into method.' But it is obvious that Dryden is simply
translating and condensing Rapin, whom he so greatly esteemed. Pope is
more likely, I think, to have taken the thought from Rapin.
[113] *Essay*, I, 144; 148.

heart, as there is no method to teach us to please; 'tis a pure effect of Nature.'[114]

'Critic learning flourished most in France,' the *Essay* asserts, but adds, as if to take away the blessing, 'the rules a nation born to serve obeys';[115] and contrasts with the docility of French writers the intractable Gothicism of the English.

> We, brave Britons, foreign laws despised,
> And kept unconquered and uncivilized;
> Fierce for the liberties of wit, and bold,
> We still defied the Romans as of old.[116]

Is this an attack on the Elizabethan poetry and the Jacobean 'metaphysicians'? If so, surely not an unmixed one. Even in this, perhaps the most servile passage in Pope's criticism, there is present a thrill of pride only partly concealed by the censure it bears on its surface. Like Dryden, Pope esteemed the proper models, French rules and French criticism, without surrendering his sense that there was something greater than regularity, something greater than the current age could produce, in the works of the 'giant race before the Flood.'[117] Dryden characterized the contrast:

> Our age was cultivated thus at length,
> But what we gained in skill, we lost in strength.
> Our builders were with want of genius curst;
> The second temple was not like the first.[118]

Similarly, in his Preface to Shakespeare, Pope sets in antithesis the old and new in the drama, by no means to the discredit of the old. One looks upon Shakespeare's works 'in comparison with those that are more finished and regular, as upon an ancient majestic piece of Gothic architecture compared with a neat modern building: the latter is more elegant and glaring, but the former is more strong and solemn.' The older 'theater' contained in one of its plays 'materials enough to make many of the other. It has much the greater variety and much the nobler apartments. . . . Nor does the whole fail to strike us with greater reverence. . . .'[119] Even the maligned Augustans could distinguish between 'great' and 'correct,' and if they could not reconcile their admirations, they would surrender neither. The few verses on French criticism in

---

[114] *Works*, II, 173. The translation which I quote—that by Basil Kennett—was first published in 1705. It seems likely that Pope made use of it.

[115] *Essay*, III, 153-4.

[116] *ibid.*, III, 156-9.

[117] Dryden: *To My Dear Friend, Mr. Congreve*, 5.

[118] *ibid.*, 11-14.

[119] E-C, X, 549.

---

the *Essay* need to be interpreted, as they seldom are, in the light
of the whole body of Pope's criticism; but even taken by themselves, as has been suggested, they are not so partisan as is sometimes supposed.

Hamelius, who insists upon regarding Pope as the typical neo-
classicist, interprets the just discussed passage as an attack on
Dryden's criticism, which he thinks of as opposing to the authority
of foreign critics the native art and taste of the English.[120] This is
certainly a rather gratuitous assertion. There is not the slightest
evidence that any of Pope's near contemporaries so understood the
passage. Nowhere does Pope attack Dryden as a critic; and there
was no such disparity in their views as would warrant an attack.
For all the latter's genuine enthusiasm for the great English
writers, he was anxious to be 'correct': says Professor Saintsbury,
truly, 'he copies, with a half ludicrous deference, the stock opinions
of the critics and criticasters in vogue; he gives us pages on pages
of their pedantic trivialities instead of his own shrewd and racy
judgments.'[121] Dryden was at his freest in his dramatic criticism,
where he had personal experience of the restraints of 'correctness':
he says, for example, that 'many of the tragedies in the former age
[the Elizabethan] among us were without comparison beyond
those of Sophocles and Euripides.'[122] But even in dramatic criticism,
he is often orthodox: the Preface to *Troilus and Cressida* gravely
informs us of 'the first rule which Bossu prescribes to the writer of
an heroic poem, and which holds too by the same reason in all
dramatic poetry. . . .'[123] In his discussions of the other *genres*—
particularly the epic—he is invariably 'correct.' The introduction
to the *Aeneid* is based on all the 'best authorities'; and even in the
Essay on Satire he takes occasion to point out that the epic poet
'must have exactly studied Homer and Virgil as his patterns,
Aristotle and Horace as his guides, and Vida and Bossu as their
commentators, with many others, both Italian and French. . . .'[124]
I need not labor the case: sufficient to remind the reader that
Dryden had a heavy ballast of neo-classicism. Nor is it necessary to
suppose, as modern commentators are fond of doing, that he was
sincerely attached only to the English worthies, particularly
Shakespeare. Even the great, as we like to delude ourselves into
forgetting, were of their time as well as beyond it.

As regards the particular relation of Dryden's to Pope's criticism, the evidence for its being rather a close one is good. Oldmixon

[120] Hamelius, 122.
[121] *History of Literary Criticism*, II, 373.
[122] Ker, II, 5.
[123] *ibid.*, I, 213.
[124] *ibid.*, II, 43.

expressly charges Pope with borrowing in the *Essay on Criticism* from 'Dryden's Prefaces and his *Essay on Dramatic Poetry*.'[125] Dr. Johnson points out that in the Preface to his Shakespeare, Pope 'expanded with great skill and elegance the character which had been given of Shakespeare by Dryden.'[126] Besides many phrases borrowed or imitated, there are three or four more significant instances of indebtedness to Dryden in the *Essay*. The notion that the rules are 'made only to reduce Nature into method' was probably taken by Pope direct from Rapin, but it is reinforced by Dryden.[127] Quite certainly the passage which contrasts the Greek critics who were the friends of the poets with the present generation, of quite another temper, comes, as Wakefield points out, from some remarks in the Dedication to Dryden's *Ovid*: the earlier critics 'were defenders of poets, and commentators on their works, to illustrate obscure beauties, to place some passages in a better light, to redeem others from malicious interpretations. Are our auxiliary forces turned our enemies? Are they from our seconds become principals against us?'[128] Equally certainly, it would seem, we may trace Pope's

> the ancients thus their rules invade,
> As kings dispense with laws themselves have made,

to Dryden's remark that 'Virgil might make this anachronism by superseding the mechanic rules of poetry, for the same reason that a monarch may dispense with or suspense his laws.'[129] The notion that those should be 'praised who but endeavored well' had also been expressed by Dryden. Presumably in both it was an 'occasional' and unmeditated sentiment.[130] The world has long said with Horace,

> mediocribus esse poetis
> Non homines, non di, non concessere columnae.[131]

and Pope believed with the world, as his long war with the 'dunces' gave him opportunity to testify, that 'Middling poets are no poets at all.'[132]

More important than the furnishing of a few specific passages was the general influence of Dryden's position. Even more pro-

[125] *Arts of Logic and Rhetoric*, xx.
[126] *Lives of the Poets*, III, 139.
[127] E-C, II, 39, n.
[128] *Essay*, I, 92-107. E-C, II, 39, and n.
[129] *ibid.*, I, 161-2. E-C, II, 43, and n.
[130] E-C, II, 65 and n.
[131] *Ars*, 372-3.
[132] Spence, 199.

nouncedly than Boileau and Rapin he was a mediator. Scholars like Hamelius who divide seventeenth century criticism into suspiciously neat categories find difficulty with Dryden: he belongs to all their categories, and hence to none. He had the advantage over the great French critics of feeling a warm devotion to earlier national literature; and it was this devotion which was, it seems to me, Dryden's chief gift to Pope. From the others he could learn that there were graces beyond the reach of the rules; from Dryden he could learn to love Chaucer and Spenser and Shakespeare, and find in their 'Gothic' greatness examples which must permanently liberalize his doctrine.

Of other Post-Restoration critics, Pope knew at least Sheffield, Roscommon, Rymer, and Walsh. These were all men of some ability and men who thought for themselves; they were not mere echoes of French criticism. Lord Roscommon attacked rhyme, praised blank verse and Milton, esteemed the English language and genius above the French; on the other hand, he had much at heart the improvement of his native tongue: like Swift at a later time, and Arnold still later, he was interested in the formation of an Academy.[133] Pope seems to have studied his *Essay on Translated Verse* with great care. He commends its 'noble' author in his roster of his critics; he is six or seven times in the course of the *Essay on Criticism* indebted to him for lines and couplets.[134]

John Sheffield, Duke of Buckingham,

> the Muse whose rules and practice tell
> 'Nature's chief masterpiece is writing well.'[135]

in general follows the French criticism: he devotes the body of his *Essay upon Poetry*, like Boileau, to a discussion of the *genres*. But he finds occasion to mention the great English poets, and to prefer Spenser over Tasso.[136] His extravagant eulogy of Homer anticipated Pope;[137] and his definition of wit as 'T'express agreeably a thing that's fit'[138] combines, with those of Boileau and Dryden, to suggest Pope's celebrated 'Nature to advantage dressed.'

'Pope thought highly of Rymer; and Rymer, no less than Dryden and Boileau, must be considered in tracing his intellectual ancestry.'[139] 'Rymer a learned and strict critic?' said Pope to Spence, 'Ay, that is exactly his character. He is generally right, though

---

[133] See Gayley and Kurtz, 401.
[134] E-C, II, notes to 37, 40, 41, 44, 56, 75.
[135] *Essay on Criticism*, III, 723-4.
[136] Spingarn, II, 296.
[137] *ibid.*, II, 295.
[138] *ibid.*, II, 294.
[139] *ibid.*, I, lxxvi.

rather too severe in his opinion of the particular plays he speaks of; and is, on the whole, one of the best critics we ever had.'[140] Pope in his capacity as Shakespearean differed 'with most of the individual comments of Rymer';[141] but he esteemed his erudition (upon several occasions he commended the account of the old French poets given in *A Short View of Tragedy*);[142] and, more important, he found in him, as well as in Boileau the emphasis on 'good sense' and reason which has wearied some in the *Essay on Criticism*.

Walsh, 'the muse's judge and friend,'[143] was one of Pope's first literary advisers. He now lives, like the other gentlemen we have just been discussing, only in the studies of scholars; but he was called by Dryden 'without flattery, the best critic of our nation';[144] and he was an 'elegant' student of *belles lettres*, with a considerable knowledge of the Italian poets at a time when they were generally neglected by Englishmen. He and Pope carried on an improving correspondence with one another. Every one remembers Walsh's exhortation to Pope to become a 'correct poet.' There was more to Walsh than that. His letters are still worth reading: they are well written and sensible. He feels the classical abhorrence of the 'conceit' and the 'metaphysical' poetry, 'in which there is no design or method, or anything natural or just . . . in all writings whatsoever (not poetry only) Nature is to be followed; and we should be jealous of ourselves for being fond of similes, conceits, and what they call saying fine things.'[145] Nature being far more to be desired than novelty, modern poets are rather to follow the *loci communes* of the ancients than to be original at the cost of eccentricity. But there is rationality in this classicism: 'Indeed, in all the common subjects of poetry the thoughts are so obvious, at least if they are natural, that whoever writes last must write things like what have been said before: but they may as well applaud the ancients for the arts of eating and drinking, and accuse the moderns of having stolen those inventions from them; it being evident in all such cases that whoever lived first must find them out.'[146] In other words, the ancients are to be 'followed,' not be-

[140] Spence, 172.
[141] Spingarn, I, lxxx.
[142] *e.g.*, Spence, 172.
[143] *Essay on Criticism*, III, 729.
[144] Ker, II, 244.
[145] E-C, VI, 55.
[146] *ibid.*, 53. Compare the passages from Addison and Johnson quoted on p. 4 and n. Fontenelle has developed Walsh's thought more fully, *Oeuvres*, V, 285.

cause they are the ancients, but because they anticipated us in following Nature.

These were Pope's predecessors in the long line of classical criticism. The survey just completed does not pretend to be a history of this criticism: it has treated the various names on the list purely from the point of view of their connection with Pope; it has attempted to trace, as far as possible, their influence upon him. But I hope that from the survey emerges the suggestion that these predecessors, so often characterized and so infrequently read, have long suffered from injustice; that not only was Pope himself more liberal and eclectic than is often supposed, but that the critics whom he read and from whom he learned were themselves men whose theories allowed for exceptions.

It is now time to discuss some of the terms most frequently employed in the *Essay* and in criticism contemporary with it: in a very real sense to understand the terminology and its history is to understand the whole intellectual point of view of the period.

The idea of Nature was not a new one in criticism. The Augustans inherited it from Seneca, Vida, Montaigne, and Charron; it was the watchword of classicism. By the time of Dryden it had come to be used in a sense which was derived partly from philosophy, partly from society, partly from literature. The rationalism of Descartes and the sensationalist philosophy of Hobbes conceived of the universe as governed by law, 'with general human nature as a microcosm of this mechanical order on the one side, man's mere whim on the other.'[147] The metaphysics of a mechanical (not in the modern sense mechanistic) universe produced an analogous conception of human nature: this, too, was a world of law and order. Men and women were classifiable by types: the whole doctrine of *decorum* was based upon this generalization, and the deduction thence that they are always to be represented 'true to type.' The miser, the senile old man, the fop, the coquette: such they are and not otherwise.[148] Then besides being types, men and women are human beings; and humanity itself is a constant factor. Human nature is the same in all ages and in all climes.

Cartesianism did not, however, take the emotions into sufficient account. It sought for a more special sort of constancy than could there be found. There are a hundred ways of feeling about a thing, it said, but the truth about it is one. The feelings vary with tem-

---

[147] Spingarn, I, lxvi.

[148] The study of human nature was often identified with knowledge of the types. Having enjoined the author 'Que la nature donc soit votre étude unique,' Boileau proceeds to specify that he means knowing 'ce que c'est qu'un prodigue, un avare, un honnête homme, un fat, un jaloux, un bizarre' (*Art Poétique*, III, 359; 363-4).

perament and special circumstances, but reason is the same in all
men. But the 'natural' in the microcosm is that which exhibits law
and order; it is the rational: 'qu'entend-on par la nature dans
l'ordre intellectuel, sinon ce qu'il y a de semblable et d'identique
dans tous les hommes, c'est-à-dire la raison?' It follows that a
'natural' person is one 'dont tous les mouvements sont réglés, qui
est vraie et judicieuse, qui parle et agit selon la vérité et la raison.'
To live 'conformably to nature' 'n'est pas s'abandonner à tous ses
mouvements, à tous ses instincts; c'est suivre la raison. Pour être
naturel, il faut se rendre libre de toutes les impressions, de tous les
jugements qui nous viennent du dehors, et qui substituent une
fausse nature à la véritable.'[149] In other words, to Augustan France
and England to 'follow nature' was not to abandon yourself to
your instincts—that would be to allow a 'false' or individual
nature—but to subordinate yourself to the commands of the one
thing which was the same in all men,—the reason.

Nature had, too, its social implications. The Latin peoples,
among which the conception originated, are socially minded.[150]
Their ideal of life is not to be attained in any richness except in
cities and (in earlier days) in courts. Here human relations
through their very complexity are required to submit to codifica-
tion: a society of extent and subtlety soon comes to have its own
inviolable laws, its canons of decorum and propriety. What deduction more easy than that these laws, so necessary for the
maintenance of social relations between men in their highest state,
the state in which they seem first to realize all the possibilities of
their humanity, should be regarded as expressing, not something
arbitrary, but something 'natural,' something inviolably stamped
upon men's hearts? Again, society and individualism (in any
vigorous sense) are sworn foes. From the point of view of society,
the natural is what cultivated people have in common, the unnatural that in which they differ. Society does not favor whim,
caprice, and eccentricity: it rebukes the assertion of the personal
as above the social man. Equally with the rationalist, then, society means by nature something which is thought of as universal:
it means the social code, the sentiments and manners of which men
have in common. Of course, the Augustans used *society* in its narrower sense: they distinctly meant by it the life of the upper
classes—the nobility and the gentry. 'Étudiez la cour et connoissez
la ville,' wrote Boileau.[151] Only when the social code rules human

[149] Nisard, II, 86-7.
[150] cf. Brunetière's interesting essay 'sur le caractère essentiel de la
littérature française' (*Études Critiques sur l'Histoire de la Litterature
Française*, 5ᵉ Série (Paris, 1893), 251-76).
[151] *Art Poétique*, III, 391.

life does it seem to attain to at once the universality and the order of the mechanical universe.

Augustan literature might have derived its conception of Nature from either of the sources discussed above. In some instances, it did so derive it. Dennis, for example, bases his aesthetics upon his cosmology: 'As man is the more perfect the more he resembles his Creator,' he tells us, 'the works of man must needs be more perfect the more they resemble his maker's. Now the works of God, though infinitely various, are extremely regular.'[152] But the classics afforded a third approach to the conception. In them one found—or seemed to find—a portrait of human nature for which the whole world appeared to have sat. One found universality, restraint, the social sense, all the things one esteemed in life, collected, as it were, into a treasury upon which one might make endless draught. Rapin reminds us that Demetrius and Longinus perpetually propose the Greek poets 'for models to those who study the sublime style; and it is in these great originals that our modern poets ought to consult nature, to learn how to raise their wits and be lofty';[153] he refers us to 'the good authors of antiquity, whose works are the only true sources whence these riches so necessary to poetry may be drawn.'[154]

The term Nature, which is used twenty-one times in the *Essay on Criticism*, bears in almost all cases this sense, derived from three points of view, of a regular and ordered world, with the emphasis commonly on human nature, the microcosm. The constancy of Nature and its universality are proclaimed. Her 'just standard' is 'still the same':

> Unerring Nature, still divinely bright,
> One clear, unchanged, and universal light,
> Life, force, and beauty must to all impart,
> At once the source, and end, and test of Art.[155]

But in the classics, as we have said, Nature is found in pre-eminent degree. When the Augustans thought of the ancients and their balanced, humanistic literature, they put in contrast to it the mediaevalism from which they felt their Northern countries just emergent, the barbarousness of the 'Gothic taste,' where fancy had free rein, and men studied not mankind but angels and 'monsters.' Bishop Hurd had in mind this contrast when he spoke of the later seventeenth century as the period when 'reason was but dawn-

[152] *Select Works*, II, 418.
[153] *Works*, II, 162.
[154] *ibid.*, II, 172.
[155] *Essay*, I, 68-73. cf. A. O. Lovejoy's 'E 17' definition of Nature as 'The universal and immutable in thought, feeling, and taste' (*M.L.N.*, XLII, 447).

ing, as we say, and just about to gain the ascendant over the portentous spectres of the imagination.' From 'spectre-haunted Europe with its romantic literature, its superstitions, its fanaticisms, and its religious wars,'[156] the Age of Reason had escape to the literature which depicted men, and gods made in their likeness. The Middle Ages had banished Nature in favor of the supernatural. When the Renaissance and later the *Aufklärung* wished to 'return to Nature,' where should they find so just a standard by which to *frame* their *judgment* as by that of the Age before the Flood, before the deluge of 'the Gothic and monkish ignorance and barbarity?'[157] In point of fact, to what generation since the Augustans has not the 'return to Nature' meant a return to the classics and their conception of life? As Goethe, the most eminent of literary Hellenists said, 'If we set our gaze on antiquity and earnestly study it in the desire to form ourselves thereon, we get the feeling as if it were only then that we really became men.'[158]

Of all the classics, Homer was the most natural: he was the poet of Nature, as Virgil was the poet of Art. To study him was 'to contemplate Nature in the place where she was seen to most advantage, collected in all her charms in the clear mirror of Homer.'[159] Pope's thought is clear enough, but he falls into confusion, as Dennis was prompt to note, when he attempted to illustrate his thesis that 'Nature and Homer were . . . the same.' Virgil is represented as first scorning to draw 'but from Nature's fountain'; and that being the case, it is certainly hard to see why the discovery that he might have followed Homer rather than the Nature there 'collected' should necessitate the checking of his 'bold design,' its confinement to strict rules. Is not Nature, then, identical with herself?[160]

Besides its conception of Nature, neo-classicism had its rules. How were these two standards to be reconciled? By the device which reconciled Nature and the ancients. We are to 'imitate' the authors of antiquity because they 'followed Nature'; and we are to obey the rules because they are simply the codifications of the regular and ordered scheme of things. The rules were not invented or 'devised': they were, like the 'laws' of modern science, 'discovered.' They do not supplant; they 'methodize' Nature.

> Nature, like Liberty, is but restrained
> By the same laws which first herself ordained.[161]

[156] L. P. Smith, *Four Words*, 7.
[157] Gildon (Durham, 42).
[158] *Maxims and Reflections*, 445.
[159] Warburton, E-C, II, 90.
[160] For sensible comment on the confusion see Dennis' *Reflections upon a Late Rhapsody* (in Durham, 223) and E-C, II, 42, n.
[161] *Essay*, I, 88-91.

No neo-classical doctrine has been more frequently misrepresented than that of 'the rules.' It seems sometimes to be thought that they were believed to be in and by themselves efficacious. As a matter of fact, their advocates almost invariably 'bottomed' them (to use Locke's homely term) upon Nature and reason. Countless illustrations might be given; I will select a few. D'Aubignac, who wrote an admired treatise, *Pratique du Théâtre*, 'qui passe pour le farouche et servile exécuteur des decisions d'Aristote, ne réclame aussi pour les fameuses règles d'autre autorité que celle qui leur vient de la raison.'[162] Dennis 'insisted even more strongly than his master [Dryden]' that 'the rules of Aristotle are nothing but nature and good sense reduced to method.'[163] In his *Grounds of Criticism* the same critic rationalizes very sensibly: 'If it [poetry] is an art, it follows that it must propose an end to itself, and afterwards lay down proper means for attaining that end. For this is undeniable, that there are proper means for the attaining of every end, and those proper means in poetry we call the rules.'[164] Rapin agrees with Pope's 'Just precepts thus from great examples given':[165] 'Aristotle,' he says, 'drew the platform of these rules from the poems of Homer and other poets of his time by the reflections he had a long time made on their works.'[166] He finds the advantage of the rules in the fact that they methodize the means of pleasing: 'because poetry is only profitable so far as it is delightful, 'tis of the greatest importance in this art to please; the only certain way to please is by the rules.'[167]

Pope, as we have seen, relates the rules to Nature; he also relates them to the end of poetry, the gaining of the heart.[168] 'Rules,' he says, 'were made but to promote their end,'[169]—to please. Rapin had asked 'Whether one may please in poetry against the rules?', and had given the plausible answer: 'I pretend that neither he [Molière] nor any others shall ever please, but by the rules. They have some natural draughts whereby they are successful, and these draughts are the strokes of art; for art, as I have said, is nothing else but good sense reduced to method. 'Tis only these strokes that are taking in irregular pieces, where what is irregular never pleases because 'tis never natural.'[170] Pope gives a different, but equally conciliatory answer: If there are not rules

[162] Lanson, 520.
[163] Paul, 148.
[164] *Select Works*, II, 417.
[165] *Essay*, I, 98.
[166] *Works*, II, 145.
[167] *ibid.*, II, 144.
[168] See *Essay*, I, 156-7.
[169] *ibid.*, I, 147.
[170] *Works*, II, 240. Similarly Gildon (Durham, 23): 'no play did ever please for any time, but by those parts of it which were conformed to the rules.'

for securing the desired effect, a 'lucky license' will 'answer to the full'; indeed, it in its turn, may become a rule for future writers,[171] since the rules simply methodize past success, simply act as convenient guide.

Pope will go farther. There are 'beauties' which 'no precepts can declare'; there are felicities, 'nameless graces which no methods teach' and to which only genius (the 'master-hand') can attain.[172] 'Invention's aid' is necessary and no amount of 'dull receipts how poems may be made'[173] will help him who is without it. Not only are there beauties which cannot be taught, but there are beauties which transgress the rules.

> Great wits sometimes may gloriously offend,
> And rise to faults true critics dare not mend.[174]

The ancients themselves 'their rules invade':[175] as kings, they may dispense with their own laws. Thus they produce 'freer beauties' which some presumptuous critics call faults, but which require only to be seen 'proportioned to their light or place'[176] to be recognized as beauties which make for variety.

Thus far Pope's treatment of the rules has been sensible and consistent. Unfortunately, at this point in the discussion he is disposed to forget his generally balanced position and his counsel to critics not to prize the classics only.[177] We are instructed that the ancients may violate the rules because they made them (though earlier we had been told that the great critics drew the rules from the practice of the great poets: the poets did not, in solemn conclave, agree upon laws which should bind them all); but that the moderns must 'beware': disobey 'seldom, and compelled by need'; and be able always to vouch the precedent of an ancient.[178] Here, indeed, we get that arbitrary conservatism which the hasty are apt to suppose the general characteristic of neo-classicists. Yet even here there is a touch of rationalism: if one must transgress let it be 'against the precept' (i.e., the specific rule) and not against its 'end,' the objective it proposes.[179]

Perhaps of all the terms in the vocabulary of Augustan critics *wit* was the most ambiguously as well as copiously employed. Pope uses it forty-two times in the *Essay on Criticism*, and in a multi-

---

[171] *Essay*, I, 145-9.
[172] *ibid.*, 141-4.
[173] *ibid.*, 114-15.
[174] *ibid.*, 152-3.
[175] *ibid.*, 161-2.
[176] *ibid.*, 170-4.
[177] *ibid.*, III, 194-5.
[178] *ibid.*, I, 161-6.

[179] *ibid.*, I, 163-4. Let me add, in leaving the subject, that I emphatically deny Hamelius' assertion that the 'French rules' 'Popes ganzes Evangelium bildeten' (105).

tude of meanings. 'A wit in the reign of Queen Anne,' remarks Mr. Elwin, 'was not only a jester, but any author of distinction; and wit besides its special signification was still sometimes employed as synonymous with mind. The ordinary generic and specific meanings, already confusing, and fruitful in ambiguity, were not sufficient for Pope. A wit with him was now a jester, now an author, now a poet, and now, again, was contradistinguished from poets. Wit was the intellect, the judgment, the antithesis to judgment, a joke, and poetry.'[180] Surely these tangles demand an explication.

'It was about the time of Cowley,' says Dr. Johnson, 'that Wit, which had been till then used for Intellection, in contradistinction to Will, took the meaning, whatever it be, which it now bears.'[181] These last clauses show that even in the Doctor's age the term continued to be one of many possibilities. But while new senses were added, it still retained the primary meaning just assigned, and is frequently used by Pope in that sense.[182]

From the intellectual powers in general, the term came to admit of a narrower interpretation as the creative faculty in man or its product, art. Dr. Johnson prefaces his remarks on the 'metaphysical' poetry with that observation that 'Wit, like all other things subject by their nature to the choice of man, has its changes and fashions, and at different times takes different forms.'[183] Pope considers it fitting that Aristotle, 'who conquered Nature, should preside o'er Wit.'[184] Contrasting authors and critics, he remarks that the former are 'partial to their wit' as the latter to their 'judgment.'[185] He speaks of the 'schools' of literary taste as 'parties in wit.'[186]

In a yet narrower sense, the term came to be used of the characteristic 'invention' of Donne and Cowley and those who followed in their train. Wit consisted in the discovery of unexpected and startling analogies, forced and esoteric figures, 'conceits,' as they were called. Wit was approximately synonymous with 'fancy' in the familiar contrast of the fancy and the imagination attributed to Coleridge; it was antithetical to 'judgment.' The 'metaphysical' poetry was not, as is well-known, confined to England; it had not so much sources as analogues in Italian Marinism, Spanish Gon-

---

[180] E-C, II, 25, n.
[181] *Lives of the Poets*, I, 36.
[182] e.g., *Essay*, I, 52-3; 60-1: II, 9-10; 228-9.
[183] *Lives of the Poets*, I, 18.
[184] *Essay*, III, 93.
[185] *ibid.*, I, 17-18.
[186] *ibid.*, II, 256.

garism, and the cult of the Pléiade in France. The conception may then be illustrated from Continental as well as English criticism. Rapin speaks of 'those who are furnished with *a naked wit only*, and who to be great poets rely principally on their *fancy*, as Chevalier Marino among the Italians, Theophile among the French.'[187] The same school of poets is hit at in the account of those 'that have *wit* and little judgment; they endeavor to hide what is irregular in their works by *glittering faults* and *false beauties*.'[188] Dr. Johnson defines this conception: 'Wit, abstracted from its effects upon the hearer, may be more rigorously and philosophically considered as a kind of *discordia concors*; a combination of dissimilar images, or discovery of occult resemblances in things apparently unlike. Of wit, thus defined, they [the 'metaphysical' poets] have more than enough. The most heterogeneous ideas are yoked by violence together; nature and art are ransacked for illustrations, comparisons, and allusions. . . .'[189] A passage in the *Essay* trenchantly characterizes the poets and their audience:

> Some to conceit alone their taste confine,
> And glittering thoughts struck out at every line;
> Pleased with a work where nothing's just or fit,
> One glaring chaos and wild heap of wit.
> Poets, like painters, thus unskilled to trace
> The naked nature and the living grace,
> With gold and jewels cover every part,
> And hide with ornaments their want of art.[190]

The last doctrine in our series is expressed in what is almost the best-known of Pope's couplets:

> True wit is nature to advantage dressed,
> What oft was thought, but ne'er so well expressed;[191]

This introduces us to Pope's distinction between *true* and *false* wit, by which latter he means the extravagances of the seventeenth century poets. It is to be noted that the celebrated couplet follows immediately upon the account of those who confine their taste to 'conceit alone.' Pope was not the first to attempt such a definition of wit as would restore to this good old word a sounder denotation. Addison had labelled the contending conceptions *true* and *false*, and others had suggested a sense approximating Pope's union of

[187] *Works*, II, 151.
[188] *ibid.*, II, 185. The italics are mine.
[189] *Lives of the Poets*, I, 20.
[190] *Essay*, II, 89-96.
[191] *ibid.*, II, 97-8.

the natural in thought with the felicitous in expression. Dryden had asserted that "The definition of wit which had been so often attempted, and ever unsuccessfully, by many poets is only this, that it is a propriety of thoughts and words.'[192] And the Duke of Buckingham in his admired *Essay upon Poetry* had twice given a 'hint':

> wit only should be brought
> To turn agreeably some proper thought.

> 'tis the top of wit
> T'express agreeably a thing that's fit.[193]

But it was certainly Pope who, agreeably to the sentiment of his definition, made the thought his property by giving it the perfect expression; and it was Pope who proceeded to exemplify the ideal by casting the *loci communes* of the classics and the wisdom of the world into a permanent English form.

It may be noted here that in the letters to Wycherley which were not published until 1735, but allegedly dated from the period prior to the composition of the *Essay*, there are two approaches to the passage there. One contrasts the *true* and the *false*: 'if by wit you mean no more than fancy or conceit; but in the better notion of wit, considered as propriety. . . .'[194] The other defines 'true wit' as 'a justness of thought and a facility of expression; or, in the midwives' phrase, a perfect conception with an easy delivery.'[195]

Dennis waxed gleeful over the lines,[196]

> Some, to whom Heaven in wit has been profuse,
> Want as much more to turn it to its use.[197]

But Pope is only indulging in a 'turn' on the two senses of the word. As Spingarn has remarked before me,[198] 'under rationalistic influence, wit, from being opposed to judgment, came to include it.' The wit which 'some' have in profusion is 'false wit,' and the 'as much more' of which they stand in need is 'judgment.' Fancy, or invention, plus judgment equals 'true wit.' Perhaps the 'turn' is hardly justifiable, but Pope might plead that in addition to the two senses just mentioned there was, still in use, the older interpretation of the intellective (as contrasted to the volitional) which included both.

---

[192] Ker, I, 190.
[193] Spingarn, II, 294.
[194] E-C, VI, 34. 'Propriety' will be recalled as Dryden's definition.
[195] *ibid.*, VI, 16.
[196] Durham, 228-9.
[197] *Essay*, I, 80-1.
[198] I, xxvii.

Two more terms remain to be noted. We have already seen that Pope's emphasis on 'sense' (variants, 'good sense,' 'common sense') derives from Rymer and through him from the rationalist school of criticism founded in France on Descartes and in England on Hobbes. *Le bon sens* was constantly employed in French criticism during the last thirty years of the seventeenth century, from the time of the Abbé d'Aubignac. Molière adopted it as a standard 'sufficient in itself for the critical discussion of literature.' Common sense furnished the arrows which reached home in Buckingham's *Rehearsal*. In his *Tragedies of the Last Age*, Rymer can dispense with learning, knowledge of critical theory, and experience: *common sense suffices.*[199] The celebrated *Querelle des Anciens et des Modernes* had as its 'modernists' the followers of Descartes, who defied the notion of authority in literature, could not find the enthusiasm of Boileau and Racine for Homer and Euripides entirely 'reasonable.' The classicists were fond of alleging in support of their favorites the universal consent of all ages; but Abbé Terrasson asserted[200] that 'le principe propre et naturel par lequel on doit juger d'un ouvrage de belles-lettres n'est pas l'antique et constante admiration qu'on a eue pour cet ouvrage, c'est la conformité réelle qu'il doit avoir avec la droite raison et la belle nature. . . .' According to the 'modernists,' each man is at liberty to judge the great works of antiquity for himself by the rule of the evident. Reason is always identical with itself and common to all men. Hence, what is true will, in all times and places, appear evident to the reason of men. One has the right to condemn what is to him unintelligible. 'Toutes les critiques que Perrault, Fontenelle, La Motte dirigent contre les oeuvres particulières des anciens sont fondées sur ce principe, ce que je ne comprends pas ne saurait être raisonnable.'[201]

There was a real issue at stake between classicism and rationalism: the principles represented were essentially at variance. But a temporary *rapprochement* was possible. In the seventeenth century, as Lanson shows, Cartesianism, classicism, and the Christian religion were compatible, even friendly: the eighteenth century saw the dissolution of the alliance. Boileau and Pope, eclectically desirous of including all that was good in both classicism and rationalism 'speciously reconciled' them 'by the assumption that, since nature and reason were best exemplified in the ancients, classical practice rather than reason or nature itself should be the

---

[199] Spingarn, I, lxix-xx.
[200] Terrasson, I, iv.
[201] Lanson, 536.

guide of the poet and critic.'[202] Pope uses 'sense' and its variant phrases, 'good sense,' 'men of sense,' 'superior sense,' etc. eighteen times in the *Essay on Criticism*, but without implying thereby any antithesis to the classics or the 'received critics.'

Like *wit* and unlike *sense*, the critical term *taste* shows change of conception. Originally it meant 'a mere instinct or sentiment of the mind, without order or authority,'[203] the product of the heart rather than the head, the sentiment rather than reason; it was the personal equation. Again, it was the aesthetic faculty which enabled the man of discernment to enjoy beauties for which no rules gave warrant, to delight in the mysterious felicities of art. The characteristic phrase of the 'school' was *Je ne sais quoi*: one's rapture admits of no definition; it is indescribable. At this stage, the conception achieved great popularity: it represented individual as distinguished from social appreciation; it was a criterion capable, by its expression of the impulse of the heart, of antithesis to the rules and to 'good sense'; it lent itself to a dilettante toying with art which masked as a more exquisite, because inexpressible, enjoyment. We get echoes of this popularity in some of the dialogue of Gildon's *Art of Poetry*, where the ladies play with the phrases very prettily. 'The general judgment of the town,' we are told, 'is . . . made and formed on *Je-ne-sais-quois*, they *know-not-what*, their beautiful extravagancies and many such empty sounds. . . .' One lady actually prefers the 'wild and confused productions of blind' fancy, such as a sampler from the days of Queen Bess, to works of order and harmony in accordance with the rules: 'the wretched creature replied that there was something, she *did not know what*, of Antiquity in the other that made it venerable. That she did not know the art, or the nicety of the stitches, and happy mixture of the colors and the like;[204] but her eye was much more pleased with a *Je ne sais quoish* beauty of the old piece without order, beauty, or harmony of the parts than with all the correspondence and *ordonance* of mine.'[205]

We now see the affiliations of some passages in Pope's *Essay* already cited in other connections. From the liberalizing doctrines of the 'school of taste' derive the 'beauties no precepts can declare,' the 'nameless graces,' the 'lucky license,' the 'grace beyond the reach of art.'

But it was possible so to define *taste* as to make it approximate the criteria of the other contemporary 'schools'; and there are

---

[202] Spingarn, I, lxxxi.
[203] *ibid.*, I, xci.
[204] i.e., the technical side of art.
[205] Durham, 40.

never wanting in any age those who are pleased to synopsize, harmonize, reconcile conceptions on the face of them opposite. It was possible to rationalize taste, to divorce it from individual whim, and erect it into another principle constant in all persons of culture, though independent of the rules.[206] Surely, however many tastes there may be, there is only one proper taste, one 'good' taste. And 'good taste,' the natural feeling of all persons of culture, manifestly will not depart from that other universal faculty, the reason. But the rules, the symbol of classicism, are not arbitrary: they are founded on reason; they are Nature reduced to method. Whatever the critics' first principles in the Augustan age, their backgrounds and their ideals were not very different, and this consonancy tended to neutralize the individualization of the terms themselves. The process is already complete when Abbé Batteux can speak of that neo-classical compendium, the *Ars* of Horace, as 'good taste reduced to principle.'[207]

The *Essay on Criticism* is expressive of this later stage in the history of the term: 'in Pope the poetical principle "wit," and the critical principle, "taste," are virtually identified with sense.'[208] The term is used only five times; but four of its occurrences are in important passages, as where the 'true genius' which is necessary to poets is parallel with the 'true taste' which ought to distinguish critics, and where the critic is advised to know the reach of his own 'genius, taste, and learning.'[209]

In the two preceding sections of this chapter, we have been studying the *Essay on Criticism* in the light of its background of critics and critical schools. We have studied Pope's 'sources' and the use he made of them; it remains to consider his originality. The point of view was suggested in some introductory remarks:[210] Part One of the *Essay* is a compendium of 'sound' doctrine culled from many sources and representing not only neo-classicism proper but rationalism and the 'school of taste,' in which Pope's task was to select, to harmonize, and to express with precision and finality. In the Second and Third Parts, on the other hand, his indebtedness is only for occasional phrases; his plan—the discussion of the biases which warp critical sanity, his 'character' of the true critic, and his history of criticism—and his substance are his own. He had no model to follow here; and he drew his material not from books but from observation and experience. The types

[206] Spingarn, I, xcviii.
[207] Quoted in Cook, *The Art of Poetry* (1892), xix.
[208] Spingarn, I, lxxvi.
[209] *Essay*, I, 12; 49.
[210] *ante*, pp. 1-3.

discussed are universal, but on that very account they could be and were copied from life. We shall be able to see in later chapters whether Pope's own criticisms were guided by the principles here enunciated; it is sufficient now to remark that these principles are full, to a degree seldom recognized, of balance, moderation, and justness.

Let me illustrate by Pope's exposition of the causes which prevent correct judgment in criticism. The first is pride, which is ever ready to supply the deficiencies of 'wit': in order to remove which we should make use of the criticism of our foes as well as of our friends.

The second is superficial knowledge: 'A little learning is a dangerous thing'; the critic is tempted to presumption which the really erudite are above: 'drinking largely sobers us again.'[211]

The third is the vice of judging by parts rather than by the whole. Criticism should not be petty and captious, mindful of small defects and oblivious to large excellences.

> And if the means be just, the conduct true,
> Applause, in spite of trivial faults, is due.[212]

The virtues of poetry are not negative: if we cannot censure them, we can fall asleep over

> such lays as neither ebb nor flow,
> Correctly cold and regularly low.[213]

Great poetry is that in which 'Nature moves and rapture warms the mind';[214] it must sometimes 'neglect the rules each verbal critic lays,'[215] the minute prescriptions of criticasters, in order to avoid graver faults. A true critic will accordingly 'survey the whole'[216] of a work, not judge it by its conformity to a 'loved' folly of his own. He will read in 'the same spirit that its author writ,'[217] not pedantically conclude that

> all were desperate sots and fools
> Who durst depart from Aristotle's rules.[218]

The fourth vice is caring only for one particular element of poetry. Some critics fancy only conceits, 'glittering thoughts,' and are pleased with a work which contains these false brilliants though it include nothing 'just' or 'fit.' Others care only for 'language,' style, eloquence, and pay no attention to the thought;

[211] *Essay*, II, 15, 18.
[212] *ibid.*, 57-8.
[213] *ibid.*, 39-40.
[214] *ibid.*, 36.
[215] *ibid.*, 61.
[216] *ibid.*, 35.
[217] *ibid.*, 34.
[218] *ibid.*, 71-2.

forgetting that where words are most abundant, sense is apt to be absent, and that eloquence is not appropriate to all subjects.[219] Some of these lovers of language belong to the cult of the archaic: they are

> Ancients in phrase, mere moderns in their sense;
> Such labored nothings, in so strange a style,
> Amaze th' unlearned, and make the learned smile.[220]

But most critics judge a poem by its versification: 'smooth or rough with them is right or wrong.'[221] They care to please only their ears; they are pleased with dulcetly monotonous rhymes, and have a fondness for the Alexandrine.[222] They forget the law of decorum, that manner should suit matter.

The fifth is what we may call literary chauvinism.

> Some foreign writers, some our own despise;
> The ancients only, or the moderns prize.[223]

Yet genius cannot be confined to any age or territory.

> Meanly they seek the blessing to confine,
> And force the sun but on a part to shine,
> Which not alone the southern wit sublimes,
> But ripens spirits in cold northern climes;
> Which from the first has shone on ages past.
> Enlights the present, and shall warm the last.[224]

The sixth and the seventh are opposites. Some critics simply borrow the judgments of others, 'reason and conclude by precedent,'[225] not by independent thought. They estimate the value of new works by the reputations of their authors. Worst of all of

---

[219] *Essay*, II, 105-19.   [221] *ibid.*, 138.
[220] *ibid.*, 125-7.   [222] *ibid.*, 140-57.
[223] *ibid.*, 194-5.

[224] This passage is another evidence of Pope's eclecticism. The thought here expressed, that genius is as constant as human nature, not limited to Greece and Italy ('not alone the southern wit sublimes') but operative in France and England, not limited to antiquity ('ages past') but a force in the present and a surety for the future, was a favorite with the rationalists, or modernists, in their controversy with the classicists. Perrault says:

> A former les esprits comme à former les corps
> La Nature en tout temps fait les mesmes efforts,
> Son estre est immuable, et cette force aisée
> Dont elle produit tout ne s'est point épuisée.

(*Parallèle*, I, 186); and Fontenelle: 'Les siècles ne mettent aucune différence naturelle entre les hommes. Le climat de la Grece ou de l'Italie, et celui de la France, sont trop voisins pour mettre quelque différence sensible entre les Grecs ou les Latins et nous. . . .' *Oeuvres*, V, 284.

[225] *Essay*, 210.

this sort are those who sell their judgments to the rank of a patron;
who 'fetch and carry nonsense for my lord.'[226] But on the other
hand, the 'learned' often err 'by being singular': they are so desirous of thinking the reverse of the crowd

> that if the throng
> By chance go right, they purposely go wrong.[227]

The eighth and last is party spirit. Some 'valuing those of their
own side,'[228] praise only writers who adhere to the Tory party;
some only Whigs.

> Parties in wit attend on those of state,
> And public faction doubles private hate.[229]

It would be difficult, it seems to me, to find a discussion of what
is to be avoided in criticism which surpasses that just outlined for
inclusiveness, catholicity, and balance. Nowhere is there better
evidence that the *Essay on Criticism* is not a party document: an
opponent would be hard put to it to find instances of neo-classical
narrowness here. And similarly catholic is the portrait of the ideal
critic in Part Three, which Sainte-Beuve said every professional
critic should frame and hang up in his study:[230]

> But where's the man who counsel can bestow,
> Still pleased to teach, and yet not proud to know?
> Unbiassed or by favor or by spite;
> Not dully prepossessed, nor blindly right;
> Though learned, well-bred, and though well-bred, sincere;
> Modestly bold, and humanly severe;
> Who to a friend his faults can freely show,
> And gladly praise the merit of a foe;
> Blessed with a taste exact, yet unconfined,
> A knowledge both of books and humankind;[231]
> Generous converse; a soul exempt from pride:
> And love to praise with reason on his side?[232]

Of course, when I speak of the originality of Pope as exhibited
in the Second and Third Parts of the *Essay*, I do not mean to imply

[226] *Essay*, 217.

[227] *ibid.*, 225-7.

[228] *ibid.*, 252.

[229] *ibid.*, 256-7.

[230] In his review of Taine's *English Literature, Nouveaux Lundis*, May
30, 1864.

[231] The ideal of the *honnête homme*: cf. Boileau's

> Que les vers ne soient pas votre éternel emploi,
> Cultivez vos amis, soyez homme de foi.
>
> (*Art*, IV, 121-2.)

[232] *Essay*, III, 72-83.

that the views there expressed were novel; that our pleasure in them proceeds from our surprise. 'When I was a young man,' Goldsmith wrote, 'I was perpetually starting new propositions; but I soon gave that over; I found that generally what was new was false.'[233] Pope would have agreed with this conclusion, though unlike the quoted speaker, he was born to wisdom. According to modern conceptions, originality seems sometimes to be thought of as the new even when it is the false or the 'unnatural.' Obviously Pope does not possess it if it must be so defined: he 'followed Nature everywhere, but was not so bold to go beyond her.'[234] And Nature is, as humanists believe, constant in all ages and climes.

In what sense, then, may a classicist be original? In seeing Nature for himself rather than, or as well as, through 'the spectacles of books.' Even the *Essay* exhibits abundant evidence that Pope had done this. 'He was certainly in his early life a man of great literary curiosity,' says Dr. Johnson; but he adds with yet greater assurance that 'he studied in the academy of Paracelsus, and made the universe his favorite volume. He gathered his notions fresh from reality; not from the copies of authors, but the originals of Nature.'[235] The *Essay on Criticism* has been misconceived when it has been judged in the light of the First Part alone. In that, a young man digests what he has read, attempts to harmonize the opinions of the 'received critics'; in the rest of the poem, he is giving us, on his own account, an empirical study of the 'psychology' of critics.

To the doctrine of the *Essay*, all the 'authorities' have contributed, especially Vida, Boileau, Rapin, and Dryden. Part One attempts, as Boileau and Dryden had done, to reconcile the so-called schools of classicism, rationalism, and taste. In the *Essay*, classicism 'transcends by including' the others; but the result is far from the rigid arbitrary dogmatism so often attributed to it. The classics are not the only literature to be admired. Rules are not *a priori* but empirical, convenient formulations of the successful usage of the past. Intelligent criticism is criticism in the light of the *end* and *spirit* of the author. It is not to concern itself unduly with *minutiae* but to estimate by the total effect of the work considered. A creed in which these tenets appear can hardly be judged grossly illiberal.

What Pope borrows in the *Essay* he makes his own; he adds what only he has to give.

---

[233] In a passage, admired by Dr. Johnson, included in the first draft of the *Vicar of Wakefield*, but later deleted. See Boswell, III, 376.
[234] Ker, II, 258.
[235] *Lives of the Poets*, III, 216.

CHAPTER II

I

IN the place of the 'arts of poetry' which his predecessors in the line of the classical tradition wrote, Pope essayed the variant of a treatise on criticism. But manifestly he was a poet who was interested in the technique of his craft,—who had his views on how to write. The purpose of the present chapter is to collect these views into something like the form they might have taken in a veritable *Ars Poetica*.

Pope took the profession of poet seriously. There was, in his opinion, a vast separation to be made between those who write for their own diversion and those who devote their life to their art. The demarcation appears in his remarks on Crashaw: the application is hardly apt, but the generalization is sound. 'I take this poet,' he says, 'to have writ like a gentleman,—that is, at leisure hours, and more to keep out of idleness than to establish a reputation—so that nothing regular or just can be expected from him. . . . No man can be a true poet who writes for diversion only. These authors ['the mob of gentlemen who wrote with ease'] should be considered as versifiers and witty men rather than as poets. . . .'[1]

One can, to be sure, find passages in which Pope affects to take his poetry lightly. 'I take up with the Muses for want of your better company,' he writes Cromwell.[2] In his genteel 'Author's Preface' he 'confess[es] it was want of consideration that made me an author: I writ because it pleased me . . .';[3] he speaks of the advantages of 'a genius to poetry' as 'the agreeable power of self-amusement when a man is idle or alone' and 'the privilege of being admitted into the best company.'[4] The *Epistle to Dr. Arbuthnot* makes composition the leniment of ill-health:

> The Muse but served to ease some friend, not wife,
> To help me through this long disease, my life.[5]

[1] E-C, VI, 116.
[2] *ibid.*, VI, 127.
[3] *ibid.*, I, 7.

[4] E-C, I, 6.
[5] ll. 131-2.

But this was the polite affectation of the time. The older, still sincerely felt, devotion to 'a poet's dignity'[6] was in conflict with the ideal of the *honnête homme*, who, according to La Rochefoucauld, 'picques himself on nothing.' Boileau had advised the poet,

> Que les vers ne soient pas votre éternel emploi;
> Cultivez vos amis, soyez homme de foi.
> C'est peu d'être agréable et charmant dans un livre,
> Il faut savoir encore et converser et vivre.[7]

Should not the writer be lost in the gentleman? It will be recalled that when Voltaire came to pay his respects to the admired Congreve, the latter begged him to look upon him not as an author but as a 'gentleman.' The *Epistle to Dr. Arbuthnot* is a long protest against the popular reduction of man into poet:

> Heavens! was I born for nothing but to write?
> Has life no joys for me? or (to be grave)
> Have I no friend to serve, no soul to save?[8]

The letters Pope wrote in later life studiously avoid the shop-talk of the study: they dally with the delights of gardening; they announce a stoical detachment from the world; they swear undying friendship.

No one was ever deceived by the graceful pose. In a real sense, Pope was nothing if, and when, not a poet.[9] He was constantly preoccupied with composition. 'Swift complains that he was never at leisure for conversation because he "had always some poetical scheme in his head." It was punctually required that his writing box should be set upon his bed before he rose; and Lord Oxford's domestic related that in the dreadful winter of 'Forty, she was called from her bed by him four times in one night to supply him with paper lest he should lose a thought.'[10] Pope himself wrote of his absorption in his art to Jervas: 'I have the greatest proof in nature at present of the amusing power of poetry, for it takes me up so entirely that I scarce see what passes under my nose, and hear nothing that is said about me. To follow poetry as one ought, one must forget father and mother, and cleave to it alone.'[11] He describes the Muses to Cromwell as those '*Quae nobiscum pernoctant, peregrinantur, rusticantur.*'[12]

---

[6] *ibid.*, 263.   [8] ll. 272-4.

[7] *Art Poétique*, IV, 121-4.

[9] Dr. Johnson asks, 'of what could he be proud but of his poetry?' (*Lives*, III, 208).

[10] *Lives of the Poets*, III, 208-9.   [11] E-C, VIII, 6.

[12] *ibid.*, VI, 127. Pope is, of course, adapting Cicero's celebrated eulogy of books in the Oration *Pro Archia Poeta*.

Pope was fully aware that genius was necessary to a poet; that poetry could not be produced by effort and training alone. The frequent references to the Muses and their inspiration do not constitute a mere decorative device borrowed from the ancients. Pope would have agreed with Shelley that 'Poetry is not, like reasoning, a power to be exerted according to the determination of the will. A man cannot say, "I will compose poetry".'[13] True genius derives from heaven its light;[14] it is not produced by effort. Pope knew as well as another the psychology of 'inspiration,' the visits of the

> sacred Nine, that all my soul possess,
> Whose raptures fire me, and whose visions bless,[15]

He does not confuse the imagination (in the modern sense) with the understanding. His later correspondence is full of the lament that the one has failed as the other has gained. '*Non sum qualis eram!*' he writes Swift;[16] 'My understanding indeed, such as it is, is extended rather than diminished; I see things more in the whole, more consistent, and more clearly deduced from, and related to, each other. But what I gain on the side of philosophy, I lose on the side of poetry: the flowers are gone when the fruits begin to ripen. . . .' The poetic gift disappears, or is transmuted, with the passage of youth: 'As the Psalmist says on another occasion, the age of a Muse is scarce above five and twenty: all the rest is labor and sorrow.'[17]

Pope emphasizes, as we should expect, the necessity for the 'limae labor et mora'[18]; he agrees with Horace,

> Nec rude quid prosit video ingenium. . . .[19]

He apologizes to Caryll for sending him 'thoughts just warm from the brain, without any polishing or dress, the very *déshabille* of the understanding.'[20] He instructs Broome to be sure his Miscellany is 'Carefully and correctly done.'[21] The task of polishing was agreeable to him: 'I corrected because it was as pleasant to me to correct as to write'[22]; and he believed in its efficacy. Dr. Johnson reprints some transcripts of passages from the manuscript of 'Pope's Homer'[23] which sufficiently evidence the meticulousness of the poet's composition; and when Spence 'was looking on his foul copy of the *Iliad* and observing how very much it was corrected

[13] *A Defense of Poetry.*
[14] *Essay on Criticism*, I, 13.
[15] *Windsor Forest*, 259-60.
[16] E-C, VII, 342.
[17] *ibid.*, IX, 433.
[18] Horace: *Ars*, 291.
[19] *ibid.*, 410.
[20] E-C, VI, 170.
[21] *ibid.*, VIII, 119.
[22] *ibid.*, I, 7.
[23] *Lives*, III, 120-5; E-C, III, 206 ff., prints a facsimile of one of Pope's minutely corrected manuscripts.

and interlined, he said, "I believe you would find, upon examination, that those parts which have been the most corrected read
the easiest".'[24] But he regarded industry as the necessary supplement to genius, not as its substitute. 'You do not need any man to
make you a good poet,' he wrote Broome, 'you need no more than
what every good poet needs,—time, and diligence, and doing
something every day. *Nulla dies sine linea.*'[25] Industry and attention cannot produce, but they can develop, a 'good poet.'

Pope undoubtedly held, with all the poets of the Renaissance
and the Enlightenment, that poetry is to instruct as well as please.
But, as we have seen, he did not confuse poetry with philosophy.
It is true that in his later period he was in a rather definite sense
a 'moral poet,' and that he was greatly admired in this capacity.
Swift, for example, writes him of the *Epistles*, 'I am often wonder-
ing how you come to excel all mortals on the subject of morality,
even in the poetical way';[26] and again, 'I am amazed to see you
exhaust the whole science of morality in so masterly a manner.'[27]
Pope himself remarked, 'No writing is good that does not tend to
better mankind in some way or other.'[28] But there is no need to take
utterances like this last to imply the limitation of poetry to didacticism; and such a limitation was far indeed from the poet's intention. In this connection we may usefully recall Pope's description of himself:

> That not in fancy's maze he wandered long,
> But stooped to truth, and moralized his song.[29]

The contrast in both these passages is not so much between the
didactic and the creative in art as between the views implied in
those baffling terms, the *classic* and the *romantic*. Classical art is
built on *vraisemblance*, decorum, truth to nature: it 'follows
Nature everywhere,' but is 'never so bold to go beyond her.'[30]
Romantic art is the escape to the ivory tower; it dallies in
'fancy's maze'; it blows air-bubbles of sentiment and aspiration;
it builds, with Shelley, a 'many-colored haze of words and images,

> Pinnacled dim in the intense inane.'[31]

Pope asserts the classical view of art: it bears relation to human
life; it is a 'criticism of life.'

[24] Spence, 265.
[25] E-C, VIII, 49.
[28] Spence, 203.
[26] *ibid.*, VII, 358.
[27] *ibid.*, 344.
[29] *Epistle to Dr. Arbuthnot*, 340-1.
[30] Dryden's happy account of Chaucer. Ker, II, 258.
[31] Arnold: *The Study of Poetry* (*Essays in Criticism*, Second Series).

II

All poetry is divided *in tres partes*. 'There are,' said Pope, 'three distinct *tours* in poetry,—the design, the language, and the versification.'[32] Let us consider at some length Pope's attitude toward them.

Under 'design' we are concerned with 'invention' and 'imitation,' both of which are the agencies for the production of the scheme or 'fable,' which is the 'soul of poetry.'[33] Pope, like his contemporaries used these terms with some looseness. *Invention* was employed by the Latin critics in its strictly etymological denotation: 'the question of originality hardly ever arose in our modern sense, because the ancient authors adopted a different attitude towards the function of *inventio*, or invention. I mean that the ancient author found (*invenit*), but did not fabricate (*fingit*) his material. There is, therefore, no exact technical equivalent in ancient literature for our term *fiction*.'[34] But the term 'find' is itself ambiguous: if the neo-classicist may be thought of as drawing his subjects from literature, the classicist discovers his in Nature: he copies rather than creates. In the Preface to Homer, where Pope speaks most of 'invention,' he uses it in what may be called its genuine, or Aristotelian, sense. Invention is not appropriation from the works of others; neither is it the production of something which never was on land or sea, the evocation of vagrant desire. It is the creation of a microcosm in the image and likeness of the macrocosm. Homer, 'wanting yet an ampler sphere to expatiate in, opened a new and boundless walk for his imagination, and created a world for himself in the invention of fable.'[35] But this new world is not without the bounds of Nature: it but expands those bounds. It creates by copying archetypal patterns.

It will be seen that the conception is capable of being approached from the side either of creation or 'imitation.' In his Preface, Pope emphasized particularly, and with much warmth, that aspect of it with which moderns are most struck,—the creative: 'It is the invention that in different degrees distinguishes all great geniuses; the utmost stretch of human study, learning, and industry, which masters everything besides, can never attain to this. It furnishes Art with all her materials, and without it, judgment itself can at best but *steal wisely*, for Art is only like a prudent steward that lives on managing the riches of Nature.' Judgment may select, control, prune; yet 'Whatever praises may be given to works of

[32] Spence, 23.
[33] Aristotle's phrase; quoted by Pope in the Preface to the *Iliad*.
[34] Fiske, 42.   [35] Durham, 325.

judgment, there is not even a single beauty in them but is owing to the invention. . . .'³⁶ The poet is primarily 'maker': as long as Homer's 'invention,' 'which is indeed the characteristic of poetry itself, remains unequalled by his followers, he still continues superior to them.'³⁷

'Imitation,' like 'invention,' is a term susceptible of varying interpretations. Aristotle meant by *mimesis*, as we know, the copying of Nature, or the universals of human experience: 'The primary objects of artistic imitation,' he says, "are human beings in action, men performing or undergoing something.'³⁸ Art is an expression of life and experience. 'Imitation' reminds the artist that it is not his function to wander in 'fancy's maze,' but to 'copy Nature.' But of course the term was easy to misinterpret. The literature of Rome was, as we have so often been told, a derivative literature; it was a literature of models and standards, whose ambition was to produce in Latin the equivalents of the Greek classics.³⁹ The steps were easy, first to extend the 'imitation' to cover the copying of earlier poets, and then habitually to limit it to that sense. Renaissance critics pretty generally, particularly the more devout Maronolatrists, were zealous preachers of 'imitation' in this secondary sense. The worship of Virgil and the exaltation of the epic as a form which had its set rules and prescriptions led, naturally enough, in Scaliger and Minturno and Tasso, to 'the formation of a kind of poetical stockroom of metaphors and figures, regulation poetic devices and tricks for the production to order of epic, tragedy, sonnet and epigram.'⁴⁰ Castelvetro, perhaps alone, understood 'imitation' in its Aristotelian sense.

Vida, whom Pope attentively read and assiduously praised, was of all Renaissance critics the most insistent on the modern poet's dependence upon the ancients. He enjoined a 'lawful' robbery. One is to 'steal in broad day, and glory in the theft,' 'strip the ancients, and divide the spoils.'⁴¹

³⁶ Durham, 323.
³⁷ *ibid.*, 341.
³⁸ *Poetics*, II.
³⁹ 'Thus by the Augustan age . . . the works of certain masters had attained a sort of canonical literary authority. Virgil, for example, is in his *Eclogues* a Roman Theocritus, in his *Georgics* a Roman Hesiod, in his *Aeneid* the continuator in the main of the Homeric epic and the Ennean *Annales*. Propertius regards himself as a Roman Callimachus. Horace's lyric poetry is modelled on the Aeolic lyrics of Sappho, Alcaeus, and Anacreon. . . .' Fiske, 42.
⁴⁰ Charlton, 27.
⁴¹ The phrases are from Pitt's translation. I will append some passages from the original *Ars*:

But no one, not even Vida, supposed that a modern poem might be simply a mosaic of stolen beauties:

> Non tamen omnia te priscis fas fidere, qui non
> Omnia sufficient: quaerenti pauca labore
> Attentanda tuo, nondum ulli audita, supersunt.[42]

Certainly neither Pope nor Sir Joshua Reynolds, both of whom were sincerely interested in understanding the classical tradition in criticism, held for a moment to a theory so extreme and absurd. In the first place, both had some acquaintance with the sounder conception of 'imitation': Pope defines the Pastoral as 'an imitation of the action of a shepherd, or one considered under that character';[43] Reynolds' *Discourses* are throughout a development of the Aristotelian conception of art, even though their author commonly uses the term 'imitation' in the sense which it more generally conveyed at the period.[44]

Pope and Reynolds were concerned to reconcile 'imitation' with 'invention.' It is not enough to borrow: creation must come in somewhere. Pope gives several solutions. He writes Walsh, 'I would beg your opinion too as to another point: it is how far the liberty of borrowing may extend? I have defended it sometimes by saying that it seems not so much the perfection of sense to say things that had never been said before as to express those best that have been said oftenest. A mutual commerce makes poetry flourish; but then poets, like merchants, should repay with something of their own what they take from others; not, like pirates, make prize of all they meet.'[45] It is the poet's function, in other words, to express not the thoughts and feelings which are peculiar to him, but those which are common to mankind; to give perfect

> Haud tamen interea reliquum explorare labores
> Abstiteris vatum, moneo, suspectaque dicta
> Sublegere, et variam ex cunctis abducere gazam.
> (III, 193-5.)

> Saepe palam quidam rapiunt, cupiuntque videri
> Omnibus intrepidi, ac furto laetantur in ipso
> Deprensi. . . .   (III, 223-5.)

> Ergo agite o mecum securi accingite furtis
> Una omnes, pueri, passimque avertite praedam.
> (III, 243-4.)

[42] *Ars Poetica*, III, 264-6.
[43] E-C, I, 258.
[44] 'By imitation, I do not mean imitation in its largest sense, but simply the following of other masters, and the advantages to be drawn from the study of their works.' *Discourses*, 90.
[45] E-C, VI, 52.

utterance to those *loci communes* which sum up human experience and human wisdom.[46] The poet can only be said to plagiarize when he is not able to assimilate what he has borrowed; when he copies without improving.

The thought is amplified by Reynolds. 'We come now,' he says, 'to speak of another kind of imitation,—the borrowing of a particular thought, an action, attitude, or figure, and transplanting it into your own work: this will either come under the charge of plagiarism, or be warrantable, and deserve commendation, according to the address with which it is performed. . . . It is generally allowed that no man need be ashamed of copying the ancients: their works are considered as a magazine of common property always open to the public, whence every man has a right to take what materials he pleases; and if he has the art of using them, they are supposed to become to all intents and purposes his own property. . . . He who borrows an idea from an ancient or even from a modern artist not his contemporary, and so accommodates it to his own work that it makes a part of it, with no seam or joining appearing, can hardly be charged with plagiarism. But an artist should not be contented with this only; he should enter into a competition with his original and endeavor to improve what he is appropriating to his own work.'[47]

Again, Pope urges that without 'borrowing' one is limited to a narrower range both of experience and of subject. We secure catholicity and variety by appropriating the thoughts of our fellows. 'Writers in the case of borrowing from others are like trees which of themselves would produce only one sort of fruit, but by being grafted upon others may yield variety.'[48] And Reynolds tells us that 'The mind is but a barren soil,—a soil which is soon exhausted, and will produce no crop, or only one, unless it is continually fertilized and enriched with foreign matter.'[49] 'The greatest natural genius cannot subsist on its own stock; he who resolves never to ransack any mind but his own will be soon reduced, from mere barrenness, to the poorest of all imitations: he will be obliged to imitate himself, and to repeat what he has before often repeated.'[50]

In some remarks prefaced to his *Observations*,[51] Pope expressly attempts to reconcile 'imitation' with 'invention.' The one 'does not hinder' the other, he assures us. 'We may observe the rules of

---

[46] The classical poet does not, like Rousseau, pride himself upon being 'different.'

[47] Reynolds, 105.   [49] Reynolds, 96.

[48] E-C, VI, 52.   [50] *ibid.*, 97.

[51] *Observations on the First Book of the Iliad.*

Nature and write in the spirit of those who have best hit upon them, without taking the same track, beginning in the same manner, and following the main of their story almost step by step, as most of the modern writers of epic poetry have done, after one of these great poets.' Here Pope has dismissed the 'imitation' of special beauties and detached passages for a larger consideration. The modern poet may invent for himself 'in the spirit of' Nature and the great poets of antiquity who have most perfectly apprehended it. It is the temper and conception of the masters which is to be followed, not the particularity of their detail. Once more to parallel from the *Discourses on Art*, we are advised, 'Instead of copying the touches of those great masters, copy only their conceptions. Instead of treading in their footsteps, endeavor only to keep the same road. Labor to invent on their general principles. Possess yourself with their spirit.'[52]

Though he was committed by the temper of his genius, the age in which he lived, and the tradition in which he grew up, to the classical theory of art as an 'imitation of Nature,' Pope seems sometimes to have fretted at the confines thus imposed upon him. There is considerable truth in Professor Phelps' contention that Pope has suppressed leanings toward the romantic,[53] though Professor Phelps was not aware of the extent to which Pope's own sincere belief in classical theory was in agreement with the faith of the time. A letter to Swift laments, or plays at lamenting, the poet's confinement to Nature: 'my system is a short one, and my circle narrow. Imagination[54] has no limits, and that is a sphere in which you may move on to eternity; but where one is confined to truth,[55] or, to speak more like a human creature, to the appearances of truth, we soon find the shortness of our tether.'[56]

Eighteenth century 'romanticism' was variously instigated. Pope seems to have derived the impulse from Orientalism. He greatly

[52] Reynolds, 25.

[53] The following are excerpts from *The Beginnings of the English Romantic Movement*: 'I think that Pope, notwithstanding his manifest limitations, had more imagination and enthusiasm than he generally has credit for; but he was forced to bow to the public opinion which he himself had done so much to form . . . (8). Matthew Arnold's remark that Gray would have been another man in a different age would be much nearer the truth if spoken of Pope; for the great wit and satirist did have occasional touches of emotion and imagination which, in another age, he would have fostered rather than repressed . . . (14). Pope chafed a little under this rigid exclusion of romanticism . . .' (18).

[54] In the modern sense of *fancy*,—the imagination released from its obligation to copy Nature.

[55] That is, to Nature and probability.

[56] E-C, VII, 330.

relished the letters of Lady Mary Wortley Montagu, with their descriptions of the exotic, and in his replies emulates their tone. He read, admired, and loaned to Atterbury some Arabian Tales of which that learned prelate was forced to say, 'Indeed they do not please my taste; they are writ with so romantic an air, and, allowing for the difference of Eastern manners, are yet, upon any supposition that can be made, of so wild and absurd a contrivance (at least to my Northern understanding) that I have not only no pleasure but no patience in perusing them.'[57] 'After reading the *Persian Tales* . . . ,' Pope told Spence, 'I had some thought of writing a Persian fable in which I should have given a full loose to description and imagination. It would have been a very wild thing. . . .'[58] Of the same project he wrote Miss Cowper, 'I have long had an inclination to tell a fairy tale, the more wild and exotic the better; therefore a *vision*, which is confined to no rules of probability, will take in all the variety and luxuriance of description you will. . . .'[59] But the inclination was never fulfilled: distrust of his powers 'in that kind,' timidity of departure from the probable,—something frustrated the desire.

III

Thus far we have been considering Pope's conception of the larger aspects of composition—what he called 'design'; what others have called 'invention.' We proceed now to the second division of our *Ars*, which deals with diction. This is a subject which was of serious interest in the seventeenth and eighteenth centuries. It was felt that the vernacular languages were yet under construction, yet changing. Pope, like the wits of the Restoration, had still the distrust that

> Poets that lasting marble seek
> Must carve in Latin or in Greek.[60]

He feared that Dryden's language would presently, like Chaucer's, appear archaic,—that to another generation even his own diction would seem 'failing.'[61] He was pleased to safeguard himself by having some of his more important poems translated into Latin.

But there was hope that the rapid transformation of the language might be checked. The ages which immediately succeeded

[57] E-C, IX, 22.
[58] Spence, 140.
[59] E-C, IX, 431-2.
[60] Waller: *Of English Verse.*
[61] *Essay on Criticism*, II, 282-3. In the Preface to his *Poems*, Pope wrote: 'A mighty foundation for our pride! when the utmost we can hope is but to be read in one island, and to be thrown aside at the end of one age.' E-C, I, 8.

the Renaissance, those of the Pléiade in France and the Elizabethans in England, loved words, gloried in amassing them,
prized a rich and florid vocabulary. They preached and practised
the enlargement of the vernacular by the adoption of words from
other languages and from the trades and professions, the revival
of suitable archaisms, and the coinage of new terms. Upon all
these expansive tendencies the 'classical age' pronounced a sharp
volte face. From Malherbe on there was in progress constant retrenchment as well as standardization. Poetry must speak, not a
specialized language, but the language of cultivated people who
pique themselves on nothing—that is, the courtiers. Language
must be purged of archaic, dialectal, and professional terms.
'Ainsi toute la doctrine de Malherbe sur le vocabulaire est essen-
tiellement restrictive. Là, surtout, il a bien été un "docteur en
négative." Sans abandonner l'idée qu'il doit exister une langue
littéraire distincte de la langue courante, il veut qu'on la con-
stitue de tout autre façon que faisaient ses prédécesseurs : ce ne
sont pas des additions, ce sont des retranchements qu'il s'agit d'y
faire.'[62]

The French Academy, which had its informal beginning in
1625, adopted the improvement of the national language as its
'declared grand aim.' The English have never had a similar arbiter
of the elegancies of diction, 'a recognized authority, imposing on
us a high standard in matters of intellect and taste.'[63] But the
notion of such a tribunal has found lodgment in other hearts
than that of Arnold. Swift, who was a rigorous purist in diction,
printed in 1712 an extensive *Proposal for Correcting, Improving,
and Ascertaining the English Tongue*, in which he comments upon
French industry—'the French [language] for these last fifty
years has been polishing as much as it will bear'—and contrasts
with it the backward state of his own vernacular: 'But the
English tongue is not yet arrived to such a degree of perfection as
to make us apprehend any thoughts of its decay; and if it were
once refined to a certain standard, perhaps there might be ways
found to fix it forever. . . .'[64] Swift felt, like Pope, the transi-
ency of the English tongue: 'what I have most at heart is that
some method should be thought on for ascertaining and fixing our
language forever. . . . For I am of opinion, it is better a
language should not be wholly perfect than that it should be per-

[62] Brunot, III, *Première Partie*, 6.
[63] Arnold: *The Literary Influence of Academies* (*Essays in Criticism*,
First Series).
[64] *Works*, XI, 9.

petually changing. . . .'[65] 'How then,' he asks despondently, 'shall any man who has a genius for history equal to the best of the ancients, be able to undertake such a work with spirit and cheerfulness when he considers that he will be read with pleasure but a very few years, and, in an age or two, shall hardly be understood without an interpreter?'[66]

One solution of the difficulty was the production of a dictionary based upon the usage of the best English writers. A dictionary, by recording correct speech, could do much to 'fix' and perpetuate it; and much of the slowing up of change in our language is, it is a commonplace, due to the influence which lexicographers have, ever since Johnson, exerted. Swift favored an academy; but for standards was able to suggest only the King James Bible and the Book of Common Prayer: 'for those books being perpetually read in churches have proved a kind of standard for language, especially to the common people.'[67] But Pope conceived the idea both of a dictionary and of founding that, and such rules as might be drawn up for writing, upon the usage of the accepted authors. 'There is hardly any laying down particular rules for writing our language,' he told Spence; 'even Dean Swift's, which seemed to be the best I ever heard, were, three in four of them, not thoroughly well grounded. In most doubts whether a word is English or not, or whether such a particular use of it is proper, one has nothing but authority for it. Is it in Sir William Temple,[68] or Locke, or Tillotson?[69] If it be, you may conclude that it is right, or at least won't be looked upon as wrong.'[70]

Pope amused himself on one occasion by drawing up rather

[65] *Works*, XI, 15.

[66] *ibid.*, 18.

[67] *ibid.*, 15.

[68] Dr. Johnson said of Temple that he was 'the first writer who gave cadence to English prose. Before his time they were careless of arrangement, and did not mind whether a sentence ended with an important word or an insignificant word, or with what part of speech it was concluded' (Boswell, III, 257). Mr. Gosse thinks that in Temple 'we feel that English prose has come to the birth,' that 'we shall probably come to the conclusion that the tradition of the last century [the eighteenth] did not err very wildly in considering him the first prose-writer of his age' (*History*, 88).

[69] By Dr. Johnson's day, the informal, at times colloquial, style of Archbishop Tillotson had come to seem dated, though the lexicographer feels a caution in 'objecting to what has been applauded by so many suffrages' (Boswell, III, 247). But, according to Congreve, Dryden used to 'own with pleasure that if he had any talent for English prose, it was owing to his having often read the writings of the great Archbishop Tillotson' (Ker, I, xxvii). He was still eminently 'standard' in Pope's day.

[70] Spence, 291.

definitive lists of writers whose sanction might be regarded as rendering words 'correct.' 'In talking over the design for a dictionary that might be authoritative for our English writers, Mr. Pope rejected Sir Walter Raleigh twice, as too affected.—The list for prose authors from whose works such a dictionary should be collected was talked over several times, and quite settled. There were eighteen of them named by Mr. Pope, but four of that number [Ben Jonson, L'Estrange, Congreve and Vanbrugh] were only named as authorities for familiar dialogues and writings of that kind.'[71] The list comprised Bacon, Hooker, Hobbes, Clarendon, Barrow, Tillotson, Dryden, Temple, Locke, Sprat,[72] Atterbury,[73] Addison, Swift, and Bolingbroke. Spence's suggestion secured the addition of Hooke and Middleton,[74] after which the canon was declared closed: 'I think there's scarce any more of the living that you need name.'

'The list of writers that might serve as authorities for poetical language was begun upon twice, but left very imperfect. There were but nine mentioned, and two of these [Butler and Swift] only for the burlesque style.' The poets sanctioned were Spenser, Shakespeare, Fletcher, Waller, Butler, Milton, Dryden, Prior, and Swift; Fletcher was 'only mentioned as an authority for familiar dialogue and the slighter kinds of writing.'[75] Here, as in the list of prose writers, it is to be noted that Pope has not confined himself to the neo-classicists, but has drawn from the great authors of the English Renaissance like Bacon, Hooker, and Spenser.

Pope did not follow Malherbe into all his finesse of 'retrenchment': on the matter of diction as on so many other matters he took a sensible middle ground. He did not fancy the excessive and manneristic use of archaisms; he ridicules those who

> by old words to fame have made pretence,
> Ancients in phrase, mere moderns in their sense.[76]

He prudently cautions that

---

[71] Spence, 310.

[72] Sprat (1636-1713), Bishop of Rochester, was the admired biographer of Cowley.

[73] Atterbury (1662-1731), also Bishop of Rochester, was Pope's devoted friend. Dr. Johnson (Boswell, III, 247) commended him as one of the best pulpit stylists.

[74] Nathaniel Hooke, a 'Papist' and Pope's friend, was, according to Warton (*Essay*, II, 202) 'a mystic and a quietist, and a warm disciple of Fénelon.' Conyers Middleton (1683-1750), a Deist, wrote a polished *Life of Cicero*.

[75] Spence, 310-11.

[76] *Essay on Criticism*, II, 124-5.

> In words as fashions the same rule will hold,
> Alike fantastic if too new or old.
> Be not the first by whom the new are tried,
> Nor yet the last to lay the old aside.[77]

But he does not disapprove 'a style judiciously antiquated': 'A just and moderate mixture of old words may,' he says, 'have an effect like the working old abbey stones into a building, which I have sometimes seen give a kind of venerable air, and yet not destroy the neatness, elegance, and equality requisite to a new work. . . .'[78] Following, though at a distance, the doctrine of Horace, he counsels:

> Mark where a bold expressive phrase appears
> Bright through the rubbish of some hundred years;
> Command old words that long have slept to wake,
> Words that wise Bacon or brave Raleigh spake . . .[79]

There is no justification for coining or borrowing new terms when the old are adequate; but, on the other hand, the expansion of a language in the interests of great precision and fuller expression is to be commended:

> Or bid the new be English ages hence
> (For Use will father what's begot by Sense). . . .[80]

Of course there was much difference of opinion among the Augustan critics upon the propriety of drawing for the apt expression upon other languages. But both Dryden and Pope upheld the use. Says the former, in his *Dedication of the Aeneid*, 'If sounding words are not of our growth and manufacture, who shall hinder me to import them from a foreign country?'[81] It was borrowing from the Latin which he was here concerned to defend; but Dryden also made use of French words—according to Dr. Johnson, in order to show the rank of company he kept.[82]

Pope does not find in his original the injunction he promulgates that poets shall enrich the English language by loans:

[77] *Essay*, 133-6.
[78] *Postscript* to the *Odyssey* (*Odyssey*, V, 278).
[79] 'Second Epistle of the Second Book of Horace,' 165-8. The original:
> Obscurata diu populo bonus eruet atque
> Proferet in lucem speciosa vocabula rerum,
> Quae priscis memorata Catonibus atque Cethegis
> Nunc situs informis premit et deserta vetustas (115-18).
[80] *ibid.*, 169-70; a paraphrase of Horace's
> Adsciscet nova, quae genitor produxerit usus (119).
[81] Ker, II, 234.
[82] *Lives*, I, 463.

Pour the full tide of eloquence along,
Serenely pure, and yet divinely strong,
Rich with the treasures of each foreign tongue.[83]

He gave himself warrant, perhaps under the authority of Dryden,
for rather free introduction of the *mot juste* in French, particularly
in his *Observations on the Iliad*, as Oldmixon, in his English expansion of Bouhours, took malicious note: 'But I think what follows has no parallel in any tongue for a babel of languages:
"Nothing is more lively and picturesque than the attitude Patroclus is here described in. The pathetic of the speech is finely contrasted[84] by the *fierté* to that of Achilles." Which, in plain English,
is, "Nothing is more lively and picturelike, or picturish, than the
posture Patroclus is here described in; the tenderness of this speech
being a fine opposition to the fierceness of that of Achilles".'[85]

In another passage, Oldmixon accuses the poet of disloyalty to
his country: he adds to his 'Popery' devotion to 'out-landish' diction: 'Besides *ensanguined*, we have *picturesque*, *riant*, *fierte*, *com-
partements*, *traits*, etc., without the least necessity for it,—as good
English all as are his political principles and religion.'[86] This affectation of exceeding gentility was noted also by Dr. Johnson,
who remarks that in Pope's 'later productions the diction is sometimes vitiated by French idioms, with which Bolingbroke had
perhaps infected him.'[87]

Neo-classical taste in both France and England was exceedingly
averse to the use of the technical terminology of trades and professions. It was thought to smack of pedantry or affectation: the
poet should be an *honnête homme*, not a specialist; and he should
discourse in language which will be immediately intelligible to
cultivated people. 'I will not give the reasons why I writ not always
in the proper terms of navigation, land-service, or in the cant of
any profession,' writes Dryden in his *Dedication of the Aeneid*.
'I will only say that Virgil has avoided those proprieties because
he writ not to mariners, gardeners, peasants, etc., but to all in
general, and in particular to men and ladies of the first quality,
who have been better bred than to be too nicely knowing in the
terms.'[88]

---

[83] 'Second Epistle of the Second Book of Horace,' 171-3.
[84] Oldmixon elsewhere (167) gibes, '*contrasted*, as Mr. Pope calls it.'
[85] Oldmixon, 417. This is an interesting exhibit of linguistic development. All of Pope's terms, except the obviously unidiomatic *fierté*, have
become naturalized.
[86] *ibid.*, 415.
[87] *Lives*, III, 250.
[88] Ker, II, 236.

In the Preface to his *Annus Mirabilis*, however, the inconsistent Dryden argued in favor of the use of technical details; and even in his translation of the *Aeneid*, in which we were led to expect only the general language of ladies and gentlemen, he fell into reprehensible practices. Pope declares his own orthodoxy on the subject by agreeing heartily with Cromwell in a 'censure of the use of sea-terms in Mr. Dryden's Virgil; not only because Helenus was no great prophet in those matters, but because no terms of art, or cant-words, suit with the majesty and dignity of style which epic poetry requires. *Cui mens divinior atque os magna soniturum.* The tarpaulin phrase can please none but such *qui aurem habent Batavam*; they must not expect *auribus Atticis probari. . . .*'[89]

IV

The third of what Pope called the '*tours* in poetry' is 'versification.' Under this head there is available a full and interesting analysis which the poet worked out for Cromwell and afterwards published 'with some alterations and considerable additions' as a letter to Walsh. But before entering upon this, it may be pertinent to say a few words of the contest, much waged in the eighteenth century, between blank verse and rhymed. It has often been hastily assumed that both Pope and his contemporaries were strictly limited in their talent and their appreciation to the latter. But such was not the case. 'Undoubtedly . . . most readers liked rhyme, as they do today . . . and, other things being equal, preferred rhymed poetry.' But it is a striking fact that 'after the first quarter of the century the poems most widely and enthusiastically read were those in blank verse,'—the *Seasons*, *Night Thoughts*, *The Grave*, and *Pleasures of the Imagination*.[90] When Pope and others disliked blank verse it was not by any means on purely *a priori* grounds. The form had frequently the misfortune of being the instrument for unsuccessful copies of the Miltonic style; and 'The imitators of Milton, like most other imitators, are not copies but caricatures of their original; they are a hundred times more obsolete and cramped than he. . . .'[91] It has been suggested that 'Fastidious writers like Pope and Gray, antagonized by the slovenly workmanship and unmelodious imitations of *Paradise Lost*, naturally concluded . . . that blank verse was another bow of Ulysses.'[92]

Whatever may have been Pope's inmost feelings, he nowhere

[89] E-C, VI, 107.
[90] Havens, 46.
[91] *Postscript* to the *Odyssey* (*Odyssey*, V, 278).
[92] Havens, 47.

condemns blank verse *in toto*: indeed his devotion to Milton would hardly have admitted of that. He continued to use the style of versification he had learned and mastered in youth; he no doubt distrusted risking his powers in another form, and one in which he would have had Milton for rival. But 'when Lyttleton expressed surprise that Pope had not used blank verse for his *Iliad*, the master of the heroic couplet did not defend his measure, but answered that rhyme was easier for him.'[93]

To Spence, he vouchsafed a more objective 'apology' for rhyme; but even here it is interesting to note the air of defence, the negative character of the argument. 'I have nothing to say for rhyme, but that I doubt whether a poem can support itself without it in our language, unless it be stiffened with such strange words as are likely to destroy our language itself. The high style [Arnold's variant is the 'grand style'] that is affected so much in blank verse would not have been borne even in Milton had not his subject turned so much on such strange, out-of-the-way things as it does.'[94] In the epic and the tragedy, the elevation of emotion admits with propriety of the use of a heightened style and figurative diction; but there are, Pope makes the point, other sorts of poetry. And these less elevated *genres* find it difficult to sustain themselves at the poetic level without the frame of rhyme. 'Rhyme, without any other assistance,' Addison confirmed, 'throws the language off from prose, and very often makes an indifferent phrase pass unregarded; but where the verse is not built upon rhymes, there pomp and energy of expression are indispensably necessary to support the style and keep it from falling into the flatness of prose.'[95]

Though he published no blank verse, Pope was not averse to experimenting with it; and it seems probable that had he succeeded in mustering the courage necessary for the venture of a tragedy or an epic poem he might have ventured also to adopt the medium which to the Augustans as well as us seemed appropriate.[96] In his youth he was half persuaded to attempt a tragedy on the subject of Lady Jane Grey;[97] and under the sheltering mask of burlesque he essayed a few lines to Cromwell which for all their parallelism are undeniably in the untried measure:

[93] Percival Stockdale; quoted, *ibid.*, 324.
[94] Spence, 200.
[95] *Spectator*, no. 285.
[96] It should be recalled that for all his oft-expressed devotion to rhyme, Dr. Johnson's tragedy, *Irene*, was in blank verse. So was Addison's *Cato*, and so were the tragedies of Pope's correspondents, Thomson and Hill.
[97] E-C, VI, 129, n. See also Gildon's *The New Rehearsal*, 48.

Tell me, by all the melting joys of love,
By the warm transports and entrancing languors,
By the soft fanning of the wafting sheets,
By the dear tremblings of the bed of bliss;
By all these tender adjurations, tell me:
Am I not fit to write a tragedy ?[98]

We have another specimen of Pope's powers in blank verse which dates from a much later period. The following lines, which are obviously modelled on the cadences of Milton, though free from the so-called Miltonic diction, avoided the regularly recurring caesuras and the end-stopped lines of the couplet, and seem to me exceedingly beautiful. They are the invocation to a projected epic on the theme of the Trojan Brutus, the colonizer of Britain.

The patient chief, who lab'ring long arriv'd
On Britain's coast, and brought with fav'ring gods
Arts, arms, and honor to her ancient sons:
Daughter of Memory! from elder time
Recall; and me with Britain's glory fir'd,
Me far from meaner care or meaner song
Snatch to the holy hill of spotless bay,
My country's poet, to record her fame.[99]

One wishes he had possessed the courage to persevere in so auspiciously undertaken an enterprise: perhaps he might have discovered to himself and the world powers unsuspected.

The 'thoughts . . . on the subject of English versification' deal, as Pope says, with 'certain niceties which, though not much observed even by correct versifiers, I cannot but think deserve to be better regarded.' And the first of these concerns the poet's favorite doctrine of the adaptation of sound to sense. 'It is not enough that nothing offends the ear, but a good poet will adapt the very sounds, as well as words, to the things he treats of. So that there is, if one may express it so, a style of sound: as in describing a gliding stream, the numbers should run easy and flowing; in describing a rough torrent or deluge, sonorous and swelling; and so of the rest. This is evident everywhere in Homer and Virgil, and nowhere else that I know of to any observable degree. The following examples will make this plain, which I have taken from Vida: [he quotes eight detached verses from Book III of Vida's *Ars Poetica*]. This, I think, is what very few observe in

[98] E-C, VI, 129.
[99] Printed by Snyder, *Journal of English and Germanic Philology*, XVIII, 583, from Brit. Mus. MS. Egerton 1950.

practice, and is undoubtedly of wonderful force in imprinting the image on the reader. We have one excellent example of it in our language, Mr. Dryden's Ode on St. Cecilia's Day, entitled *Alexander's Feast.*'[100]

In the *Essay on Criticism* the same doctrine was enunciated with the enrichment of examples, practice illustrating precept:

'Tis not enough no harshness give offence;
The sound must seem an echo to the sense.
Soft is the strain when zephyr gently blows,
And the smooth stream in smoother numbers flows;
But when loud surges lash the sounding shore,
The hoarse, rough verse should like the torrent roar.
When Ajax strives some rock's vast weight to throw,
The line, too, labors, and the words move slow;
Not so when swift Camilla scours the plain,
Flies o'er th' unbending corn and skims along the main.[101]

Pope's notes on the 'beauties' of Homer gave him opportunity for calling to the reader's attention many instances of this 'adaptation'; as, for example, where he remarks, 'there is a very remarkable beauty in the run of the verse in Homer; every word has a melancholy cadence, and the poet has not only made the sands and the arms but even his very verse to lament with Achilles.'[102] In his translation of the *Iliad*, Pope himself endeavored to emulate his original in this respect: 'I have followed the significance of the numbers and the adapting them to the sense much more even than Dryden, and much oftener than any one minds it, particularly in the translation of Homer, where 't was most necessary to do so, and in the *Dunciad* often, and indeed in all my poems.'[103]

Pope found the doctrine in both Dionysius of Halicarnassus and Vida: the latter critic treats it with particular fullness of illustration.[104] These authorities gave assurance to a doctrine which will not, I fear, permit of too rigorous inspection. Dr. Johnson, with even more than his usual shrewdness and sagacity, saw the subjectivism which can scarcely be separated from the appreciation of 'representative metre.' 'There is nothing in the art of versifying so much exposed to the power of the imagination,' he remarks, 'as the accommodation of the sound to the sense, or the representation of particular images, by the flow of the verse in which they are expressed. Every student has innumerable passages in which he, and perhaps he alone, discovers such resemblances.'[105] 'It is

[100] E-C, VI, 56.
[101] *Essay*, II, 164-73.
[102] *Observations*, XXIII: II.
[103] Spence, 316.
[104] *Ars Poetica*, III, 367-439.
[105] Brown, 259.

scarcely to be doubted that on many occasions we make the music
which we imagine ourselves to hear; that we modulate the poem by
our own disposition, and ascribe to the numbers the effects of the
sense.'[106] Pope's illustrative lines in the *Essay* were 'labored with
great attention'; yet they are themselves sufficient evidence of the
futility of the device. 'The verse intended to represent the whisper of
the vernal breeze must be confessed not much to excell in softness
or volubility; and the smooth stream runs with a perpetual clash
of jarring consonants.'[107] It seems as if particular vowel and consonant successions might do something; the speed of a line might
be retarded by the use of monosyllables heavily freighted with consonants. But there are difficulties in the way of application. It is
exceedingly doubtful if, without attention to the sense, it takes
longer to read

> The line, too, labors and the words move slow

than to read

> Not so when swift Camilla scours the plain.

Pope was on much safer ground when he proclaimed, as he
frequently did, the necessity for the more general adaptation
which we may call *decorum* of style. Modern critics have complained that Pope gives to Homer an artificial and unvarying
'grand style' which does not adapt itself to the plain details in
which parts of the narrative abound. 'A literary and intellec-
tualized language is,' says Arnold, 'in its own way well suited to
grand matters; and Pope, with a language of this kind and his
own admirable talent, comes off well enough as long as he has
passion, or oratory, or a great crisis to deal with. . . . It is when
he comes to level passages, passages of narration or description,
that he and his style are sorely tried and prove themselves
weak.'[108]

This is, I think, an eminently just criticism; but it is interesting
to know that the translator prided himself on making just that
adaptation of style in which the critic found him deficient. Pope
feared he had sacrificed the attention of his audience to his
artistic conscience. 'I am going to tell the world,' he writes to Lord
Oxford, 'that if they do not keep quite wide awake over part of
my Homer it is because I thought it my duty to observe a certain
mediocrity[109] of style agreeable to conversation and dialogue which

[106] Brown, 260.
[107] *ibid.*, 426. For a defense of Pope see Lotspeich, *The Metrical Technique
of Pope's Illustrative Couplets, J.E.G.P.*, XXVI, 471-4.
[108] *On Translating Homer*, 158.
[109] i.e., mean.

is called the narrative, and ought to be low, being put into the mouths of persons not of the highest condition, or of a person acting in the disguise of a poor wanderer, as Ulysses must in reason be supposed to do, or Ulysses was not the wise man we are to take him for.'[110]

Having approved his own conduct, he proceeds to censure that of others: 'our modern poets,' we are told, 'preserve a painful equality of fustian throughout their whole epic or tragic works, like travelling all along on the ridge of a hill, which is not half so pleasant as sometimes rising and sometimes descending gently into the vale, as the way leads, and as the end of the journey directs. To write thus upon low subjects is really the true sublime of ridicule,—it is the sublime of *Don Quixote*; but it is strange they should not see it is by no means so of the humbler and narrative parts of poetry. It leaves no distinction between the language of the gods, which is when the muse or the gods speak, and that of men in their conversations and dialogues. Even in set harangues or orations, this painted, florid style would be ridiculous.'[111] Our critic was, it will be observed, exceedingly sound in his theory.

However much stress Pope may have laid upon the doctrines of 'representative metre' and adaptation, he had weightier points in his Law. 'The great rule of verse is to be musical; this other ['representative metre'] is only a secondary consideration, and should not jar too much with the former.'[112] The remaining 'thoughts' on versification are all directed toward the production of what Dr. Johnson called the 'mellifluence of Pope's numbers.'[113]

Rule Two deal with the position of the *caesura*. 'Every nice ear must, I believe, have observed that in any smooth English verse of ten syllables there is naturally a *pause* at the fourth, fifth, or sixth syllable. It is upon these that the ear rests; and upon the judicious change and management of which depends the variety of versification.' Examples follow: after which a caution: 'Now I fancy that to preserve an exact harmony and variety, the pause at the fourth

---

[110] E-C, VIII, 218.

[111] *ibid.*, 219. Pope also objects to the lack of adaptation in the style of contemporary tragedy, 'where one continued sameness of diction runs through all their characters . . .' (*ibid.*, 218). The writers of tragedy are to use a 'lower style' when occasion demands, 'if they would copy Nature; whereas that painted and poetical diction which they perpetually use would be improper even in orations designed to move with all the arts of rhetoric' (*Postscript* to the *Odyssey*: *Odyssey*, V, 275).

[112] Spence, 316. This rule its promulgator obeyed. As Dr. Johnson reminds us (*Lives*, III, 248), 'his poetry has been censured as too uniformly musical, and as glutting the ear with unvaried sweetness.'

[113] *Lives*, I, 453.

or sixth should not be continued above three lines together without
the interposition of another, else it will be apt to weary the ear
with one continued tone—at least it does mine. That at the fifth
runs quicker, and carries not quite so dead a weight, so tires not
so much though it be continued longer.'[114] Dr. Johnson saw also the
necessity for placing the *caesura* as near the middle of a verse as
possible, and in his 'rule' rather particularizes than departs from
Pope's. 'It may be, I think, established,' he says, 'that a pause which
concludes a period should be made for the most part upon a strong
syllable, as the fourth and sixth; but those pauses which only sus-
pend the sense may be placed upon the weaker [i.e., the fifth].'
'The noblest and most majestic pauses which our versification
admits are upon the fourth and sixth syllables. . . . But far
above all others, if I can give any credit to my own ear, is the rest
upon the sixth syllable, which, taking in a complete compass of
sound, such as is sufficient to constitute one of our lyric measures,
makes a full and solemn close.'[115] Pope's practice exhibits a preference for the earlier pause: 'The *caesura* after the fourth syllable
varies in frequency from one-third to one-half of the whole;' but
is generally more near the half than the third.[116] Warton charged
the theorist with failure to follow his own good counsel of varying
the pauses: 'he continued the pause at the *fourth* syllable sometimes through six verses together.'[117] Undoubtedly it is difficult to
secure as much variety with the closed couplet as with some less
constrained forms, but Pope's meticulous attention increased its
range. 'In this manipulation of pauses, Pope had certainly no
superior.'[118]

Earlier writers of the heroic couplet,—Waller, Denham, and
Dryden had free resort to such expletives as *do*, *does*, and *did*.[119]
One undoubted improvement which Pope wrought upon the form
was the avoiding of this confession of inadequacy. 'Another nicety,'
Rule Three states, 'is in relation to expletives—whether words or
syllables—which are made use of purely to supply a vacancy. *Do*
before verbs plural is absolutely such; and it is not improbable but
future refiners may explode *did* and *does* in the same manner,
which are almost always used for the sake of the rhyme. The
same cause has occasioned the promiscuous use of *you* and *thou* to
the same person, which can never sound so graceful as either one
or the other.'[120]

[114] E-C, VI, 57.   [115] Brown, 259.
[116] Mead, 25-6. The latter page exhibits a table.
[117] E-C, VI, 57, n.   [119] *ibid.*, 36.
[118] Mead, 38.   [120] E-C, VII, 57.

One of the more delicate points of controversy in Augustan days was the admissibility of those variants of heroic versification, the triplet and the Alexandrine. Pope was in theory against both: 'I would also object to the irruption of Alexandrine verses of twelve syllables, which, I think, should never be allowed but when some remarkable beauty or propriety in them atones for the liberty. Mr. Dryden has been too free of these, especially in his latter works. I am of the same opinion as to triple rhymes.'[121] The *Essay on Criticism* sneers,

> A needless Alexandrine ends the song,
> That, like a wounded snake, drags its slow length along.[122]

The Alexandrine is 'very rare in Pope's later works, and infrequent in all;'[123] but the triplet found a moderate employment, especially in the translations and modernizations, where a certain latitude was convenient. Swift, who was a purist in versification as well as in diction, asserts that his friend 'never used them [triplets] till he translated Homer,[124] which was too long a work to be so very exact in; and I think in one or two of his last poems he has, out of laziness, done the same thing, though very seldom.'[125] But as a matter of fact, there are eight triplets in the *Essay on Criticism*, and many more in the *Merchant's Tale* and the First Book of the *Thebaid*.[126] Though there is no abstract argument against what Swift calls this 'vicious way of rhyming,' it cannot be said often to produce felicities; the result of the three consecutive rhymes is frequently only monotony. In Pope's later original work he again nearly abandoned the triplet.

The *Essay on Criticism* holds up to ridicule poets who

>   ring round the same unvaried chimes
> With sure returns of still expected rhymes.
> Where'er you find 'the cooling western breeze,'
> In the next line it 'whispers through the trees';
> If crystal streams 'with pleasing murmurs creep,'
> The reader's threatened, not in vain, with 'sleep.'[127]

---

[121] E-C, VII, 57-8.
[122] II, 156-7. The second line exemplifies 'representative metre' as well as the Alexandrine: the series of monosyllables with which it terminates is supposed to induce a drawling delivery.
[123] Mead, 11.
[124] Pope was still translating Homer when he wrote Swift in 1733. 'But these things shall lie by till you come to carp at them, and alter rhymes and grammar and triplets and cacophonies of all kinds' (E-C, VII, 307).
[125] Letter to Beach, 1735 (*Correspondence*, V, 162).
[126] Pope's use of the triplet is tabulated in Mead, 44-5.
[127] II, 148-53.

And in Pope's 'thoughts' on versification we are told, 'I would equally object to the repetition of the same rhymes within four or six lines of each other as tiresome to the ear through their monotony.'[128] But rhymes do not abound in English; and Pope himself has been taken to task by critics from Dennis to Elwin for failure to heed his own counsel. 'He was perhaps not aware how often he had repeated himself. It was always dangerously easy for him, even in his best work, to bestow his chief care upon the antithesis and to let the end-syllables shift for themselves.'[129]

Dr. Johnson has expressed himself as finding a line of monosyllables almost always harsh in English, because 'being of Teutonic origin, or formed by contraction' these words 'commonly begin and end with consonants.'[130] But Pope's disapproval was qualified by his love for 'representative metre.' 'Monosyllable lines, unless very artfully managed, are stiff or languishing,' he admits; 'but may,' he adds, 'be beautiful to express melancholy, slowness, or labor.'[131] He reprehends the 'Ten low words [which] oft creep in one dull line';[132] but he prided himself on attaining the ponderation of

When Ajax strives some rock's vast weight to throw.[133]

The seventh and longest of the 'thoughts' concerns the use of the *hiatus*. 'To come to the *hiatus*, or gap between two words which is caused by two vowels opening on each other . . . ; I think the rule in this case is either to use the *caesura*,[134] or admit the *hiatus*, just as the ear is least shocked by either; for the *caesura* sometimes offends the ear more than the *hiatus* itself, and our language is naturally overcharged with consonants. . . . The *hiatus* which has the worst effect is when one word ends with the same vowel that begins the following; and next to this, those vowels whose sounds come nearest to each other are most to be avoided: *o*, *a*, or *u* will bear a more full and graceful sound than *e*, *i*, or *y*.' Some people, Pope knows, will 'think these observations trivial'; but he can 'corroborate them by some great authorities' which he has met with in 'Tully' and Quintillian. With this warning, we are off upon a train of learned quotations from the *Rhetoric to Herennius*,

128 E-C, VI, 58.
129 Mead, 47.
130 Brown, 257.
131 E-C, VI, 58.
132 *Essay on Criticism*, II, 147.
133 *ibid.*, 170.
134 Pope is obviously misusing *caesura* to mean *elision*. Cf. Saintsbury (*Historical Manual of English Prosody*, 274): 'At one time, in the earlier writers on English prosody (e.g., Dryden) there grew up a strange habit of using the term "caesura" to express elision or hiatus—to neither of which has it the least proper reference.' The *N.E.D.* has no record of this misuse.

the *Orator*, and the *Institutes* and a citation of 'Turnebus on Quintillian.' The Latin over, we return to modernity with Malherbe, who, it is comforting to know, 'of all the moderns has been the most scrupulous' in his avoidance of the hiatus: 'I think Ménage[135] in his observations upon him says he has not one in his poems.' The scholar concludes, 'I believe the *hiatus* should be avoided with more care in poetry than in oratory; and I would constantly try to prevent it unless where the cutting it off is more prejudicial to the sound than the *hiatus* itself.'[136]

Milton shared Pope's aversion to vowels 'opening upon each other';[137] and it is apropos of the Miltonic versification that Dr. Johnson undertakes his attack on elision as unsuited to 'the genius of the English tongue,' which is already overstocked with consonants.[138] But whatever the point of view of the critic, it is hard to see anything beyond an academic interest which was involved in the doctrine. Pope, who so warmly preaches the liberty of elision, makes very little use of his right. In practice, only the definite article is clipped; and an occasional 'th egregious' or 'th all-beauteous' need not occasion fears that 'our harsh cadences' are to be made 'yet harsher.'[139]

With the liberalization of English 'numbers' which the nineteenth century effected, the portentousness of the particular problems to which Pope's 'thoughts' addressed a solution may have been dissipated. More important than any doctrine advanced is the spirit in which the proponent approached his task,—the interest in the technical problems of the poet. 'The numerous passages in his works that expressly speak of his art show to what extent the theory of versification had taken possession of his thinking.'[140]

---

[135] Gilles Ménage (1613-1692) was a French scholar whose wit and learning gathered about him the critics of the time, such as Chapelain and Sarrazin; his sarcasm caused his exclusion from the Academy, and he suffered from the satire of Boileau and Molière.

[136] E-C, VI, 58-9. E. A. Abbott has noted the poet's practice: 'Pope often elides *e* in *the*, but not, as Milton does, before a metrically accented syllable' (*Concordance*, xiv).

[137] So did Dryden, from whom Pope may have inherited the doctrine. He censures Hobbes for not employing the '*synaloepha*' (elision); finds in the phrase 'the army' 'a most horrible ill-sounding gap betwixt those words' (*Examen Poeticum*; Ker, II, 11). He prides himself that in his translation of the *Aeneid* 'there is not, to the best of my remembrance, one vowel gaping on another . . . in this whole poem' (*Dedication*; Ker, II, 216).

[138] Brown, 257.

[139] *ibid.*, 257.

[140] Mead, 2. In this, as in so many other respects, Pope resembled his instructor, Dryden, who never lost an opportunity for discussing the technical aspects of his art. In the *Dedication to the Aeneid* he tells us,

V

Most *Artes Poeticae* devote a section, sometimes the principal, to description of the *genres* and rules for their accomplishment. Some of these were generally neglected by the Augustans, noticeably the various species of lyric poetry. Others were attempted in pursuance of dogmatic critical theories, and in imitation of the practice of the ancients, regardless of their suitability to the talent of the poet and the taste of the times. The Augustan genius ran to satire and what we sometimes loosely call 'didacticism'; but it had been an accepted dictum with generations of critics that the epic and the tragedy were the greatest of 'forms,' and in consequence the Augustans admired and sometimes essayed.

If Pope nowhere repeats the saying, it is because it was a commonplace of criticism that 'A heroic poem, truly such, is undoubtedly the greatest work which the soul of man is capable to perform.'[141] He thoroughly shared the orthodox veneration of the epic. He had read Le Bossu's treatise; and his set pieces of criticism, the Preface to Homer and the *Examen* of Voltaire's *Henriade*, follow the systematical treatment of *Traité du Poème Épique*: the former discusses Homer's 'fable,' natural and allegorical; his characters; his speeches; his sentiments and descriptions; his expression and versification, all in the approved fashion. But Pope saw the absurdity of the system of the 'mechanical' epic when carried to extremes; the *Receipt to Make an Epic Poem* and the burlesque analysis of the *Dunciad*, *Martinus Scriblerus of the Poem*,[142] are sufficient warrant for this. The Homeric essays nowhere mention Le Bossu's theory that Homer first selected a moral, then chose a plot to illustrate it;[143] Pope accepts rather than credits the supposed allegory of the poet: in the main he certainly treats Homer as we should treat him, as a great narrator who told his story for the pleasure it gave him.

Both Dryden and Pope were sincerely ambitious of the high

'I have long had by me the materials of an English *Prosodia*, containing all the mechanical rules of versification, wherein I have treated with some exactness of the feet, the quantities, and the pauses' (Ker, II, 217). There are many books one could better have spared than this.

[141] Ker, II, 154.

[142] E-C, IV, 77-82.

[143] Dryden, whom it is customary to consider more 'liberal' than Pope, accepted the theory of Le Bossu. We are solemnly told in the *Dedication to the Aeneid*, (Ker, II, 167) that 'Homer's moral was to urge the necessity of union and of a good understanding betwixt confederate states and princes engaged in a war with a mighty monarch; as also of discipline in an army and obedience in the several chiefs to the supreme commander of the joint forces.'

dignity of 'heroic' poets;[144] but both dallied with translations of the ancients and burlesque- and mock-epic, while lesser men like Cowley and Davenant made the venture, and inconsequential persons like Sir Richard Blackmore and Leonidas Glover poured forth 'heroic' strains in floods. One of Pope's youthful essays was an epic of which the hero is 'variously stated' to have been Deucalion and Alcander, Prince of Rhodes.[145] In mature life, he was again possessed with the idea of 'heroic' composition. He liked to feel that if he had not engaged in the translation of Homer, he would 'certainly have written an epic poem. . . .'[146] 'I should,' he adds proudly, 'have sat down to it with this advantage, that I had been nursed up in Homer and Virgil.'[147] In 1743-1744—that is, just before his death—he was busy with the project of an epic upon the subject of the Trojan Brutus. 'The idea that I have had for an epic poem of late turns wholly on civil and ecclesiastical government.' The consecrated model of the *Aeneid* is followed in the next: 'The hero is a prince who establishes an empire. That prince is our Brutus from Troy. The plan of government is much like our old original plan, supposed so much earlier; and the religion introduced by him is the belief of one God and the doctrines of morality. Brutus is supposed to have travelled in Europe, and there to have learned the unity of the deity and the other purer doctrines afterwards kept up in the mysteries.' When this account was given, none of the poem had yet been written, though its projector assured Spence, 'what I look upon as more than half the work is already done, for 't is all exactly planned.' Execution would, he thought, occupy 'much less' than ten years.[148] A little later, progress was reported to the extent that 'even some of the most material speeches [were] written in prose';[149] and from time to time further reports were made: 'that nothing might be wanting to perfect it as an epic composition, our poet had prepared his machinery and given names to his good and evil spirits.'[150]

Of course one may take the affair upon its face value and con-

---

[144] Dryden planned an epic on King Arthur.

[145] E-C, V, 16.

[146] Spence, 259.

[147] *ibid.*, 284.

[148] Spence, 288. A full outline of the 'fable,' characters, etc., is given in Ruffhead, 316-27.

[149] Spence, 315. Of Pope's other works, at least the *Essay on Criticism* was first 'digested' in prose (Spence, 142). Racine's tragedies were composed after similar preparation.

[150] Ruffhead, 325. Pope followed, it will be seen, Dryden's advice that the angels and devils of the Christian system might appropriately supplant the heathen 'machines' of Homer.

sider that, as Pope said, only the translation of Homer prevented him from writing an epic; or, again, that, had he lived, he would have completed the *Brutus*. One may; but I like to see in this frustration other forces at work: an instinctive feeling that the age of the epic had passed and the age of other and more sophisticated forms had arrived; the sense that his own powers were better suited to satire and its derivatives, the mock-epic and the burlesque. He could not surrender the idea of some day writing a serious heroic poem without, perhaps, surrendering his right to be considered a poet of the first rank. But at the same time his artistic sense and his always admirably just estimate of his own powers restrained him from the venture. There is something symbolic of the departure of the old conception of classicism in the fact that the greatest of the Augustan poets dared not rise to full epic dignity, but sheltered himself under its shadows: adapted, paraphrased, modernized, burlesqued.

Much the same may be said of Pope and tragedy. Here again one may seek an interpretation more or less external according as he chooses. Again we have a record of essays and frustrations. It has often been said, and no doubt with considerable rightness, that the aversion to the stage and players Pope exhibited in later life was due to the unfavorable reception accorded the *Three Hours after Marriage* in which he collaborated.[151] But there is also plausibility in the poet's own assertions that he disliked to subject himself to the personal fancies of the actors and the fickle and undiscriminating taste of audiences. In the eighteenth century, it would seem, the theatrical conditions were much what they are today: the hapless playwright, if he is really desirous of staging his play, has to sacrifice to its ruthless alteration in the interests of popular appeal and the exploitation of the 'star'; and as for the public, experienced managers regard its reactions to any given 'entertainment' as more or less of a gamble. A sensitively organized poet who had been able to secure, and who prized, his independence might well decide it was not worth his pains to write for the stage.

'When I was very young,' said Pope, 'I wrote something toward a tragedy, and afterwards an entire one. The latter was built on a very moving story in the legend of St. Genevieve. After I had got acquainted with the town, I resolved never to write anything for the stage, though I was solicited by several of my friends to do so, and particularly by Betterton. . . . I had taken such strong resolutions against anything of the kind from seeing how much everybody that did write for the stage was obliged to subject themselves

[151] For an interesting account of this play see Winchelsea (ed. Reynolds), lxii-lxx.

to the players and the town.'[152] Ruffhead, deriving his information from Warburton, adds a few details: 'During his residence in the Forest, our poet, being between the years of thirteen and fifteen, composed a comedy[153] and a tragedy. With regard to the subject of the former we are wholly in the dark. . . . But whether he distrusted his talent for dramatic poetry, or whether he was cautious of hazarding his fame on the fickle taste of a captious audience, he could never be prevailed upon to write for the stage. . . .'[154] Nevertheless Pope liked to dally with the idea of tragedy. Cromwell encouraged his dramatic ambitions; and in 1707 the poet seems to have been meditating a tragedy on the Gracchi.[155] The subject was surrendered, but not the inclination. 'In his latter days he told a particular friend that he had a strong propensity to the tragic drama, and should certainly have made it his principal study had not the moral and intellectual characters of the players of his time, so different from that of Betterton,[156] always deterred him from putting his design in execution.'[157]

It certainly cannot be said that the taste of early eighteenth century theatre-goers invited the attention of serious dramatists. Legitimate drama frequently yielded, and was always in danger of yielding, to the Italian opera, the farce, the masque, the spectacle. The inclination of the *pecus vulgum* was ever toward what should amaze and divert; they loved not the 'proper sentiments and expressions' of the poetry but the 'dresses and decorations of the stage';[158] they preferred the lion to Nicolini. The *Epistle to Augustus* brilliantly points up Horace's attack on the audiences of his day to fit the sensation-loving public of London.

> The many-headed monster of the pit,
> A senseless, worthless, and unhonored crowd
> Who, to disturb their betters, mighty proud,
> Clattering their sticks before ten lines are spoke,
> Call for the farce, the bear, or the black-joke.[159]

[152] Spence, 197.
[153] This is the only mention we have of a comedy of Pope's sole contrivance.
[154] Ruffhead, 18-19. Pope burned his plays, as he did his epic *Alcander*, the latter at Atterbury's request. *ibid.*, 21.
[155] E-C, VI, 64 and n.
[156] Pope, who seems greatly to have admired Betterton, once painted, or copied, his portrait (E-C, VI, 95, n).
[157] Ruffhead, 19.
[158] See Addison's attack on English theatrical taste in the *Spectator*, nos. 42 and 44.
[159] The *Coalblack Joke* was the name of an indecent popular song.

What dear delight to Britons farce affords!
Ever the taste of mobs, but now of lords.[160]

Audiences pay no attention to the dramatic construction of a piece;
the plot is useful only, as Bayes says in *The Rehearsal*, 'to bring in
fine things.' 'Yes,' says Smith, 'but the play stands still.'[161]

The play stands still; damn action and discourse!
Back fly the scenes, and enter foot and horse;
Pageants on pageants, in long order drawn,
Peers, heralds, bishops, ermine, gold, and lawn.[162]

The 'thunder of the pit' is silent when some grand passage of
eloquence is uttered, but aroused when there is some novelty of
scene or dress to engage the eye:

Such is the shout, the long applauding note
At Quin's white plume, or Oldfield's petticoat,
Or when from court a birthday suit bestowed
Sinks the lost actor in the tawdry load.
Booth[163] enters—hark, the universal peal!

'But has he spoken?'—Not a syllable.
'What shook the stage, and made the people stare?'
Cato's long wig, flowered gown, and lacquered chair.[164]

It is difficult to make out how frequent a theatre-goer Pope was.
Ruffhead tells us that 'While he was at the school near Hyde Park
Corner, the attention paid to his conduct was so remiss that he was
suffered to frequent the playhouse in company with the greater
boys;' and thinks this must have made a great impression on him.
During his stay in London to study the 'polite languages' and his
visits with Wycherley he must have frequented the playhouse, but
there is no express mention of it; and the *Farewell to London*
which in 1715 announced the poet's enforced retirement from the
enervating pleasures of the gay city bids

[160] *To Augustus*, 304-11.
[161] Act III. Buckingham's *Rehearsal*, with which Pope must have been
familiar, is a delicious satire on the art of dramatic composition as practised by the 'heroic' dramatists of the Restoration.
[162] *To Augustus*, 314-17.
[163] Earlier in the same Epistle Pope sneers at 'well-mouthed Booth'
(123). He had a personal grievance at the actor for his unfavorable comment on *Windsor Forest;* but in addition Pope really did dislike 'the
solemn and formal style of the old school of acting, and was enthusiastic
in his praise of Garrick, who was the first to introduce a more free and
natural manner' (E-C, III, 357-8, n).
[164] *To Augustus*, 330-7.

Luxurious lobster-nights, farewell,
For sober, studious days!
And Burlington's delicious meal
For salads, tarts, and peas!

but says nothing of the sacrifice of Drury Lane. We know that Pope never entirely gave up trips to the theatre when something by one of his friends was to be produced. He mentions seeing Aaron Hill's *Athelwold* acted in 1731; and, in February, 1739, he witnessed David Mallet's *Mustapha*.[165] But apparently these trips were not frequent. Pope always affected an ignorance of the practical aspects of the drama. 'No man,' he wrote Broome, 'knows less of anything relative to the seasons propitious or the aspects unfavorable to the stage.'[166]

In spite of such avowals on Pope's part as, 'But it is no more than honesty to tell you . . . that in dramatic poetry I am less [of a critic] than in any other,'[167] his friends who were engaged upon the composition of correct, now defunct, tragedies besought his advice. This, which was modestly given, may surprise the reader by its emphasis on the qualities which alone give plays vitality—emotional appeal, effective construction, and plenty of action. 'To say truth, I think any common reader judges these [plays] of the most material part as well as the most learned—*that is, of the moving the passions*; and you'll agree with me that if a writer does not move them, there is no art to teach him.' He writes to Hill of his *Athelwold*, 'Nothing but trifles have I to object, and which were such as did not once stop me at the first reading,—the spirit, design, and characters carrying me on without stop, check or even intermission. You certainly are master of the art of the stage in the manner of forming and conducting the design, which I think impossible to be mended. *Of that great part, and of the other, the raising the passions*, I will say nothing to you who know them so much better than myself.'[168] He questions whether Dodsley's *Toyshop* '*has action enough* to please on the stage,' even though he thinks 'the morality and satire ought to be relished by the *reader*.'[169]

---

[165] E-C, X, 39, 93.
[166] *ibid.*, VIII, 59.
[167] *ibid.*, X, 80.
[168] *ibid.*, X, 25.
[169] *ibid.*, IX, 535. The italics in the foregoing quotations are mine. A note on Robert Dodsley (1703-64) may interest. Pope kindly recommended his play to the theatrical manager, Rich; it was produced and had a successful run, upon the proceeds of which Dodsley set up the book-seller's shop which published Johnson's *London*.

Occasionally the criticisms are a little more academic—take note of correctness and regularity, 'frequency of sentence' and sentiment; he writes to Mallet of his *Eurydice*, 'As to the particular conduct, the incidents, the working up of those incidents, and the gradation of the scenes to that end, as far as I can judge . . . you proceed judiciously and regularly. The single sentiments and expressions are surely generally correct. . . .'[170] He praises Hill for excelling 'throughout in the greatness of sentiment; and I add that I never met with more striking sentences[171] or lively short reprizes.'[172]

For Pope's theory of the Pastoral, we need not resort to patchwork and inference. The 1717 edition of his *Pastorals* was prefaced by a *Discourse* of theory. In this, the poet was avowedly setting forth no original view, but collating and summarizing what had been said by the 'received' critics. The prefaces of authors are apt to assume the form of *apologiae* for what follows; but Pope's was to give the rules of the game which had been set by others and to which he agreed: 'it is my design to comprise in this short paper the substance of those numerous dissertations that critics have made on the subject without omitting any of their rules[173] in my own favor. You will also find some points reconciled about which they seem to differ,[174] and a few remarks which, I think, have escaped their observation.'[175] There is something of a parade of authorities in the footnotes—the Preface to the *Pastorals* in Dryden's Virgil, Rapin's *Discourse on Pastorals*,[176] Rapin *Sur l'Art Poétique d'Aristote*, Fontenelle's *Discourse on Pastorals*,[177] and even—once—Heinsius *In Theocrito*.

The general conception of the pastoral held by Pope follows Fontenelle pretty closely. This amiable and cultivated French critic was desirous of taking a middle ground between the view that it was the function of the *genre* to copy the humble and rustic life of ordinary shepherds and the extreme view on the other hand that one need pay no attention to *verisimilitude*, but might make

[170] E-C, X, 80.

[171] i.e., *sententiae*.

[172] E-C, X, 61.

[173] These rules have been drawn from 'the only undisputed authors of Pastoral,' Theocritus and Virgil (E-C, I, 260).

[174] This 'ministry of reconciliation' is characteristic of Pope's temper on matters political, literary, philosophical, and theological.

[175] E-C, I, 257.

[176] Published a few years before in Creech's translation of Theocritus (Warton: *Works of Pope*, I, xiv).

[177] This was added to the English translation of Le Bossu *On the Epic Poem*.

the pastoral a vehicle for wit and courtly compliment. 'Entre la grossièrté ordinaire des bergers de Théocrite, et le trop d'esprit de la plupart de nos bergers modernes, il y a un milieu à tenir.'[178] Realistic portrayal of peasants cannot please: we are not interested in the routine of their life; it is only the attractive and idyllic features of it which the pastoral should develop—the leisure and peace which attach to such a life, or did in the Golden Age. 'Entendre parler de brebis et de chèvres, des soins qu'il faut prendre de ces animaux, cela n'a rien par soi-même qui puisse plaire; ce qui plâit, c'est l'idée de tranquillité attachée à la vie de ceux qui prennent soin de brebis et de chèvres. . . .'[179] 'L'illusion et en même temps l'agrément des bergeries consiste donc à n'offrir aux yeux que le tranquillité de la vie pastorale, dont on dissimule la bassesse; on en laisse voir la simplicité, mais on en cache la misère.'[180]

Pope similarly adopts a middle ground. The manners are to be 'not too polite nor too rustic; the thoughts are plain, yet admit a little quickness and passion, but that short and flowing; the expression humble, yet as pure as the language will afford; neat, but not florid; easy, and yet lively.'[181] 'If we would copy Nature, it may be useful to take this idea along with us, that Pastoral is an image of what they call the Golden Age; so that we are not to describe our shepherds as shepherds at this day really are, but as they may be conceived to have been when the best of men followed the employment.'[182] Some 'knowledge in rural affairs' is to be discovered; yet 'what is inviting in this sort of poetry . . . proceeds not so much from the idea of that business as of the tranquillity of a country life. We must therefore use some illusion to render a pastoral delightful; and this consists in exposing the best side only of a shepherd's life and in concealing its miseries.'[183]

The form as well as the subject matter of the Pastoral should mediate between realism and romanticism. It 'ought to preserve some relish of the old way of writing: the connections should be loose, the narrations and descriptions short, and the periods concise. Yet it is not sufficient that the sentences only be brief: the whole eclogue should be so too, for we cannot suppose poetry in those days to have been the business of men, but their recreation at vacant hours.'[184] On the other hand, art must shape the Eclogue:

[178] *Oeuvres*, V, 26.
[179] *ibid.*, 9-10.
[180] *ibid.*, 16.
[181] E-C, I, 258.
[182] *ibid.*, 258.
[183] *ibid.*, 259. Pope will be observed to follow Fontenelle rather closely in these last sentences.
[184] *ibid.*, 259.

each of a set must have its own 'particular beauty' and be different
from every other. 'Besides, in each of them a designed scene or
prospect is to be presented to our view, which should likewise have
its variety,' obtained by 'frequent comparisons drawn from the
most agreeable objects of the country' and by 'elegant turns on
the words, which render the numbers extremely sweet and pleasing.'[185]

No doubt the day of 'reconciliations' has passed. If there must
be the pastoral, a modernist would say, why not either copy the life
of actual shepherds, or else abandon the notion of *verisimilitude*
entirely and frankly employ it for whatever grace and decorative
quality there is in its convention; surely there is no middle ground
of theory logically to be justified. Realism or aestheticism: one
must choose. But must one? There are still those who conceive the
possibility of a soundly humanistic art which shall, without forgetting circumstance and detail, somehow see through and beyond
them to universal experience; see in shepherds and shop-people
neither a sentimental projection of one's own emotions nor yet
merely the external and the animal, but human nature, shaped
by, and yet transcending, particularities of rank and profession.
Though Pope would not so have expressed it, was there not a
similar conception of art and its function in his mind when he discoursed of the Pastoral?

So much for Pope's connections with and views upon, the principal *genres* of his time. The conclusion remains. Pope was a
serious student of the poetic craft: he felt a keen interest in the
technique of composition, and took the pride of one who had mastered his art in discoursing upon its niceties. His sense of proportion was here, as in his practice, firm and just: he conceived of design as the soul of poetry, but he paid due attention to the details of
versification. In the matter of diction he stood, on the whole, with
the neo-classical advocates of a retrenched diction; but he did not
object to the use of revived archaisms and loan-words from the
French and Latin in moderation. He made decided improvements
in the 'heroic' versification by the omission of gap-filling expletives
and attention to the *caesura*. For concern with aspects large and
small, Pope belongs to the company of the poets who are conscious
of their aims and methods, who have seriously pondered their art.

[185] E-C, I, 260.

CHAPTER III

POPE'S 'Homer' is a focal point for many lines of interest. It is the English poet's *magnum opus*; it established his right to the rank of most eminent man of letters of the day; and it gave him financial independence of patrons and public—the first such independence in literature. Its success was the most impressive thing in Pope's career. It takes its place as the most celebrated and brilliant of the great number of translations from the classics with which both French and English literature provided themselves in the seventeenth and early eighteenth centuries; it succeeded Dryden's versions of Virgil, Juvenal, and Persius.

On another side, it connects us with the celebrated Quarrel of the Ancients and the Moderns, which lent zest to French criticism of the Classical Age, and was echoed in England by the controversy between Bentley and Temple. Pope was not merely translator: he was critic as well; and he could not read, by way of preparation, the contemporary French critics without to some extent taking sides in the Quarrel. If, then, the translation has its connections with Pope's personal history and with the systematic assimilation of the classics into English literature, the critical material accompanying it calls us to a study of the long line of Homeric critics; for it was not Pope alone who felt that the cause of classicism stood or fell with the cause of Homer.

Before we are fairly started upon a consideration of the theoretical interests involved, it may be useful briefly to trace the history of Pope's undertaking. From a child, Homer was a favorite with his future translator: 'he was,' says Pope, 'the first author that made me catch the itch of poetry when I read him in my childhood.'[1] Ogilby's version, in a large edition embellished with 'sculptures,' was the poet's great delight at eight;[2] at twelve the boy wrote a play for his schoolmates which included in paraphrase many speeches from the *Iliad*;[3] and in his epic, *Alcander*, written

---

[1] E-C, VIII, 37.
[2] Spence, 276.
[3] E-C, V, 9.

at the same age, he imitated Homer besides other ancient and modern poets.

Among the early and fragmentary translations which Pope executed for practice in versification was one of the episode of Sarpedon; and upon receipt of this, his early patron, Sir William Trumbull, wrote exhorting him to continue the venture: 'I am confirmed in my former application to you; and give me leave to renew it upon this occasion, that you would proceed in translating that incomparable poet, to make him speak good English, to dress his admirable characters in your proper, significant, and expressive conceptions. . . .'[4]

The exhortation did not remain unheeded. In 1713, when Pope was still, according to our standards, a very young man to undertake a work so vast and requiring powers so varied and considerable, he issued Proposals for a complete translation of the *Iliad*. It was an audacious venture, but the spirit of the time moderated its audacity. 'There was reason to believe that Pope's attempt would be successful. He was in the full bloom of reputation, and was personally known to almost all whom dignity of employment or splendor of reputation had made eminent'; he 'conversed indifferently' with both political parties; and, since both boasted of their literary zeal, might reasonably expect to receive encouragement from both.[5]

His Proposals offered to the public an English *Iliad* in six quarto volumes at six guineas—a price, according to Dr. Johnson,[6] greater than had yet been asked for a work of the sort. A considerable number of book-sellers made application to undertake the edition; the highest bidder was Lintot, who agreed to pay £200 for each volume and in addition supply the subscribers' copies free. The Proposals were 'very favorably received, and the patrons of literature were busy to recommend his [Pope's] undertaking and promote his interest'; Swift made particular exertions on his behalf. The list of subscribers almost constituted a roll of all persons of eminence in Church and State; the King and the Prince of Wales and the libraries of ten Oxford Colleges were included.

A few dissenting voices were, to be sure, raised against the undertaking: some ventured to call into question the translator's qualifications for his task. Thomas Burnet, in his *Homerides*, called it 'bold and almost prodigious for a single man to undertake a work which not all the poets of our island durst jointly attempt. . . .'[7] Charles Gildon, in his *New Rehearsal*, represented Sir Indolent as remarking to Sawney Dapper (i.e., Pope), 'I did not know

[4] E-C, VI, 3.
[5] Johnson: *Lives*, III, 109.
[6] *ibid.*, III, 110.
[7] Burnet, *Homerides*, 5.

that you understood Greek,' and Sawney as replying, 'Why, Sir
Indolent, if I did not understand Greek, what of that? I hope a
man may translate a Greek author without understanding Greek.'[8]

But these were the taunts of enemies. No doubt it is in the main
true that in the easy-going days of Queen Anne ignorance of
Greek was not regarded as any serious obstacle to the carrying
out of such an undertaking. Even Dr. Johnson is disposed to
minimize the handicap. With 'an irregular education, and a
course of life of which much seems to have passed in conversation,
it is not very likely that he overflowed with Greek. But when he
felt himself deficient, he sought assistance; and what man of
learning would refuse to help him?' Homer's glory is his 'invention'—his design; the nice details of style are by comparison inconsequential. 'Minute enquiries into the force of words are less
necessary in translating Homer than other poets, because his
positions are general, and his representations natural, with very
little dependence on local or temporary customs. . . .'[9]

There were plenty of literal translations into Latin at hand from
which he 'could easily obtain his author's sense with sufficient certainty;'[10] 'If more help was wanting, he had the poetical translation of Eobanus Hessus . . . , the French *Homers* of La Valterie
and Dacier, and the English of Chapman, Hobbes, and Ogilby.'[11]
Perhaps even so there were difficulties. Pope told Spence that during
the translation of the *Iliad*, and 'particularly the first part of it, I
was often under great pain and apprehension. Though I conquered the thoughts of it in the day, they would frighten me in the
night. I sometimes, still even, dream of being engaged in that
translation, and got half-way through it, and being embarassed
and under dread of never completing it.'[12] But the task gradually
grew easier. The same forms and *formulae* 'were constantly recurring.' Even the occasional collation of modern versions with
the Greek would in time build up some knowledge of the original
tongue.

In a letter Pope wrote his friend Bridges, he acknowledges his
inadequacy at Greek; but, like Johnson, feels that the supreme

[8] Act III, p. 41.
[9] *Lives*, III, 113-14. The Doctor is certainly incorrect in his last statement. The Homeric customs are no more emancipated from the limitations
of time and space than any other.
[10] Dr. Johnson adds, at this point, the amazing remark that 'among the
readers of Homer the number is very small of those who find much in
the Greek more than in the Latin, *except the music of the numbers*'
(Italics mine).
[11] *Lives*, III, 114.
[12] Spence, 283.

merit of Homer lies not in his niceties of style but in such larger
elements of composition as a fairly free translation can convey.
After speaking of himself as one 'who values the authority of one
true poet above that of twenty critics or commentators,' he proceeds: 'But though I speak thus of commentators, I will continue
to read carefully all I can procure, to make up that way for my
own want of critical understanding in the original beauties of
Homer, *though the greatest of them are certainly those of invention
and design, which are not at all confined to the language*: for the
distinguishing excellences of Homer are, by the consent of the best
critics of all nations, first, in the manners (which include all the
speeches, as being no other than the representatives of each person's manners by his words), and then in that rapture and fire
which carries you away with him with that wonderful force that
no man who has a true poetical spirit is master of himself while
he reads him.'[13]

The translation by itself could hardly be counted upon to occupy
the promised six volumes; notes must be provided. 'What the mere
perusal of the text could suggest, Pope wanted no assistance to
collect or methodize; but more was necessary: many pages were to
be filled, and learning must supply materials to wit and judgment.'[14] Madame Dacier had appended a full course of notes to her
French translation of Homer; but dignity, if nothing else, seemed
to require the culling of material from other and less accessible
sources. Accordingly resort was had to Eustathius'[15] *Commentary
on the Iliad and Odyssey of Homer*, which included numerous extracts from the *scholia* of critics whose writings have perished.
There was at the time no Latin version of Eustathius: Pope hired
Broome to translate such notes as fitted his plan. He remarks in his
Observations that 'of all the commentators upon Homer, there is
scarcely one whose principal design is to illustrate the poetical
beauties of the author.'[16]

His intention is to supply this need; and accordingly he directs
Broome to 'read over in order the commentaries of Eustathius . . .
and place a mark upon all the notes which are purely critical,
omitting the grammatical and geographical and allegorical ones.
. . .' 'Be so kind as to take this method: translate such notes only
as concern the beauties or art of the author. . . . What are alle-

[13] E-C, VI, 12. Italics mine.
[14] Johnson: *Lives*, III, 115.
[15] Eustathius was a Byzantine scholar, probably a native of Constan-
tinople, who flourished in the second half of the twelfth century. He was
incumbent successively of the episcopal sees of Myra in Lycia and Thes-
salonica.
[16] *Observations on the First Book of the Iliad.*

gorical, if obvious and ingenious, abstract; if far-fetched, omit;
but leave out none of the art or contrivance of the poet, or beauties,
it being on account of those alone that I put you to this task.'[17] In
the midst of his labors, Broome married a rich widow: the labor of
compilation was suspended, and the later celebrated Dr. Jortin,
then an undergraduate at Cambridge, 'supplied' for a time.

Pope's friend, Dr. Parnell, was the poet's invaluable assistant
throughout his labors. He wrote an introductory *Life of Homer*,
and assisted, upon visits to Binfield, in the elucidation of the
'learned languages.' The indebtedness is humorously indicated in
a letter dispatched just after the coadjutor has left: 'the minute
I lost you,' our translator writes, 'Eustathius, with nine hundred
pages and nine thousand contractions of the Greek character, arose
to my view! Spondanus,[18] with all his auxiliaries, in number, a
thousand pages (value, three shillings); and Dacier's three volumes; Barnes' two; Valterie's three; Cuperus, half in Greek; Leo
Allatius, three parts in Greek; Scaliger; Macrobius; and (worse
than all) Aulus Gellius.'[19]

Pope announced in an introductory *Observation* that 'Whatever
in the following notes is extracted from others is constantly
owned . . .'; but neither he nor his collaborator felt wholly bound
by the declaration. He accused Madame Dacier of stealing materials: 'Her *Remarks upon Homer* are an example, where Eustathius
is transcribed ten times for once that he is quoted,' and says he has
left unexposed hundreds of her thefts.[20] But he professed shock
at discovering Broome at the same practice: 'I must only at present
warn you of one point. . . . I find, upon comparing your notes
with Dacier's, many of them much more directly—indeed, entirely
—copied from her, besides what she takes from Eustathius—than
I expected, or than is consistent with the plan laid down and the
declaration I made in the introduction to the notes on the *Iliad*,

---

[17] E-C, VIII, 32-3.

[18] Spondanus, or Jean de Sponde, a French critic, in 1583 published a
Homer with Latin translation and commentary—this latter 'die erste
zusammenhängende ästhetische Erklärung Homers' to be written in
Europe (Finsler, 125).

[19] E-C, VII, 451-2. Joshua Barnes' edition of Homer, published in 1711,
'alle frühern übertraf'; 'Die Aufgabe ist für lange Zeit grundlegend ge-
worden' (Finsler, 309). De la Valterie translated both epics into French
in 1681. His version 'die Sitten der homerischen Zeit dem Zartgefühl des
Barocks anzunähern bestrebt' (*ibid.*, 155); Pope praised the 'elegance' of its
style (E-C, X, 146). Cuperus, Professor at Deventer in the seventeenth
century, elucidated the then just discovered relief known as 'The Apothe-
osis of Homer.' Allatius, an Italianized Greek, Librarian of the Vatican,
composed in 1640 a Latin work on the 'Fatherland' of Homer.

[20] E-C, X, 145-6.

which you also declare in yours to these on the *Odyssey*[21] to make your model.'[22]

There is good reason to suppose that Pope himself had profited by, while he condemned, Madame Dacier's example. When, in spite of his profession that he had concealed the lady's thefts, he comments, 'Madame Dacier should have acknowledged this remark to belong to Eustathius,' the critic Wakefield is provoked to surprise: 'our translator,' he says, 'has borrowed from others every note that contains one particle of ancient learning, without exception, to the best of my belief, and yet does not acknowledge the obligation one time in six.'[23]

Besides his observations upon particular passages of the text, Pope wrote a number of set essays for insertion between books: notable are those on Achilles' Shield (in which the author shows his taste for the art of painting), on the Catalogues in Homer, and on the Battles. Two projected essays on the Theology and Morality of Homer and the Oratory of Homer and Virgil were left unfinished.[24] He also 'designed four very laborious and uncommon sort of indexes to Homer,' of which only three were completed—one of 'Persons and Things,' another of 'Arts and Sciences,'[25] and a third, called a 'Poetical Index,' which tabulates the 'Fable'[26] and its assisting Episodes, the Allegories,[27] the 'Characters or Manners,' Theological[28] and Heroic,[29] the 'most considerable' Orations,[30] the

[21] The notes to the *Odyssey* were entirely furnished by Broome.
[22] E-C, VIII, 113.   [23] *ibid.*, 114, n.   [24] *ibid.*, IX, 71.
[25] That Homer gathered into himself and his poems all the learning, Egyptian and Greek, of his time was a commonplace of neo-classical criticism. We are not to be surprised, then, at lists headed, 'Art Military,' 'Agriculture and Rural Arts,' 'Architecture,' 'Astronomy,' 'Divination,' 'Gymnastics,' 'Geography,' 'History,' 'Music,' 'Mechanics,' 'Policy' (i.e., Politics), 'Physic' (Medicine), 'Painting,' 'Sculpture,' etc., and 'Theology.'
[26] Under which we are given, following Le Bossu, the stages in the rise and fall of the 'wrath of Achilles,' and the 'great moral of the *Iliad*, that concord among governors is the preservation of states, and discord the ruin of them.'
[27] The 'Allegorical Fables' are divided into the 'moral,' such as 'Prudence restraining Passion represented in the machine of Minerva descending to calm Achilles,' and the 'physical or philosophical,' such as 'the quality of salt preserving dead bodies from corruption [represented] in Thetis, or the sea, preserving the body of Patroclus.'
[28] Here again the allegories enter: the list is of the 'characters of the Gods of Homer as acting in the physical or moral capacities of those deities'; e.g., Juno, 'as an element of air'; Mars 'as mere martial courage without conduct' (i.e., prudence); Minerva, 'as martial courage with wisdom.'
[29] Their qualities are tabulated, with supporting proof-texts.
[30] Divided generically into the 'Exhortatory or Deliberative,' the 'Vituperative,' the 'Narrative,' the 'Pathetic,' and the 'Sarcastic,' with a con-

'most remarkable' Descriptions, the Similes,[31] and the passages of 'representative metre, 'Expressing in the sound the thing described.' Tabulations of this sort are bound to seem quaint if not grotesque today. The epithets 'laborious' and 'uncommon' cannot, however, be denied them. Dryden's Virgil, nearest prototype to Pope's Homer, was lacking both notes and indexes.

So much for the preparation of the translation and its accompanying apparatus. In 1715 the first volume of the *Iliad* was issued from the press—in form, a substantial quarto, equipped with portrait, preface, introduction, maps and notes. A chorus of acclamation greeted its appearance; and succeeding volumes attained the same favor. A few critics attacked—notably Dennis, who charged Pope's translation with being barbarous, flat, obscure, affected, and unnatural where the original was pure, clear, lofty, simple, and unaffected;[32] and Bentley, whose famous gibe is almost as well-known as either Pope or Homer; but otherwise the praise was unmixed. The scholarly Theobald, not yet the King of Dunces, praised with as much enthusiasm as did the 'gentlemen': 'The spirit of Homer breathes all through this translation,' he said, 'and I am in doubt whether I should most admire the justness of the original or the force and beauty of the language, or the sounding variety of the numbers; but when I find all these meet, it puts me in mind of what the poet says of one of his heroes, that he alone raised and flung with ease a weighty stone that two common men could not lift from the ground: just so one single person has performed in this translation what I once despaired to have seen done by the force even of several masterly hands.'[33] And the learned Spence, not until afterward the friend and biographer of the poet, charged Pope with often violating the simplicity of Homer, but decided that the great beauties of the translation were more than equalled by its defects, and that Pope had greatly enriched his original: 'his faults are the faults of a man; his beauties are the beauties of an angel.'[34]

Defenders of the translation have been wont to urge that it is a great original poem, poetic, spirited, and eminently readable; de-

cluding list of 'Speeches to Horses'! (This recalls Richardson's *dramatis personae* for *Sir Charles Grandison*, which comprises men, women, and Italians.)

[31] Tabulated according to subjects, as drawn from 'beasts,' 'lions,' 'birds,' etc.

[32] *Remarks upon Mr. Pope's Translation of Homer*, 11. On page 12, Dennis takes Bentley's position: 'the Homer which Lintot prints does not talk like Homer, but like Pope.'

[33] Lounsbury, 188-9.

[34] *An Essay on Pope's Odyssey* (1726), 156.

nunciators, to emphasize its unfaithfulness to the spirit of the
original. Dr. Johnson, whose view of the whole matter is perhaps
the most balanced and sensible of all, took a mediating third position in which he emphasized the necessity of taking the historical view. 'Time and place will always enforce regard. In es-
timating this translation, consideration must be had of the nature
of our language, the form of our metre, and, above all, of the
change which two thousand years have made in the modes of life
and the habits of thought.' Even Virgil had to 'embellish' what he
borrowed from Homer—'the demand for elegance [was] so much
increased that mere Nature would be endured no longer.' Admittedly, Pope has similarly touched up his original. 'Homer
doubtless owes to his translator many Ovidian graces not exactly
suitable to his character. . . . Elegance is surely to be desired if it
be not gained at the expense of dignity.' The Doctor will be yet
more of an opportunist: 'To a thousand cavils, one answer is sufficient: the purpose of a writer is to be read. . . . Pope wrote for
his own age and his own nation: he knew that it was necessary to
color the images and point the sentiments of his author. He therefore made him graceful, but lost him some of his sublimity.'[35]

Let us turn now from the history of Pope's translation to the
Quarrel of the Ancients and the Moderns and the connection with
it of Pope's Homeric criticism. Two tempers and two spirits were
contending in this literary anticipator of many a modern struggle.
Both parties, it is true, repudiated the 'barbarous' Middle Ages.
But the conservative, or classical, party clung to the worship of the
ancients which had been the progressivism of the Italian and
French Renaissance; while the modernist party, fired by the triumphs of Descartes and his 'scientific' philosophy and the 'law' of
human progress, moved on to assert the emancipation of the reason
even from its emancipators, the ancients. The propaganda on
both sides was apt to be *a priori*: as today, few were able to command impartial criticism; the dogma of tradition and received
opinion was in combat not with disinterested enquiry but with the
dogma of 'science' and the dogma of progress. The classicists
sought to silence their opponents by exhibiting in behalf of their
clients the universal approbation of the ages: 'c'est le temps et le
consentement général des hommes qui consacrent nos productions.'[36] But what, argued the modernists with some point, means
the approbation of the ages if the poem has nothing to say to me?
Am I to be overawed by the centuries? What of the new-found

[35] *Lives*, III, 238-40.
[36] Madame Dacier: *Des Causes de la Corruption du Goût* (in Vial and
Denise, II, 15).

rights of the individual to judge for himself? 'Nous ne devons le sacrifice de notre jugement qu'à l'autorité divine,' says La Motte piously; 'et c'est une espèce d'idolâtrie que d'accorder à des décisions humaines ce sacrifice que Dieu s'est réservé pour lui seul.'[37] Unfortunately, the modernists were not content with demanding the right of private judgment: they tended, with their great teacher, Descartes, to an inordinate contemporaneity and a rationalism too insensitive to cultural tradition, to a belief in the 'indefinite progress of the human spirit'[38] which applied to the history of the arts the very different norm of the development of the sciences.

Large intellectual issues were, then, involved;[39] but in the second and more heated stage of the quarrel, the immediate subject of most of the essays and dissertations was Homer, the chief representative of ancient literature, as Aristotle was of ancient philosophy. Descartes had ended the reign of the latter; were not the modernists presently to dismiss the other king from his throne? 'Ne voyez-vous pas . . . dans l'histoire du long règne d'Aristote l'image de celui d'Homère? La chute de celui-là ne vous fait-elle pas pressentir la chute prochaine de celui-ci? La cause de M. de La Motte n'est assurément pas moins victorieuse que celles de Descartes. . . .'[40]

Fifteen years after the termination of the contention between Perrault and Fontenelle in behalf of the moderns and Boileau and La Fontaine in behalf of the ancients, the controversy was renewed over the publication of Madame Dacier's translation of the *Iliad* with accompanying defense of Homer. This good lady was the most rigorously orthodox classicist who will come to our attention. Her devotion to her poet knew no bounds of reason: she believed in his inerrancy; and woe to those whose admiration was not capable of such a height.

Her doctrine provoked, and encountered, attack from a series of shrewd, rationalistically-minded critics. Houdar La Motte produced a translation of the *Iliad* in which he had the impudence to abridge the original into twelve books and make all manner of corrections. In his *Discours sur Homère* he asserts that this great author, like others, is open to the exercise of the reader's judgment, vigorously attacks the morals, manners, and wit of the 'heroes,'

[37] Vial and Denise, II, 20.
[38] See particularly Abbé Terrasson, *Dissertation*, I, xiii.
[39] The Quarrel of the Ancients and the Moderns 'n'est pas une frivole question de préséance. Au fond du débat il y avait une idée philosophique, une des plus grandes qui puissent être proposées a l'esprit humain, parce qu'elle intéresse la dignité de sa nature, l'idée du progrès intellectuel de l'humanité.' Rigault, II.
[40] Vial and Denise, II, 17. The passage is quoted from the Abbé de Pons.

and doubts whether moderns are qualified to judge of the 'beauties' of Homer's poetry.[41] His assault was followed by those highly rationalistic clerics, Abbé de Pons, who proclaimed, 'on jugera Homère un grand génie, et le premier homme de son siècle rustique, en même temps qu'on jugera son poème très défectueux pour un siècle aussi éclairé que le nôtre,'[42] and Abbé Terrasson.

The various charges brought against Homer by the modernists are reviewed and 'answered' by Pope in his Preface to the *Iliad*, and frequently also in the notes. Our poet's position is clear. He declares himself on the side of the classicists: he wrote in his *Postscript* to the *Odyssey*, 'I have fought under Madame Dacier's banner, and have waged war in defence of the divine Homer against all the heretics of the age.'[43] We could hardly expect less from the writer of the *Essay on Criticism*. But Pope was in this, as in all other matters, inclined to moderation. In his younger days, he altered the verse which originally read, 'Nor Homer nods so often as we dream' to the blunt 'Nor is it Homer nods but we that dream,'[44] thereby, as Dennis pointed out,[45] presuming to differ with Horace. But the *Observations* confess to having surrendered belief in an inerrant Homer.

'I sometimes think,' wrote Pope *à propos* of the death of Patroclus, 'I am in respect to Homer much like Sancho Panca [*sic*] with regard to Don Quixote. I believe upon the whole that no mortal ever came near him for wisdom, learning, and all good qualities. But sometimes there are certain starts which I cannot tell what to make of, and am forced to own that my master is a little out of the way, if not quite beside himself. The present passage of the death of Patroclus, attended with so many odd circumstances to overthrow this hero (who might, for all I can see, as decently have fallen by the force of Hector) are what I am at a loss to excuse, and must indeed (in my own opinion) give them up to the critics. I really think almost all those parts which have been objected against with most clamor and fury are honestly defensible; and none of 'em (to confess my private sentiment) seem to me to be faults of any consideration, except this conduct in the death of Patroclus, the length of Nestor's discourse in Lib. 11, the speech of Achilles' horse in the nineteenth, the conversation of that hero with Aeneas in Lib. 20, the manner of Hector's flight round the walls of Troy and his death in Lib. 22.

[41] Vial and Denise, II, 6-10.
[42] *ibid.*, 17.
[43] *Odyssey*, V, 281.
[44] E-C, II, 44-5 and n.
[45] In *Reflections upon a Late Rhapsody* (Durham, 232).

'I hope,' he concludes, 'after so free a confession no reasonable modern will think me touched with the 'ομηρομανία of Madame Dacier and others. I am sensible of the extremes which mankind run into in extolling and depreciating authors. We are not more violent and unreasonable in attacking those who are not yet established into fame than in defending those who are, even in every minute trifle. Fame is a debt which when we have kept from people as long as we can, we pay with a prodigious interest which amounts to twice the value of the principal. Thus 't is with ancient works as with ancient coins : they pass for a vast deal more than they were worth at first; and the very obscurities which time has thrown upon them are the sacred rust which enhances their value with all true lovers of antiquity.'[46]

Madame Dacier was hardly likely to be pleased with the tone of this,[47] nor with the dubious and mixed praise Pope bestowed upon her at the beginning of his *Observations* on the First Book : 'I am obliged to say, even of Madame Dacier, that she is either more beholden to him [Eustathius] than she has confessed, or has read him less than she has confessed. She has made a farther attempt than her predecessors to discover the beauties of the poet, though we have often only her general praises and explanations instead of reasons.[48] But her remarks all together are the most judicious collection extant of the scattered observation of the ancients and moderns,[49] as her Preface is excellent and her translation equally careful and elegant.'

The second edition of her version afforded the lady opportunity for making a number of attacks on Pope's Preface. Pope, in the *Postscript* to the *Odyssey*, attributes these attacks to the faulty French translation which the lady read.

But he takes occasion nevertheless to distinguish his devotion to Homer from hers. 'I offer *opinions*, and she delivers *doctrines*,' he

[46] *Observations*, XVI: LI.

[47] If we are to believe Rigault (443)—and his theory seems plausible— Pope had much earlier, in the *Essay on Criticism*, indulged in his first fling at Madame Dacier. Her doctrine that 'Il y a des nations plus heureusement situées et plus favorisées du soleil que les autres' was attacked in Pope's

> Meanly they seek the blessing to confine,
> And force that sun but on a part to shine
> Which not alone the southern wit sublimes,
> But ripens spirits in cold northern climes.
> (*Essay*, II, 198-201.)

[48] Pope elsewhere in several places ridicules critics who rhapsodize and 'have no reasons.'

[49] Study of Pope's notes is evidence of the copious 'acknowledged' use he made of this collection. After Eustathius it was his chief source of information.

says; 'my imagination represents Homer as the greatest of human poets, whereas in hers he was exalted above humanity; infallibility and impeccability were two of his attributes.' Madame Dacier flatly prefers the manners of the ancient world to those of the modern; Pope cannot take so unjudicious a position. 'I confessed that in my own opinion the world was mended in some points, such as the custom of putting whole nations to the sword, condemning kings, and their families to perpetual slavery, and a few others. Madame Dacier judges otherwise in this. . . .'[50]

With these reservations, however, he will join her: 'as to the rest particularly in preferring the simplicity of the ancient world to the luxury of ours . . . she owns we agree.' But his spirit will still differ from hers: though as 'great' he cannot be 'as passionate an admirer as herself.' Reason sets its bounds. 'Though I am a poet, I would not be an enthusiast; and though I am an English-man I would not be furiously of a party.'[51]

The contention was ended by courtesy rather than the surrender of either point of view. After a time Pope wrote her 'a very genteel and obliging letter'; she answered pleasantly; 'so that these two great admirers and translators of Homer ever after maintained towards each other the most perfect appearance of esteem and regard.'[52]

Though he was not able to believe in the infallibility of Homer, and was therefore obliged to dissent from some of Madame Dacier's extreme views, Pope was certainly on the whole correct when he described himself as having fought under the lady's banner, and 'waged war in defence of the divine Homer against all the heretics of the age.' The second part of the Preface to the *Iliad* consists of an answer to the chief accusations preferred against Homer by the modernists, which mentions by name Rapin, Perrault, and LaMotte besides that earlier villifier in the interests of Virgil, J. C. Scaliger.

Pope draws his general line of defense from the thesis that the glory of Homer is his 'invention,' and the contrast, which had already been made by Addison, between the natural and the learned

---

[50] *Odyssey*, V, 284-5. This is pretty heavy irony. Madame Dacier was, how-ever, a resolute proponent of the Homeric manner of life, which she com-pared to that of the Patriarchs. She tells us, 'Pour moi . . . , je trouve ces temps anciens d'autant plus beaux qu'ils ressemblent moins au nôtre' (Dacier, I, xxiii). Rigault remarks. (445), 'Mme. Dacier . . . ne distingue pas entre Homère, ses héros, ses dieux, et son siècle: elle les confond tous dans une égale admiration, et, toute bonne catholique qu'elle était devenue, elle aurait vécu volontiers chez les Phéaciens, au siècle d'or de Nausicaa.'

[51] *Odyssey*, V, 288.

[52] Ruffhead, 152.

genius. The chief objections against Homer 'proceed from so noble a cause as the excess' of his genius for 'invention.' It 'is with great parts as with great virtues: they naturally border on some imperfection, and it is often hard to distinguish exactly where the virtue ends or the fault begins; and as magnanimity may run up to profusion or extravagance, so may a great invention to redundancy or wildness.'[53]

To some of the charges, then, Pope brings an explanation rather than a defence. He cannot pretend to be pleased with 'speaking horses' and similar marvels and will not attempt to palliate the distress they occasion to 'judicious' readers: 'methinks the commentators are at too much pains to discharge the poet from the imputation of extravagant fiction by accounting for wonders of this kind,' he says. 'I am afraid that next to the extravagance of inventing them is that of endeavoring to reconcile such fictions to probability. Would not one general answer do better—to say once for all that the above cited authors lived in the age of wonders: the taste of the world has been generally turned to the miraculous; wonders were what the people would have, and what not only the poets but the priests gave 'em.'[54]

One explanation, then, is simply that Homer gave his hearers what they wanted. Another involves calling to attention again the fertility and profusion of his 'invention': 'Perhaps it may be with great and superior souls as with gigantic bodies which, exerting themselves with unusual strength, exceed what is commonly thought the due proportion of parts to become miracles in the whole; and, like the old heroes of that make, commit something near extravagance amidst a series of glorious and inimitable performances.'[55]

Perrault had derided the Homeric similes—'comparaisons à longues queues,' as he profanely called them.[56] Pope explained this antiquated length as he had done the improbable. 'It is owing to the same vast invention that his similes have been thought too exuberant and full of circumstances. The force of this faculty is seen in nothing more than its inability to confine itself to that single circumstance upon which the comparison is grounded. . . . The same will account for his manner of heaping a number of comparisons together in one breath, when his fancy suggested to him at once so many various and correspondent images.'[57] Similar is the remark of the *Observations*[58] that it is 'usual with our author to heap his similes very thick at the conclusion of a book. . . . 'Tis

[53] Durham, 336.
[54] *Observations*, XIX: XXI.
[55] Durham, 336.
[56] Rigault, 200.
[57] Durham, 336-7.
[58] XX: XXX.

the natural discharge of a vast imagination, heated in its progress, and giving itself vent in this crowd of images.'

A principal accusation which critics directed against the Homeric poems curiously confounded the poet and the poet's time: 'Ces temps qualifiés d'héroïques,' charged La Motte, 'paraîtront le règne des passions les plus injustes et les plus basses, et surtout le triomphe de l'avarice.'[59] 'Les héros d'Homère sont de forts mauvais railleurs; ils ne disent jamais rien, en ce genre, d'ingénieux ni de bien choisi.'[60] The manners of the time were gross and crude; 'leurs religion n'était qu'un tissu monstrueux de fables aussi ridicules que les contes de fées; leur philosophie n'avait rien que de vain et de superstitieux.'[61] The gods of the Homeric theogony 'semblent inventés tout exprès par l'ennemi du genre humain pour autoriser tous les crimes, et pour tourner en dérision la Divinité.'[62]

In general, Pope's answer to these charges is the sensible, and to us, obvious one: Homer is not responsible for the theology and the 'manners' he depicted; he was of his time as we are of our times:[63] 'il devait représenter les hommes selon les moeurs qui régnaient alors dans la Grèce et dans l'Asie Mineure.'[64] If there are other critics who 'seem rather to charge him with a defect or narrowness of genius than an excess of it, those seeming defects will be found upon examination to proceed wholly from the nature of the times he lived in. Such are his grosser representations of the gods and the vicious and imperfect manners of his heroes. . . .'[65]

Sometimes, however, he distinguishes carefully between the morality exhibited by this or that particular hero and the morality of Homer himself. 'This inhumanity of Achilles in dragging the dead body of Hector has been severely (and I think indeed not

[59] Vial and Denise, II, 7.
[60] *ibid.*, 8.
[61] Fénelon, 144.
[62] *ibid.*, 146.
[63] The *Essay on Criticism* originally contained an answer to Perrault's sneers at the Homeric 'manners.' The advice to know the 'religion, country, genius of his age' of each ancient before judging him was followed by:

> Zoilus, had these been known, without a name
> Had died, and Perrault ne'er been damned to fame;
>
> . . . .
>
> And sacred Homer yet been unprofaned;
> None e'er had thought his comprehensive mind
> To modern customs, modern rules confined,
> Who for all ages writ, and all mankind.

(E-C, II, 40, n.)

[64] Fénelon, 150.
[65] Durham, 337.

without some justice) censured by several both ancients and moderns,' he remarks; 'but methinks it is a great injustice to Homer to reflect upon the morals of the author himself for things which he only paints as the manners of a vicious hero.' 'Homer as often describes *ill* things in order to make us avoid them, as *good* to induce us to follow them (which is the case with all writers whatever). But what is extremely remarkable and evidently shows the injustice of Plato's censure is that many of those very actions for which he blames him are expressly characterized and marked by Homer himself as evil and detestable by previous expressions or cautions.'[66]

Sometimes Pope fears—as when he reads of Idomeneus taunting the dead—that 'whatever we may see of his superior genius in other respects, his [Homer's] own views of morality were not elevated above the barbarity of his age. I think indeed the thing by far the most shocking in this author is that spirit of cruelty which appears too manifestly in the *Iliad*.'[67]

In his general view of the Homeric 'manners,' Pope balanced carefully, as we have seen, between Madame Dacier and her opponents. The Preface to the *Iliad* develops this mediating position on 'a point generally carried into extremes, both by the censurers and the defenders of Homer.' Who, asks our critic, can be so prejudiced 'as to magnify the felicity of those ages when a spirit of revenge and cruelty reigned through the world; when no mercy was shown but for the sake of lucre; when the greatest princes were put to the sword, and their wives and daughters made slaves and concubines?'

But Pope thinks equally unjustifiable, on the other hand, the contempt for simple manners and primitive conventions which some of his contemporaries affect. 'I would not be so delicate as those modern critics who are shocked at the servile offices and mean employments in which we sometimes see the heroes of Homer engaged. There is a pleasure in taking a view of that simplicity, in opposition to the luxury of succeeding ages; in beholding monarchs without their guards, princes tending their flocks, and princesses drawing water from their springs.' Homer is the 'most ancient author in the heathen world'; and in reading him we have the pleasure of 'stepping almost three thousand years back into the remotest antiquity' and witnessing 'a clear and surprising vision of things nowhere else to be found, the only true mirror of that ancient world.'[68] It is only a 'false delicacy' which occasions shock

[66] *Observations*, XXII: XXXIII.
[67] *ibid.*, XIII: XXXI.
[68] Durham, 337.

at the emphasis on the pleasures of the table, one of Pope's *Observations*[69] assures us. 'Indeed to a common reader who is more fond of heroic and romantic than of just and natural images this at first sight may have an air of ridicule; but I'll venture to say that there is nothing ridiculous in the thing itself, nor mean and low in Homer's manner of expressing it.'

Madame Dacier was fond of justifying Homer's manners by remarking their similarity to those of the Patriarchs in the Bible. 'Homère parle souvent de chaudrons, de marmites, de sang, de graisse, d'intestins, etc. On y voit des princes, dépouiller eux-mêmes les bêtes et les faire rôtir. Les gens du monde trouvent cela choquant; mais on fait voir que tout cela est entièrement conforme à ce que l'on voit dans l'Ecriture sainte.'[70] 'Les Patriarches travaillent eux-mêmes de leurs propres mains; les filles les plus considérables allaient elles-mêmes à la fontaine. . . . J'aime à voir les héros d'Homère faire ce que faisaient les patriarches, plus grands que les rois et que les héros.'[71] Pope followed her comparisons to considerable lengths. He quotes the likenesses of custom and language she has discovered, and adds a good many from his own reading. For example: 'This is conformable to the custom of the Orientals: Achilles will not be induced to wash, and [after the death of Patroclus] afterwards retires to the seashore and sleeps on the ground. It is just thus that David mourns in the Scriptures; he refuses to wash or take any repast, but retires from company and lies upon the earth.'[72] He generalizes, 'I have often observed with pleasure the similitudes which many of Homer's expressions bear with the Holy Scriptures, and that the oldest writer in the world except Moses[73] often speaks in the idiom of Moses.'[74] Illustrative quotations from the Old Testament, sometimes in the Vulgate, but more frequently in the Authorized Version, are at least as numerous as those from Virgil and Milton.

But Pope finds it necessary to reprove Madame Dacier for the extremes to which she carries her parallels: she must not hope to justify the Homeric theology on the basis of the more anthropomorphic passages of the Old Testament. 'I must confess that in

[69] XIX: VIII.

[70] Dacier, I, xxiv.

[71] *ibid.*, xxv.

[72] *Observations*, XXIII: V.

[73] A modern dating may interest. Scott, in his *Unity of Homer* (3-4) says, 'My belief is that Homer . . . lived approximately 900 B.C., or about one hundred years after David composed his *Songs* and Solomon his *Proverbs*. The greatest period of Hebrew literature would roughly correspond with the age of Homer.'

[74] *Observations*, XXI: III.

comparing passages of the sacred books with our author [Homer]
one ought to use a good deal of caution and respect. If there are
some places in Scripture that in compliance to human understanding represent the Deity as acting by motives like those of men,
there are infinitely more that show Him as He is, all perfection,
justice, and benevolence, whereas in Homer the general tenor of the
poem represents Jupiter as a being subject to passion, inequality,
and imperfection. I think Madame Dacier has carried these comparisons too far, and is too zealous to defend him upon every
occasion in points of theology and doctrine.'[75]
The Preface goes on to answer the charge that the Homeric
'constant use of the same epithets to his gods and heroes, such as
the *far-darting* Phoebus, the *blue-eyed* Pallas, the *swift-footed*
Achilles, etc.,' is impertinent and tediously repeated.' Pope explains that the titles of the gods 'depended upon the powers and
offices then believed to belong to them'; that they were 'a sort of
attributes that it was a matter of religion to salute them with on
all occasions, and an irreverence to omit.' He has the authority of
the great Boileau for his statement that the epithets of the heroes
'were in the nature of surnames, and repeated as such'; and is able
to add parallels from English history in such names as 'Harold
Harefoot, Edmund Ironside, Edward Longshanks, Edward the
Black Prince, etc.'[76]
Many of the cavils raised against Homer 'have been occasioned
by an injudicious endeavor to exalt Virgil': Rapin, for example,
in his *Parallel* of the two great poets, is manifestly partisan. The
critics seem to forget, says Pope, that Homer wrote before Virgil
and served as his model. They 'prefer the fable and moral of the
Aeneid to the *Iliad* for the same reasons which might set the *Odyssey* above the *Aeneid*,—as that the hero is a wiser man and the
action of the one more beneficial to his country than that of the
other; or else they blame him for not doing what he never designed,—as because Achilles is not as good and perfect a prince as
Aeneas, when the very moral of his poem required a contrary
character. . . .' This is Rapin's method of attack; Scaliger's[77] is to
select passages from Homer which are not as 'labored'—that is,
polished—'as some that Virgil drew out of them.'[78] Perrault finds
'low and mean expressions' in Homer, partly because of a 'false
delicacy and refinement'; partly through mistranslation of the

[75] *Observations*, VIII: II.
[76] Durham, 338-9.
[77] Scaliger 'who is seldom just to our author [Homer].' *Observations*,
II: XXIII.
[78] Durham, 340.

original. And, finally, La Motte, 'pretending to a fairer proceeding,' distinguishes 'between the personal merit of Homer and that of his work,'[79] but nevertheless assigns the cause of the great reputation of the *Iliad* to 'the ignorance of his times, and the prejudice of those that followed.'[80]

'What other cavils have been raised against Homer are such as hardly deserve a reply, but will yet be taken notice of as they occur in the course of the work,' promises the Preface;[81] and the promise is kept: we are not allowed to forget for long in the *Observations* that a controversy is on, and that it is the duty of a 'true commentator, if not a true critic,' to 'excuse, if not to defend' the lapses of his author.[82]

The charges of the critics are variously met: sometimes with explanation or apology; sometimes with admission. Homer's custom of 'giving his reader a sketch of the principal events he supposes' 'may to many appear no way artful'; and indeed 'this is a principal article of the charge brought against him by some late French critics,' notably La Motte; but Pope replies with a distinction between the *genres* of epic poetry on the one hand and tragedy and romance on the other. In the epic, a foreshadowing summary but excites our anticipation: 'the most judicious poets never fail to excite their reader's curiosity by some small sketches of their design; which, like the outlines of a fine picture, will necessarily raise in us a greater desire to see it in its finished coloring.'[83] Rapin and others had found the design of the *Iliad* defective: 'This and the following book (XXIII and XXIV) . . . are undoubtedly superadded to the grand catastrophe of the poem.' 'Many judicious critics have been of the opinion that Homer is blameable for protracting it.' But in the poet's justification Pope can allege 'that what he undertook was to paint the anger of Achilles; and as that anger does not die with Hector, but persecutes his very remains, so the poet still keeps up to his subject. . . .'[84]

[79] La Motte heads a section of his *Discours sur Homère, Du mérite personnel d'Homère.* His disciple, the Abbé de Pons, wrote: 'si l'on fait attention au siècle grossier dans lequel naquit Homère, si l'on a égard aux moeurs rustiques qui régnaient alors . . . , on jugera Homère un grand génie, et le premier homme de son siècle rustique, en même temps qu'on jugera son poème très défectueux pour un siècle, aussi éclairé que le nôtre' (Vial and Denise, II, 17).

[80] Durham, 340.

[81] *ibid.*, 339.

[82] E-C, X, 147.

[83] *Observations*, XV: VI.

[84] *ibid.*, XXIII: I. Pope does not succeed in meeting the critic's charge: he fails to distinguish between the 'wrath' against Agamemnon and that against Hector. Rapin's criticism of the structural defects of the *Iliad* is on

We are warned that '*little exactnesses* are what we should not look for in Homer,' and the reason given is that 'the genius of his age was too incorrect, and his own too fiery, to regard them.'[85]

That purity of taste which was distressed by such confusions of the *genres* as tragi-comedy could scarcely relish the interspersion of comic elements in the epic. Thersites 'may give us a taste' of Homer's 'vein in this kind. But whether ludicrous descriptions ought to have place in the epic poem has been justly questioned. Neither Virgil nor any of the most approved ancients have thought fit to admit them into their compositions of that nature, nor any of the best moderns, except Milton, whose fondness for Homer might be the reason of it.'[86] Madame Dacier, objecting to a similar passage, chooses to think it added to the original by a critic or rhapsodist; Pope will not defend the passage, but will produce in its behalf the suffrage of others, including again the English epic poet. 'I must just take notice,' he says, 'that however mean or ill-placed these railleries may appear, there have not been wanting such fond lovers of Homer as have admired and imitated 'em. Milton himself is of this number, as may be seen from those very low jests which he has put into the mouth of Satan and his angels in the Sixth Book.'[87]

As we have seen before, our critic does not require us to find his author inerrant. Sometimes the case is quite frankly given over. Adversaries have censured Homer for bringing Achilles on the battle-field and then disappointing the reader by having him turn his hand to no mighty deed. Eustathius and Madame Dacier have attempted to defend Homer. But Pope admits the censure; 'And to show that this is really a fault in the poet, I believe I may appeal to the taste of every reader, who certainly feels himself disappointed.' 'Neither is it any excuse to say he has given us a piece of ancient history. We expected to read a poet, not an historian. In short, after the greatest preparation for action imaginable, he suspends the whole narration, and from the heat of a poet cools at once into the simplicity of an historian.'[88]

its own plane unanswerable. If the subject of the *Iliad* is the Trojan war, 'then is that action defective and imperfect, for that war has not, in the *Iliad*, either beginning or end.' If it is the wrath of Achilles, it is still defective: 'that anger has indeed a beginning, but it has neither end nor middle, for it is effaced by a new anger of the same person against Hector upon the death of Patroclus.' 'And the greatest default is, that the rest of the poem has no connection with that anger' (Rapin, *Works*, I, 142).

[85] *Observations*, III: VII.
[86] *ibid.*, II: XIII.
[87] *ibid.*, XVI: XLVII.
[88] *ibid.*, XX: XIII.

The foregoing pages make it clear, I think, that the critical matter appended to Pope's *Iliad* was not all of it written in the calm air of the study. The translator composed at a time when the name of Homer was still something of a battle-cry in literary circles; when one's admiration or disparagement of the poet unavoidably had party significance, aligned one with classicists or modernists. And Pope's own position is clear. In the Quarrel of the Ancients and the Moderns he fought for the divine Homer; but he did so with moderation and judgment: though a poet, he would not be an enthusiast. The presupposition with him was that Homer, who had stood the test of the centuries, would, in any disputed matter, be found defendable: but, on the other hand, the contention of the modernists that even Homer must be submitted to the judgment of the individual's reason could not be denied. Pope is capable, as we have just seen, of putting a case to the tribunal of 'the taste of every reader.' His classicism is itself restrained by his good sense.

The positive argument of Pope's Preface is a beautifully neat development of the thesis that 'invention' is the great glory of Homer and the source of all his merits, and of the contrast between Homer and Virgil. Neither of these themes was original: Homer, says our critic, is *universally allowed* to have had the greatest *Invention* of any writer whatever.' Parallels between suitably contrasting men of letters were as favorite a form of amusement in the Augustan Age as in the Victorian. The Jesuit Father Rapin wrote a whole series of paired studies, which included Cicero and Demosthenes, Thucydides and Livy, and Plato and Aristotle. His elaborate essay on Homer and Virgil, which decidedly favors the latter, contrasts the prolixity of the one with the other's economy of speech, the defective, ill-mannered and cruel gods and heroes of the *Iliad* with the amiable *dramatis personae* of the *Aeneid*—pious Aeneas, and the gods themselves, as he quaintly puts it, 'persons of some quality and good repute.'[89] Virgil surpasses Homer in *thoughts*, but in *diction* Homer has the superiority. 'Homer has more spirit, and Virgil more judgment.'[90] Dryden makes much of the same sort of antithesis between the two greatest poets of antiquity in his Preface to the *Fables*: 'Virgil was of a quiet, sedate temper; Homer was violent, impetuous, and full of fire. The chief talent of Virgil was propriety of thoughts and ornament of words; Homer was rapid in his thoughts, and took all the liberties, both of numbers and of expressions, which his language and the age in which he lived allowed him. Homer's invention was more copious, Virgil's more

[89] *Works*, I, 156.
[90] *ibid.*, 210.

confined . . . if invention be the first virtue of an epic poet, then
the Latin poem can only be allowed the second place.[91] In one
of Addison's papers on the *Pleasures of the Imagination*, he contrasts by similes: 'Reading the *Iliad* is like travelling through a
country uninhabited, where the fancy is entertained with a thousand savage prospects of vast deserts, wide uncultivated marshes,
huge forests, misshapen rocks and precipices. On the contrary, the
Aeneid is like a well-ordered garden, where it is impossible to
find out any part unadorned, or to cast our eyes upon a single spot
that does not produce some beautiful plant or flower.'[92]

But if the themes are not original, the treatment is at once fresh
and artistic. No other essay on Homer had similarly developed its
whole conception of the poet from his 'invention'; none had so
clearly seized upon the distinctive 'characters' of the contrasted
epics; none, perhaps, had succeeded in grasping the idea that to
antithesize need not be to depreciate one of the objects of antithesis
—that each virtue, each scheme of things, has its corresponding
defects, or at any rate imperfections.

Invention and Nature, the foundations of poetry—to begin
an analysis of the body of the Preface—are in preeminent degree
Homer's. In judgment and art, Virgil may justly contest with
him; but these are dependent upon nature for their materials:
'Art is only like a prudent steward that lives on managing the
riches of Nature. Whatever praises may be given to works of judgment, there is not even a single beauty in them but is owing to
the invention, as in the most regular gardens, however Art may
carry the greatest appearance, there is not a plant or flower but is
the gift of Nature.'[93] Art's function is merely that of arrangement,
—of reducing the beauties of Nature 'into a more obvious figure
which the common eye may better take in.' The reason why 'most
critics are inclined to prefer a judicious and methodical genius
[i.e., Virgil] to a great and fruitful one [Homer] is because they
find it easier for themselves to pursue their observations through
a uniform and bounded walk of Art than to comprehend the vast
and various extent of Nature.'

Without mentioning the names which the contrast would im-

[91] Ker, II.

[92] *Spectator*, no. 417 (June 28, 1712).

[93] This was possibly suggested by Shakespeare's lines (*Winter's Tale*,
IV, 3):

> Yet Nature is made better by no mean
> But Nature makes that mean: so, over that Art
> Which, you say, adds to Nature, is an Art
> That Nature makes.

mediately suggest, Pope borrows a 'hint' from Addison[94] and improves it into the metaphors of 'natural' and 'regular' gardens. Homer's work is a 'wild paradise,' not an 'ordered garden.' "Tis like a copious nursery, which contains the seeds and first productions of every kind, out of which those who followed him have but selected some particular plants, each according to his fancy, to cultivate and beautify.' The figure of the tropical wilderness is pursued. 'If some things are too luxuriant, it is owing to the richness of the soil: and if others are not arrived to perfection or maturity, it is only because they are overrun and oppressed by those of a stronger nature.'[95]

Somewhat later in the Preface the contrast between Homer and Virgil is specifically developed in a series of graceful antitheses. The express purpose of the passage is to avoid creating the impression that the praise of one implies derogation of the other. 'No author or man ever excelled all the world in more than one faculty; and as Homer has done this in *Invention*, Virgil has in *Judgment*.' 'Homer was the greater genius; Virgil the better artist.' 'Homer hurries and transports us with a commanding impetuosity, Virgil leads us with an attractive majesty; Homer scatters with a generous profusion, Virgil bestows with a careful magnificence. Homer, like the Nile, pours out his riches with a sudden overflow; Virgil, like a river in its banks, with a gentle and constant stream.'[96]

Which of these types of poetic genius did Pope prefer? We cannot tell. Must there have been a preference? I wonder if our critic has not given us his honest answer in the sort of passage just quoted. No writer and no species of art can give us all the kinds of pleasure we are capable of deriving from art; each is to be enjoyed for that particular and characteristic pleasure it alone can give. Perhaps it is not romanticizing to find an anticipation of Pater's doctrine in Pope's direction for studying the poets: 'We ought to have a certain knowledge of the principal character and distinguishing excellence of each: it is in that we are to consider him, and in proportion to his degree in that we are to admire him.'[97]

The prime characteristic of Homer, springing from 'the strength of this amazing invention' of his, is 'that unequalled fire and rapture which is so forcible in Homer that no man of a true poetical spirit is master of himself while he reads him.'[98] In this remark speaks a different Pope than he whose favorite maxim was *Nil admirari*.[99] The Preface is, as Warton says, 'a declamatory

[94] *Spectator*, no. 417.
[95] Durham, 324.
[96] *ibid.*, 335.

[97] *ibid.*, 335.
[98] *ibid.*, 324.
[99] See *supra*, Chapter I, p. 12.

piece of criticism in the way of Longinus';[100] and the critic who, in other moods and upon other subjects, would ridicule 'enthusiasm' insists that no one who really appreciates poetry can remain without ecstasy in the presence of Homer's *efflatus*. In the *Observations*, Pope expressly praises his author for breaking out into a description 'with an air of enthusiasm which greatly heightens the image in general, while it seems to transport him beyond the limits of an exact comparison. And this daring manner is particular to our author above all the ancients, and to Milton above all the moderns.'[101]

In Pope's *Observations on the Catalogue*,[102] he laughs at the critics of the 'school of taste' who are unable to give articulate expression to their aesthetic enjoyment but take refuge in 'the *simplicitas*, the *nescio quo modo*, the *genio antiqui poetae digna*,' 'excellent general phrases for those who have no reasons.' We are told that 'the term of the *Je ne sçay quoy* is the very support of all ignorant pretenders to delicacy; and to lift up our eyes and talk of the genius of an ancient is at once the cheapest way of showing our own taste and the shortest way of criticizing the wit of others, our contemporaries.' But our critic himself seems to approach dangerously near the ecstasy so neatly censured. He is not always willing to condescend to exposition and argument: sometimes, like modern as well as Augustan critics, he merely damns us as persons utterly without cultivation if we do not acquiesce in his judgment. 'A man must have no taste for poetry that does not admire this sublime description,' he remarks at one point;[103] and of the Twenty-Second Book his comment is, 'Terror and pity are here wrought up in perfection; and if the reader is not sensible of both in a high degree, either he is utterly void of all taste, or the translator of all skill in poetry.'[104]

It is Homer's *fire* which produces these flights above the domain of exact and rational analysis. In works where 'exact disposition, just thought, correct elocution,' and elegant versification are absent, 'this can overpower criticism and make us admire even while we disapprove.' All the great poets have had this *vivida vis animi*; but Homer, preeminently and uniquely. 'This *fire* is discerned in Virgil, but discerned as through a glass, reflected, and more shining than warm, but everywhere equal and constant; in Lucan and Statius, it bursts out in sudden, short, and interrupted flashes; in Milton, it glows like a furnace kept up to an uncommon fierceness by the force of art; in Shakespeare, it strikes before we are aware,

[100] *Genius of Pope*, II, 400.
[101] II: XXXVI.
[102] Following Book Two.
[103] *Observations*, XXIV: XVIII.
[104] *ibid.*, XXII: I.

like an accidental fire from Heaven; but in Homer, and in him
only, it burns everywhere clearly, and everywhere irresistibly.'[105]

There are three sorts of 'fable': the probable, the allegorical,
and the marvellous. The 'probable fable' of the *Iliad* is built
upon 'the anger of Achilles, the most short and single subject that
ever was chosen by any poet.'[106] Pope does not admit the charge
brought against this epic by critics from Rapin down to the School
of Wolf, that the *Iliad* is clumsily constructed and that the wrath
of Achilles occupies only a small part of the epic.[107] He seems to
feel assurances that all the varied materials which Homer produces
bear recognizable relation to the theme. He speaks of this last as
'supplied with a vaster variety of incidents and events,' councils,
speeches, and battles, 'than are to be found even in those poems
whose schemes are of the utmost latitude and irregularity.' Virgil,
'lacking so warm a genius' was not able to turn a slight theme to
so fertile an account; but had to aid himself 'by taking in a more
extensive subject as well as a greater length of time.' Later epic
poets have been yet more at a loss: they have tended to 'superin-
duce a multiplicity of fables, destroy the unity of action, and lose
their readers in an unreasonable length of time.'[108]

There is, in the next point Pope makes, the sort of inconsistency
which Dryden, Addison, and Johnson were all guilty of. It is
charged to the discredit of the epic poets who succeeded Homer that
not only 'in the main design . . . have they been unable to add to
his invention, but they have followed him in every episode and part
of story.'[109] Virgil and Statius both imitate the funeral games of
Patroclus (the latter at the expense of unity of action). 'If
Ulysses visit the shades, the Aeneas of Virgil and the Scipio of
Silius[110] are sent after him. If he be detained from his return by
the allurements of Calypso, so is Aeneas by Dido, and Rinaldo by
Armida.' But it was not through lack of inventive power that these
later poets copied: it was because the belief had grown up that
each of the *genres* had consecrated models which were to be fol-

[105] Durham, 325.

[106] 'The plan of this poem is formed upon anger and its ill effects; the
plan of Virgil's upon pious resignation and its rewards; and thus every
passion or virtue may be the foundation of an epic poem' (*Observations*,
I: prefatory to I).

[107] Rapin remarks, 'Virgil never wanders from his subject; Homer
seldom keeps so much as within distance of his. There is not a single blow
given in the heat of an engagement, but he must from thence take an occasion to tell stories and derive genealogies' (*Works*, I, 153).

[108] Le Bossu makes Statius an instance of these faults.

[109] Durham, 326.

[110] Scipio and Hannibal are the heroes of the *Punica*, an epic imitative of
Homer and Virgil, on the theme of the Second Punic War.

lowed. The classical epic, Latin, French, English, was by its very origin and constitution *imitative*—or as we now say, *literary*. The pleasure it gave the cultivated reader was that which derived from its traditional structure and themes, its overtones of a whole epic convention. All the greater Augustans saw in the power to create, to 'invent,' the distinctive power of the poet: 'It is the invention that in different degrees distinguishes all great geniuses.'[111] 'No man ever yet became great by imitation. Whatever hopes for the veneration of mankind must have invention in the design or the execution; either the effect itself must be new, or the means by which it is produced.'[112] But they also believed in the rules for writing epics and pastorals, which were drawn from the practice of the masters. The loyalties remained unfused: the Augustans, like the Victorians, had their compromises.

In Pope's day it was, as the translator says in his Preface, 'generally supposed' that Homer had 'wrapped up in . . . Allegories' 'innumerable knowledges,' 'secrets of Nature and physical philosophy'; that his imagination 'was able to clothe all the properties of elements, the qualifications of the mind, the virtues and vices, in forms and persons, and to introduce them into actions agreeable to the nature of the things they shadowed.'[113] Homer's learning and Homer's allegory were not doctrines to which Pope attached any great importance, or upon which his case for the genius of his poet depended. But they were still the 'received doctrines,' and as they contributed to the glory of the poet it was useful to repeat them.[114] He has read in Rapin that 'we know little or nothing of the person of Homer, only that he undertook a voyage into Egypt to study the sciences under that people, who were the first masters of learning in the world . . .'[115] and both Le Bossu and Rymer, favorite critics with him, taught the allegorical sense of Homer. The latter points out that the Bible as well as the epic poet offers difficulties, such as contradictions and anthropomorphisms, in the letter; and that in the early centuries of Christian apologetic, both believers and pagans had recourse to

[111] Durham, 251.
[112] *Rambler*, no. 154.
[113] Durham, 327.
[114] 'There can be no doubt that in this Preface Pope occasionally lauds Homer for qualities which existed only in the imagination of certain scholars. The . . . deification of Homer's learning, of his influence on science and philosophy, were the extravagances of scholarly fanatics. Pope knew too little about Homer to deny such statements. He cared too little about such matters to investigate them [the second clause is the truer]; so he includes them, but only as further evidence, somewhat irrelevant, of his central thesis.' Durham, p. xxxiii.
[115] *Works*, I, 118.

the 'spirit.' 'As for the fables which in Homer, or on the stage, give
offense, the ancients had a thing called allegory which went a great
way towards stopping the mouth of many a pert observer.'[116] 'So we
see what Lactantius objected against Homer and the heathen
tragedies is by the heathens objected against our Bible and religion.' 'But we need not be so angry on either hand. Find but out
the allegory, and we are all to rights again.'[117]

Pope's *Observations* find it a convenience in filling space, as well
as in reconciling difficulties and answering the objections of the
captious, to borrow from earlier commentators their allegorical
interpretations of various passages. The existence of this 'inner
sense' is nowhere, even in the passage of doctrine I shall now quote,
dogmatically affirmed; it is merely suggested as, in the light of the
customs of the time and the tradition of critics, a plausible assumption. 'Homer, like most of the Greeks, is thought to have
travelled into Egypt and brought from the priests there not only
their learning, but their manner of conveying it in fables and
hieroglyphics. This is necessary to be understood by those who
would thoroughly penetrate into the beauty and design of many
parts of this author. For whoever reflects that this was the mode
of learning in those times will make no doubt but there are several
mysteries both natural and moral,[118] philosophy involved in his
fictions which otherwise in the liberal meaning appear too trivial
or irrational; and it is but just when these are not plain or immediately intelligible, to imagine that something of this kind may
be hid under them.' But Homer was not primarily 'writing philosophy or theology,' so that we may suppose that frequently these
'fables and traditions' are used 'as embellishments of his poetry
only, without taking the pains to open their mystical meaning to
his readers, and perhaps without diving very deeply into it
himself.'[119]

Pope cannot pretend to patience with the extremes of which allegorical interpretation was capable. Having retailed at length the
exegesis of Eustathius and Heraclides Ponticus,[120] he concludes,
'All these refinements (not to call 'em absolute whimsies) I leave
just as I found 'em, to the reader's judgment or mercy.'[121] In

[116] *A Short View of Tragedy*, 45.
[117] *ibid.*, 46.
[118] Some of the allegories shadow forth operations of the physical
universe; others, those of the moral world of man. See examples quoted
from the Index, *supra*, p. 81, nn. 27-8.
[119] *Observations*, VIII: I.
[120] Heraclides, *floruit* fourth century, B.C., was a pupil of Plato and
Aristotle.
[121] *Observations*, XVIII: XXXVII.

principle, he believed that 'allegories ought to be disguised, but not obscured: An allegory should be like a veil over a beautiful face,—so fine and transparent as to show the very charms it covers.'[122] But the necessities of the apologist sometimes necessitate recourse to an inner sense which is not very apparent. A passage in Book Twenty-One (line 567, *ff.*) occasions the comment, 'Homer never better deserved than in this place the censure passed upon him by the ancients, that as he raised the characters of his men up to gods, so he sunk those of gods down to men. Yet I think it but reasonable to conclude from the very absurdity of all this, supposing it had no hidden meaning or allegory, that there certainly must be some. Nor do I think it any inference to the contrary that it is too obscure for us to find out.'[123] Another exegetical difficulty suggests having 'recourse to allegory (which softens and reconciles everything)': it may, for example, be imagined that 'by the congress of Jupiter and Juno is meant the mingling of the ether and the air (which are generally said to be signified by those two deities).'[124]

The third division of 'Fable' comprises 'whatever is supernatural, and especially the machines of the gods.'[125] Pope does not attempt to justify the morality of the Homeric deities; he takes the safer position that there were never 'machines' so suitable to poetry. Homer may not have been, he remarks, the inventor of the Greek theogony; but he was 'the first who brought them into a system of machinery for poetry, and such a one as makes its greatest importance and dignity.' Yet more to the point: 'whatever cause there might be to blame his [Homer's] *machine* in a philosophical or religious view, they are so perfect in the poetic, that mankind have been ever since contented to follow them: none have been able to enlarge the sphere of poetry beyond the limits he has set. Every attempt of this nature has proved unsuccessful; and after all the various changes of times and religions, his gods continue to this day the gods of poetry.'[126] Of this very felicitous statement of the case, Professor Scott, eminent contemporary scholar, writes: 'No one has ever more thoroughly grasped the meaning of the Homeric gods than Pope. . . . In these few words Pope has given all that need be said about Homeric religious beliefs. Homer drew the portraits of his gods with the hand of a poet; and as poetic portraits they are still the delight and envy of poets.'[127]

---

[122] *Observations*, XXI: XXX.

[123] *ibid.*, XXI: XXX. Origen similarly argues the presence of a mystical sense in the Scriptures from the 'impossibilities and incongruities' of some passages in the literal text. See *De Principiis*, Book IV, cap. I.

[124] *ibid.*, XIV: XV.   [126] *ibid.*, 253.

[125] Durham, 328.   [127] *Unity of Homer*, 178.

The same student of Homer has also praised the note Pope strikes in his remarks upon the *characters* in the *Iliad* : the poet's power of individuating them. 'Here again,' he says, 'Pope furnishes just the necessary words.'[128] These 'necessary words' tell us that no author has drawn so many and such varied characters, or 'given us such lively and affecting impressions of them.' But particularly it is to be noted that 'Every one has something so singularly his own that no painter could have distinguished them more by their features than the poet has by their manners.'[129] Even though a number of persons may be characterized by a single predominant quality, yet it will be discovered that Homer has distinguished and individuated them all, Achilles, Diomed, Ajax, Hector, Agamemnon, Menelaus, Idomeneus, and Sarpedon—all of these may be said to exemplify 'the single quality of *courage*'; yet how 'wonderfully diversified' they are. But Homer does not make his characters the abstractions of a morality play or limit them to variations upon a single theme; besides the 'ruling passion,' each hero has his appropriate admixture of other qualities. Pope concludes his paragraph on Homer's characterization by noting that none of the later epic poets, such as Virgil and Statius, were able to equal the diversity of his creation.[130]

We should expect Pope, who was so masterly a psychologist, to take an especial interest in Homer's characterization; and the opening books of the *Observations* prove that he did. Each of the many persons who play a rôle in the *Iliad* serves, upon his introduction, to occasion an analysis. Some of these are exceedingly good, particularly for the way in which the critic, like a true classicist, penetrates the superficial 'local color' to discover the unchanging human types.

Of Idomeneus, he remarks: his 'character (if I take it right) is such as we see pretty often in common life: a person of the first rank, sufficient enough of his high birth, growing into years, conscious of his decline in strength and active qualities, and therefore endeavoring to make it up to himself in dignity, and to preserve the veneration of others. The true picture of a stiff old soldier, not willing to lose any of the reputation he has acquired; yet not inconsiderate in danger, but by the sense of his age, and by his experience in battle become too cautious to engage with any great odds against him. Very careful and tender of his soldiers, whom he had commanded so long that they were become old acquaintances (so that it was with great judgment Homer chose to intro-

[128] *Unity of Homer*, 179.
[129] Durham, 328.
[130] *ibid.*, 329-30.

duce him here in performing a kind office to one of 'em who was wounded). Talkative upon subjects of war, as afraid that others might lose the memory of what he had done in better days.'[131]

'The picture here given of Paris' air and dress,' Pope comments on III, 26, 'is exactly correspondent to his character: you see him endeavoring to mix the fine gentleman with the warrior.'[132] Paris 'is a master of civility, no less well-bred to his own sex than courtly to the other. . . . Homer draws him . . . soft of speech —the natural quality of an amorous temper; vainly gay in war as well as love; with a spirit that can be surprised and recollected— that can receive impressions of shame or apprehension on the one side, or of generosity and courage on the other: the usual disposition of easy and courteous minds which are most subject to the rule of fancy and passion. Upon the whole, this is no worse than the picture of a *gentle knight*, and one might fancy the heroes of the modern romance were formed upon the model of Paris.'[133]

The 'character' of Helen ought also to be quoted. She, 'the main cause of this war, is drawn by this great master with the finest strokes, as a frail but not an abandoned creature. She has perpetual struggles of virtue on the one side, and softnesses, which overcome them on the other. Our author has been remarkably careful to tell us this: whenever he but slightly names her . . . she is represented at the same time as repentant. . . .'[134]

Closely related to characterization is *dramatic propriety*, as we call it—in Augustan terminology, *decorum*. 'The *speeches* are to be considered as they flow from the characters, being perfect or defective as they agree or disagree with the manners of those who utter them. As there is more variety of characters in the *Iliad*, so there is of speeches, than in any other poem.'[135] Here again, Homer has the supremacy over Virgil, whose 'speeches often consist of general reflections or thoughts which might be equally just in any person's mouth upon the same occasion'; and many of his persons have no character so sufficiently marked as to demand appropriate speech.

Pope delights to illustrate the *decorum* of the *Iliad*. 'As Homer's invention is in nothing more wonderful than in the great variety of characters with which his poems are diversified, so his judgment appears in nothing more than in that propriety with which each character is maintained.'[136] 'The image . . . of the amusements of

[131] *Observations*, XIII: XIX.
[132] *ibid.*, III: III.
[133] *ibid.*, III: XI.
[134] *ibid.*, III: Introduction. Cf. also III: XVIII.
[135] Durham, 330.
[136] *Observations*, XI: I.

the Myrmidons while Achilles detained them from the fight has
an exquisite propriety in it. Though they are not in action, their
very diversions are military and a kind of exercise of arms.' There
is nothing 'finer than the manly concern of the captains, who, as
they are supposed more sensible of glory than the soldiers, take no
share in their diversions, but wander sorrowfully round the camp,
and lament their being kept from the battle. This difference betwixt the soldiers and their leaders (as Dacier observes) is a
decorum of the highest beauty.'[137]

Propriety of speech to character is frequently exhibited for our
admirations. 'Homer is in nothing more excellent than in that distinction of characters which he maintains through his whole poem.
What Andromache here says can be spoken properly by none but
Andromache. There is nothing general in her sorrows; nothing
that can be transferred to another character. The mother laments
the son, and the wife weeps over the husband.'[138] The lamentations
of Priam and Hecuba remind our critic of 'a judicious stroke in
Milton with regard to the several characters of Adam and Eve.
When the angel is driving them both out of Paradise, Adam
grieves that he must leave a place where he had conversed with
God and his angels; but Eve laments that she shall never more
behold the fine flowers of Eden. Here Adam mourns like a man,
and Eve like a woman.'[139]

The observation of Homer's *decorum* frequently affords opportunity for a vignette characterization, as in the comments I
shall quote upon Nestor and Priam. 'This speech,' Pope remarks,[140]
'is admirably well adapted to the character of Nestor. He aggran-
dizes, with an infirmity peculiar to age, his own exploits; and one
would think Horace had him in his eye,

                laudator temporis acti
        Se puero—

Neither is it any blemish in the character of Nestor thus to be a
little talkative about his own achievements. To have described him
otherwise would have been an outrage to human nature, inasmuch
as the wisest man living is not free from the infirmities of man,
and as every stage of life has some imperfection peculiar to itself.'
Priam's petulancy after Hector's death has also to be defended
against the attacks of hostile criticism. 'Rapin has censured this
anger of Priam as a breach of the manners, and says he might have

[137] *Observations*, II: XXXV.
[138] *ibid.*, XXII: XXXVII.
[139] *ibid.*, XXII: VII.
[140] *ibid.*, XXIII: XXXIII (ll. 718 *ff.*).

shown himself a father otherwise than by this usage of his children. But whoever considers his circumstances will judge after another manner.' 'This last blow sinks him quite, and changes him so much that he is no longer the same. He becomes impatient, frantic, unreasonable! The terrible effect of ill fortune! Whoever has the least insight into Nature must admire so fine a picture of the force of adversity on an unhappy old man.'[141]

Pope's Preface next calls the reader's attention to the dramatic character of the *Iliad*: 'everything is acted or spoken. It is hardly credible in a work of such length how small a number of lines are employed in narration. In Virgil the dramatic part is less in proportion to the narrative. . . .' As a result of this, 'We oftener think of the author himself when we read Virgil than when we are engaged in Homer. . . . Homer makes us hearers, and Virgil leaves us readers.'[142] One of the notes calls attention again to this contrast in dramatic invention. 'There is,' it observes, 'a great deal more dialogue in Homer than in Virgil. The Roman poet's are generally set speeches; those of the Greek, more in conversation. What Virgil does by two words of a narration, Homer brings about by a speech: he hardly raises one of his heroes out of bed without some talk concerning it. There are not only replies but rejoinders in Homer,—a thing scarcely ever to be found in Virgil; the course whereof is that there must be in the *Iliad* many continued conversations . . . a little resembling common chit-chat. This renders the poem more natural and animated, but less grave and majestic. However, that such was the way of writing generally practised in those ancient times appears from the like manner used in most of the books of the Old Testament; and it particularly agreed with our author's warm imagination, which delighted in perpetual imagery and in painting every circumstance of what he described.'[143]

We should today perhaps hardly single out for comment Homer's 'sentiments,' or *sententiae*; but Pope's generation, like Horace's, was pleased to find in the epic poet one

> Qui quid sit pulchrum, quid turpe, quid utile, quid non,
> Planius ac melius Chrysippo et Crantore dicit.[144]

---

[141] *Observations*, XXIV: XIV. Pope 'always was particularly struck with that passage in Homer were he makes Priam's grief for the loss of Hector break out into anger against his attendants and sons; and could never read it without weeping for the distress of that unfortunate old prince' (Spence, 260).

[142] Durham, 330.

[143] *Observations*, XIII: XXIV.

[144] *Epistles*, Book I: II, 3-4.

Homer teaches one more 'of moral evil and of good Than all the
sages can.' Longinus, our Preface tells us, 'has given his opinion
that it was in this part Homer principally excelled.' And the
'grandeur and excellence of his sentiments' is proved by their
having so remarkable a parity with those of the Scripture: 'Duport,
in his *Gnomologia Homerica* has collected innumerable instances
of this sort.'[145] Nor do the *Observations* fail to point out the instruction to be derived from the *Iliad*. 'The poet is very happy in
interspersing his poem with moral sentences; in this place he steals
away his reader from war and horror and gives him a beautiful
admonition of his own frailty.'[146] 'This,' it is commented in
another place, 'is one among a thousand instances of Homer's in-
direct and oblique manner of introducing moral sentences and instructions. These agreeably break in upon his reader even in
descriptions and poetical parts where one naturally expects only
painting and amusement. We have virtue put upon us by surprise,
and are pleased to find a thing where we should never have looked
to meet with it.'[147] And finally, Pope makes a concluding generalization on Homer's distribution of poetic justice. 'Homer now
begins, after a beautiful and long fable, to give the moral of it,
and display his poetic justice in rewards and punishments. Thus,
Hector fought in a bad cause, and therefore suffers in the defence
of it; but because he was a good man, and obedient to the gods in
other respects, his very remains become the care of Heaven.' He
concludes: 'If the reader does not observe the morality of the *Iliad*,
he loses half, and the nobler part of its beauty. He reads it as a
common romance, and mistakes the chief aim of it, which is to
instruct.'[148] Pope can hardly have put very deep faith in this last:
the whole tenor of his Preface and notes contradict, or at any rate
interpret, the remark. But it was the received doctrine with critics
as reputable as Le Bossu and Madame Dacier, and Pope passes it on
to his reader.

Of course Homer's 'descriptions, images, and similes' call for
attention in both Preface and notes. They, too, illustrate Pope's
theme—his poet's 'invention.' 'To what else,' he asks, 'can we
ascribe that vast comprehension of images of every sort, where we

[145] Durham, 330-1. Duport, whose book appeared in 1660, was a Professor at Cambridge. He illustrated his collection of the gnomic passages,
or *sententiae*, from Homer with parallels from ancient and modern
authors and particularly the Old Testament. He 'findet die Übereinstim-
mung zwischen Homer und den heiligen Schriftstellern überraschend
gross . . .' (Finsler, 146).

[146] *Observations*, XXI: XXVI.

[147] *ibid.*, XVI: XXXIII.

[148] *ibid.*, XXIV: XXI.

see each circumstance of art and individual of nature summoned together by the extent and fecundity of his imagination . . . ?'

The similes afford frequent subjects for comment—sometimes generalization, sometimes analysis of the particular at hand. The genteel are cautioned 'not to be shocked at the frequency of . . . similes taken from the ideas of a rural life.'[149] The learned are advised that 'It is Homer's design in his comparisons to apply them to the most obvious and sensible image of the thing to be illustrated; which his commentators too frequently endeavor to hide by moral and allegorical refinements.'[150] Some critics have found Homer's similes drawn too exclusively from lions and like animals. Pope explains that his poet is 'a great observer of natural imagery that brings the thing represented before our view. It is indeed true that lions, tigers, and beasts of prey are the only objects that can properly represent warriors; and therefore 'tis no wonder they are so often introduced. The inanimate things, as floods, fires, and storms, are the best and only images of battles.'[151] As to the degree of relation in detail between simile and subject, 'One may make a general observation that Homer in those comparisons that breathe an air of tenderness is very exact, and adapts them in every point to the subject which he is to illustrate. But in other comparisons, where he is to inspire the soul with sublime sentiments, he gives a *loose* to his fancy and does not regard whether the images exactly correspond.'[152]

The *Observations* aimed, as we have seen, at aesthetic appreciation. 'It is something strange,' Pope remarks, 'that of all the commentators upon Homer there is scarcely one whose principal design is to illustrate the poetical beauties of the author. They are voluminous in explaining those sciences which he made subservient to his poetry, and sparing only upon that art which constitutes his character. This has been occasioned by the ostentation of men who had more reading than taste, and were fonder of showing their variety of learning in all kinds than their single understanding in poetry.'[153] Pope endeavors to assist the reader to greater enjoyment of the *Iliad's* poetic delights; and his chief contribution to this, aside from the analysis of character, consists in his somewhat rhapsodic paraphrases or interpretations of descriptive passages. These are somewhat wearisome in abundance: a

[149] *Observations*, XIII: XLI.
[150] *ibid.*, XVI: XXIX.
[151] *ibid.*, XVII: X.
[152] *ibid.*, VIII: XXXIV.
[153] *ibid.*, I: Introduction. Pope never misses an opportunity for a thrust at scholars.

single specimen will suffice. 'With how much dreadful pomp is Achilles here introduced! How noble and in what bold colors hath he drawn the blazing of his arms, the rapidity of his advance, the terror of his appearance, the desolation around him, but, above all, the certain death attending all his motions and his very looks. . . . But immediately after this follows the moving image of the two aged parents, trembling, weeping, and imploring their son. That is succeeded again by the dreadful, gloomy picture of Hector, all on fire, obstinately bent on death, and expecting Achilles; admirably painted in the simile of the snake rolled up in his den and collecting his poisons. And indeed through the whole morning this wonderful contrast and opposition of the moving and terrible is kept up, each heightening the other. I can't find words to express how so great beauties affect me.'[154]

Praise of the 'liveliness' of Homer's descriptions occasions a yet longer 'appreciative' analysis. 'I cannot conclude the notes to this book,' our critic declares, 'without observing that what seems the principal beauty of it, and what distinguishes it among all the others is the liveliness of its paintings. The reader sees the most natural night scene in the world; he is led step by step with the adventurers, and made the companion of all their expectations and uncertainties. We see the very color of the sky, know the time to a minute, are impatient while the heroes are arming; our imagination steals out after them, becomes privy to all their doubts, and even to the secret wishes of their hearts sent up to Minerva. We are alarmed at the approach of Dolon, hear his very footsteps, assist the two chiefs in pursuing him, and stop just with the spear that arrests him.' 'The marshy spot of ground where Dolon is killed, the tamarisk or aquatic plants upon which they hang his spoils, and the reeds that are heaped together to mark the place are circumstances the most picturesque imaginable. And though it must be owned that the human figures in this piece are excellent and disposed in the properest actions, I cannot but confess my opinion that the chief beauty of it is in the prospect, a finer than which was never drawn by any pencil.'[155]

Our critic's fondness, in the above descriptions, for references to painting and the 'picturesque'—a word which was just coming into use at the time and for the use of which Oldmixon took him

---

[154] *Observations*, XXII : II. Pope takes occasion now and then to ridicule the speechless ecstasies of the aesthetic critics of his day. 'Of what use,' he asks, 'is this ['perpetual rapture'] either to a reader who has a taste or to one who has not?' (*ibid.*, XV : XXXVIII). But he indulges in what he reprehends; witness as case in point the concluding sentence of the passage just quoted.

[155] *ibid.*, X : LIX.

to task[156]—will not have escaped attention. Pope seems early to have shown an inclination to the fine arts: this was encouraged by his father and his friend Caryll; and when he was still in his early twenties he took lessons in painting from Charles Jervas, pupil of the celebrated Sir Godfrey Kneller. Pope's achievement at the art never attained professional excellence;[157] but the poet retained always his interest in painting and painters, as some passages in his poems attest; he was given to allusions to the masters of the art and its technique.

Ut pictura poesis[158] is much in evidence in the *Observations*. Our critic sees pictorial possibilities: 'I fancy this interview between Priam and Achilles would furnish an admirable subject for a painter in the surprise of Achilles and the other spectators, the attitude of Priam, and the sorrows in the countenance of this unfortunate King.'[159] Or he is reminded of pictorial analogues: 'There is scarce any picture in Homer so much in the savage and terrible way as this comparison of the Myrmidons to wolves. It puts one in mind of the pieces of Spagnoletto or Salvator Rosa:[160] each circumstance is made up of images very strongly colored and horridly lively.'[161] An essay on the Shield of Achilles concludes with an extended consideration of this elaborately decorated piece of armor 'as a complete idea of painting, and a sketch for what one may call a *universal picture*. This is certainly the light in which it is chiefly to be admired, and in which alone the critics have neglected to place it.'

Pope makes use of the Shield to display at once Homer's and his

[156] *supra*, p. 56. In 1712 Pope wrote to Caryll of some verses 'which seem to me what the French call picturesque.' The word seems to have existed in French early in the eighteenth century, though the earliest instance of it noted in Hatzfeld-Darmesteter is in 1732.

[157] There is a well-known passage in one of his letters to Caryll in which Pope describes his progress in the art: 'I have been so out of conceit with my former performances that I have thrown away three Dr. Swifts, two Duchesses of Montague, one Virgin Mary, the Queen of England, besides half a score Earls and a Knight of the Garter. . . . I find my hand most successful in drawing of friends and those I most esteem, insomuch that my masterpieces have been one of Dr. Swift and one of Mr. Betterton' (E-C, V, 82).

[158] Horace: *Ars Poetica*, 361.

[159] *Observations*, XXIV: XXVII.

[160] Josef de Ribera (1588-1656), called Il Spagnoletto, was, as the name implies, of Spanish birth, but spent his life in Italy. A pupil of Caravaggio, like his master, he 'delighted in subjects of horror' and indulged in extreme contrasts of light and shadow. Salvator Rosa (1615-1673), 'greatest landscape and battle-painter of Italy,' resembled Caravaggio in the sombre violence of his style.

[161] *Observations*, XVI: XIX.

own knowledge of painting. We are assured that 'there is scarce a branch of this art which is not here to be found, whether history, battle-painting, landscape, architecture, fruits, flowers, animals, etc.'; that certainly Homer 'had, whether by learning or by strength of genius . . . a full and exact idea of painting in all its parts,—that is to say, in the invention, the composition, the expression, etc.' He was well versed in modern correctnesses: 'That he was not a stranger to aerial perspective appears in his expressly marking distance of object from object.' 'What the critics call the *three unities* ought in reason as much to be observed in a picture as in a play: each should have only one principal action, one instant of time, and one point of view.' The designs on the Shield of Achilles obey these requirements.

In the same essay there are impressive references to the great painters. We hear of 'even Raphael himself' and of Rubens, 'who has with most happiness and learning imitated the ancients in these fictitious and symbolic persons.' The themes treated on the Shield suggest those who could appropriately paint them: the graceful subject of the Dance is 'fit for Guido'; while the 'herds, dogs, and lions are put into action enough to exercise the warmth and spirit of Rubens, or the great taste of Julio Romano.'[162] And Pope concludes his little flourish with a personal acknowledgment: 'I ought not to end this essay without vindicating myself from the vanity of treating an art which I love so much better than I understand. But I have been very careful to consult both the best performers and the best judges in painting. I can't neglect this occasion of saying how happy I think myself in the favor of the most distinguished masters of that art. Sir Godfrey Kneller[163] in particular allows me to tell the world that he entirely agrees with my sentiments on this subject [the Shield].'[164]

---

[162] Guido Reni (1575-1642), 'clever and prolific' decorator, was a member of the Bolognese 'school.' Julio Romano (1492-1546), a favorite pupil of Raphael's, later developed a violent and non-natural style: his colors were vivid; his shadows equally accentuated; his characteristics, brilliancy and vigor. Pope's 'great taste' is perhaps an Englishing of the then fashionable phrase, *gusto grande*, which signifies beauty of an 'irregular' and romantic sort.

[163] This German artist was official painter to the English court. He died in 1723, and his friend Pope wrote an epitaph for his tomb in Westminster Abbey commencing:

> Kneller, by Heaven, and not a master, taught,
> Whose art was Nature, and whose pictures Thought.
> (E-C, IV, 387.)

[164] *Observations*, XVIII: III. Pope's Epistle to Mr. Jervas gives him op-

Pope's analysis of the excellences of Homer concludes with some remarks on his 'expression' and 'versification.' By the first term he means to denote phraseology and, more particularly, diction. Homer is not only the inventor of the 'poetic story'; he is 'the father of poetical diction, the first who taught that language of the gods to men.' Drawing an analogy from painting again, Pope compares his 'expression' to 'the coloring of some great masters, which discovers itself to be laid on boldly and executed with rapidity. It is indeed the strongest and most glowing imaginable, and touched with the greatest spirit.' Homer's are 'living words'; and 'there are in him more daring figures and metaphors than in any good author whatever.' 'Yet his expression is never too big for the sense, but justly great in proportion to it. It·is the sentiment that swells and fills out the diction, which rises with it and forms itself about it. . . .'

Homer's 'compound epithets' were 'affected,' Pope thinks, to 'throw his language more out of prose. . . .' They 'heightened the diction,' 'assisted and filled the numbers with greater sound and pomp,' and helped to 'thicken the images'—that is, 'they are a sort of supernumerary pictures of the persons or things they are joined to,'[165] Pope devotes several paragraphs to considering how these compound epithets are to be rendered in English;[166] and concludes that one is not bound invariably to reproduce them. 'Many . . . cannot be done literally into English without destroying the purity of our language.' Some require a 'circumlocution' to give them weight. 'Upon the whole, it will be necessary to avoid that perpetual repetition of the same epithets which we find in Homer,[167]

portunity for further impressively casual characterisations of the painters then admired :

> Each heavenly piece unwearied we compare ;
> Match Raphael's grace with thy loved Guido's air,
> Caracci's strength, Correggio's softer line,
> Paulo's free stroke, and Titian's warmth divine.

[165] Durham, 332.

[166] *ibid.*, 258.

[167] 'It is plain that too scrupulous an adherence to many of these [epithets] gives the translation an exotic, pedantic, and whimsical air which it is not to be imagined the original ever had. To call a hero the *great artificer of flight, the swift of foot*, or the *horse-tamer*—these give us ideas of little peculiarities, when in the author's time they were epithets used only in general to signify alacrity, agility, and vigor. A common reader would imagine from these servile versions that Diomed and Achilles were foot-racers, and Hector a horse-courser, rather than that any of them were heroes. A man shall be called a faithful translator for rendering πόδας ὠκύς into English *swift-footed*, but laughed at if he should translate our English word dextrous into any other language *right-handed*' (*Observations*, VIII : LIII).

and which, though it might be accommodated to the ear of those times is by no means so to ours; but one may wait for opportunities of placing them where they derive an additional beauty from the occasions on which they are employed; and in doing this a translator may at once show his fancy and his judgment.'

His versification is the last proof adduced of Homer's 'invention.' Pope tells us that the poet, 'with this particular view, to beautify and perfect his numbers,' examined all the dialects of Greece, 'considered these as they had a greater mixture of vowels or consonants, and accordingly employed them as the verse required either a greater smoothness or strength.' He chiefly made use of the 'peculiar sweetness' of the Ionic; but with it 'he mingled the Attic contractions, the broader Doric, and the feebler Aeolic. . . .' This careful selection effected 'that harmony which makes us confess he had not only the richest head, but the finest ear, in the world.' Even persons who know no Greek, if they will but harken to the 'tune of his verses,'[168] will 'find more sweetness, variety, and majesty of sound than in any other language or poetry.'[169]

Of course Pope cannot leave the subject of versification without some mention of his favorite 'representative metre,' at which both Virgil and Homer excelled. The former 'never failed to bring the sound of his line to a beautiful agreement with its sense'; and Dionysius of Halicarnassus 'has pointed out many of our author's beauties in this kind in his treatise of the *Composition of Words*. . . .'[170]

We have already, in pursuance of another purpose, considered Pope's defense of the alleged defects of Homer; the remaining section of the Preface gives us the translator's theory of his own task. This was much like that of translators before and since, with the exception of extremists on both sides—believers in *les belles infidèles* or in literalism. Pope, like Dryden, advocated a *via media*:[171] 'It is certain,' he says, that 'no literal translation can be just to an excellent original in a superior language; but it is a great mistake to imagine (as many have done) that a rash para-

---

[168] At this point Pope inserts a sneer at British fondness for opera in a tongue not understanded of the people: 'with the same sort of diligence as we daily see practised in the case of Italian opera.'

[169] Durham, 333.

[170] *ibid.*, 334.

[171] A few illustrations from Dryden's *Dedication to the Aeneid*: 'I had long since considered that the way to please the best judges is not to translate a poet literally. . . .' 'The way I have taken is not so strait as metaphrase, nor so loose as paraphrase: some things too I have omitted, and sometimes have added of my own. Yet the omissions, I hope, are but of the circumstances, and such as would have no grace in English; and the additions, I hope, are easily deduced from Virgil's sense.'

phrase can make amends for this general defect, which is no less in danger to lose the spirit of an ancient by deviating into the modern manners of expression.' 'I know no liberties one ought to take but those which are necessary for transfusing the spirit of the original and supporting the poetical style of the translation; and I will venture to say there have not been more men misled in former times by a servile dull adherence to the letter than have been deluded in ours by a chimerical insolent hope of raising and improving their author.' But though Pope seeks a middle course, when one must choose between the spirit and the letter, he advocates the former. 'It is not to be doubted that the *fire* of the poem is what a translator should principally regard. . . .'[172] 'That which in my opinion ought to be the endeavor of any one who translates Homer is above all things to keep alive that spirit and fire which makes his chief character.'[173]

Similarly one should endeavor to attain a mean in the tone with which one renders Homer: nothing that belongs to him 'seems to have been more commonly mistaken than the just pitch of his style; some of his translators having swelled into fustian in a proud confidence of the *sublime*,[174] others sunk into flatness in a cold and timorous notion of simplicity.[175] But since Homer's chief 'character' is his *fire*, 'one could sooner pardon frenzy than frigidity.'[176]

Translators' theories of their task are apt to sound pretty much alike; their practice is the best interpretation of their conception. In practice, Pope wrote, as Dr. Johnson says, 'for his own age and his own nation: he knew that it was necessary to color the images and point the sentiments of his author. . . .'[177] 'His aim is to master the general sense of what he is about to render, and then to give this in such rhetorical forms as his own style requires, omitting and even adding thoughts at his pleasure.'[178] The result was,

[172] Durham, 342.
[173] *ibid.*, 348.
[174] Presumably Chapman, of whom Pope (p. 347) gives the character 'His expression is involved in fustian, a fault for which he was remarkable in his original writings, as in the tragedy of *Bussy d'Ambois*, etc. In a word, the nature of the man may account for his whole performance, for he appears from his Preface and remarks to have been of an arrogant turn, and an enthusiast in poetry.' 'But that which is to be allowed him . . . is a daring fiery spirit that animates his translation. . . .'
[175] Hobbes and Ogilby. The former 'has given us a correct explanation of the sense in general; but for particulars and circumstances, he continually lops them, and often omits the most beautiful.' 'His poetry, as well as Ogilby's, is too mean for criticism' (*ibid.*, 347-8).
[176] *ibid.*, 343.
[177] *Lives*, III, 240.
[178] E-C, V, 165.

if not Homer, something approaching the Johnsonian estimate, 'the noblest version of poetry which the world has ever seen.'[179] For once, even though not in his own right, Pope essayed and achieved the 'grand style ornate.'

A few concluding comments may be made upon the Preface and notes to the *Iliad*. One appreciative student has described the former as follows: 'Le caractère de cette longue étude est une admiration chaleureuse mais clairvoyante, qui sait choisir ses objets, se préserver de toute hyperbole et se justifier par de bonnes raisons: c'est l'alliance singulièrement rare de l'enthousiasme et de la critique, de l'amour et de l'impartialité.'[180] Pope does combine in this, as in his Preface to Shakespeare, intense, often rapturous, appreciation of the genius of his author, with the saving grace of judgment. He will not allow Homer infallibility, but he will stop only this side idolatry; he will steadfastly believe the poems 'the best that ever human wit invented.'[181] Pope's Preface exhibits independent judgment. Materials for criticism were abundant; addition to their number was hardly useful. But there was place for an appreciative yet balanced sifting of facts and opinions, an impartial and eclectic selection and synthesis. For such a task Pope was excellently qualified. He follows no one, two, or three critics: he has read all the authorities of the age; and he judges each disputed point on its own merits as he sees them in the light of what both parties have to say. To what he derives he adds his own contribution,—common sense, and the perceptions of a poet.

Let me quote Dr. Johnson on the *Observations*. 'The copious notes with which the version is accompanied and by which it is recommended to many readers, though they were undoubtedly written to swell the volumes, ought not to pass without praise: commentaries which attract the reader by the pleasure of perusal have not often appeared; the notes of others are read to clear difficulties, those of Pope to vary entertainment.

'It has, however, been objected with sufficient reason that there is in the commentary too much of unseasonable levity and affected gaiety, that too many appeals are made to the ladies,[182] and the

---

[179] *Lives*, III, 119.

[180] Rigault, 445.

[181] *Odyssey*, V, 289 (Postscript).

[182] Pope amplifies Eustathius' account of Andromache's hair ornaments: 'I cannot pass over a matter of such importance as a young lady's dress without endeavoring to explain what sort of heads were worn [i.e., how the hair was dressed] above three thousand years ago. It is difficult to describe particularly every ornament, mentioned by the poet, but I shall lay before my female readers the bishop's explanation. . . . The ladies cannot but be pleased to see so much learning and Greek upon this im-

ease which is so carefully preserved is sometimes the ease of a trifler. Every art has its terms and every kind of instruction its proper style; the gravity of common critics may be tedious, but is less despicable than childish merriment.'[183]

On the whole this is a fair statement of the case, though the extent of the unreasonable levity is over-estimated. Pope was attempting in his *Observations*, to summarize and popularize what we should today call the 'results of recent scholarship,' and to state these 'results' with some literary grace and polish. The range in subject matter was set in the poet's direction to Broome to translate from Eustathius 'such notes only as concern the beauties or the art of the author—none geographical, historical, grammatical. . . .'[184] Pope's *Iliad* and its accompanying commentary were addressed, not to scholars, but, like Dryden's *Aeneid*, 'to all in general, and in particular to men and ladies of the first quality.'[185] The *Observations* constitute one of the first attempts to make classical scholarship palatable to those without scholarly training, and to furnish to the cultivated 'general reader' help in the aesthetic interpretation and appreciation of a great poetic monument. As such, they have very considerable historic importance. They do on an extended scale for Homer what Addison had essayed to do for Milton in his papers on *Paradise Lost*.

The high favor with which the 'English *Iliad*' was received invited the supplement of the *Odyssey*. This latter, begun in 1724 and completed in 1726, was also published by Lintot in five volumes at a guinea apiece. Pope, weary of the labor of translating, sought assistance. Broome and Fenton, amiable minor poets, did twelve books between them; and Broome, compiler from Eustathius for the *Observations on the Iliad*, furnished all the notes for the similar commentary on the *Odyssey*.[186] The whole was concluded by a *Postscript* from Pope's pen which made no pretensions to rivalling the formal elegance and fulness of treatment of the Preface, but in an easy and agreeable way sought to elucidate the

portant subject' (*Observations*, XXII: XXXIII). Another condescension: 'This passage may be of consideration to the ladies, and for their sakes I take a little pains to observe upon it. Homer tells us that the very goddesses, who are all over charms, never dress in sight of any one; the Queen of Heaven adorns herself in private, and the doors lock after her. So in Homer there are no *dieux des ruelles*, no gods are admitted to the toilet' (*ibid.*, XIV: CXLI).

[183] *Lives*, III, 240.
[184] E-C, VIII, 33.
[185] Ker, II.
[186] For the elaborate details of the partnership see E-C, V, 195-205.

'true character and style' of the *Odyssey*, and defend it from un-warranted censures.[187]

Pope adopted as his professed point of view in the *Postscript* that of so-called modern criticism: he emphasizes the necessity for keeping one's critical eye upon the work of art studied rather than upon some *a priori* standards or criteria. The 'first principle of criticism,' we are told, 'is to consider the nature of the piece and the intent of its author.' Why refuse to enjoy one epic simply because it does not follow the lines of another?

The particular occasion of the liberality is a plea for the *Odyssey*. Pope finds that adverse judgments upon it seem largely to result from its lack of conformity with its companion piece. 'Who-ever reads the *Odyssey* with an eye to the *Iliad*, expecting to find it of the same character, or of the same sort of spirit, will be griev-ously deceived. . . .'[188] And in point of fact, 'many have been misled to regard it as a continuation or second part, and thence to expect a parity of character inconsistent with its nature.' Aristotle 'constantly cites' both epics 'with equal praise,' but even so great and discerning a critic as Longinus has fallen into the mistake and seems to consider the *Odyssey* inferior because it lacks the dramatic power, fire, and sublimity of the *Iliad*.

This occasions Pope a double concern: first, to wrest the sense of Longinus, whom he obligingly quotes at length, in an attempt to make it appear that the critic does not regard the *Odyssey* as really inferior; secondly, to defend the equality in merit of the epics: the *Odyssey*, is different, but at least as good. The exegesis of Longinus is ingenious but hardly more than quibbling: Longinus tells us he speaks 'of the *Odyssey* only to show the greatest poets, when their genius wants strength and warmth for the pathetic [i.e., in old age], for the most part employ themselves in painting the manners.' Of which Pope's account is, 'After having highly extolled the sublimity and fire of the *Iliad*, he justly observes the *Odyssey* to have less of those qualities and to turn more on the side of moral and reflections on human life. Nor is it his business here to determine whether the *elevated spirit* of the one or the *just moral* of the other be the greater excellence in itself.'[189] It may be true that it was not properly the 'business' of Longinus to judge between excellences, but it seems clear from the passage quoted from him that he did; that he held the genius of Homer to have declined as

---

[187] The *Postscript* is not reprinted, either in E-C or, in its entirety, in any other modern edition. References are to the first edition.
[188] *Odyssey*, V, 264.
[189] *ibid.*, 266-7.

it cooled; and that he thought the virtues of the *Odyssey* those proper not to the epic, but to comedy.

Pope's positive argument is much more successful. 'To blame Homer for his choice of such a subject as did not admit the same incidents and the same pomp of style as his former is to take offense at too much variety, and to imagine that when a man has written one good thing he must ever after only copy himself.'[190] Each type of subject is capable of furnishing enjoyment and exhibiting art. 'To censure Homer because it [the *Odyssey*] is unlike what it was never meant to resemble is as if a gardener who had purposely cultivated two beautiful trees of contrary natures as a specimen of his skill in the several kinds should be blamed for not bringing them into pairs. . . .'[191] The whole contention of modern criticism is expressed in these sentences, and the overthrow of the *genres* at hand. The standards by which a work of art is to be judged are not exterior to itself.

The *Odyssey*, then, has its own excellences. Indeed, 'In some points, and those the most essential to the epic poem, the *Odyssey* is confessed to excel the *Iliad*; and principally in the great end of it, the *moral*. The conduct, turn and disposition of the *fable* is also what the critics allow to be the better model for epic writers to follow.'[192] Here we return to the characteristic tone of neo-classical criticism, and the rules of the epic *genre*. The *Odyssey* is a better constructed poem, a more regular poem.

Longinus' suggestion that the *Odyssey* was 'partly of the nature of comedy,'[193] by which he meant much what modern critics mean when they find in it a precursor of the romance and the novel, is happily developed in a paragraph of the *Postscript*. Pope calls our attention to the marked difference between the portrayals of Ulysses: the *Odyssey* 'shows him not in that full light of glory, but in the shade of common life. . . . As for the other persons, none of them are above what we call the higher comedy: Calypso, though a goddess, is a character of intrigue; the suitors yet more approaching to it; . . . the Cyclops, Melanthius, and Irus descend even to droll characters; and the scenes that appear throughout are generally of the comic kind—banquets, revels, sports, loves, and the pursuit of a woman.'[194]

The style of the *Odyssey* also, adapting itself to the subject matter, differs from that of the *Iliad*: it 'is not always clothed in the majesty of verse proper to tragedy, but sometimes descends into the plainer narrative and sometimes even to that familiar dialogue essential to comedy.' Sublimity is frequently lacking; but 'it always

---

[190] *Odyssey*, V, 268.   [192] *ibid.*, 269.   [194] *ibid.*, 371.
[191] *ibid.*, 271.   [193] *ibid.*, 271.

preserves a dignity, or at least a propriety. [And] There is a real beauty in an easy, pure, perspicuous description even of a low action.'[195] Pope can not 'pretend to determine' which of his styles 'was the harder task to Homer himself,—the narrative simplicity or the sublime of the epic; but he has found the former the more difficult to reproduce. He ventures to think that 'The *sublime* style is more easily counterfeited than the *natural*; something that passes for it, or sounds like it, is common to all false writers; but Nature, purity, perspicuity, and simplicity never walk in the clouds: they are obvious to all capacities, and where they are not evident they do not exist.'[196]

It will be seen that as the antithesis between Homer and Virgil formed one of the chief themes of the Preface, so a similar antithesis between Homer's own works, the *Iliad* and the *Odyssey* forms that of the Postscript. For the first antithesis, Pope finds the metaphor of the 'wild paradise' and the 'ordered garden.' A similar graceful figure sums up the second: 'The *Odyssey* is a perpetual source of poetry: the stream is not the less full for being gentle, though it is true, when we speak only with regard to the sublime, that a river foaming and thundering in cataracts from rocks and precipices is what more strikes, amazes, and fills the mind than the same body of water flowing afterwards through peaceful vales and agreeable scenes of pasturage.'[197]

The points made in this chapter may now briefly be summarized. Pope's Homer was the most signally successful of the endeavors made by seventeenth and eighteenth century French and English poets to render into the vernacular the treasures of classical literature. It made the *Iliad* and the *Odyssey* the permanent possessions of the English-speaking world. The critical matter by which it was accompanied was addressed not to scholars but to the polite world. It sought to present the results of learned study in an attractive literary form. It aimed at interesting the reader; and in place of philosophical and historical disquisitions it substituted aesthetic appreciation. Though these were Pope's immediate aims, the times forced him to take a stand on the issue of the 'quarrel' between partisans of the ancient and modern literature. This 'stand' was here, as elsewhere, mediating: he was on the side of the ancients, but his loyalty was qualified by reservations. To give to his readers a summary of the best criticism of Homer, Pope had to survey many books and writers: this he did with reliance on his own judgment. The result is, for the times, a singularly balanced and appreciative interpretation of a great poet.

[195] *Odyssey*, V, 372.   [196] *ibid.*, 376.   [197] *ibid.*, 270.

CHAPTER IV

TODAY Shakespearean scholarship is a distinct profession and a highly specialized one. But it was not always so. In the Augustan Age, there were learned men in plenty; but their labors were bestowed upon editions of the ancient classics. Few conceived that the masterpieces of English literature deserved the same careful attention, the same unremitting pains in the establishment of the text and the elucidation of diction and allusions. When the great classical scholar Bentley undertook an edition of *Paradise Lost*, he was capable of the boldest irreverence in emendation of the text. A beginning had been made at Old English scholarship by Humphrey Wanley and others, but the interest was a subject for the sneers of the cultivated.

All this has to be recalled as the background for Pope's edition of Shakespeare. We should not now expect the greatest poet of the time to appear as editor, partly because we should think his high gifts more fruitfully turned to creation, partly because we are all now at least vaguely aware of the technical demands of scholarship and understand the necessity for professional training. The first of these objections was felt by Pope's contemporaries. Lord Oxford and Lord Bolingbroke, among others, expressed their regret that the poet should spend at his translation of Homer time and energy which might have produced an original masterpiece.[1] And Pope himself, who undertook these works to gain a financial independence and establish himself, used to lament his 'ten years to comment and translate.'[2] But few doubted the ability of one poet to edit the works of another. Few were conscious of the difficulties involved, few aware of the industry and patience necessary and of the extensive reading in Elizabethan literature which could alone insure safety in interpretation. And Pope himself, who felt a real devotion to Shakespeare and a real desire to do him honor, did not count the cost before he began to build.

The Preface to Pope's edition of the works of Shakespeare has

[1] E-C, VII, 394.
[2] *Dunciad*, III, 332.

near its end this statement of the editor's purpose and method:
'In what I have done I have rather given proof of my willingness
and desire than of my ability to do him [the playwright] justice.
I have discharged the dull duty of an editor to my best judgment
with more labor than I expect thanks, with a religious abhorrence
of all innovation, and without any indulgence to my private sense
or conjecture. The method taken in this edition will show itself.
The various readings are fairly put in the margin, so that every
one may compare them; and those I have preferred into the text
are constantly *ex fide codicum*—upon authority. The alterations or
additions which Shakespeare himself made are taken note of as
they occur. Some suspected passages which are excessively bad
(and which seem interpolations by being so inserted that one can
entirely omit them without any chasm or deficience in the context)
are degraded to the bottom of the page, with an asterisk referring
to the places of their insertion. The scenes are marked so distinctly
that every removal of place is specified,—which is more necessary
in this author than any other, since he shifts them more frequently,
and sometimes without attending to this particular, the reader
would have met with obscurities. The more obsolete or unusual
words are explained. Some of the most shining passages are distinguished by commas in the margin; and where the beauty lay
not in particulars but in the whole, a star is prefixed to the scene.'[3]

These are sound and sensible principles; and, had Pope adhered
faithfully to them, the result would have been an edition of the
greatest of English 'classics' comparable to those produced in the
domains of Latin and Greek scholarship. Without the industry and
patience necessary to the undertaking, Pope seems to have conceived the task awaiting Shakespeareans, of constructing from
inaccurate and inconsistent materials as complete and careful a
text of their author as is humanly possible. He was the first to
collate with any seriousness the various versions of a given play
found in folios and quartos. And his collection of materials, chiefly
loans from 'noble' friends, was uncommonly rich. Besides the First
and Second Folios, he had, with the exception of *Much Ado*, quarto
editions of all the plays which had appeared before the publication
of the First Folio. Theobald, whose fate it became to point out the
errors and omissions of Pope's edition, was forced to work with far
less—had indeed no copy of the First Folio.[4] Pope had the materials and conceived the correct method: so much may be said to
start with. As Dr. Johnson says, 'in his edition [he] undoubtedly
did many things wrong, and left many things undone; but let him

[3] E-C, X, 548.
[4] Lounsbury, 168-9.

not be defrauded of his due praise : he was the first that knew, or at
least the first that told, by what helps the text might be improved.
If he inspected the early editions negligently, he taught others to
be more accurate.'[5]

The edition of Shakespeare was probably undertaken without
full realization of the labor to which it committed him who undertook it. The very meager payment promised Pope when he accepted
the commission from Lintot—only two hundred and seventeen
pounds and a few shillings—seems to imply that the pains and
length of time which would be involved in any adequate sort of
editing were greatly underestimated by publisher and, more particularly, by editor. It proved less easy to secure assistance in the
explication of the text than might have been thought. Elizabethan
scholarship was far more to seek than classical. Friends who could
interpret Homer for his translator there were in plenty ; but few
had yet given the same exact attention to the older English literature, and those few were not among Pope's friends.

A plea for help addressed to Bishop Atterbury brought the surprising reply, 'I protest to you, in a hundred places I cannot construe [Shakespeare] ; I do not understand him. The hardest part of
Chaucer is more intelligible to me than some of these scenes, not
merely through the faults of the edition, but the obscurity of the
writer,—for obscure he is and a little (not a little) inclined to
bombast, whatever apology you may have contrived on that head
for him. There are allusions in him to a hundred things of which
I knew nothing and can guess nothing. . . . I protest Aeschylus
does not want a comment to me more than he does. So that I begin
to despair of doing you any considerable service.'[6]

Pope also, according to his own statement, 'by public advertise-
ments did request the assistance of all lovers of this author' ;[7] but
this, too, was fruitless. The one man who might have assisted was
Lewis Theobald, and he, though an admirer of Pope's genius, 'considered,' as he wrote later, 'the labor of twelve years study upon
this author of too much value rashly to give either the profit of it
to a book-seller whom I had no obligations to or to the credit of an
editor so likely to be thankless.'[8]

As a consequence, Pope was left to his own labors with what

[5] *Lives*, III, 139. 'His judgment,' says Ruffhead (157) 'was seen in
doing what had never been done before—in giving the text from the
collated copies of the old editions of the plays.'

[6] E-C, IX, 26.

[7] Lounsbury, 316.

[8] *ibid.*, 332.

assistance Fenton[9] and Gay could give him. The laborers had no
model before them to spur them on by its example: the only earlier
'modern' edition, that of Rowe, was perfunctory in the extreme.
And none of them had acquaintance with Elizabethan drama outside the works of Jonson, Beaumont, and Fletcher. Shakespeare can
only be understood as we understand the age in which he lived, its
manners, conventions, diction. But Pope 'was not sufficiently
acquainted . . . with the works of Shakespeare's predecessors and
contemporaries.'[10] And without this background many passages in
Shakespeare must remain obscure, and many more suffer misinter-
pretation.

Work on the edition seems to have been begun as soon as the
Iliad was published and to have been carried on along with the
translation of the *Odyssey*. The Shakespeare was reported complete with Preface and index in October, 1724, but it was not before
March of the following year that it made its appearance,[11] shortly
to be followed by the first three volumes of the *Odyssey*. The edition of Shakespeare was in six handsome quarto volumes, and
contained the complete plays as the canon is now established, with
the exception of *Pericles*; the sonnets and other non-dramatic
poems were not included.[12]

What was Pope's treatment of Shakespeare's text is the first
question a modern critic wants to ask. As we have seen, his theory
of text-establishment was commendably sound. He made as rich a
collection as he could of folios and quartos, and he expressed his
consciousness that the procedure adopted by an editor should
everywhere be apparent to his readers: he should have 'a religious
abhorrence of all innovation' and make no indulgence to 'private
sense or conjecture'; should 'fairly put' all variant readings in the
margin, and print suspected passages at the foot of the page.

But there were difficulties in the way of patient adherence to this
method. Habits of meticulously accurate work had never been
formed; and without such habits consistently reliable scholarship
could hardly be expected. Haphazard industry produces haphazard
results—now a happy conjecture, now a correct emendation or

[9] Fenton received £30 14s. for his share in the editing of Shakespeare.
E-C, VII, 82, n.
[10] Warton: *Genius of Pope*, II, 400.
[11] Lounsbury, 82.
[12] That is, not by Pope. The poems were not included in Rowe's six
volume edition (1709) either; but a seventh volume containing them
was added by Charles Gildon in 1710. This supplement was reprinted in
1725 to complete Pope's edition, but the poet had no share in it. Gildon's
work was 'revised and corrected, with a Preface, by Dr. [George] Sewell'
(d. 1726), Cambridge man and booksellers' hack.

explanation; but, equally often, dangerous tampering with the text
or the omission occasioned by negligence. Added to this was a
constitutional contempt for textual criticism which the spirit of
the age fostered rather than diminished. Expressions of this contempt abound in Pope. No doubt some may be attributed to the
bitterness which was occasioned by the relative failure of his
edition of Shakespeare and Theobald's victorious *Shakespeare
Restored*. Such perhaps are the sneers at the 'verbal critics' in the
Dunciad and the *Epistle to Dr. Arbuthnot*:

> Pains, reading, study are their just pretence,
> And all they want is spirit, taste, and sense.
> Commas and points they set exactly right,
> And 't were a sin to rob them of their mite.
>
>   . . . .
>
> Each wight who reads not, and but scans and spells,
> Each word-catcher that lives on syllables,
> Ev'n such small critics some regard may claim
> Preserved in Milton's or in Shakespeare's name.[13]

But the same spirit was Pope's before his edition of Shakespeare
was ever contemplated. He missed no opportunity to deride the
more laborious commentators on Homer, and in his remarks prefaced to the *Observations on the Iliad* took special occasion for a
gibe at textual criticism.

'Even the grammarians,' he says, 'though their whole business
and use be only to render the words of an author intelligible, are
strangely touched with the pride of doing something more than
they ought. The grand ambition of one sort of scholars is to in-
crease the number of *various lections*; which they have done to
such a degree of obscure diligence that we now begin to value the
first editions of books as most correct because they have been the
least corrected. The prevailing passion of others is to discover
new meanings in an author, whom they will cause to appear mysterious purely for the vanity of being thought to unravel him.
These account it a disgrace to be of the opinion of those that preceded them; and it is generally the fate of such people who will
never say what was said before them to say what will never be
said after them.'[14]

Inaccurate scholarly habits and contempt for the scholar's profession between them effected much of a breach between the profession and the practice of Pope. He wearied of his correct method;

[13] ll. 159-62; 165-8. Bentley and Theobald are the critics pilloried in the
last line.
[14] *Observations*: I: Introduction.

he wondered whether his industry in exact details would ever receive appreciative notice; he indulged in periodical assertions of the right of his poet's intuition to deal with the text as seemed best to itself. He could not see his task 'steadily': he worked erratically, trusted too much to inspiration.

The foundation of his text was Rowe's second edition.[15] But collation was spasmodically attempted. 'His method of proceeding in general may be stated as having been about as follows. If a puzzling sentence chanced to arrest his attention, his first thought apparently was to amend it by some conjecture of his own. If no way of clearing up the difficulty presented itself to his mind, he turned to the quartos or folios for help. If a satisfactory solution of the difficulty could be derived from these sources, he availed himself of it, though assuredly not in all cases. How indifferently, how negligently this work of consultation was done, there are plenty of examples to show.'[16]

Pope was impressed with the importance of the quartos—or, as he called them, the 'old editions.' In his Preface he compares them with the First Folio to the disadvantage of the latter. The 'additions of trifling and bombast passages are in this edition far more numerous,' he tells us; 'for whatever had been added since those quartos by the actors, or had stolen from their mouths into the written parts, were from thence conveyed into the printed text, and all stand charged upon the author. He himself complained of this usage in *Hamlet*, where he wishes that *those who play the clowns would speak no more than is set down for them*.'[17] Besides, the First Folio omits 'a number of beautiful passages which are extant in the first single editions.' Pope thinks Heminge and Condell printed from copies 'which had lain ever since the author's day in the playhouse, and had from time to time been cut or added to arbitrarily.'[18]

The quartos, or 'old editions,' ordinarily served as warrant for Pope to remove or relegate to the bottom of the page passages which did not please his taste—passages of low humor, or quibbling, or bombast. His treatment of *Romeo and Juliet* may serve as case in point. This play, in Shakespeare's 'earlier manner,' afforded instances of all the poet's least Augustan traits, and there was wide variance between folio and quarto to give Pope some support in his attempt to disclaim for Shakespeare what seemed to him the worst

[15] Lounsbury, 101.
[16] *ibid.*, 106.
[17] E-C, X, 544. Cf. Lounsbury, 56-7.
[18] E-C, X, 545.

passages.[19] Unfortunately, it does not matter to Pope that the
characters are speaking 'in character' and that Shakespeare was
writing in accordance with a taste which was, if mistaken, his own.
Upon the nurse's speech beginning, 'Yes, madam. Yet I cannot
choose but laugh,' Pope's comment is, 'This speech and tautology
is not in the first editions';[20] failing to remark that tautology is a
part of the characterization. Similarly, Lady Capulet's speech in
the same scene in which Paris is compared to a book is completely
omitted: in a foot-note appended to the preceding speech of the
nurse's we are told 'In the common editions [i.e., those printed
from the folios] here follows a ridiculous speech which is entirely
added since the first.'[21] In Act II, Scene 5, a long conversation between Romeo, Benvolio, and Mercutio involving punning of an
elaborate character is relegated to a foot-note and so is the short
passage a little later in which Romeo and Mercutio banter vulgarly
with the nurse. Some verses immediately following the nurse's
return to the Capulet garden are omitted as 'not in the old edition.'
In Act III, Scene 4, from Juliet's address to the nurse beginning
'what devil art thou that dost torment me thus?' Pope omits four
lines exceedingly characteristic of the Shakespearean fondness for
'conceits' and puns:

> I am not I, if there be such an I,
> Or those eyes shut that make thee answer 'I,'
> If he be slain, say 'I'; or if not, no:
> Brief sounds determine of my weal or woe—

with the Augustan comment, 'The strange lines that follow here
in the common books are not in the old edition.' Juliet's paradoxical
compounds of 'Beautiful tyrant! fiend angelical!' and so on[22] are
removed to the bottom of the page; so are some brief passages of
punning in the next scene. After Juliet's 'And slay thy lady, too,
that lives in thee,'[23] Pope assures us, without quoting the text,
'Here follows in the common books a great deal of nonsense, not
one word of which is to be found in the first edition.' Passing over
a few minor omissions and relegations, we find the nurse again
checked in her tautology: Upon 'Oh Woe! oh woeful, woeful,

---

[19] In his Preface, Pope tells us that 'in the old edition of *Romeo and
Juliet* there is no hint of a great number of the mean conceits and ribal-
dries now to be found there' (E-C, X, 544).

[20] Act I, 4 (References are to Pope's scene-division, not to that of
the modern editions).

[21] See the *Variorum* on this 'metaphysical' passage. Steevens, in his
edition (1773) called it 'stuff.'

[22] Act III, 4.

[23] Act III, 5. Seventeen highly figurative lines are omitted.

woeful day,'[24] our editor remarks 'This speech of exclamations is not to be found in the edition above cited. Several other parts, unnecessary or tautological, are not to be found in the said edition, which occasions the variation in this from the common books.' This comment is apparently supposed to warrant the complete omission of the succeeding speeches, in rhetorically elegiac strain, by Paris and Capulet.[25] The ground for exclusion appears more boldly in the comment appended to Romeo's 'Stay not, be gone; live, and hereafter say':[26] 'Some lines are left out here and afterwards which are unworthy of Shakespeare, and no hint of them to be found in the old edition.' Under guise of doing homage to Shakespeare, Pope was at liberty to dismiss as unauthentic and foisted into the text by the actors whatever did not strike him as 'elegant.'[27]

If Pope used the 'old editions' as pretext for subtracting from the text what he did not fancy,[28] he sometimes, to give him credit, made use of them for proper addition. He was 'the first to lay the quartos under contribution for the establishment of the modern text. To *Hamlet* he added a few lines from this source; to *Lear* a great many—roughly speaking, about one hundred and fifty, including a whole scene.'[29]

But in neither case was a method given consistent application. As we have seen, passages which did not seem to him equal to the dignity of a Shakespeare were sometimes 'bottomed,' sometimes entirely omitted. The additions were on no more systematic a basis. He restored a hundred and fifty lines to the text of *Lear*; but he 'left about a hundred more to be added from the same source by Theobald.' 'No settled principles in fact determined his action in any given case.'[30]

Pope disclaims in his Preface having given 'any indulgence to my private sense or conjecture.' 'But nevertheless he allowed himself the 'unchecked license of editors of English classics before

---

[24] Act IV, 5.

[25] I should in justice add that White (*Variorum* on the passage) thinks 'In this speech of mock-heroic woe, and perhaps in the two that follow, Shakespeare seems to have ridiculed, as he has done elsewhere, the translation of Seneca's tragedies published in 1581.' See also Ulrici's comment on the same.

[26] Act V, 4.

[27] Ruffhead says (157) that Pope showed 'his elegance in banishing all the poet's and players' ribaldry and nonsense from the text.' Our editor himself was not so daring as to censure the 'poet's . . . nonsense'; instead, he attributed it entirely to the actors.

[28] It should be added that, as Lounsbury says (103), the treatment of *Romeo and Juliet* is perhaps Pope's 'worst achievement in this line.'

[29] Lounsbury, 102.

[30] *ibid.*, 102.

and after his time.'[31] The text of Shakespeare as given us in folios
and quartos has incomplete lines, redundant lines, limping lines.
Modern scholarship does not venture to 'improve' these, but Pope,
with his verse attuned to a very regular iambic versification,
attempted to reduce the irregularities as much as possible, with
which end in view he inserted or deleted words or changed their
order. These changes were exceedingly numerous, and 'they were
nearly all made silently. In scarcely a single instance where the
line has undergone alteration for the sake of the metre is there the
slightest hint furnished of the deviation which has taken place
from the original.'[32] As instances of these 'smoothings-out' of the
text may be cited from Act I of *Hamlet* the reduction of 'dared to
the combat' into 'dared to the fight' and

> things rank and gross in Nature
> Possess it merely. That it should come to this!

to

> Possess it merely that it should come thus.

Similarly,

> Let me not think on't: Frailty, thy name is woman!

becomes

> Let me not think—Frailty, thy name is woman!

The emendations of audacious conjecture are in themselves rep
rehensible enough; but it should be repeated that far more to be
condemned was this emendation unaccompanied as it was by in-
dication to the reader of where the text was as the 'old editions'
gave it, where revised, and on what authority. The Preface promised that 'the various readings are fairly put in the margin so that
every one may compare them, and those . . . preferred into the
text are constantly *ex fide codicum*. . . .' A spasmodic and erring
performance could not claim the excuse of ignorance.

Pope's assertion that 'the more obsolete or unusual words are
explained' was also scantily warranted. The explanations occur
only infrequently, in spite of the fact that the Elizabethan diction
was far more puzzling to Augustan readers than it is to us.[33] And
some of the words selected could hardly have been 'the more obsolete.' 'Where so vast a number of really difficult words were
passed over in silence, it would hardly seem worth while to inform
the reader, as did Pope, that *bolted* means *sifted*, that *budge* means

[31] Lounsbury, 109.
[32] *ibid.*, 109.
[33] The romanticists revived a good many words which had become
archaic to the narrower 'classical' vocabulary of the Augustans.

give away, that *eld* means *old age*, that *gyves* means *shackles*, that
fitchew means *polecat*, that *sometime* means *formerly*. . . .'[34]
Furthermore, the definitions and etymologies given were frequently
lamentably incorrect.[35]

It is easy, however, to deride Pope for not being what few even
professedly learned men of his time were, an English philologist.
The English language was still held to be uncertain and rapidly
changing—not yet 'fixed' so that it was capable of scholarly in-
vestigation. The notion of systematic study of dialects such as
would have dispensed illumination upon English etymologies was
not yet entertained. Gildon, in his supplementary volume to
Rowe's edition published in 1710, furnished under the heading *An
Explanation of the Old Words Used by Shakespeare in His Works*
only five pages in large type.

It ought also to be said that Pope is not always incorrect in his
definitions even according to modern authorities. A few random
instances: *Frank* is an 'old English word for hog-stye,' *yarely*
means 'nimbly,' *tarre* is an 'old English word signifying to provoke or urge on.' Nor did Pope always resort to private conjecture.
He frequently made use, as Lounsbury fails to note, of the *Ety-
mologicon Linguae Anglicanae*, giving his authority, Skinner, at
the end of the note.[36] Lounsbury is 'surprised' by Pope's 'occasional
ignorance of what from his professed religion he would be supposed fully to know,'[37] but the former's comment is not very apt
upon the passage he cites, Hamlet's father's description of himself
as cut off 'Unhouseled, unanointed [Pope's substitution for *disappointed*], unaneled.' It is ignorance of an old word rather than of
the rites of the Catholic religion which makes Pope explain *unaneled* as meaning 'no Knell rung,' for he explains *unanointed* as
'without extreme unction' and correctly defines *unhouseled* as
'without sacrament.'

It seems to me, then, that unnecessary scorn has been poured
upon Pope's meagre lexicography. Of his predecessors, Rowe gave
no notes, and Gildon but few. The study of the English language
was still in its beginnings. Pope laid no claim to philological
learning or inspiration, and had little help available. He used
Skinner's work when he could; conjectured occasionally when he
could not.

Some other editorial work must now be noted. Annotations other

[34] Lounsbury, 87.
[35] Lounsbury gives several pages of them (*ibid.*, 88-92).
[36] Stephen Skinner (1623-1667) was an Oxford man. He published his
etymological dictionary in 1671.
[37] Lounsbury, 92.

than etymological are, like all Pope's labors on his Shakespeare, erratic in their frequency. But some are useful, and many are interesting. Pope made a good beginning at the work of source attribution. *Othello* and *Measure for Measure* he traces to Cinthio's novels; to the *Decameron*, *All's Well that Ends Well* and *Cymbeline*. *Much Ado about Nothing* comes from the fifth book of *Orlando Furioso*,[38] *Romeo and Juliet* from Bandello,[39] *Winter's Tale* from 'the old story-book of *Dorastus and Faunia*.'[40] *Troilus and Cressida* is attributed to 'an old Lombard author,[41] and since by Chaucer'; the *Comedy of Errors* to the *Menaechmi* of Plautus. 'The hint of part of this play,' *Timon of Athens*, is from Lucian's Dialogue of *Timon*. *Hamlet* was 'not invented by our author, though from whence he took it, I know not.'[42] Of the historical plays, *Henry V* and *Henry VI*, Part II, are attributed to Hall's (i.e., Holinshed's) *Chronicles*,[43] *Coriolanus* to Plutarch's Life. *Macbeth* comes 'from Hector Boetius and other Scottish chroniclers.'[44]

Some of the plays are prefaced by a general comment; and there are occasional reflections of general interest appended at other points. *Two Gentlemen of Verona* induced the observation: 'It is observable (I know not from what cause) that the style of this comedy is less figurative and more natural and unaffected than the greater part of this author's, though supposed to be one of the first he wrote'; in spite of which the dialogue between Proteus and Speed in Act I is relegated to the bottom of the page with the comment, 'This whole scene, like many others in these plays (some of which I believe were written by Shakespeare and others interpo-

[38] This is still held the source of the deception of Claudio; the main plot, however, is from Bandello.

[39] Still in the succession, though the versions by Painter and Brooke are nearer Shakespeare.

[40] The later title of Robert Greene's romance, *Pandosto*.

[41] Pope got this misinformation from Dryden, who wrote in the Preface to his *Troilus and Cressida*, 'the original story was written by one Lollius, a Lombard author in Latin verse, and translated by Chaucer into English' (Ker, I, 203). Chaucer's mysterious 'myn auctour' was long supposed to be 'Lollius of Urbino.' Up to modern times 'Lombardy' was loosely used of a vaguely defined northern Italy. The fullest discussion of the Lollius problem is in Kittredge's article: *Harvard Studies in Classical Philology*, XXVIII: 47-133.

[42] Theobald pointed out that the source was Saxo Grammaticus (Lounsbury, 320).

[43] Pope's notes to *Henry V* furnish plentiful verbatim quotations from Holinshed.

[44] Hector Boece (or Boethius) (1465-1536), professor at the Universities of Paris and Aberdeen, wrote a *Scotorum Historiae* which, in the English translation of W. Harrison, supplied the chief part of the account of Scotland given in Holinshed's *Chronicles*.

lated by the players) is composed of the lowest and most trifling conceits, to be accounted for only from the gross taste of the age he lived in; *populo ut placerent.* I wish I had the authority to leave them out;[45] but I have done all I could—set a mark of reprobation upon them throughout this edition.' Valentine's surrender of Sylvia to Proteus in Act V, Scene 4, occasions Pope's wonder: 'It is (I think) very odd to give up his mistress at once, without any reason alleged. But our author probably followed the stories just as he found them in his novels as well as in his histories.' This last comment reveals a point of view toward Shakespeare's methods of work which we have only recently begun to understand: the improbabilities in Shakespeare's play arise from the closeness with which popular taste demanded that the 'old stories' be followed. The artist smoothed and rationalized what he could, but the framework retained unmanageable elements—the opening incident in *Lear*, for example.

An introductory note on *The Merry Wives* gives a brief history of the comedy. 'This play was written in the author's best and ripest years, after *Henry the Fourth*, by command of Queen Elizabeth. There is a tradition that it was composed at a fortnight's warning. But that must be meant only of the first imperfect sketch of this comedy which is yet extant in an old quarto edition printed in 1619. This which we have was altered and improved by the author almost in every speech.'[46]

The note on *King John* is also bibliographical: '*The Troublesome Reign of King John* was written in two parts by W. Shakespeare and W. Rowley and printed in 1611.[47] But the present play is entirely different and infinitely superior to it.'[48]

Pope expended considerable time and thought on *Henry V*: it is one of the most plentifully annotated of the plays. It was Pope who first realized the function of the Chorus, and set its appearances in their proper places—as his notes will certify. The introductory note gives us the unusual assistance of a dating. 'This play was

[45] He later waxed more bold and took the liberty.

[46] The old quarto to which Pope alludes must have been a reprint of the First Quarto (1602), which 'seems to have been printed from a stenographic report of an acting version of the play.' 'This which we have' is the First Folio version.

[47] It was first printed in 1591. Here again Pope's copy is a reprint.

[48] 'Yet from this admittedly spurious piece he received into the text of the genuine in one place twelve lines, in another three' (Lounsbury, 105). Pope adds a long note in justification of the longer insertion (Act III, sc. 1): the ground of the quarrel between the Bastard and Austria is 'nowhere specified in the present play.' But in 'the first sketch of this play' he finds it 'insisted upon,' and so has 'ventured to place it' in this.

writ (as appears from a passage in the Chorus to the Fifth Act) at
the time of the Earl of Essex' commanding the forces in Ireland in
the reign of Queen Elizabeth, and not 'till after *Henry the Sixth*
had been played, as may be seen by the conclusion of this play.'
Comparison of the First Quarto, almost certainly pirated, and the
text in the Folio occasions: 'This first scene was added since the
edition of 1608,[49] which is much short of the present editions,
wherein the speeches are generally enlarged and raised; several
whole scenes besides, and all the Choruses also, were since added
by Shakespeare.' One of the notes explanatory of the proper setting
of the Choruses may be quoted: 'Between this [Act I, Sc. 4] and the
foregoing scene, in all the editions hitherto is inserted the Chorus
which I have postponed. That Chorus manifestly is intended to ad-
vertise the spectators of the change of scene to Southampton, and
therefore ought to be placed just before that change and not here,
where the scene is still continued in London.' The scene in French
between Katherine and the old gentlewoman did not seem to Pope
to have a proper dignity; but for once he dared no removal. 'I
have left this ridiculous scene as I found it; and am sorry to have
no color left from any of the editions to imagine it interpolated.'

In *Henry VI*, Part I, Act I, Scene 1, there is an incomplete line,
'Than Julius Caesar, or bright——.' This occasions one of Pope's
pleasantest notes. 'I can't guess,' he says, 'the occasion of this
hemistich and imperfect sense in this place. 'Tis not impossible it
might have been filled up with *Francis Drake*—though that were a
horrible anachronism (as bad as Hector's quoting Aristotle in
Troilus and Cressida). Yet perhaps at the time that brave Englishman was in his glory, to an English-hearted audience, and pronounced by some favorite actor, the thing might be popular, though
not judicious; and therefore by some critic in favor of our author
afterwards struck out. But this is a mere slight conjecture.'

Bibliographical notes prefaced to the Second and Third Parts of
Henry VI explain that these were first written and printed under
the titles of *The Contention of York and Lancaster*, and *The True
Tragedy of Richard, Duke of York*. Pope speaks of the former as
'since vastly improved by the author': it is now thought that
Shakespeare had no hand in either of the *Contentions*. As usual, the
dates Pope gives are of reprints, not of the First Quartos.

The dating of the play is the principal concern of the introduction to *Troilus and Cressida*, of which Pope had the First Quarto.
'Before this play . . . , printed in 1609, is a bookseller's Preface
showing that first impression to have been before the play had been

[49] Reprint of Q[1] (1600).

acted, and that it was published without Shakespeare's knowledge from a copy that had fallen into the bookseller's hands. Mr. Dryden thinks this one of the first of our author's plays.[50] But, on the contrary, it may be judged from the forementioned Preface that it was one of his last; and the great number of observations both moral and politic with which this piece is crowded more than any other of his seems to confirm my opinion.'

I have quoted all Pope's introductory notes and some of the more interesting scattered through the text. It will be observed how little method is displayed. Some plays are almost void of annotation; others show evidence of a good deal of labor and study. Pope is capable of really instructive and suggestive observations, but incapable of producing them according to any system; each play is annotated on a different method. Nor does it appear that the choice of plays for the more careful treatment was based on any very deep reason. The so-called 'four great tragedies' received less attention than some of far less interest or significance.

A few more features of the editing remain to be noted. The division into acts and scenes of Shakespeare's plays was 'haphazard and imperfect' in the folios: six plays begin with the heading *Actus Primus, Scaena Prima* and have no further indications. Rowe, in his edition, was the first to make a systematic division of the plays. Pope carried on this work, subdividing the acts into scenes according to the fashion of the French stage: a new scene is begun whenever a new character is introduced. Thus Rowe makes two scenes of the First Act of the *Tempest*, Pope six; in the Fourth and Fifth Acts of the same play Rowe makes no division at all, Pope five and six scenes respectively.

Pope was the first to call into question the Shakespearean canon as set by the Third Folio, in which had appeared *Pericles, Locrine, Sir John Oldcastle*, the *Yorkshire Tragedy, Lord Cromwell, The Puritan*, and *The London Prodigal*, all of which were reprinted in the Fourth Folio and the two editions of Rowe.[52] These seven were omitted from his edition, and, with the exception of *Pericles*, from all subsequent. The Preface judges 'from all the distinguishing marks' of Shakespeare's style and 'his manner of thinking and writing' that 'those wretched plays' are not his. Pope adds, 'I should conjecture of some of the others (particularly *Love's Labor Lost*,

[50] In the Preface to his play, *Troilus and Cressida*, Dryden speaks of Shakespeare as having written his play of the same name 'in the apprenticeship of his writing . . .' (Ker, I, 203).

[51] *Troilus and Cressida* is one of the plays in which Pope marks most speeches for admiration.

[52] Lounsbury, 113.

the *Winter's Tale*, and *Titus Andronicus*) that only some characters, single scenes, or perhaps a few particular passages were of
his hand.' Our critic adduces in behalf of his general theory what
has since come to be generally recognized: the Elizabethan practice
of floating plays under the names of great and popular authors. 'It
is very probably what occasioned some plays to be supposed
Shakespeare's was only this—that they were pieces produced by
unknown authors, or fitted up for the theatre while it was under
his administration, and no owner claiming them, they were ad-
judged to him. . . .' In behalf of his rejection of the seven plays
he can cite the authority of Heminge and Condell, who did not
allow them entry into the First Folio. He gives as a particular
reason for the rejection of *Titus* that Ben Jonson openly expressed
his contempt for this play in the Induction to *Bartholomew Fair* in
1614, when Shakespeare was still living: he cannot believe that
Jonson would so have spoken had the play been his friend's.

Pope added to his Shakespeare, as to his *Iliad*, a series of quaintly
impressive indexes.[53] The first comprises 'Characters of Historical
Persons,' such as 'Arthur, a hopeful young Prince, unfortunate,'
'Brutus, reserved and melancholic,' 'Constance, a mother passion-
ately fond,' 'Henry VI, meek, religious, unfortunate,' and 'Lear,
King, choleric, fickle, mad, miserable.' The second lists passages on
'Manners, Passions, and their External Effects': 'Avarice and
cruelty. *vid.* Shylock,' 'Child, the duty it owes a father,' 'Chastity
scandalized beautifully painted in Hero,' 'Joy, excess produceth
tears' are examples. The 'Index of Fictitious Persons with the
Characters Ascribed to them' parallels the first. The fourth is an
'Index of Thoughts or Sentiments'—that is, of the gnomic passages
in the plays. The topics discussed may surprise us by their variety:
among them are 'Astrology ridiculed,' 'Bastardy defended,' 'Dying
words, their force,' 'Eclipses, their influence,' 'King-killing detested,' and 'Fruition more languid than expectation.' A fifth index
arranges the 'speeches' in Shakespeare according to their rhetorical
'kinds' as Exhortatory, Vituperative, Execrative, Deliberative,
Narrative, Pathetic, or Soliloquy. In the sixth are catalogued all the
'Descriptions' of 'Places,' 'Persons,' and 'Things,' ranging from
'Bank, flowery' and 'Vale, a dark and melancholy one' to 'A Bishop
in arms,' 'Young lady playing on the lute and singing' and 'Beautiful person petitioning.' The series is concluded with an 'Index of
Some Similes and Allusions.'[54]

Pope's editing was, as we have seen, unmethodical and incom-

[53] Fenton seems to have assisted in their compilation. See E-C, VIII, 82.
[54] Theobald, strange to say, reprints this series of indexes in his edition;
no other Shakespearean editors have done so.

plete. Much was proposed and much begun; but little was pursued with regularity. But the new edition of Shakespeare could boast one feature not soon to be surpassed—a Preface at once 'judicious' and appreciative which has hardly, since the eighteenth century, been given its due. Dr. Johnson recognized its merit. 'Once when a lady talked of Johnson's Preface to Shakespeare as superior to Pope's: "I fear not, madam, (said he), the little fellow has done wonders".'[55] In his own Preface, the Doctor calls Pope's 'valuable alike for elegance of composition and justness of remark, and containing a general criticism on his author so extensive that little can be added, and so exact that little can be disputed.' A work of this sort, he continues, 'every editor has an interest to suppress, but that every reader would demand its insertion.'

Justice is coming tardily to be given to the eighteenth century appreciation of the great English classics, Shakespeare, Spenser, and Milton. Because it understood him differently, because it was perfervid and rhapsodic instead of deliberative, the nineteenth century liked to believe that it was 'the first to recognize and explain the greatness of Shakespeare.' The Schlegels, Coleridge, Hazlitt, and Lamb felt themselves explorers. But German romanticists had no need to awaken Englishmen to a belief in the greatness of Shakespeare. To the Augustan as much as to the Victorian, he was 'the glory of English letters.' At no time in the eighteenth century was he unpopular. Rowe's edition came out the year the *Tatler* was begun. Dennis 'read him over and over and still remained unsatiated.' Gibbon speaks of 'the idolatry for the gigantic genius of Shakespeare which is inculcated from our infancy as the first duty of an Englishman.'[56] Augustan appreciation was not less than Victorian simply because it was different.

It is true, however, that the eighteenth century did not hold to the doctrine of Shakespeare's infallibility. The rule followed by the romanticists was 'To justify all the faults of which Shakespeare had been accused by former critics.'[57] They found prodigious and

[55] *Lives*, III, 139, n.
[56] Pope himself bears testimony to the national veneration of Shakespeare in his *To Augustus*:
> On Avon's bank where flowers eternal blow
> If I but ask if any weed can grow,—
> One tragic sentence if I dare deride
> Which Betterton's grave action dignified,
> Or well-mouthed Booth with emphasis proclaims
> (Though but, perhaps, a muster-roll of names)—
> How will our fathers rise up in a rage
> And swear, all shame is lost in George's age!
[57] Stapfer, 18.

overwhelming beauties in what had been supposed defects: irregularities and the lapses of carelessness seemed strokes of genius, to be venerated, not criticized. Such a point of view was, it now seems to us, manifestly untenable. One of the most striking phenomena of recent Shakespearean criticism is the extent to which it has returned to the judgment of the eighteenth century. The writings of Schücking and Stoll and such a chapter from a more conservative critic as that on *Construction in Shakespeare's Tragedies* by Professor Bradley represent a point of view surprisingly close to that adopted by Pope in his Preface.

Shakespeare, says Pope, is 'of all English poets' 'the fairest and fullest subject for criticism,' and he affords 'the most numerous as well as most conspicuous instances both of beauties and faults of all sorts.'[58] 'It must be owned that with all these great excellencies, he had almost as great defects; and that as he has certainly written better, so he has perhaps written worse than any other.'[59] The Preface follows the favorite design of the times—the tabulation of beauties and defects; but the framework is easily forgotten in the richness and variety of the edifice.

Pope finds Shakespeare's prime 'character' in his unequalled perception of Nature. Not even Homer, he thinks, 'drew his art so immediately from the fountains of Nature,' for Homer's 'proceeded through Egyptian strainers and channels': it had 'some tincture of the learning or some cast of the models of those before him.' But Shakespeare is truly an 'Original': indeed, he 'is not so much an imitator of Nature as an instrument of Nature; and it is not so just to say that he speaks from her as that she speaks through him.'[60]

Thus Shakespeare's characters 'are so much Nature herself that 't is a sort of injury to call them by so distant a name as copies of her.' And, like those in Nature, they are infinitely diversified. Those of other poets bear a family resemblance to their creator; 'But every single character in Shakespeare is as much an individual as those in life itself: it is an impossibility to find any two alike. . . .'

Pope believes the *decorum* of each character is so perfectly preserved in Shakespeare 'that, had all the plays been printed without the very names of the person, I believe one might have applied them with certainty to every speaker.' Dr. Johnson agrees with caution: 'I will not say with Pope that every speech may be as-

[58] E-C, X, 534.

[59] *ibid.*, X, 536. Dr. Johnson parallels: 'Shakespeare with all his excellencies has likewise faults, and faults sufficient to obscure and overwhelm any other merit' (Smith, 122).

[60] E-C, X, 535.

signed to the proper speaker, because many speeches there are which have nothing characteristical; but perhaps though some may be equally adapted to every person, it will be difficult to find that any can be properly transferred from the present possessor to another claimant.'[61] Our maintenance of the thesis would be even more reserved. Shakespeare is quite capable of creating characteristic speech for his persons, but often he does not trouble to do so but gives them his own rich, highly-figured language. Bradley admits, 'Once more, to say that Shakespeare makes all his serious characters talk alike, and that he constantly speaks through the mouths of his *dramatis personae* without regard to their individual natures would be to exaggerate absurdly; but it is true that in his earlier plays these faults are traceable in some degree, and even in *Hamlet* there are striking passages where dramatic appropriateness is sacrificed to some other object.'[62]

Dryden tells us that when Shakespeare 'describes anything you more than see it: you feel it.'[63] One of the most beautiful, if quaintly beautiful, passages in Pope's prose is his account of his great subject's 'power over our passions.' It was 'never possessed in a more eminent degree or displayed in so different instances. Yet all along there is seen no labor, no pains to raise them,—no preparation to guide our guess to the effect, or be perceived to lead toward it; but the heart swells, and the tears burst out, just at the proper places. We are surprised the moment we weep; and yet upon reflection find the passion so just that we should be surprised if we had not wept and wept at that very moment.'[64] And as he induces our tears, so Shakespeare commands our laughter and our 'spleen': 'he is no more a master of the great than of the ridiculous in human nature; of our noblest tendernesses than of our vainest foibles; of our strongest emotions than of our idlest sensations!'

Pope's taste for *sententiae* found ample scope in Shakespeare. 'His *sentiments* are not only in general the most pertinent and judicious upon every subject, but by a talent very peculiar, something between penetration and felicity, he hits upon that particular point on which the bent of each argument turns or the force of each motive depends.'[65] Such philosophic grasp seems to our critic 'perfectly amazing'; for Shakespeare was 'a man of no education or experience in those great and public scenes of life which are usually the subject of his thoughts.' It is generally granted that poets are born such, but here is 'the only author that

[61] Nichol Smith, 116.
[62] Bradley, 74.
[63] Ker, I, 80.
[64] E-C, X, 535.
[65] *ibid.*, X, 536.

gives ground for a very new opinion,'—that 'the philosopher and even the man of the world' may too be created what they become. Shakespeare, says Dryden, 'needed not the spectacles of books to read Nature; he looked inward and found her there.'[66] Says Pope, 'he seems to have known the world by intuition, to have looked through human nature at one glance. . . .'

How is it that with virtues so amazing Shakespeare has 'almost as great defects'? Pope devotes the second section of his Preface to accounting for these as far as possible on such grounds as shall extenuate the poet's responsibility. He thinks it 'hard to imagine that so large and so enlightened a mind could ever have been susceptible of' such defects: he will attribute them to the times in which the poet lived, the exigencies of the stage, the necessity for pleasing a popular audience. In all this, Pope is taking much the point of view which has been advocated in recent years by Schücking and Stoll.

In writing for the stage, Shakespeare was subjecting himself to the taste of a miscellaneous and not wholly enlightened audience. Lyric and epic poetry find their own readers, appeal to select persons; 'stage poetry . . . is more particularly levelled to please the populace, and its success more immediately depending upon the common suffrage.'[67] When Shakespeare began to write for the stage, he had 'no other aim in his writings than to procure a subsistence':

> Shakespeare, whom you and every play-house bill
> Style the divine, the matchless,—what you will—
> For gain, not glory, winged his roving flight
> And grew immortal in his own despite.[68]

He could not write to please himself; he must direct 'his endeavors solely to hit the taste and humor that then prevailed.' 'There must have been,' says a modern critic, 'spectators who were to some extent capable of following the elevated flight of his thought and measuring the depth and delicacy of his feelings'; but 'Shakespeare did not write for one small circle; he was careful always to keep the general public before his eyes.'[69] Particularly before the turn of the century, the public theatre made its appeal chiefly to the

---

[66] Ker, I, 80.

[67] E-C, X, 536. Today plays are written for specialized audiences; the moving pictures have taken the place of the stage in having to include something for all tastes and particularly in 'depending upon the common suffrage.'

[68] To Augustus, 69-72.

[69] Schücking, 18-19.

middle and lower classes: as Pope puts it, 'The audience was generally composed of the meaner sort of people. . . .'

Much in Shakespeare's plays that offends an educated and sensitive taste may be attributed to the playwright's obligation to furnish his audiences what they wanted. Shakespeare followed his fellows in appealing to the 'meaner sort of people' by depicting scenes from low life: 'not our author's only, but almost all the old comedies have their scene among tradesmen and mechanics. . . .'[70] The historical plays are under necessity of strictly following 'the common old stories or vulgar traditions' to which the people are accustomed, and from the details of which they will suffer no departure.

Popular taste relishes the sensational and exaggerated: 'In tragedy, nothing was so sure to *surprise* and *cause admiration* as the most strange, unexpected, and consequently most unnatural events and incidents, the most exaggerated thoughts, the most verbose and bombast expression, the most pompous rhymes and thundering versification.' Pope does not directly lay these sins upon Shakespeare: his caution describes popular taste and leaves us to draw the inference that a playwright who would be successful must needs have complied. There is no reason, however, for doubting that Pope believed his subject fairly to be charged with the offenses cited.

The accusation of bombast[71] was openly made to Spence: 'Shakespeare generally used to stiffen his style with high words and metaphors for the speeches of his kings and great men: he mistook it for a mark of greatness. This is strongest in his early plays; but in his very last, his *Othello*, what a forced language has he put into the mouth of the Duke of Venice.'[72] So thought Bishop Atterbury: the poet is 'a little—not a little—inclined now and then to bombast, whatever apology you [Pope] may have contrived on that head for him.'[73] The orthodox Professor Bradley is forced to agree: 'the early critics [i.e., Pope and Johnson] were no doubt often provokingly wrong when they censured the language of particular passages in Shakespeare as obscure,[74] inflated, tasteless, or pestered with metaphors; but they were surely right in the general state-

---

[70] E-C, X, 537.

[71] First, perhaps, made by Dryden, who speaks of Shakespeare's serious 'wit' as 'many times . . . swelling into bombast' (Ker, I, 80).

[72] Spence, 173-4. 'This was the way,' adds Pope, 'of Chapman, Massinger and all the tragic writers of the day.' Bombast was Elizabethan.

[73] E-C, X, 26-7.

[74] Atterbury: 'The obscurity of the writer—for obscure he is. . . .' *ibid.*, IX, 26.

ment that his language often shows these faults.'[75] In an appended
'Note F' on the Player's Speech in *Hamlet*, Bradley speaks out
boldly. 'The truth is that the two defects of style in the speech are
the very defects we do find in his writings. When he wished to
make his style exceptionally high and passionate he always ran
some risk of bombast.' The second defect is what Pope called 'exaggerated thoughts'—that is, elaborate and strained figures. 'And
he was even more prone to . . . a use of metaphors which sound
to our ears "conceited" or grotesque.'[76] Bradley devotes several
succeeding pages to copious illustrations.

As regards the sensational in the plays, Schücking thinks Shakespeare retained 'those *more popular* elements which some of the
contemporary playwrights, even when writing for the popular
theatre, were beginning to reject.' 'Only hesitatingly does he yield
to the taste of the more educated part of the audience which since
the commencement of the seventeenth century had begun to rebel
against the excessive bloodshed, the noise of battle, the riotous
soldiery on the stage, and the practice of strewing the boards with
corpses at the end of the piece.' For an example, 'in *King Lear* the
way in which the eyes of the aged Gloster were trodden out in view
of the public was but a survival of the old atrocity plays, and not
much to the liking of the more advanced taste of the age.'[77]

So much for the popular demands in tragedy and the compliance
of Shakespeare with them. In comedy, too, the subtle and delicate
could not be expected to satisfy the body of the audience; and
'nothing was so sure to please as mere buffoonery, vile ribaldry,
and unmannerly jests of fools and clowns.'[78] Pope disliked to believe that the great poet could have stooped so low; and in his
edition was fond, whenever he could, of relegating to the bottom of
the page passages of the sorts characterized. His taste was not
always infallible in what it chose to dismiss; but, on the other
hand, the nineteenth century to the contrary, Shakespeare was not
above using primitive and even vulgar means in order to please.
His 'striving after popularity is most clearly visible in his use of
the clown.'[79] This frequently effected neither contrast nor relaxa-
tion, but disturbance. The clowns had a traditional privilege of
improvising to which Hamlet's injunction that they 'speak no more
than is set down for them' bears testimony; they were also at
liberty to insert timely allusions and local 'hits': Shakespeare
himself seems to have indulged in such lapses at times.[80] Here

[75] Bradley, 73.   [78] E-C, X, 537.
[76] *ibid.*, 416.   [79] Schücking, 22.
[77] Schücking, 19.

again, the greatest of the Elizabethan playwrights was retaining traditional popular elements when some of his fellows and the 'educated spectators of that time' had rebelled in behalf of a purer taste.

The desire to please, and please by old and tried methods, could not, however, conceal or repress the genius of Shakespeare. Pope beautifully palliates the insinuated charges with the assurance that even in low comedy 'our author's wit buoys up and is borne above his subject; his genius in those low parts is like some prince of a romance in the disguise of a shepherd or a peasant: a certain greatness and spirit now and then break out which manifest his higher extraction and qualities.'[81]

One of the topics which no eighteenth century writer on Shakespeare could omit was his neglect of the 'rules' of the drama—in particular, the unities of time, place, and action. Was Shakespeare ignorant of these, or did he consciously choose to disobey them? Today it seems pretty certain that the latter was the case. There was a vigorous school of 'classical' critics in the age of Elizabeth from Sidney in his *Defense of Poesy* on. 'Is it likely that the greatest dramatic genius of his time should have been ignorant of what must have been discussed by every playwright whom he was in the habit of meeting daily? Could the intimate friend of Ben Jonson have been unacquainted with Ben Jonson's opinion . . . ?'[82] 'Shakespeare came up to London in 1586 when he was between twenty-two and twenty-three years of age, and here he lived for about twenty-five years, mixing in good society as well as that of the stage. His friends in the world of fashion were the highly educated men of Elizabeth's court, and great lords, all partisans of the classical revival and of the imitation of the ancients: his companions at the theatre were scholars, graduates of either Oxford or Cambridge, so that he must assuredly have been well informed as to the doctrines of the neo-classical school, and was, doubtless, warmly urged on all sides to follow its precepts and examples.'[83]

It has also for some time been recognized by all students of the subject that there are occasional references in Shakespeare's plays to classical doctrine—the unities and purity of *genre*, and that at

[80] Schücking, 24.

[81] E-C, X, 537.

[82] Lounsbury: *Shakespeare as a Dramatic Artist*, 102. Presumably the 'wit-combats between Shakespeare and Ben Jonson' of which Fuller speaks in a celebrated passage must frequently have been waged over the 'classical' doctrine.

[83] Stapfer, 57.

least in the *Tempest*, Shakespeare showed that he was quite able to conform to the rules if he chose. The following passage sums up many longer discussions of this subject. 'Shakespeare did not escape the current talk about the "unities." There is an allusion to the unity of time, and to dramatic "law" and "custom" in the Prologue to *Henry V* (1599); while Polonius (*Hamlet* II: 2) prates technically of "scene individable, or poem unlimited," mentions Seneca and Plautus, stock examples for the theorists, and says of the actors: "For the law of writ and the liberty, these are the only men." Time, the Chorus in *The Winter's Tale* (?1610) says (Act 4): "It is in my power to o'erthrow law." The "laws" of place and time in this "poem unlimited" are manfully overthrown by an artist who regards action as the important thing. In Shakespeare's last play, however, *The Tempest* (?1611), we have "scene individable," and the action is comprised within three hours.'[84]

Pope's answer to the question 'whether Shakespeare knew the unities and rejected them by design or deviated from them by happy ignorance'[85] is not direct. The implication is that he knew of the rules, but had no incentive to follow them, since the irregular drama met with a warmer reception from popular audiences. Before 'Ben Jonson, getting possession of the stage, brought critical learning into vogue,' 'not only the common audience had no notion of the rules of writing, but few even of the better sort piqued themselves upon any great degree of knowledge or nicety that way. . . .'[86] Of course Pope is mistaken if he thinks that none of 'our authors had . . . thoughts of writing on the model of the ancients' before Ben Jonson: though most of the academic imitations of Seneca and Plautus must have perished, Pope knew at least *Gorboduc*.[87] But his description is correct if he is referring only to the writers for the public theatre that 'their tragedies were only histories in dialogue and their comedies followed the thread of any novel as they found it no less implicitly than if it had been true history.' Shakespeare, writing for the suffrage of the people, and 'at first without patronage of the better sort and therefore without aims of pleasing them, without assistance or advice from the learned, as without the advantage of education or acquaintance among them,' naturally followed the old established methods.

Is it then fair to judge Shakespeare's writing by the 'rules of Aristotle,' asks Pope. His answer is at once daring and cautious. He

[84] Lane Cooper: *Poetics of Aristotle*, 133.
[85] Dr. Johnson: Preface to Shakespeare (Nichol Smith, 130).
[86] E-C, X, 537.
[87] E-C, IX, 67-8.

does not deny the importance and value of the rules, in which almost all his literary contemporaries believed. But upon sufficient grounds he was willing to make an exception. 'He regarded it as a misfortune that Shakespeare was not so circumstanced as to be able to write on the model of the ancients, but, unlike the pedant theorists, he refused to judge Shakespeare by the rules of a foreign drama.'[88] The Renaissance critic had asserted in the course of the dispute over the lawfulness of Ariosto's *Orlando*, 'Aristotle did not know romance, and therefore his rules do not and cannot apply to it. . . .'[89] Similarly Pope, without denying the general right of Aristotelian canons, is able to venture the defense of Shakespeare on the ground that to judge him by the 'rules' is 'like trying a man by the laws of one country who acted under those of another.'[90]

The compliance of Shakespeare with the taste of his audience serves also to explain, Pope thinks, the improvement which is manifest in the 'works of his riper years.' In time 'his perform-ances had merited the protection of his Prince,' and 'the encourage-ment of the court had succeeded to that of the town'; and though our critic has no exact information as to when each play was com-posed, he thinks that their differences in quality could be 'in every instance' explained by the audience for which they were written—'whether . . . for the town or the court.'[91]

Besides the necessity for pleasing popular audiences, Shake-speare suffered under another disability which may serve to exten-uate his defects. He was an actor; and he presumably formed himself 'first upon the judgments of that body of men whereof he was a member.' And actors are not men of exact taste and learn-ing. 'They have ever had a standard to themselves upon other principles than those of Aristotle. As they live by the majority, they know no rule but that of pleasing the present humor and com-plying with the wit in fashion. . . .' They are 'just such judges of what is right as tailors are of what is graceful.' Shakespeare sac-rificed right judgment 'as a poet' to 'right judgment as a player.' He knew what would 'take,' what would be effective on the stage; and he was willing to achieve it at the risk of incorrectness.

[88] Nichol Smith, xviii.
[89] Saintsbury, II, 58.
[90] E-C, X, 537. It should be noted that Pope does not rest his defense on Shakespeare's ignorance of the rules. Rowe wrote: 'it would be hard to judge him by a law he knew nothing of' (Smith, 15). Pope's position is simply that Shakespeare complied with popular taste in allowing irregu-larity.
[91] E-C, X, 538.

Later in the Preface Pope returns to make some further remarks on the 'players.' He has been crediting them with the defective state of Shakespeare's text. Among other accusations, he suggests that where speeches seem put in the mouths of the wrong persons or 'the author now seems chargeable with making them speak out of character,' it is 'sometimes perhaps for no better reason than that a governing player, to have the mouthing of some favorite speech himself, would snatch it from the unworthy lips of an underling.'[92] He remarks upon their inferior social station: 'As then the best playhouses were inns and taverns (the Globe, the Hope, the Red Bull, the Fortune, etc.), so the top of the profession were then mere players, not gentlemen of the stage. They were led into the buttery by the steward, not placed at the lord's table or lady's toilette, and consequently were entirely deprived of those advantages which they now enjoy in the familiar conversation of our nobility and an intimacy (not to say dearness) with people of the first condition.'[93]

In the Epistle *To Augustus*, Pope acquiesced in the traditional view that 'fluent Shakespeare scarce effaced a line'; but the Preface lays it to the charge of the same careless men, the 'players.' By them it was considered a point to Shakespeare's credit, and accordingly they 'industriously propagated' it.[94] But to Pope 'there never was a more groundless report, or to the contrary of which there are more undeniable evidences.'[95] The instances Pope cites hardly prove his theory—all simply emphasizing the great variation between a pirated quarto and the complete text in the First Folio.

Another topic to which Shakespearean criticism with ardor addressed itself in the eighteenth century was that of the poet's learning. Did Shakespeare know and read Latin and Greek, French and Italian? The controversy was ended by the publication in 1767 of an amazingly thorough and brilliant piece of scholarship, the *Essay on the Learning of Shakespeare*, by Dr. Farmer, Fellow of Emmanuel College, Cambridge, which made it clear by the quotation of innumerable parallels that the poet had derived his classics from English translations and followed these blindly without consulting the original to avoid possible errors.[96]

[92] E-C, X, 546.
[93] Of course Pope does not distinguish between the earlier Elizabethan drama and the later development. By the turn of the century, actors and playwrights had come to be persons of station and repute. Marston, Beaumont and Fletcher, Tourneur, etc., were 'gentlemen.'
[94] E-C, X, 538.
[95] *ibid.*, 539.

But while a good deal of learning in Elizabethan literature was necessary to prove the point, Dr. Johnson's common sense anticipated Dr. Farmer's erudition: 'Some have imagined that they have discovered deep learning in many imitations of old writers; but the examples which I have known urged were drawn from books translated in his time, or were such easy coincidences of thought as will happen to all who consider the same subjects, or such remarks on life or axioms of morality as float in conversation and are transmitted through the world in proverbial sentences.'[97]

Pope as usual is cautious and guarded; 'But though he records the evidence brought forward by those who believed in Shakespeare's knowledge of the ancients, he does not fail to convey the impression that he belongs to the other party.'[98] And, indeed, in another passage of the Preface he says quite definitely that Shakespeare was 'without assistance or advice from the learned, as without the advantage of education or acquaintance among them, without that knowledge of the best models, the ancients, to inspire him with an emulation of them.'[99]

When controversialists discussed Shakespeare's learning they meant his acquaintance with the languages, Pope, however, chooses to import 'a vast difference between *learning* and *languages*. How far he was ignorant of the latter, I cannot determine; but 't is plain he had much reading at least, if they will not call it learning.'[100] He cannot see that it matters, 'if a man has knowledge, whether he has it from one language or another.'[101] And it is clear enough that Shakespeare 'had a taste of natural philosophy, mechanics, ancient and modern history, poetical learning, and mythology. We find him very knowing in the customs, rites, and manners of antiquity. In *Coriolanus* and *Julius Caesar*, not only the spirit but manners of the Romans are exactly drawn; and still a nicer

[96] The *Essay* is reprinted in Nichol Smith, 162-215.

[97] Smith, 135. Dr. Johnson's Preface to Shakespeare was first published in 1765.

[98] Smith, xxiii.

[99] E-C, X, 538.

[100] *ibid.*, 539.

[101] *ibid.*, 540. 'If we take the word *learning* in its large and liberal sense, and no longer reduce the question to a miserable pedantic wrangling over his more or less of Latin and Greek, then of all men that ever lived Shakespeare is one of the most learned.' Stapfer, 105. See also *ibid.*, 76-7, for a sympathetic development of Pope's distinction between *learning* and *languages*. 'Few men have been as learned as Goethe; few men have imbibed the Greek spirit and have understood it as he did, yet Goethe did not know Greek.'

distinction is shown between the manners of the Romans in the time of the former and of the latter.'[102] 'The manners of other nations in general, the Egyptians, Venetians, French, etc. are drawn with equal propriety.'

The extent of Shakespeare's learning is sketched. 'Whatever object of nature or branch of science he either speaks of or describes it is always with competent . . . knowledge. . . . When he treats of ethic or politic, we may constantly observe a wonderful justness of distinction as well as extent of comprehension.[103] No one is more a master of the poetical story or has more frequent allusions to the various parts of it.'[104]

Among authors, he seems to have known Ovid, translations from whom 'We have . . . published in his name, among those poems that pass as his.[105] He appears also to have been conversant in Plautus, from whom he has taken the plot of one of his plays; he follows the Greek authors, and particularly Dares Phrygius, in another[106] (although I will not pretend to say in what language he read them). The modern Italian writers of novels he was manifestly acquainted with;[107] and we may conclude him to be no less conversant with the ancients of his own country from the use he

---

[102] This is intended as a reply to the charges of Dennis and others. Dr. Johnson, in his Preface, tells us that Shakespeare's 'adherence to general nature has exposed him to the censure of critics who form their judgments upon narrower principles. Dennis and Rymer think his Romans not sufficiently Roman. . . . But Shakespeare always makes nature predominate over accident; and, if he preserves the essential character, is not very careful of distinctions superinduced and adventitious. His story requires Romans or kings, but he thinks only on men' (Smith, 117). Dr. Johnson's point of view is of course the one which has prevailed.

[103] Dryden says of Shakespeare and Homer that in them both 'We find all arts and sciences, all moral and natural philosophy, without knowing that they ever studied them' (Ker, II, 18).

[104] The 'poetical story' is classical mythology. For other instances of the use of this phrase and the similar 'poetic history' see Dr. Farmer's *Essay* (Smith, 184-5). Some critics had employed Shakespeare's frequent allusions to mythology as proof of his learning, though as Bishop Hurd sagely pointed out, 'They who are in such astonishment at the *learning* of Shakespeare forget that the pagan imagery was familiar to all the poets of his time, and that abundance of this sort of learning was to be picked up from almost every English book that he could take into his hands' (Smith, 185).

[105] 'The seventh or supplementary volume of Rowe's and Pope's editions contained, in addition to some poems by Marlowe, translations of Ovid by Thomas Heywood.' Translations of two of Ovid's Epistles were attributed to Shakespeare (*ibid.*, 312).

[106] *Troilus and Cressida*; see Smith, 187 and 312.

has made of Chaucer in *Troilus and Cressida* and in the *Two Noble Kinsmen*, if that play be his. . . .'[108]

But whether Shakespeare read these sources in the original or not, whether he had *languages* or only *reading*, Pope thinks the 'common opinion of his want of learning' proceeded not from any proof but from the assertions of actors and others who thought it redounded to Shakespeare's credit by enhancing his 'originality' and 'natural' genius,[109] or who wanted a neat antithesis between Jonson and Shakespeare and 'endeavored to exalt the one at the expense of the other. It is ever the nature of parties to be in extremes; and nothing is so probable as that because Ben Jonson had much the more learning it was said on the one hand that Shakespeare had none at all. . . .'[110]

And again, Pope believes that another cause for the *allegation* of a 'want of learning' was the 'many blunders and illiteracies of the first publishers of his [Shakespeare's] works. In these editions their ignorance shines in almost every page: nothing is more common than *Actus tertia*, *Exit omnes*, Enter three witches *solus*.[111] Their French is as bad as their Latin. . . . Their very Welsh is false.' There was much discussion in Pope's day, as ever since, of Shakespeare's anachronisms:[112] the abbess in the *Comedy of Errors*, the clock in *Julius Caesar*, pudding and pistols in *Pericles*. 'These faults,' says Dr. Johnson, 'Pope has endeavored, with more zeal than judgment, to transfer to his imagined interpolators': Pope had remarked, 'Nothing is more likely than that those palpable blunders of Hector's quoting Aristotle with others of that gross kind sprung from the same root [the 'blunders and illiteracies of the first publishers'].' The Doctor continues, 'We need not wonder to find Hector quoting Aristotle when we see the loves of Theseus and Hippolyta combined with the Gothic mythology of fairies. Shakespeare, indeed, was not the only violator of chronology, for in the same age Sidney, who wanted not the advantages of

[107] As Pope has indicated in his attributions of sources to the plays, which include Cinthio, Bandello, and Boccaccio. Of course Shakespeare read them in Painter's *Palace* and other English collections.

[108] E-C, X, 540-1. Pope did not include the *Two Noble Kinsmen* in his edition, but he tells us here that he thinks it 'has little resemblance of Fletcher and more of our author than some of those which have been received as genuine' (E-C, X, 541).

[109] E-C, X, 539.

[110] *ibid.*, 541.

[111] According to Steevens, 'This blunder appears to be of Mr. Pope's own invention' (Smith, 313).

[112] There is an excellent chapter devoted to the subject in Stapfer (107-26).

learning, has, in his *Arcadia*, confounded the pastoral with the feudal times. . . .'[113]

However Shakespeare's learning may be estimated, Pope does not think his faults are to be attributed to a want of it, for 'the most [of these] are not properly defects but superfoetations, and arise not from want of learning or reading but from want of thinking or judging—or rather, to be more just to our author, from a compliance to those wants in others.'[114]

Pope is willing to assign most of the faults which he has just mentioned, and which he has admirably characterized as faults of excess—a too abundant fancy—to Shakespeare's modest submission to the taste of others 'against his own better judgment.' Today the highly figurative style of Shakespeare, his resounding lines, his obscurity seem primarily characteristic of the man rather than the age. 'Most of the defects in his writings must be due,' thinks Bradley, 'to indifference or want of care.' But 'it seems hardly doubtful that his perception was sometimes at fault, and that, though he used the English language like no one else, he had not that *sureness* of taste in words which has been shown by some much smaller writers.'[115] Whether one agree with this judgment or not, there seems little reason for doubting that in matters of style Shakespeare chose his own way.

So much for a survey of the Preface. It is perhaps, all things considered, the best criticism Pope ever wrote. Dr. Johnson has done it an injustice in giving the impression that it is a mere expansion, even though achieved 'with great skill and elegance of the character which had been given of Shakespeare by Dryden,'[116] as one has only to compare the two to see. It was rather inspiration than information that Pope drew from the justly celebrated but brief passage in the *Essay of Dramatic Poesy*: Dryden had shown that a just appreciation of the surpassing greatness of Shakespeare could be combined with candid admission of his faults.

The tone of Pope's Preface is pitched higher than that of Dryden. In this, as in the Preface to Homer, the neo-classical poet displays the capacity for an almost ecstatic appreciation of great excellence very different from the sort he himself possessed. The power of judicial analysis displayed in frank discussion of the poet's faults is no greater than the power of warm acknowledgment of his merits. This singular balance with Pope, most of all the Augustans, preserved in his criticism did not interfere with the same final

[113] Smith, 124.
[114] E-C, X, 539.
[115] Bradley, 75.
[116] *Lives*, III, 139.

/

estimate of Shakespeare as that of the most fanatical of romanticists. Like Ben Jonson, Pope exalts the English playwright not
only above all his fellows but above the great Greek tragedians:
'he is justly and universally elevated above all other dramatic
writers.'[117]

After the rhapsodies of nineteenth century criticism we are
coming to take a more judicial view of Shakespeare, to feel that, as
Schücking says, his 'incomparable genius is rich enough to stand
in no need of borrowed renown.'[118] This faith will enable us to see
in the best of Augustan criticism of Shakespeare,—such prefatory
essays as those of Pope and Johnson—a synthesis of critical balance with genuine appreciation which illuminates and honors its
subject. Pope's Preface expresses the mind of a critic who was
thoroughly familiar with critical theory and standards and with
the great classical tradition, but who was, at the same time, able
and willing to deal justly with a great poet who cared little for
any of these things.

One feature of the edition we have been considering yet remains
for description. In the Preface, Pope wrote, 'Some of the most
shining passages [in the plays] are distinguished by commas in the
margin; and where the beauty lay not in particulars but in the
whole, a star is prefixed to the scene. This seems to me a shorter
and less ostentatious method of performing the better half of criticism—namely, the pointing out an author's excellencies—than to
fill a whole paper with citations of fine passages. . . .'[119] The collection and arrangement of these 'most shining passages' constitutes what we have good right to consider a neo-classical antecedent
of the Victorian *Beauties of Shakespeare* or *Elegant Extracts*.
Pope's selection should give us an insight into what he really found
to admire in the greatest of his predecessors.

Pope's Preface, like Johnson's, is a notable piece of literary catholicity. But the student of these two great critics will observe that
their principles are frequently chivalrously modern in advance of
their practice. They are philosophical in their generalities, but
pedantic in their application: it is as if speculation had exhausted
their generosity. One must be prepared for a considerable disparity
between the spirit of the *Essay on Criticism* and the Preface to
Shakespeare—a spirit large enough to include a surprising range

[117] E-C, X, 534.
[118] Schücking, 28.
[119] E-C, X, 548. The concluding slur seems to be directed at Gildon,
who in his seventh volume of the Rowe edition devoted a section to in-
dexing the more extended 'admired passages' and to quotation of the
shorter 'gems.'

of modern literature—and the more restricted and personal taste
exhibited in the choice of 'beauties.' With these cautions I proceed
to discuss the types of passages which appealed to Pope.

There is no evidence that he felt the music of Shakespeare's
verse. It is noticeable that the Preface, with all its range of topics,
says nothing of the dramatist's poetic style, if we except its regret
at the indulgences in 'false thoughts' and 'forced expressions.' The
free and flexible versification approaching an elegant conversa-
tional prose which grew upon Shakespeare can hardly be expected
to have pleased an ear trained on end-stopped lines and closed
couplets; and we know from notes to the plays and from the ruthless relegations to the bottom of the page as unworthy of
Shakespeare of passages in the Renaissance 'conceited' or metaphysical manner, the distaste of our Augustan for the 'heightened'
style of poetry. We should expect to find, however, some marked
passages in versification approaching Pope's own ideal of line
co-terminous with sense, or exemplifying the favorite rhetorical
device of parallelism. Such, though not in great abundance, there
are; and some would seem to have been chosen for that analogy alone. I cite five lines from the *Comedy of Errors*, Act II,
Scene 2:[120]

> The time was once when thou unurg'd wouldst vow
> That never words were music to thine ear,
> That never object pleasing in thine eye,
> That never touch well welcome to thy hand,
> That never meat sweet-savor'd in thy taste,
> Unless I spake, or look'd, or touch'd, or carv'd to thee.

and *Henry the Sixth*, Part III, Act IV, Scene 8.

> I have not stopp'd mine ears to their demands,
> Nor posted off their suits with slow delays;
> My pity hath been balm to heal their wounds,
> My mildness hath allay'd their swelling griefs,
> My mercy dried their water-flowing tears;
> I have not been desirous of their wealth:
> Nor much oppress'd them with great subsidies,
> Nor forward of revenge, though they much erred.

A portion of a speech of King Henry's from the same play, Act II,
Scene 5, has two very elaborate sets of variations on a constant

---

[120] For the reader's convenience, my references to the 'beauties' are
given according to the act and scene assignment of the modern editions,
not that of Pope's, which subdivides acts according to the classical use of
France—a new scene whenever one of the *dramatis personae* makes
entrance or exit.

phrase theme. An ingeniously elaborate parallelism between the
speeches of Troilus and Cressida in which each pledges constancy
may also have been approved for this 'regularity.'

From all the plays but two lyrics are marked. (Pope, it will be
remembered, did not include the sonnets and other non-dramatic
poems in his edition): the *Take, oh take those lips away*, from
Measure for Measure, and the *Fear no more the heat of th' sun*
from *Cymbeline*. One is disappointed at this almost total neglect
of the wealth of lovely songs, but perhaps one has no right to be
surprised that a poet who was not himself to any extent a practitioner of the lyric, and who flourished in the period of English
literary history when the form was most neglected, should want
the ear for these.

We turn now to categories of content. Pope had noted in his
Preface Shakespeare's 'power over our passions,' his command of
pathos, laughter and spleen. Though he seems not to labor in
preparation, 'the heart swells and the tears burst out, just at the
proper place'; yet 'he is not more a master of the *great* than of
the *ridiculous* in human nature; of our noblest tenderness, than
of our vainest foibles; of our strongest emotions, than of our
idlest sensations.' Pope's own verse, particularly in the so-called
romantic poems, shows him not devoid of pathos; and in Shakespeare he admires Constance's beautiful

> Grief fills the room up of my absent child
> Lies in his bed, walks up and down with me;
> Puts on his pretty looks, repeats his words.[121]

He marks, too, Tirrel's moving description of the death of the
Royal Babes in the Tower:

> girdling one another
> Within their alabaster innocent arms.
> Their lips were four red roses on a stalk
> Which in their summer beauty kiss'd each other.[122]

In *Cymbeline* he has marked the lengthy series of elegiac laments in
which Arviragus and Guiderius weep the supposed death of
Imogen; while in *Antony and Cleopatra* he admires the touching
abasement of Cleopatra's

> No more but a mere woman, and commanded
> By such poor passions as the maid that milks.[123]

[121] *King John*, Act III, Scene 4.
[122] *Richard* III, Act IV, Scene 3.
[123] Act IV, Scene 13.

and her last

                    peace, peace!
        Dost thou not see my baby at my breast
        That sucks the nurse asleep?[124]

As evidences of the comic powers of Shakespeare, Pope has cited
several addresses of Launce to his dog Crab in *Two Gentlemen of
Verona*, and all the important speeches of Falstaff in *Henry IV*,
Part I, a scanty but representative selection of the humor. The
comic wit of Shakespeare took expression in a fondness for punning and other varieties of verbal word-play which were repugnant
to Pope's taste, and of which he was disposed, when he had the
slightest pretext, to deny the authenticity.

But perhaps the spleen was a passion to which Pope was far
more susceptible than to the pathetic and the comic. A profound
vanity accentuated if not in part produced by the long disease of
his life, and constantly acerbated by controversy, could not but
find expression in ill-temper, melancholy, and cynicism. This ascending series was actuality as well as pose. Lowell has written of
that 'period of Pope's correspondence with his friends, when Swift,
his heart corroding with disappointed ambition at Dublin, Bolingbroke raising delusive turnips at his farm, and Pope, pretending
not to feel the lampoons which embittered his life, played together
the solemn farce of affecting indifference to the world by which it
would have agonized them to be forgotten.'[125] Pope has marked in
his Shakespeare the 'Tomorrow and tomorrow' which ends in 'a
tale told by an idiot, full of sound and fury signifying nothing'
and Macbeth's 'I gin to be a weary of the sun'; and the fool's reply
to Lear's 'Dost thou call me fool?' 'All men are fools'; and the
misogyny of Posthumus' 'We are bastards all' (*Cymbeline*, Act 2).
His love for *Measure for Measure* and *Timon of Athens* is striking, and in them his approving pencil has been enamored of black
melancholy, as, for example, when it marks the Duke's discourse
on the evils of life, beginning

            Reason thus with life:
        If I do lose thee, I do lose a thing
        That none but fools would keep.[126]

and Claudio's 'Ay, but to die and go we know not where,'[127]
Timon's *résumé* of his past to Apemantus,[128] and the entire solilo-

---

[124] Act V, Scene 2.
[125] *My Study Windows: Pope* (1871 ed., 408).
[126] *Measure for Measure*, Act III, Scene 1.
[127] *ibid.*, Act III, Scene 2.
[128] *Timon*, Act IV, Scene 3 (ll. 250-77).

quy of Timon in which he begs the earth henceforth to produce not men but beasts.[129]

Pope's characterization of Shakespeare's *sentiments* as 'the most pertinent and judicious upon every subject' will be recalled from the Preface, and so too the quaint Index of 'Thoughts.' The category under which by far the greatest number of marked passages may be listed is that of didactic utterance, ranging from the commonplace to what it is sometimes difficult to distinguish from it—the wisdom of the ages. 'Who steals my purse steals trash,' etc. would seem to be a commonplace; but in Polonius' *catena* of instruction there would seem to be more genuine wisdom than some critics and the current stage clowning of the part would allow. Without insisting on this distinction, I may cite here as other marked 'thoughts' Lorenzo's thesis[130] that since many fools have good memories, the memory is no distinguishing mark of the wise; and Macbeth on the misery of old age unaccompanied by friends.

In his index, Pope has a separate table for 'the most considerable speeches,' but the speeches marked are commonly what may be described as set pieces—rhetorical amplifications of a thought, poetical essays upon a theme. Of these marked set pieces, examples are the King's great speech on death in *Richard II*,[131] Portia on 'The quality of mercy,' the soliloquy on sleep in *Henry IV*, Part II,[132] the Agincourt exposure of .'Thou idol ceremony'[133] the rhetorical harangues of Wolsey against ambition ('Farewell, a long farewell to all my greatness,' and the 'Fling away ambition' speech which begins: 'And when I am forgotten as I shall be And sleep in dull cold marble'),[134] the Duke Vincentio on the evils of high position,[135] Leonato on No philosophy a match for grief,[136] and Timon's two long harangues against the *radix malorum*.[137] Among set pieces, oratorical efforts not so topical in character, Pope has approved the dissertations of Brutus and Antony over the body of Caesar, the dagger soliloquy in *Macbeth* and the king's prayer in *Hamlet*.

In description, another category allotted a separate compartment

129 *ibid.*, ll. 177-97.
130 *Merchant of Venice*, Act III, Scene 5.
131 Act III, Scene 2.
132 Act III, Scene 1.
133 *Henry V*, Act IV, Scene 1.
134 *Henry VIII*, Act III, Scene 2.
135 *Measure for Measure*, Act IV, Scene 1.
136 *Much Ado about Nothing*, Act V, Scene 1.
137 *Timon*, Act IV, Scene 3 (ll. 30-44).

in the index, Pope prefers the grim characterization and the sombre
scene. He likes the description of Pinch in the *Comedy of Errors*,
as 'a hungry lean-fac'd villain,

> A mere anatomy, a mountebank,
> A threadbare juggler, and a fortune-teller,
> A needy, hollow-ey'd, sharp-looking wretch,
> A living-dead man.[138]

and the similar but more extensive and better-known picture of the
apothecary in *Romeo and Juliet*; Ulysses' portrait of Cressida:

>   Fie, fie upon her!
> There's language in her eye, her cheek, her lip,
> Nay, her foot speaks; her wanton spirits look out
> At every joint and motive of her body.
> O! these encounterers, so glib of tongue
> That give a coasting welcome ere it comes,
> And wide unclasp the tables of their thoughts
> To every tickling reader. . . .[139]

He likes, in *Titus Andronicus*, the strange drab picture of

> A barren and detested vale . . .
> The trees, though summer, yet forlorn and lean,
> O'ercome with moss and baleful mistletoe:
> Here never shines the sun; here nothing breeds
> Unless the nightly owl or fatal raven. . . .[140]

He likes the dizzy view from Dover Cliff.

The Augustan school in its revolt against the extravagant metaphor, the conceit, witnessed by such documents as the *Essay on
Criticism*, did not go to the extreme of dispensing with the similes
which arose naturally from the subject and had the authority of
Homer and Virgil behind them. The before-mentioned index has a
section of similes, and in *Titus Andronicus* and *Troilus* as well as
in more frequented sources Pope has marked some of these. I will
give three of the approved similes in *Titus*.

> Upon his bloody finger he doth wear
> A precious ring, that lightens all the hole,
> Which, like a taper in some monument,
> Doth shine upon the dead man's earthly cheeks,
> And shows the ragged entrails of the pit.[141]

---

[138] Act V, Scene 1.
[139] *Troilus and Cressida*, Act IV, Scene 5.
[140] Act II, Scene 3.
[141] Act II, Scene 3.

> For now I stand as one upon a rock
> Environ'd with a wilderness of sea,
> Who marks the waxing tide grow wave by wave
> Expecting ever when some envious surge
> Will in his brinish bowels swallow him.[142]
>
>   Why dost not speak to me?
> Alas! a crimson river of warm blood,
> Like to a bubbling fountain stirr'd with wind
> Doth rise and fall between thy rosed lips
> Coming and going with thy honey breath.[143]

We should not expect, in spite of the melodramatic sensibility of the *Eloisa to Abelard*, and the *Elegy*, that Pope would admire many of the characteristically romantic 'beauties' of Shakespeare, nor does he. He does not give us the

>   wild dedication of yourselves
> To unpath'd waters, undream'd shores

nor 'the poet's eye in a fine frenzy rolling' (which Warburton added in his accretionary markings[144]). We are surprised, though pleased, when he gives us Prospero's

>   We are such stuff
> As dreams are made on

and Prospero's dismissal of his fairy servants when he decides

>   I'll break my staff,
> Bury it certain fathoms in the earth,
> And deeper than did ever plummet sound
> I'll drown my book.[145]

the harmony of moonlight and music in the fifth act of the *Merchant of Venice*, the dialogue of Romeo and Juliet at the chamber window in Act III, and Juliet's soliloquy before drinking the potion. We should, I think, be less surprised that the inventor of the Rosicrucian 'machines' in the *Rape of the Lock* was an admirer of Mercutio's inspired anatomy of the high state of Queen Mab and her descents into mischief.[146]

The pastoral motif was common to Elizabethan and classical

[142] Act III, Scene 1.

[143] Act II, Scene 4.

[144] In the Preface to his edition (1747), Warburton tells us that 'the most beautiful passages [are] distinguished, as in his [Pope's] book with inverted commas. In imitation of him, I have done the same by as many others as I thought most deserving of the reader's attention, and have marked them with double commas.'

[145] *Tempest*, Act V, Scene 1 (ll. 33-50).

[146] *Romeo and Juliet*, Act I, Scene 4.

literature. If in Virgil and Mantuan and Sannazaro country scenes and country people have become a conventional device for conveying sentiments and personalities far from rustic, the Elizabethans for the most part shared the position that rusticities are not of interest in themselves but as background and vehicle for city persons of exalted station. In Shakespeare, with all his gift for the sympathetic description of nature—flowers in particular, no play has the country life of country people as its theme. In the *Winter's Tale* and *Cymbeline* and *As You Like It*, we have no serious studies of peasant life such as a Hardy or a T. F. Powys gives us, but ever so delicate and humanized examples of the conventional pastoral.

This urban illusion, this idyllic depiction of the simple life continued to be attractive into the Augustan Period—indeed, was only permanently dispelled by the realism of Crabbe, though it was caricatured by Gay in his *Shepherd's Week*. Pope himself wrote four graceful pastorals; he studied and enjoyed the Italian pastoralists of the Renaissance; and in his estate at Twickenham, in his garden and his grotto, he tasted the pleasures of the convention for himself. It is not strange, then, that we find him marking the King's soliloquy on the pleasures of the pastoral life in *Henry VI*, Part III,[147] and the speech of Bellarius which contrasts with the city and its vices the charms and the innocencies of country life;[148] or that *As You Like It* was a favorite play with him.

This graceful romantic comedy of the adventures and the meditations of a company of noble Brook Farmers I shall take as a concrete illustration of the foregoing topical arrangement of the subject, and from it shall cite, with a word of comment, each of the marked passages.

First comes the Duke's speech which opens Act II, with its contrast of the 'painted pomp' of the 'envious court' and the 'sweet' life of the Forest; ending with the sermonic 'Sweet are the uses of adversity' and the life exempt from public haunt which

> Finds tongues in trees, books in the running brooks,
> Sermons in stones and good in everything.'[149]

The Duke's optimism, as well as his sententiousness, was echoed in the *Essay on Man*, for Pope, who found particulars so disheartening, was blandly optimistic about the whole. Next comes Adam's picture of cheerful old age relying upon the divine providence and

---

[147] Act II, Scene 5.
[148] *Cymbeline*, Act III, Scene 3.
[149] Act II, Scene 1.

total abstinence, a set moral speech which Orlando is prompt to commend.

Silvius' rebuke to Corin[150] falls into a series of three neat parallel conditions with refrain:

> If thou remember'st not the slightest folly
> That ever love did make thee run into,
> Thou hast not lov'd:
> Or if thou hast not sat as I do now
> Wearing thy hearer with thy mistress' praise
> Thou hast not lov'd:
> Or if thou has not broke from company
> Abruptly, as my passion now makes me,
> Thou hast not lov'd.

Then comes Jaques' melancholy recital of the fool's reduction of life to the decadent succession of the hours:

> And so, from hour to hour we ripe and ripe,
> And then from hour to hour we rot and rot
> And thereby hangs a tale.[151]

Orlando's

>   But whate'er you are
> That in this desert inaccessible

consists largely of a series of parallelisms:

> If ever you have looked on better days,
> If ever been where bells have knoll'd to church,
> If ever sat at any good man's feast,
> If ever from your eyelids wip'd a tear.[152]

Jaques' The Seven Ages of Man[153] is, of course, one of the best set pieces in Shakespeare, full of psychology and pointed description such as Pope could both appreciate and himself perform. In his *Essay on Man* he played his own variations on the theme of 'one man in his time plays many parts,' and in this famous passage concluding 'And beads and prayer books are the toys of age' gave expression to the futility of life with a disillusionment which Jaques does not equal.

In Act III, Scene 2, Corin's brief prose 'Sir, I am a true laborer: I earn that I eat, get that I wear, owe no man hate, envy no man's happiness, glad of other men's good, content with my harm' is a sturdy declaration of independence which reminds one of Pope's own similar pronouncements and no doubt so reminded him.

---

[150] Act II, Scene 4.   [152] *ibid.*
[151] Act III, Scene 7.   [153] *ibid.*

Next comes a bit of graceful description—not a play upon words but a discrimination:

> There was a pretty redness in his lip,
> A little riper and more lusty red
> Than that mix'd in his cheek; 'twas just the difference
> Betwixt the constant red and mingled damask.[154]

And then a delightfully spirited anticipation of the humors of Millamant expressed in crisp parallelisms: 'No, no, Orlando; men are April when they woo, December when they are wed: maids are May when they are maids, but the sky changes when they are wives. I will be more jealous than a Barbary cock-pigeon over his hen; more clamorous than a parrot against rain; more new-fangled than an ape; more giddy in my desires than a monkey: I will weep for nothing, like Diana in the fountain, and I will do that when you are disposed to be merry; I will laugh like a hyen, and that when you are inclined to sleep.'[155]

There is a brief account of Cupid, 'that same wicked bastard of Venus,' which Rosalind gives a little later in the same scene. Then comes, Act IV, Scene 3, a long, strange passage of sombre, meagre description: Orlando's brother is lying under a decadent oak, a snake about his neck, a 'lioness with udders all drawn dry' couched by him:

> Under an oak, whose boughs were mossed with age
> And high top bald with dry antiquity,
> A wretched, ragged man, o'ergrown with hair,
> Lay sleeping on his back.

In Act V, Scene 2, Pope has marked three passages from an elaborate but regular dialogue in which Phebe, Silvius, Orlando, and Rosalind engage. The voices weave a pattern like a madrigal.

> Phe. Good Shepherd, tell this youth what 'tis to love.
> Sil. It is to be made of sighs and tears:
>   And so I am for Phebe.
> Phe. And I for Ganymede.
> Orl. And I for Rosalind.
> Ros. And I for no woman.
> Sil. It is to be all made of faith and service:
>   And so am I for Phebe.
> Phe. And I for Ganymede.
> Orl. And I for Rosalind.
> Ros. And I for no woman.

[154] Act III, Scene 5.
[155] Act IV, Scene 1.

And to conclude with, we have a brisk set of parallelisms in prose from Touchstone :

> 'I have trod a measure; I have flattered a lady; I
> have been politic with my friend; smooth with my
> enemy; I have undone three tailors; I have had
> four quarrels and like to have fought one.'[156]

Though Pope does not profess to have marked *all* the 'beauties' of the plays, it may interest to learn from which plays he quotes most and from which least. Those in which ten or more speeches or parts of speeches are checked are *Troilus and Cressida*, *Timon of Athens*, *Cymbeline*, *Julius Caesar*, *Romeo and Juliet*, *As You Like it*, and *Macbeth*. To venture a word of explanation on the secondary plays—the passages from *Timon* are almost entirely from the fourth act, which consists of a succession of sententious and misanthropic speeches; the passages from *Troilus* consists largely of short generalizations or generalization and illustrative similes. There are but two passages cited from *Winter's Tale*, one from *Twelfth Night*, three and an entire scene from *Othello*, but two each from *Hamlet* and *King Lear*. Of these *lacunae* I can offer no explanation : there is some charming pastoralism in the *Winter's Tale* which ought to have appealed; and as for sententiousness and sententious melancholy it would seem that for these there was God's plenty in *Hamlet*.

Every man hears only what he understands, said Goethe. Of course, Pope did not escape from this limitation. He was a man of his time; and in addition his ideas and his education derived from an alien literary tradition with its own sharply defined requirements. In his critical principles he shows a considerable emancipation, and in particular appreciations we have found him now and then admiring the 'beauties' of another temper and another school. But in the main his appreciations seize upon what in Shakespeare was most akin in spirit to the eighteenth century, not his rhapsody but his reason; not his lyric or dramatic art or his characterizations, but his 'judicious' sentiments, his humanism, his wisdom, in the verse, not upon his songs but upon his occasional balance and parallelism and antithesis. There is not the time for a defense of eighteenth century choice and eighteenth century limitation, were a defense in order. I shall content myself with remarking that, though Shakespeare is indeed not for an age but for all time, each age must necessarily perhaps focus its attention predominantly upon a particular aspect. The nineteenth century was interested in

[156] Act V, Scene 4.

the characters of Shakespeare; the twentieth century is studying the dramatic technique of Shakespeare in itself and in relation to the technique of contemporaries. and predecessors. And the eighteenth century came to Shakespeare as to a treasury of human wisdom. Each of these must be regarded as a valid approach.

CHAPTER V

POPE AND THE DUNCES

THE War of the Dunces has long since been dismissed to the dusty oblivion of other literary wars; its occasional resurrection only bears evidence to the enduring interest of a great, savage satire which pursued a host of minor men of letters. The *Dunciad* is a museum of specimens: under glass cases, securely lodged for such eternity as the classics can ensure, lie empaled the victims.

> 'Pretty! in amber to observe the forms
> Of hairs, or straws, or dirt, or grubs, or worms,'[1]

The unfortunate were not nonentities: 'the charge that the men satirized in the *Dunciad* were really dunces becomes particularly absurd the moment we turn our attention away from literature proper. No small number of those whose names appear in this poem had attained prominence in occupations in which dulness may be considered an absolute barrier to success.'[2] But none of them were great poets; and, as Pope told Spence, 'Middling poets are no poets at all.' None except Defoe were great writers of prose. It was certainly possible for Pope, in whom the faculty common to humankind of believing what one chooses to believe was so strong, to suppose that artistic and critical zeal prompted his war against mediocrity. And it is certainly true that the personal grievances, the affronts, real and fancied, which suggested revenge, did not dull Pope's critical faculty. As there is a type of insight which springs from love and devotion, so there is another which is the issue of malice. Part of the truth about us is known only to our enemies.

Hence there is no reason to discount in advance the value of criticism which, it is to be admitted, cannot pretend to precise impartiality, to freedom from all save aesthetic criteria. The chief objection to the *Dunciad* is simply to the futility of so carefully

---

[1] *Epistle to Dr. Arbuthnot*, 169-70.
[2] Lounsbury, 268.

devised an attack on ephemeral mediocrities who survive only in
the dubious immortality of lampoon. 'Take care,' wrote Swift to
the persecutor, 'the bad poets do not outwit you, as they have the
good ones in every age, whom they have provoked to transmit their
names to posterity. Maevius is as well known as Virgil, and
Gildon will be as well known as you if his name gets into your
verses.'[3] A satire, however great, suffers with posterity if its subjects are so obscure, so strictly contemporary in interest, that the
text must trickle through spacious margins of annotation. The
Dunciad and its companion works conceal what is a real universality of appeal under a specious concreteness. The present chapter is
mainly concerned with the larger aspects of the satire.

Though the first version of the *Dunciad* did not appear until
May 1728, projects of a similar nature had long been in Pope's
mind. Contemporaries charged the poem with being a metamor-
phosis of an earlier satire entitled the *Progress of Dulness*.[4] There
were various preliminary studies. Before the dispersal of the club
including 'some of the greatest wits of the age,' Swift, Arbuthnot,
and Pope together composed the first book of the *Memoirs of
Martinus Scriblerus*,[5] which recounts, in a vigorous and vivacious
prose suggestive of Swift, Sterne, and Rabelais in mixture, the
education of the hero-pedant.[6] The work was never completed; and
the accomplished section was not published until much later;[7] but
from hints in this germinal work sprang the treatise on *bathos*,
Gulliver's Travels, and the *Dunciad*.

A suggestion in one of the notes to the *Dunciad* that the poem
was six years in preparation was indignantly repudiated by Pope
as ironical, but the materials were certainly accumulated over a
period of years. Some of the attacks on the poets for which the
culprits were sentenced to exposure had been made as far back as
the *Essay on Criticism*. With all his consciousness of power and
station, and his boasted lofty purposes, Pope was desirous, as the
time for the publication of the *Dunciad* drew near, to make it in
every way appear as if his satire were done only in self-defense
against the constant assaults upon him of the jealous 'dunces.'
Accordingly, he exercised himself to provoke assault:[8] he printed

[3] E-C, VII, 64.
[4] *ibid.*, IV, 7.
[5] *ibid.*, X, 272.
[6] Probably drawn from Bentley.
[7] First included in the octavo edition of Pope's works, 1742.
[8] E-C, V, 213-15.

in the third and last volume of the Miscellanies got out by him in collaboration with Swift in March, 1728, the prose work entitled *A Discourse on the Profund, or the Art of Sinking in Poetry*.[9] This is, as the name implies, a burlesque inversion of the celebrated treatise of 'Longinus on the Sublime.' *Bathos*, a word apparently never before employed in its current sense, and originating in a misprint in an edition of Longinus for *pathos*,[10] was rendered in English by *profund*—there was a differentiation of spelling in the first edition, but not consistently thereafter—a word intended as an antonym for sublime. While no close parallel to 'Longinus' is attempted, there is a general similarity, particularly in the emphasis laid in each upon the formal figures of rhetoric, and occasionally parody of a particular sentence.

The tone of Pope's treatise is throughout ironic. He professes himself to be of the noble company of batheticians about whom he writes, and for whose instruction he professes to systematize into a critical manual the practice of earlier great masters of the *bathos*. He begins by metaphorizing the present state of things literary under a figure somewhat resembling that used by Swift in his *Battle of the Books*. The mountains are the home of the great poets who write for the taste of the discriminating few; in the lowlands resides the multitude of bad writers who please the common herd.[11] Taste, like virtue, requiring a vigilant struggle against the propensities of the natural man, humanity tends irresistibly downward. 'It is with great pleasure I have observed of late the gradual decay of delicacy and refinement among mankind, who are become too reasonable to require that we should labor with infinite pains to come to the taste of these mountaineers, when they without any may condescend to ours.'[12] So easy, so normal to undisciplined humanity is the descent (*Facilis descensus Averni*) that without the guide of ancient rule and practice the writers of the mountain—'had it not been for that mistaken opinion they all entertained that the rules of the ancients were equally necessary to the moderns'—would surely have descended. Indeed, goes on the critic, 'when any of these have gone so far as by the light of their own genius to attempt new models, it is wonderful how nearly they have approached us in those particular pieces, though in their others they differed *toto coelo* from us.'[13] After all, goes on the irony, since *bathos* is the natural taste of man and particularly

[9] For the evidence in favor of Pope's authorship of the *Art of Sinking* see E-C, VIII, 159, n.

[10] *ibid.*, X, 344, n.
[11] E-C, X, 345-6.

[12] *ibid.*, 346.
[13] E-C, X, 347.

of the present age, and since poetry is to divert and instruct, should one not prefer that which diverts and instructs the greatest number? ' 'Tis a fruitless undertaking to write for men of a nice and foppish *gusto*,[14] whom, after all, it is almost impossible to please; and it is still more chimerical to write for posterity, of whose taste we cannot judge and whose applause we can never enjoy.'[15]

In Chapter Four, Pope asserts that as there is an art of the sublime so there is an art of the *profund*, and proceeds to analyze that art. As the true sublime is above the common, so the *profund* is below it. Nature's sublime is sky, sun, moon; her *profund*, gold and pearls; her middle, corn, flowers, animals, 'of mean price, and so common as not to be greatly esteemed by the curious; it being certain that any thing of which we know the true use cannot be invaluable; which affords a solution why common sense hath either been totally despised or held in small repute of the greatest modern critics and authors.'[16] This common sense, as much above the low as beneath the great, must accordingly be eschewed by true batheticians, for common sense is the avowed foe of the fine conceits and figures so dear to the heart of poetasters. One remembers the classical injunction to 'follow nature' and the far-flown comparisons of the 'metaphysical' school as the background for the injunction Pope next lays upon the bathetic poet. 'He must acquire' a most happy uncommon, unaccountable way of thinking. He may not imitate the regularities of Nature or make uniform designs, but must mingle *genres*, his end being 'to glare by strong opposition of colors and contrariety of images.'[17] He will achieve the surprising by 'contradicting common opinion.' He will affect the marvellous: 'draw Achilles with the patience of Job; a prince talking like a jack-pudding; a footman speaking like a philosopher; and a fine gentleman like a scholar.'[18] The world is weary of natural things. It loves the relief of conjurers who can turn a coach into a wheelbarrow and tumblers who invert head and heels. This 'happy and anti-natural way of thinking' masters of the *bathos* ought to command. They ought to be able to find comparisons beneath the object, as Blackmore did when he compared the sky to a blue lustring or a child's mantle, and likened God to a painter, a chemist, a wrestler, a recruiting officer, a guarantee, an

[14] A nice example of the word in its now obsolete sense of taste.
[15] E-C, X, 348.
[16] *ibid.*, 353.
[17] E-C, X, 354.
[18] *ibid.*, 355.

attorney, a goldbeater, a fuller, a mercer, a butler, and a baker.[19]
Several Kinds of Genius in the Profund divides the bad poets
into nine classes, each typified by some grotesque variety of 'animated nature.' To the generic titles were annexed initials which
were, it was pretended, chosen at random: in point of fact, they
happened to be the initials of real people who had displeased Pope;
and thanks to the industry of Professor Courthope, they have all
been identified.[20] It was probably for this chapter and these allegedly random initials that the treatise was written. The Flying
Fish are those who now and then fly out of the *profund* (Stepney,
Hill, Gildon);[21] the Swallows skim and flutter up and down but
expend their energy only in catching flies (Theobald, Pulteney(?),
Lord Hervey);[22] the Ostriches are too heavy to fly, but run very
fast on foot (Daniel Defoe, Eusden, Hon. E. Howard);[23] the
Parrots are the plagiarizers and imitators who repeat the words of
others in a hoarse odd voice (Broome, Cibber, Dean Daniel);[24] the
Didappers are usually under water but come up now and then
when you least expect them (Welsted, Duckett, Yonge);[25] the
Porpoises, shapeless, ugly monsters, put all their number in tur-
moil by their unwieldy size (Dennis, Gildon, Oldmixon);[26] the

[19] E-C, X, 355-9.

[20] *ibid.*, 361-2, notes.

[21] George Stepney (1663-1707) contributed to Dryden's *Miscellany Poems* and his translation of Juvenal. Aaron Hill (1685-1750), dramatist, was in later years friend and correspondent of Pope's. Charles Gildon (1665-1724) was the author of several books of neo-classical criticism, especially *The Art of Poetry.*

[22] William Pulteney afterwards became Earl of Bath. Baron Hervey (1696-1743) was satirized by Pope as 'Lord Fanny' and 'Sporus' (*Epistle to Dr. Arbuthnot*).

[23] Lawrence Eusden (1688-1730) was made poet-laureate in 1718. Edward Howard (*floruit* 1669), a dramatist, was ridiculed in Bucking-ham's *Rehearsal.*

[24] Wm. Broome (1689-1745) collaborated with Pope and Fenton in translating the *Odyssey.* Dr. Daniel, dean of Armagh, was detested by Dean Swift, who called him 'a damnable poet, and consequently a public enemy to mankind' (Swift to Pope, March 6, 1728-1729).

[25] Leonard Welsted (1688-1747), a Cambridge graduate, translated 'Longinus on the Sublime.' George Duckett (d. 1732) was co-author with Burnet of *Homerides* and co-author with Dennis of *Pope Alexander's Supremacy and Infallibility Examined* (1729). Sir William Yonge, the 'Sir Billy' of the *Essay on Man* (IV, 278), was a place-hunting courtier.

[26] John Dennis (1657-1734) attacked Pope's *Essay on Criticism* and his Homer. John Oldmixon (1673-1742) was historian, pamphleteer, and literary critic.

Frogs neither walk nor fly but leap and bound into admiration: they lie in the bottom of the ditch, and make a great noise upon emergence; the Eels are obscure authors wrapped in their own mud, mighty nimble and pert (Welsted, Theobald, Motteux, Gen. Codrington);[27] and the Tortoises are low and chill and fond of gardens; their fine shell has a heavy lump under it (Philips, Broome, Eusden, and Selkirk).[28]

The Profund Consisting in the Circumstances, and of Amplification in General advises bathetic writers to choose such circumstances as will elevate their subject: 'far-fetched, unexpected, hardly compatible'; such will 'surprise prodigiously.' And they must be prolix—exhibit the selected image under its every aspect: 'choice and distinction' not only curb the spirit but 'lessen the book.'[29] The bathetic virtue of amplification is defined as 'making the most of a thought'; metaphorized as 'the spinning wheel of the Bathos, which draws out and spreads it in the finest thread';[30] and amusingly illustrated by examples from the epics of Blackmore. One of these is an expansion of the verse in the 104th Psalm, 'He looks on the earth, and it trembles; He touches the hills, and they smoke' into—

> The hills forget they're fixed, and in their fright
> Cast off their weight, and ease themselves for flight.
> The woods, with terror winged, outfly the wind,
> And leave the heavy, panting hills behind.

Pope contributes an 'appreciative' analysis: 'You see here the hills not only trembling, but shaking off the woods from their backs, to run the faster. After this, you are presented with a foot-race of mountains and woods, where the woods distance the mountains that, like corpulent, pursy fellows, come puffing and panting a vast way behind them.'[31]

Chapter Nine proclaims the duty of imitation. True authors of the *profund* are diligent to copy examples 'in their own way.'[32]

---

[27] Peter Motteux (1660-1718) translated Rabelais and *Don Quixote*. I am unable to identify General Codrington.

[28] Charles Hamilton, Earl of Selkirk, is the 'Harpax' of Pope's Third Epistle.

[29] E-C, X, 266.

[30] *ibid.*, 268.

[31] *ibid.*, 269.

[32] It should be observed that Pope is not attacking 'imitation' in this mock-advice: he is simply making a humorously logical application of the doctrine. Good poets have their models and 'originals' as have bad ones.

Defoe was the poetical son of Withers, Tate of Ogilby,[33] and Eusden of Blackmore; 'therefore when we sit down to write, let us bring some great author to our mind, and ask ourselves this question: How would Sir Richard have said this? Do I express myself as simply as Ambrose Philips?[34] Or flow my numbers with the quiet thoughtlessness of Mr. Welsted?'[35] In this amusing series of interrogatories Pope is parodying Longinus, who asks in the fourteenth section of his treatise: 'How would Homer, Plato, or Demosthenes have expressed themselves on this subject?' The bathetician is also to read the *sublime* authors (Shakespeare, Milton, Dryden), but only for the purpose of 'burying their gold in his own dunghill.' 'The book of *Job* is acknowledged to be infinitely sublime, and yet has not the father of the Bathos reduced it in every page?'[36] There are two kinds of imitation: forcing to our own purpose the thoughts of another, and 'copying the blemishes of celebrated authors.'[37] As instances of this latter type of imitation, Pope cites a play 'professedly writ in the style of Shakespeare,[38] where the resemblance lay in one single line: "And so good morrow to ye, good master Lieutenant"; and poems in imitation of Milton' 'where with the utmost exactness, and not so much as one exception, *nevertheless* was constantly *nathless, embroidered* was *broider'd, hermits* were *eremites,' 'sweet, dulcet, orchards, orchats.'*[39]

We pass now to two long and full chapters on Tropes, or figures of speech, in which each type is illustrated by ludicrous instances from contemporary poets. I give one section for its realistic reference to the popular stage: *Catachresis:—'Mow the beard, Shave the grass, Pin the plank, Nail my sleeve;* From whence results the same kind of pleasure to the mind as to the eye when we behold Harlequin trimming himself with a hatchet, hewing down a tree

---

[33] George Wither (1588-1677) was called by Denham 'the worst poet in England.' Nahum Tate (1652-1715) collaborated with Brady in versifying the Psalms. John Ogilby (1600-1676) translated both Virgil and Homer. The latter was an early favorite with Pope (Spence, 276).

[34] Ambrose Philips (1671-1749) published his *Pastorals* almost simultaneously with Pope's. See Pope's gibes at Philips' 'beautiful rusticity' in his *Guardian* essay, no. 40 (E-C, X, 507-14).

[35] E-C, X, 370.

[36] *ibid.*, 371.

[37] *ibid.*, 372.

[38] Rowe's *Lady Jane Grey.*

[39] 'He alluded particularly to [John] Philips' *Cyder*, of which he often expressed a strong disapprobation. . . .' Warton, ed. *Works of Pope*, VI, 230, n.

with a razor, making his tea in a cauldron, and brewing his ale in a teapot, to the incredible satisfaction of the British spectator.'[40] Of *Aposiopesis* Pope says, 'An excellent figure for the ignorant; as, "What shall I say?" when I have nothing to say.'[41] He draws instances of *Anticlimax* from Dennis:

> Nor Art nor Nature has the force
> To stop its steady course,
> Nor Alps nor Pyrenaeans keep it out
> Nor fortified redoubt.[42]

and from 'everlasting' Blackmore, who compared the tempestuous ocean to a pot of boiling ointment. Of the *Infantine* he says: 'This is when a poet grows so very simple as to think and talk like a child'; and with the remark, 'I shall take my examples from the greatest master in this way' he quotes from Ambrose Philips, such gems as 'Teach me to grieve with bleating moan, my sheep.'[43] Warton thinks the instances of *Redundancy*, such as 'the umbrageous shadow and the verdant green,' were intended to hit Thomson.[44]

The great Addison furnishes an example of *tautology* in a line from the *Campaign*, 'Break thro' the billows—and divide the main.'[45] One fancies that Pope particularly enjoyed the insertion into his *expurgatorius* of four or five blunders in syntax from the rival translation of Homer, published under the name of Tickell; and dexterous use of the relative pronoun implies that he attributed the real authorship of this vexing work to Addison.[46]

Under *How to Make Dedications, Panegyrics, or Satires*, Pope attacks the adulation of the mighty practised by denizens of Grub Street. With heavy irony, he points out that for purposes of panegyric, all ministers and noblemen are virtuous: the office itself implies and confers the virtue. On the other hand, satire finds a fitting subject in whoever has lost his office and, with it, the virtue it automatically bestows.[47]

Chapter Fifteen, *A Receipt to Make an Epic Poem*, appeared first in the *Guardian* of June 10, 1713. Warton finds in this a 'severe

---

[40] E-C, X, 375.
[41] *ibid.*, 376.
[42] *ibid.*, 381-2.
[43] *ibid.*, 383.
[44] *ibid.*, 385 and n. Pope told Spence (*Anecdotes*, 139) that 'It is a great fault in descriptive poetry to describe everything,' and added, 'That is the fault in Thomson's *Seasons*.'
[45] E-C, X, 385-6.
[46] *ibid.*, 387-8.
[47] *ibid.*, 398-400.

animadversion' on Le Bossu, especially for imagining that Homer and Virgil first fixed on a moral truth or axiom and then added a fable or story;[48] but he is mistaken, for in the Prefaces to Homer, Pope has expressly recommended Le Bossu's treatise and doctrine.[49] It is not the doctrine but the abuse and mechanical application of it which is satirized. The 'receipt' commences with the 'comfortable words' that epic poems, 'the greatest work human nature is capable of,' may be made without genius, or even learning.[50] It proceeds with direction as to the selection and arrangement of the 'fable.' One is to draw from any old poem, history, romance, or legend, such as *Geoffrey of Monmouth* or *Don Belianis of Greece*, those parts that are suited to long description, throwing all the adventures one fancies into one tale. For episodes one may use any material absolutely void of connection with the hero. As for this just-named adjunct to any properly made epic, Pope instructs us to choose him for the sound of his name; to make him work for twelve books; and then to let him off with conquest over his enemies, or marriage. For his proper constitution, one is to take all the good qualities attributed to the epic heroes of antiquity, and 'if they will not be reduced to a consistency, lay them all on a heap upon him,' making sure all the while that they are the virtues which one's own patron professes. Of those important elements, the moral and allegory, the advice is, 'extract out of the fable afterwards at your leisure.[51] Be sure you strain them sufficiently.' One is eclectic in his choice of machines: he takes his gods from Homer, his devils from Milton, and his spirits from Tasso. As to their proper use—'When you cannot extricate your hero by any human means or by your own wit, seek help from Heaven, and the gods will do your business very readily.'[52] Of the ready-made recipes for epic descrip-

[48] *Works of Pope*, ed. Warton, VI, 267, n.

[49] The Preface to the *Iliad* advises the reader to turn to 'Bossu's admirable treatise of the Epic Poem' for 'the justest notion of his [Homer's] design and conduct' (Durham, 349). A rather full abstract of the *Traité du Poème Épique* was prefixed to the translation of the *Odyssey*.

[50] Pope himself is popularly supposed to have held that 'the rules' were sufficient to make a poet, but of course neither he nor less liberal contemporaries actually held any such view. 'That there was in this period any critic of importance who actually believed that one could make a poet by teaching rules, or that art could replace genius, or any such silly stuff, I emphatically deny' (Durham, xvi).

[51] E-C, X, 402. Le Bossu is not satirized here: according to that estimable critic, one should form the moral and allegory of one's epic before devising the 'fable.'

[52] *ibid.*, 403.

tions, I cite that for a Tempest: 'Take Eurus, Zephyr, Auster and Boreas, and cast them together in one verse: add to these of rain and lightning and thunder (the loudest you can) *quantum sufficit*; mix your clouds and billows well together till they foam, and thicken your description here and there with a quicksand. Brew your tempest well in your head before you set it ablowing.'[53]

The *Art of Sinking* ends with a satirical *Project for the Advancement of the Stage*, against which Pope is thought to have borne a grudge ever after the failure of his (and Gay's) *Three Hours after Marriage*. Colley Cibber, later hero of the *Dunciad*, incurs here the title of master of *bathos* in recognition of his capacity of theatrical manager.

I have already mentioned the interspersion throughout the treatise of specimens of contemporary *bathos*. Some of these are listed as anonymous; but Warton tells us that many of these were drawn from Pope's own early works, particularly from his epic, the *Alcander*: 'So sensible of its own errors and imperfections is a mind truly great.'[54] Fourteen other poets are represented, including the revered Waller and the soon-to-be-celebrated Theobald. But by far the greatest number of absurdities are drawn from Sir Richard Blackmore[55] and Ambrose Philips.[56] The latter's offense has already been mentioned. Sir Richard, now nearing his grave, had bitterly antagonized both Swift and Pope by denouncing the irreligious character of the *Tale of a Tub* and of a travesty of the First Psalm attributed to Pope. That denunciation, though made half a score of years before, was enough to have justified his fate; but, in addition, Blackmore was a really atrocious poet, a prolix physician who poetized to while the time away; and neither Professor Saintsbury, who can find some good in nearly every poet, nor Professor Lounsbury, who is disposed to think well of all whom Pope attacked, has attempted to rehabilitate him. He was the unaided author of six epic poems, *Prince* and *King Arthur* (twenty books), *Alfred* (twelve), *Eliza* (ten), *The Creation* (seven), *The Redeemer* (six), and *Job* (in folio), the badness of which the forty-three specimens in the *Bathos* sufficiently attest.[57]

---

[53] E-C, X, 403-4.
[54] *Works of Pope*, ed. Warton, VI, 219, n.
[55] Forty-three in number.
[56] Eleven.
[57] I should take note, however, that, at Dr. Johnson's own suggestion, Blackmore was included in the *Lives of the Poets*. The Knight is there treated to the most generous treatment he ever received; of him the

The treatise, to take leave of it, is really an ingenious and sprightly piece of writing, still good reading, and justly characterized by Warton as 'this little treatise in which the justest rules are delivered under the mask of ridicule, *fortius et melius*, than in professed and serious critical discourses.'[58]

When in May of the same year the first edition of the *Dunciad* was brought out anonymously, the publisher alleged that during the preceding two months the town had been full of attacks of all sorts upon Mr. Pope. Professor Lounsbury is able to point out, however, that there were only twenty of these attacks counting even letters and brief paragraphs, and no pamphlets. And of these twenty, four came directly or indirectly from Pope.[59]

The 1728 edition was without the notes or the inscription to Swift. Its title page bears the representation of an owl sitting on a pile of books,—Dennis' works, Cibber's plays, the *Shakespeare Restored* of Theobald, and Blackmore's *Prince Arthur*. After the immense success of this edition, Pope ventured to bring out a new one in 1729 with full *variorum* readings, copious annotations identifying the victims of the satire, and a title page figured by an ass laden with the works of Welsted, Ward, Dennis, Theobald, Oldmixon, and Eliza Haywood, and *Mist's Journal*.[60]

The *Dunciad* was perhaps suggested by Dryden's *MacFlecknoe*, to which, as Pope justly says in a note, it 'bears some resemblance, though of a character more different from it than that of the *Aeneid* from the *Iliad*, or the *Lutrin* of Boileau from the *Défaite des Bouts Rimées* of Sarasin.'[61] From the earlier poem satirizing Shadwell, Pope borrowed the notion of Dulness as a force embodying all one disliked, also the coronation of the hero; he also utilized a number of phrases as subjects for 'imitations'; but his invention is in part adaptation from the ancients, in part of his own contrivance; and there is the utmost disparity between the lengths of the two poems.

Pope never wrote the serious epic he planned,—as a substitute

Doctor ventures to assert that 'by the unremitted enmity of the wits, whom he provoked more by his virtue than his dulness, [he] has been exposed to worse treatment than he deserved . . .' (*Lives*, II, 252).

[58] *Works of Pope*, ed. Warton, VI, 254, n. Pope himself remarked, '*The Profound* [*Profund*], though written in so ludicrous a way, may be very well worth reading seriously as an art of rhetoric' (Spence, 176).

[59] Lounsbury, 207.

[60] Both title pages are reproduced in E-C, IV.

[61] E-C, IV, 129, n.

for it he gave us his Homer; but he achieved perfection in the mock
heroic by his *Rape of the Lock* and came very near a similar tri-
umph in the burlesque epic with his *Dunciad*. This latter suffers
from having no real plot or fable, but succeeds, or nearly succeeds,
in making up for this by a vivacious succession of incident and
episode imitated from Virgil and Homer. Of these structural 'imitations' may be noted in Book One the proposition, the invocation,
the inscription, and the subject (the re-establishment of a great
empire); in Book Two, the games (as in the *Iliad*, *Odyssey*, and
Aeneid); in Book Three, the visit to the lower world, as in Homer
and Virgil, and the Pisgah-view of past and future, as in *Paradise
Lost*. In addition, there are poetical paraphrases and parodies,
most of which Pope credited to their sources in foot-notes. An
enumeration of these may interest. Of those the poet acknowledged,
there are sixty-five from Virgil, twelve from Milton (all from
Paradise Lost), seven each from Homer and Ovid, three from
Dryden, two each from Addison, Waller, Denham, Persius, Dr.
Garth, and Spenser, and one each from Lucian, Juvenal, Roscommon, Blackmore, Young, Butler, Claudian, Jonson, Propertius,
Catullus, and Lucretius. Additional attributions made by Wakefield
in his *Observations on Pope*, enumerate twenty from Dryden
(these are chiefly from his translations of the classics, and are
frequently taken over by Pope with next to no alteration), eleven
from Milton, five from Homer, four from Ovid, three from Garth's
Dispensary,[62] two apiece from Butler and Gay, and one apiece
from Addison, Parnell, Creech, Tickell, Sheffield, Young, Boileau,
Persius, and Juvenal. Whatever else these lists suggest, they evidence acquaintance with and assimilation of a considerable body of
ancient and modern literature.

Turning now to the text of the *Dunciad*, I shall select for comment only such passages as contribute more or less directly to
literary criticism.

There is an interesting paragraph in Book One which protests,
with perfect orthodoxy, against a number of kinds of 'confusion-
ism.' Neo-classical insistence on the 'unities' is universally familiar; equally characteristic was the insistence on purity of *genre*
(e.g., the abhorrence at the favorite Elizabethan tragi-comedy). It
is 'Dulness' who watches with delight the 'irregularities' of the
Grub Street *Literati*:

[62] Dr. Garth was a personal friend of 'our author,' as well as the most
successful practitioner of satire between Dryden and Pope.

There motley images her fancy strike,
Figures ill-paired, and similes unlike.
She sees a mob of metaphors advance,
Pleased with the madness of the mazy dance;
How tragedy and comedy embrace;
How farce and epic get a jumbled race;[63]
How time himself stands still at her command,
Realms shift their place, and Ocean turns to land.
Here gay description Egypt glads with showers,
Or gives to Zembla fruits, to Barca flowers;

. . . .

In cold December fragrant chaplets blow,
And heavy harvests nod beneath the snow.[64]

Book One limns also the full length portrait of Theobald, hero of the 1728 *Dunciad*, to whose life and works Professor Lounsbury has devoted a large part of his valuable if misleadingly named *Text of Shakespeare*. Always poor, but even as a young man undeniably learned, this maligned scholar tried his hand at every variety of literary work, including the composition of some original plays and the translation of parts of Aeschylus and Sophocles: today he is chiefly remembered for a few happy emendations of the text of Shakespeare. It was his misfortune that Pope had preceded him as editor of Shakespeare, and that the poet was particularly sensitive on the subject of this, the least esteemed of his labors. Theobald incurred undying wrath by his *Shakespeare Restored: or a Specimen of the Many Errors as Well Committed as Unamended by Mr. Pope in his Late Edition of this Poet*. The justice of many of Theobald's emendations, some of which Pope silently adopted in the second edition of his own text,[65] and the general acceptance

[63] Pope's own note upon these lines: 'Alludes to the transgressions of the unities in the plays of such poets. For the miracles wrought upon time and place, and the mixture of tragedy and comedy, farce and epic, see *Pluto and Proserpine* [probably Theobald's *Rape of Proserpine*, 1725], *Penelope*, etc., if yet extant' (E-C, IV, 106, n). Addison shared the reprehension of tragedy and comedy in an 'embrace': Tragi-comedy, he says, 'is one of the most monstrous inventions that ever entered into a poet's thoughts. An author might as well think of weaving the adventures of Aeneas and Hudibras into one poem as of writing such a motley piece of mirth and sorrow' (*Spectator*, no. 40).

[64] *Dunciad*, I, 65-78. Pope is here, according to his appended note, representing 'the inconsistencies in the descriptions of poets who heap together all glittering and gaudy images, though incompatible in one season, or in one scene' (E-C, IV, 106, n.).

[65] Lounsbury, 315-17.

with which his Preface met, added to the torment of the poet.[66]
Goading his genius with his resentment, Pope so completely de-
molished the reputation of Theobald for his contemporaries and
succeeding generations that Professor Lounsbury despairs of its
rehabilitation. The *Dunciad* reduces the hapless victim to the
dimensions of a pedant, a critic without perspective or sense or
proportion, whose whole energy goes into learning what wise men
are glad to forget. In Book One, he is represented as sitting in a
purely antiquarian library,

> A Gothic Vatican! of Greece and Rome
> Well-purged . . .[67]

stocked in plenty with 'The classics of an age that heard of none'—
Caxton, Wynkyn de Worde,[68] De Lyra,[69] and Philemon Holland.[70]
Theobald invokes the goddess Dulness, and calls to her remembrance his merits. Some of her disciples have busied themselves
with editions of the ancient poets:

> thy good scholiasts with unwearied pains
> Make Horace flat, and humble Maro's strains.

But Theobald has applied equal industry with equal results:

> Here studious I unlucky moderns save,
> Nor sleeps one error in its father's grave,[71]
> Old puns restore, lost blunders nicely seek,
> And crucify poor Shakespeare once a week.[72]
> For thee I dim these eyes and stuff this head,
> With all such reading as was never read.

. . . .

[66] Lounsbury, 176-7.

[67] E-C, IV, 274.

[68] Theobald had pointed out, in his *Shakespeare Restored*, that the
source of a certain speech in *Troilus and Cressida* was not in Homer but 'in
an old chronicle originally printed by Caxton and subsequently by
Wynkyn de Worde' (Lounsbury, 213).

[69] De Lyra (Nicholas Harpsfield, 1519-1575), was a scholar and ecclesi-
astic whom Pope takes as typical of the heavy commentator. Incidentally,
the poet, in his note, dated De Lyra a century too early.

[70] Voluminous translator of the Elizabethan period.

[71] Pope's own note to the first edition reads: 'As where he [Theobald]
labored to prove Shakespeare guilty of terrible anachronisms, or low
conundrums which Time had covered; and conversant in such authors as
Caxton and Wynkyn rather than in Homer or Chaucer.' Pope's edition of
Shakespeare, as we have seen, liked to label as spurious passages of the
sort above described.

[72] Again according to a note of Pope's, Theobald 'For some time, once a
week or fortnight . . . printed in *Mist's Journal* a single remark or poor
conjecture on some word or pointing of Shakespeare. . . .'

> For thee explain a thing till all men doubt it,
> And write about it, Goddess, and about it.[73]

Especially interesting in the above passage is the attack on old English reading. Pope would have the study of our literature begin, except for Chaucer, with the Elizabethans; he is always ready for satire at the expense of those who delight in black-letter and the writers of a 'Gothic' age.

It is not quite fair to set down all the *animus* of the attack on Theobald to wounded vanity and the desire for revenge. Undoubtedly Pope and his friends did feel the contempt of the *honnête homme*, the humanist, for antiquarianism. They felt that men of taste read the classics and the great modern authors of 'polite literature,' not the minor writers of unprofitable ages: they were not interested in the 'by-paths' of literature, in 'such reading as was never read.' The scorn which enveloped the scholar enveloped also all other sorts of specialists and *virtuosi*—natural scientists, collectors. Humanism so defined tends to superficiality, perhaps; but does not specialized 'research' sometimes end in a deplorable lack of perspective and proportion? Pope and his friends were in possession of at least a half truth.

Theobald's plays share the fate of his criticisms: he is made to remark:

> Not that my pen to critiques was confined;
> My verse gave ampler lessons to mankind.
> So written precepts may successless prove,
> But sad examples never fail to move.[74]

The dramatist saves his *Perfidious Brother* and *Proserpine* from becoming wrapping paper only by sacrificing them 'un-stalled, unsold' to the flames.[75]

In Book Two, which parodies in mildly amusing, sometimes indelicate, fashion the Homeric games, the subjects selected for particular censure are 'the base flattery of authors to worthless wealth or greatness'[76]—dedications written for money and the like; the coarseness of some of the minor playwrights' productions; and the ignominy of 'party-writers'—that is, hacks in the service of the political parties—whose three chief qualifications, according to Pope, are 'to stick at nothing, to delight in flinging dirt, and to slander in the dark by guess.'[77]

One of the games is a contest between the critics to see who can

[73] E-C, IV, 275.
[74] E-C, IV, 275.
[75] *ibid.*, 276.
[76] *ibid.*, 146, n.
[77] *ibid.*, 150, n.

keep awake longest while the somniferous works of the world's worst writers are being read :.

> Which most conduce to soothe the soul in slumbers,
> My Henley's periods, or my Blackmore's numbers.[78]

As mentioned earlier, the Third Book 'looks before and after' with a vision which discerns Dulness constantly endeavoring to reassert in history the ancient dominion that was hers when Chaos enveloped the world, and at length succeeding in the suppression of all intelligence. The historical survey purports to show how periods of enlightenment have been followed by catastrophe and darkness.

Writ largest was the fall of Rome, when the works of classic art were destroyed or appropriated to ecclesiastical purposes :[79] the Middle Ages sat in the darkness of ignorance and superstitious faith, while their priests regaled themselves with 'damning books unread':

> See Christians, Jews, one heavy Sabbath keep,
> And all the Western world believe and sleep.[80]

It is hard for us who, whether we share the enthusiasm or not, live in a world where neo-mediaevalists abound, fully to realize the bitterness mixed with contempt in the view of the Middle Ages held by devoted believers in the Enlightenment. Pope and those like-minded feel so strong an indignation at mankind's having been so long ignorant of the literature and the rationalism of the ancients that their classicism tends to be half anti-mediaevalism,[81] as so many good people's Protestantism is half 'No Popery.'

Perhaps the most pointed short characterization in the *Dunciad* is that of Leonard Welsted, put in the stocks for a satire on Pope and his friends published in 1718. The verses parody the once greatly admired couplets of Denham's *Cooper's Hill*:

---

[78] *Dunciad*, II, 369-70. For an interesting account of 'Orator Henley' see Hillhouse, 120-32.

[79] 'Till Peter's keys some christened Jove adorn,
   And Pan to Moses lends his pagan horn;
   See graceless Venus to a Virgin turned,
   Or Phidias broken, and Apelles burned.
                                   (*Dunciad*, III, 109-12.)

[80] *ibid.*, III, 99-100.

[81] Observe the satirically graphic picture of the friars, pilgrims, palmers, etc. in *ibid.*, III, 113-16.

> Flow, Welsted, flow! like thine inspirer, beer,
> Though stale, not ripe; though thin yet never clear;
> So sweetly mawkish, and so smoothly dull;
> Heady, not strong; o'erflowing, though not full.[82]

Then comes the satire on the antiquary Hearne, which parodies the archaic language affected by such lovers of 'the old English Saxon tongue.'[83]

> But who is he, in closet close y-pent,
> Of sober face, with learnéd dust besprent?
> Right well mine eyes arede the myster wight,
> On parchment scraps y-fed, and Wormius hight.[84]

Hearne had objected to the modernization of diction in current reprints of early works; Pope ironically agrees: 'Little is it of avail to object that such words are become unintelligible. Since they are truly English, men ought to understand them; and such as are for uniformity should think all alterations in a language strange, abominable, and unwarrantable.' The implied doctrine is clear. Had Pope lived today, he would have favored the modernization of spelling and punctuation in the English classics: would have wished to interpose no bar of 'quaintness' in appearance between authors of the seventeenth and eighteenth centuries and their readers of today.

Hearne was not the only Old English scholar who aroused Pope's derision. Humphrey Wanley,[85] the private librarian of the poet's friend, Lord Oxford, echoed his deep studies of dusty manuscripts in his ordinary talk, fashioned 'upon the ceremonious formalities of the old letters and other documents which were his habitual world.' Pope, who loved to mimic the oddities of others, used to convulse companies with laughter when he would 'take off Wanley's stilted turns of phraseology and elaboration of manner.'[86] Two of the poet's letters to the old librarian survive; and both are couched in the most pseudo-archaic of styles. The humor has badly evaporated, but the satirical intent remains clear.[87]

---

[82] *Dunciad*, III, 169-72.
[83] Hearne's own phrase (E-C, IV, 175, n.).
[84] *Dunciad*, III, 185-8.
[85] Wanley (1672-1726), an Oxford man, prepared a famous catalogue of Old English MSS and another of the Harleian MSS.
[86] E-C, VIII, 206-7, n.
[87] I will quote the first of the letters: 'To my worthy and special Friend, Maistre Wanley, dwelling at my singular goode Lord's, my Lord of Oxford, kindly present.
'Worthy Sir,—I shall take it as a singular mark of your friendly disposition and kindness to me, if you will recommend to my palate, from the

The antiquarian is followed, in the list of 'dunces,' by the textual critic, or scholiast:

> There, dim in clouds, the poring scholiasts mark,
> Wits who, like owls, see only in the dark,
> A lumber-house of books in every head,
> Forever reading, never to be read.[88]

'These few lines,' adds a foot-note of Pope's, 'exactly describe the right verbal critic: the darker his author is, the better he is pleased, like the famous quack doctor who put up in his bills, *he delighted in matters of difficulty*. Somebody said well of these men that their heads were *Libraries out of order*.'[89] From the point of view of one sort of humanism, scholarship consists in the labor of elucidating and annotating what deserves neither; the scholar is one who has filled his head 'with all such reading as is never read'; whose information is as useless and ill-digested as it is copious; whose barbarous style prohibits the 'general reader' from gaining any profit from his research. Whether Bentley or Theobald actually deserved the acid characterization above given may be a question; but beyond dispute, in this and similar passages, Pope has for all time satirized Professor Dryasdust and his works.

The last piece of criticism to be noted in Book Three is a condemnation of the extravagant and sensational appeals to the eye—novelties in the way of scene, and pantomime, and spectacle—which were delighting the theater-goers of Pope's time. The dignity of the stage and the dramatic art seemed outraged by this emphasis on everything but the play itself. Addison complained in the *Spectator*[90] that audiences seemed to lack not only good taste but common sense. In the performances of the opera *Hydaspes* neither the music nor the play was the attraction, but 'Signor Nicolini's combat with a lion,' 'which has been very often exhibited to the general satisfaction of most of the nobility and gentry in the Kingdom of Great Britain.' Pope's verses for the most part take off absurdities actually produced upon the stage in farces on Faustus and Harlequin and in Theobald's *Rape of Proserpine*:

experienced taste of yours, a dousaine quartes of goode and wholesome wine, such as yee drink at the Genoa Arms, for the which I will in honorable sort be indebted, and well and truly pay the owner thereof, your said merchant of wines at the said Genoa Arms. As witness this myne hand, which also witnesseth its master to be, in sooth and sincerity of heart, goode Sir, yours ever bounden' (E-C, X, 115).

[88] *Dunciad*, III, 191-4.
[89] E-C, IV, 176, n.
[90] No. 13.

All sudden, gorgons hiss, and dragons glare,
And ten-horned fiends and giants rush to war.
Hell rises, heaven descends; and dance on earth
Gods, imps, and monsters, music, rage, and mirth,
A fire, a jig, a battle and a ball,
'Till one wild conflagration swallows all.
    Thence a new world to Nature's laws unknown,
Breaks out refulgent, with a heaven its own;
Another Cynthia her new journey runs,
And other planets circle other suns.
The forests dance, the rivers upward rise,
Whales sport in woods, and dolphins in the skies.[91]

Theobald's[92] *Proserpine* is said to have afforded the spectacle of a corn-field set on fire; to match which the rival playhouse burned down a barn.

Of course Pope's enmity to Theobald may have had something to do with this diatribe against theatrical 'monsters,' but it need hardly be invoked for all. Even though Pope was no lover of the stage, he must have felt shame at a time when 'for no inconsiderable while the legitimate drama held the second place.'[93] Classicism, common sense, and taste alike demanded the banishment of plays which, instead of 'holding, as 't were, the mirror up to Nature,' took refuge in 'Fancy's maze' and created an illusory 'new world, to Nature's laws unknown.'

The original *Dunciad* was complete in three books. But fifteen years after, in 1743, a year before his death, Pope brought out a new edition which included a fourth book, separately published the year before, and but loosely attached to the earlier. Pope also took advantage of the new edition to make a number of changes in the *personnel* of the 'dunces.' The most important of these was the dethronement of Theobald and the substitution for him of Colley Cibber, then poet-laureate, and hated by the creator of 'dunces' on various accounts.[94] Some of the characterization and equipment of the original hero was retained; but much was altered.

---

[91] *Dunciad*, III, 235-46.

[92] For some years Theobald was closely connected with the Drury Lane, and assisted 'in the preparation of the operas, masques, and pantomimes for which this theater in the course of time became famous' (Lounsbury, 139-40).

[93] Lounsbury, 140.

[94] 'The quarrel between Pope and Cibber originated in the allusion made by the latter, while playing Bays in the *Rehearsal*, to the Mummy and the Crocodile in [Pope and Gay's] *Three Hours after Marriage* which had been

Both Doctor Johnson and Professor Lounsbury exaggerate, I make bold to think, the defectiveness of the retouched portrait. But the make-up of the library is changed: in place of the musty old English texts are installed the dramatists from whom Cibber is alleged to have plagiarized—'poor Fletcher' of the 'half-eat scenes'[95] and 'crucified Molière.'[96] The altar to Dulness is topped by a birthday-ode, suggestive of the duties of the laureateship; and the consuming fire burns the *Cid*, *Perolla*, and 'Molière's old stubble,' the *Non-Juror*.

The satire of Book Four concerns not so much authors as various classes of persons whose intellectual pursuits are, in the opinion of the satirist and many another *honnête homme*, peripheral and eccentric; who are 'dull' only in the derived sense of making perverse or futile employment of their powers:[97] the textual critics and pedants, the hidebound schoolmasters, the *virtuosi* or collectors, and the deists.

Apropos of Hanmer, who had brought out his so-called 'Oxford' Shakespeare,[98] Benson,[99] and Theobald, Pope parodied Waller's famous verses on Old Age:

> Let standard authors, thus like trophies borne,
> Appear more glorious as more hacked and torn;
> And you, my critics, in the checquered shade,
> Admire new light through holes yourselves have made.[100]

He himself had made free with the text of Shakespeare: perhaps his anger was occasioned by the presumption of lesser persons, men who were not themselves poets at all, in venturing the same liberty. This interpretation seems suggested by a note to the 1742 edition which begins, 'The Goddess applauds the practice of

recently damned' (E-C, III, 246 n.). But the immediate cause of Cibber's enthronement as 'King Log' was a pamphlet he published after the appearance of the *New Dunciad* (Book IV), 'inquiring into the motives that might induce [Pope] to be so frequently fond of Mr. Cibber's name' (E-C, V, 334).

[95] Cibber borrowed from Fletcher's *Caesar in Egypt* (E-C, IV, 318).

[96] In a foot-note, Pope calls the *Non-Juror* 'a comedy threshed out of Molière's *Tartuffe* (E-C, IV, 120).

[97] Cf. E-C, IV, 28: 'But in the word *Dulness* Pope meant to include every sort of rebellion against right reason and good taste.'

[98] Sir Thomas Hanmer displeased Pope by giving Theobald's edition the preference over his, 'though speaking with great admiration of Pope's genius,' in the Preface to the Oxford Shakespeare (E-C, IV, 354).

[99] William Benson published in 1741 an edition of the Latin translation of the Psalms by the obscure Scotch poet, Johnston.

[100] *Dunciad*, IV, 123-6.

tacking the obscure names of persons not eminent in any branch of learning to those of the most distinguished writers. . . .'[101]

At any rate, the quoted pair of couplets might far more fittingly have been applied to the victim of a later page, the great Bentley. By his edition of Milton this scholar 'succeeded in doing something for his own reputation which the most pointed satire of the greatest satirist of the age was utterly unable to effect.'[102] Bentley had postulated a friend to whom *Paradise Lost* was dictated and who saw it through the press. This friend, he believed, had tampered with the text in words, phrases, and even whole passages. The printers had aided the work with all possible carelessness. The proof sheets were never read to the author. The result was supposed to justify Bentley in the most extravagant and outrageous emendations. He heaped the vilest abuse on Milton's style and Milton's scholarship while he was professedly censuring the purely hypothetical friend. 'Did we not know indeed that the edition of Milton was undertaken seriously, it would be no unnatural assumption that it was an elaborate device to cast ridicule on the methods of verbal criticism.'[103] The exhibition was all clear gain to Pope's warfare against professional scholars. With justification complete he might then target 'Aristarchus,' the

> mighty Scholiast, whose unwearied pains
> Made Horace dull, and humbled Milton's strains.
> Turn what they will to verse, their toil is vain,
> Critics like me shall make it prose again.[104]

Throughout the *Dunciad*, Pope has amused himself by appending solemn notes aggravating trifles into significance after what he conceives to be the manner of Bentley, endorsing them with the name of the great scholar. Nor was this his last revenge: he produced and appended to his poem a burlesque on Bentley's emendations, called *Virgilius Restauratus*, in which representative passages from the *Aeneid* are badly mangled to the tune of the most plausible of foot-note rationalizations.[105]

The text of the *Dunciad* carries on the facile sneer with the charge that, among the 'learned,'

[101] E-C, IV, 196, n.
[102] Lounsbury, 423-4.
[103] *ibid.*, 429.
[104] *Dunciad*, IV, 211-14.
[105] E-C, X, 422-9. The *Grub-street Journal* also found Bentley a ready victim; see Hillhouse, 85-95.

> on words is still our whole debate,
> Disputes of *me* or *te*, of *aut* or *at*,
> To sound or sink in *cano* O or A,
> Or give up *Cicero* to C or K.[106]

They do not relish the great authors of antiquity as much as the minor, have not the taste to know what is literature and what is mere ink and paper. Bentley, who published an edition of Manilius in 1739, put his subject on an equality with Ovid as 'the only two poets that had wit among the ancients.'[107] Accordingly a Pope-Warburton foot-note remarks, 'Some critics, having had it in their choice to comment either on Virgil or Manilius, Pliny or Solinus, have chosen the worse author, the more freely to display their critical capacity.' Or, as the text makes the pedant say,

> For me, what Virgil, Pliny, may deny,
> Manilius or Solinus shall supply.
> For Attic prose in Plato let them seek:
> I poach in Suidas for unlicensed Greek.[108]

Pope shared the contempt for the Italian opera which was felt by the other critics of his day, and to which Addison devoted three numbers of the *Spectator*. Two paragraphs of the *New Dunciad* express the standard objections to this irregular *genre*,—its foreign tongue[109] 'recitatives,' its elaborate runs, its chromatic scale, its trills, its prostitution of sense to sound. The English had not been without their own opera before the advent of the invader: Purcell, one of the greatest English composers, had written many operas in a truly national vein: diatonic in harmonies, without display; the airs usually interspersed with spoken dialogue. Italian opera seemed to Addison and Pope an affront both to their patriotism and to their good sense. But more was involved than that: as we have seen, the 'legitimate stage' was for a period second in popular attention and esteem to the opera and the farce. 'If the Italians have a genius for music above the English, the English have a genius for other performances of a much higher nature, and capable of giving the mind a much nobler entertainment. Would one think it was possible (at a time when an author lived that was

---

[106] *Dunciad*, IV, 219-22.
[107] E-C, IV, 359.
[108] *Dunciad*, IV, 225-8.
[109] 'At length the audience grew tired of understanding half the opera, and therefore to ease themselves entirely of the fatigue of thinking, have so ordered it at present that the whole opera is performed in an unknown tongue. We no longer understand the language of our own stage. . . .' *Spectator*, no. 18.

able to write the *Phaedra and Hippolitus*) for a people to be so stupidly fond of the Italian opera as scarce to give a third day's hearing to that admirable tragedy?'[110] Pope represents Opera as a prostitute who looks with scorn upon the arts whose place she has usurped:

> When lo! a harlot form soft sliding by,
> With mincing step, small voice, and languid eye;
> Foreign her air,[111] her robe's discordant pride
> In patch-work fluttering,[112] and her head aside;
> By singing peers upheld on either hand,
> She tripped and laughed, too pretty much to stand;
> Cast on the prostrate Nine a scornful look,
> Then thus in quaint Recitativo[113] spoke:
> 'O *Cara! Cara!* silence all that train;
> Joy to great Chaos! let Division[114] reign;
> Chromatic tortures[115] soon shall drive them hence,
> Break all their nerves, and fritter all their sense.[116]

[110] *Spectator*, no. 18. The merits of the particular play praised do not need to concern us: Dr. Johnson, who thought well of Edmund Smith, its author, agreed with the public which condemned his *Phaedra* (*Lives*, II, 16).

[111] Then, as now, things Continental seemed more modish than things native. Addison complains that 'in general, we are transported with anything that is not English. So it be of a foreign growth, let it be Italian, French, or high Dutch, it is the same thing' (*Spectator*, no. 18).

[112] According to a note of Pope's, this refers to 'the practice of patching up these operas with favorite songs, incoherently put together' (E-C, IV, 193, n.). The great Händel himself used to transfer airs from one work to another.

[113] Says Addison, 'There is nothing that has more startled our English audience than the Italian recitativo at its first entrance upon our stage. People were wonderfully surprised to hear generals singing the word of command, and ladies delivering messages in music' (*Spectator*, no. 29).

[114] 'Divisions, in the musical nomenclature of the seventeenth and eighteenth centuries, were rapid passages—slow notes *divided* into quick ones. . . . Hence the word can be applied to quick consecutive passages like the long semi-quaver runs in Händel's bravura songs, such as *Rejoice Greatly* and *Let the Bright Seraphim*' (Grove's *Dictionary of Music*).

[115] See *chromatic* in *N.E.D.* for interesting discussion. It suggested music which would appeal to a specially trained and over-refined audience, in distinction to the old diatonic songs which appealed to all. 'Music,' says the *Spectator* (no. 29), 'is not designed to please only chromatic ears, but all that are capable of distinguishing harsh from disagreeable notes.'

[116] Addison refers to 'an established rule . . . "that nothing is capable of being well set to music that is not nonsense".' Opera has not materially changed the character of its plots since this gibe was written. But in Addison's day the sense was additionally 'frittered' by occasional attempts to

> One trill shall harmonize joy, grief, and rage,
> Wake the dull church, and lull the ranting stage.[117]

In the foregoing survey of such sections of the *Dunciad* as chiefly interest the student of Pope's literary criticism no attempt has been made to list the many minor persons satirized. For the most part, they have hardly come down to us except as embalmed in their particular dreadful immortality. There are just about a hundred culprits in the 1729 version, and the version of 1743 adds about ten more. Certain general classes of the reprehensible emerge,—pedants, critics, theater-managers, party writers, laureates, dedicators, booksellers, and publishers, antiquarians, *virtuosi*, and freethinkers. The list is a comprehensive one; and its comprehensiveness indicates the scope of the satire: its theme, which is primarily literary mediocrity, extends to include intellectual aberration in all its contemporary varieties.

It has not generally been noted that the *Dunciad* adds to its roll of 'dunces' its necessarily shorter roll of the wise. To quote Warburton, 'Nothing is more remarkable than our author's love of praising good writers. He has in this very poem celebrated Mr. Locke, Sir Isaac Newton, Dr. Barrow, Dr. Atterbury, Mr. Dryden, Mr. Congreve, Dr. Garth, Mr. Addison—in a word, almost every man of his time that deserved it';[118] to which list one may add, also from the *Dunciad*, Swift, Gay, Prior, and Chesterfield. The arts of music and architecture contribute the great Händel and the perhaps equally great Wren.

Perhaps the 'dunces' are all entitled to another trial, as Professor Lounsbury would seem to suggest; but, if the verdict of posterity is the verdict of truth, Pope in his judgments of his contemporaries drew the line between the great and the small with amazing accuracy. I have not attempted here or elsewhere to conceal the personal grievances which prompted many of Pope's antipathies, nor would I deny that he praises his friends partly from his friendship; but there is surely a good deal to be said for the literary as well as social judgment of a man whose friends are the classics of the eighteenth century literature and whose enemies are forgotten.

translate the text of a song into English, in which case 'It oftentimes happened likewise that the finest notes in the air fell upon the most insignificant words in the sentence' (*Spectator*, no. 18).

[117] *Dunciad*, IV, 45-58.

[118] E-C, IV, 138, n.

CHAPTER VI

THE CLASSICS AND A NEO-CLASSICIST

THE extent of Pope's knowledge of the classical languages has been variously estimated by his critics. Perhaps none would assert that he was a scholar in the strict sense. Perpetual illness and the restrictions placed upon him as a Roman Catholic scarcely conduced to sound foundations of learning in boyhood; and the intensive period of self-education upon which he embarked when his brief studies with neighboring priests were over was likely to produce inaccuracy in detail. The method of his linguistic studies is well known. 'I took to reading for myself, for which I had a very great eagerness and enthusiasm, especially for poetry; and in a few years I had dipped into a great number of the English, French, Italian, Latin and Greek poets. This I did without any design but that of pleasing myself; and got the languages by hunting after the stories in the several poets I read, rather than read the books to get the languages.'[1] This was from his fifteenth to his twentieth year. 'About this time, likewise, he made a translation of Tully, *De Senectute*, a copy of which, it is said, is preserved in Lord Oxford's library.'[2] Ruffhead gives in some detail, presumably on Warburton's authority, an account of later studies between his twentieth and twenty-seventh years: 'At twenty, when the impetuosity of his spirits began to subside, and his genius grew more patient of restraint, he subjected himself to the toil of renewing his studies from the beginning, and went through the several parts of a learned education upon a more regular and well-digested plan. He penetrated into the general ground and reasons of speech; he learned to distinguish the several species of style; he studied the peculiar idiom of each language with the genius and character of each author;[3] he mastered those parts of philosophy which mostly contributed to enrich the store of sentiment; and lastly he reduced his natural talent for poetry to a science.'[4]

[1] Spence, 193.
[2] Ruffhead, 13.
[3] 'Know well each ancient's proper character.' *Essay on Criticism*, I, 119.
[4] Ruffhead, 15.

The chief extant specimen of Pope's scholarship in Latin is his early translation of the First Book of Statius' *Thebaid*. Pope 'must have been at this time, if he had no help, a considerable proficient in the Latin tongue,' thinks Dr. Johnson.[5] With this dictum De Quincey begs leave to differ. The translation of Statius, he says, exhibits 'utter ignorance of prosody' and even 'occasional inability to construe the text.' As a typical error is cited his rendering of *ruptae vices*, line 178, 'and all the ties of nature broke,' when by *vices* is indicated the alternate reign of the two brothers as ratified by mutual oaths and subsequently violated by Eteocles. Other mistakes might be cited which seem to prove that 'Pope, like most self-taught linguists, was a very imperfect one.'[6]

One might take as the test of his Greek the translation of Homer. Yet with the easily available array of versions, prose and verse, in Latin, French, and English, the poet would, one would suppose, be prevented by a mere comparison of translations from any serious blunders. De Quincey was perhaps simply concurring with this probability when he wrote, 'Criticism has not succeeded in fixing upon Pope any errors of ignorance. His deviations from Homer were uniformly the result of imperfect sympathy with the naked simplicity of the antique, and therefore wilful deviations, not (like those of his more pretending competitors, Addison and Tickell) pure blunders of misapprehension.'[7] However, the eighteenth century scholar, Gilbert Wakefield, in his comments on Pope's Homer, was certain that the translator's 'pure blunders of misapprehension' were many, and that he showed surprising ignorance of the ancient languages. 'After an experimental examination,' Wakefield concluded that Pope had 'collected the general purport of every passage from some of his predecessors—Dryden, Dacier, Chapman, or Ogilby'—and had never consulted his text to any purpose.[8]

Insinuations that the translator of Homer was unfamiliar with the language from which he was translating were in constant circulation at the time. A contemporary Epistle[9] charges that the poet

> By Fenton left, by reverend linguists hated,
> Now learns to read the Greek he once translated.

When Pope made an impressively casual reference in a letter to his co-translator, Broome, of having recently read Eustathius on the

[5] *Lives*, III, 88.

[6] De Quincey: *Works*, IV, 250.

[7] *ibid.*, IV, 247.

[8] Wakefield, I, lxi. The same critic speaks (I, lxii) of 'the strange and scandalous blunders in the typography of the Greek and Latin quotations throughout the notes on the *Iliad* and *Odyssey*. . . .'

[9] E-C, VIII, 161 and n.

Twenty-second Book of the *Odyssey*, Broome wrote to the third
'hand,' Fenton, 'he is no master of Greek; and I am so confident of
this that if he can translate ten lines of Eustathius I will own
myself unjust and unworthy.'[10] (Elwin thinks Parnell, who spent
the summer and fall of 1714 assisting the poet to go through the
Greek commentators, 'helped him to the sense of the principal remarks.')[11] The antiquarian Hearne wrote in his diary (July 10,
1729) that Pope was 'mean at Latin and can hardly read Greek.'

Still, of course antiquarians and men of letters were not, at least
in the Augustan Age, expected to be on amicable terms. Pope's
friends among the 'noble lords' had confidence in his scholarship.
Lord Bathurst told Dr. Blair that a part of the *Iliad* was translated
in his house in the country, and that 'in the morning, when they
assembled at breakfast, Mr. Pope used frequently to repeat, with
great rapture, the Greek lines which he had been translating.'[12]
But Wakefield, though no enemy, laughed at the idea that these
'sonorous spoutings' were evidence of proficiency in Greek, and
inferred that Pope descended to an 'ostentatious exhibition of
his pretended erudition before a company whose slender acquire-
ments he knew would qualify them to become the dupes of such
a solemn imposition.'[13]

Pope's Boswell, Spence, in his notes for 1742-3, reports another
instance which might at first thought seem indicative of exact
classical scholarship. 'When I consulted him [Pope] about the
Hades of the ancients, he referred immediately to Pindar's Second
Olympic Ode, Plutarch's treatise, *De Iside et Osiride*, the four
places that relate to it in the *Odyssey* (though this was many
years after he had done the translation), Plato, Lucretius, and
some others; and turned to the very passages in most of them
with a surprising readiness.'[14] But knowledge of the subject matter
of the classics is no adequate guarantee of learning in the ancient
languages, as many a classicist-in-English can testify. From the
days of Elizabeth on, translations of the great foreign masterpieces
have abounded in England, and never more copiously than in the
age after the Restoration. The *De Rerum Natura*, for example, to
which Pope several times refers, appeared in the rimed translation
of Creech in 1682 and went through six editions in the following
forty years.[15] Pope's occasional references to Plato[16] and Socrates

[10] E-C, VIII, 150.
[11] *ibid.*, VIII, 33, n.
[12] Boswell, III, 403.
[13] Wakefield, I, lxx.
[14] Spence, 285.
[15] Havens, 342.
[16] It is hardly to be supposed that the lengthy summary of Plato's *Cra-
tylus* in the *Observations* (XIV: XXXIII) was the result of 'original research.'

show no more than a casual knowledge such as might easily be gleaned from a secondary source.

To conclude this discussion of Pope's 'little Greek,' it is to be observed that the poet never directly denied the charges of linguistic inadequacy brought against him. A characteristic reply to such charges is his 'question in return' to 'Lord Fanny': 'But allowing that in the space of twelve years' acquaintance with Homer, I might unhappily contract as much Greek as your Lordship did in two at the university, why may I not forget it again as happily?'[17] No doubt the implication is correct, that Pope by degrees, through the sheer exercise of translation, acquired a 'gentleman's' knowledge of Homeric Greek; and to Attic Greek he never pretended.

In his *Temple of Fame*, the six classical authors honored by pillared inclusion are Homer, Virgil, Pindar, Horace, Aristotle, and Cicero. Pope's Homeric studies have already received treatment in their appropriate chapter. The other Greek poet honored in the *Temple* is several times characterized, once conventionally, and once with greater definiteness. In the *Temple*

> Here, like some furious prophet, Pindar rode,
> And seemed to labor with th' inspiring God,
> Across the harp a careless hand he flings,
> And boldly sinks into the sounding strings.[18]

This interpretation as the frenzied improvisator with his 'irregular numbers' was conventional: the Pindaric ode had been naturalized in England by Cowley and others. More frank is the remark to Spence that 'the works of Pindar that remain to us are by no means equal to his great character.—His Dithyrambics, which were his best things, are lost; and all that is left of his works, being on the same subject, is the more apt to be tiresome.'[19] At one time, Pope planned the translation of specimen pieces—*florilegia*, I suppose—from 'all the most celebrated Greek poets'; and besides a hymn from Homer and another from Callimachus, there was to be an ode or two of Pindar.[20] One regrets that the translation of the *Iliad* put an end to the undertaking of this as well as other experiments. The *Ode for St. Cecilia's Day*, if not equal to the Pindarics of Dryden, is evidence that Pope might have extended to the freer forms the mastery which he has in fact exhibited only in the couplet.

[17] E-C, V, 438 (*A Letter to a Noble Lord*, 1733).
[18] ll. 211-14.
[19] Spence, 178.
[20] *ibid.*, 304. See also E-C, VIII, 232.

Sappho's 'fine fragments' are twice mentioned: he attributed to one of these the partial inspiration of his *Dying Christian to his Soul*. Unfortunately, Warton and Elwin find reason to suspect he was rather borrowing from Flatman, an obscure Caroline poet.[21]

Hesiod he knew; perhaps his fondness for the *Georgics* of Virgil was the incentive to study of its professed model. Pope observed the 'imitations' as well as the allusion to Hesiod. He thinks, 'Perhaps what we call Hesiod's works at present are misnamed. The *Theogony* has little prettinesses in it, not like the greatness of antiquity.—*The Shield of Hercules* is taken from Homer's *Shield of Achilles*, and there are several lines exactly the same in both. The Hμερων has the truest air of antiquity.'[22] Hesiod is occasionally quoted.

Dryden had translated three of the Idylls of Theocritus in his *Sylvae*, and there was a complete translation by Creech. Pope seems to have read these in preparation for writing his *Pastorals*, of which the *Winter* is professedly an imitation of Theocritus, though the particular passages copied are few. The brief characterization of the father of pastoral poetry which is found in the prefixed Discourse derives from Fontenelle and Dryden: 'Theocritus excels all others in nature and simplicity. The subjects of his Idyllia are purely pastoral; but he is not so exact in his persons, having introduced reapers and fishermen as well as shepherds. He is apt to be too long in his descriptions, of which that of the cup in the first pastoral is a remarkable instance. In the manners he seems a little defective, for his swains are sometimes abusive and immodest, and perhaps too much inclining to rusticity;[23] for instance, in his Fourth and Fifth Idyllia. But it is enough that all others learned their excellencies from him, and that his dialect has a secret charm in it which no other could ever attain.'[24] Evidence

[21] E-C, VI, 397, and note; IX, 411.

[22] Spence, 216. The Hesiodic poems were translated into English by Cooke in 1728. Modern scholarship is in general agreement with Pope's conjectures. By Boetian testimony, the *Works and Days* is alone genuine; the *Theogony* is 'attributed' to Hesiod or his school; the *Shield* is clearly an imitation of the Homeric account and is now generally considered spurious.

[23] Fontenelle disapproves of 'la grossièreté ordinaire' of Theocritus' shepherds. 'Il y a encore dans Theócrite des choses qui n'ont pas tant de bassesse, mais qui n'ont guère d'agrément, parce qu'elles ne sont simplement que rustiques. La quatrième de ses idylles est toute de ce caractère.' *Oeuvres*, V, 6.

[24] E-C, I, 262. 'Even his Doric dialect has an incomparable sweetness in its clownishness, like a fair shepherdess talking in a Yorkshire tone,' says Dryden; and he goes on to point out that neither Virgil or Spenser was successful in his use of dialect (Preface to the *Sylvae*).

of the indebtedness of the *Winter* to Moschus' *Lament for Bion* in the translation of Oldham for motif and phrase has been convincingly produced by Wakefield.[25]

Warton has noted the significant absence from the *Temple of Fame* of the great tragic poets of Greece. But they are very nearly absent from the rest of the *Works* too. Sophocles is cited in the *Scriblerus*[26] for some evidence on Greek customs; but this citation may have come from Arbuthnot, and Warton is inclined to think it did. There is mention in the *Observations* of Sophocles' *Ajax* and Euripides' *Iphigenia in Tauris*. In the same notes, apropos of a mention of Alcestis, we are told, 'Euripides has a tragedy on this subject which abounds in the most masterly strokes of tenderness. In particular, the first act, which contains the description of her preparation for death and her behavior in it can never be enough admired.'[27] Whether this is the admiration of personal acquaintance or hearsay one cannot tell. The only conventional reference to the Great Three is in the Preface to Shakespeare,[28] and here it is not Pope but Dryden in quotation who exalts the English dramatist above them. 'The truth is,' says Warton,[29] 'it was not fashionable in Pope's time, nor among his acquaintance, attentively to study these poets. By a strange fatality, they have not in this kingdom obtained the rank they deserve amongst classic writers.'[30] It is noteworthy that Spence's bulky *Anecdotes*, which records the dicta of many other eminent *literati* of the time besides Pope, indexes but one (passing) reference to Sophocles, and none to Aeschylus and Euripides. Translation is one of the best means of determining the popularity of a writer; and it is significant that the tragic poets were not translated into English, except in single plays, until well into the eighteenth century,—Sophocles in 1729; Aeschylus and Euripides not until considerably later (1778 and 1781-1788).[31] In spite of Aristotle's preference for tragedy, Renaissance and later neo-classical taste was firm in its allegiance to the epic, as the most casual study of the criticism of the times will attest.[32]

Of the Greek prose writers, Pope cites in the notes to his Homer

[25] E-C, I, 292-8, notes.
[26] *ibid.*, X, 295.
[27] *Observations*, II : LII.

[28] E-C, X, 542.
[29] *Genius of Pope*, I, 361.

[30] For example, it is said of Spenser that he was well read in the Greek poetry, 'except the tragedians, so strangely neglected by the Elizabethans' (De Selincourt, in the Oxford Spenser, ix). Skipping several 'ages' to another learned Englishman, we find Dr. Johnson 'confessed himself not intimately acquainted' with the Greek dramatists (Houston, 18). An exception was Pope's enemy, Dennis, who read and admired Sophocles and Euripides (Paul, 167).

[31] Harris: *First Printed Translations into English* (London, 1909).

[32] The 'learned' Dennis was an exception. Cf. Paul, 167.

Herodotus and Thucydides[33] from the classical period and Pausanias[34] and Plutarch[35] from the post-classical. The *Opera Moralia* of the last of these is copiously employed; there are citations from the *Symposiacs*, *De Oratoribus*, the *Discourse on Curiosity*, *Of Music*, *Of Knowing a Flatterer from a Friend*, *Of the Opinions of the Philosophers*, and *Of Isis and Osiris*. These essays were available in the translation (1603) of Philemon Holland, called the 'translator general of his age.'[36]

Pope had evidently read the translation of Longus' celebrated romance published by Thornely in 1733, for, as Spence held *Daphne and Chloe* in his hand, prepared to read it when the poet should doze off (as he was in the habit of doing), the latter looked up and remarked, 'they are very innocent loves, like those of Adam and Eve in Milton.'[37]

Lucretius is twice quoted in the letters (once it is the celebrated *Tantum religio* passage), once in the notes to Homer.[38] The *Dunciad* contains a brief statement of Lucretius' conception of the Olympian deities in phrases drawn, as the Pope-Warburton note indicates, from verses in the first book of the *De Rerum Natura*.[39] The *Essay on Man* was, according to its author, modelled on the 'grave march of Lucretius' rather than on the 'familiar gaieties of Horace':[40] in other words, it was intended to be a philosophical poem of 'high seriousness.' Its model, sometimes in the translation of Dryden, furnished a few short passages for imitation;[41] and a more extensive one had been intended. Pope planned to imitate Lucretius' 'compliment to Epicurus' (*De Rerum*, I, 62-79) by an address to our Saviour at a corresponding point in the *Essay on Man*. Fortunately the good taste of Bishop Berkeley intervened to prevent the project.[42]

From Catullus is drawn the motto which prefaces the 'book of letters' got out in 1736.[43] The poet's use of diminutives is noted.[44] Unfortunately, this is the only evidence that Pope appreciated the passion against a background of pathos in, if not the greatest, the most lyric of Roman lyricists. Even the neo-classical Jonson was

---

[33] *Observations*, VI, 3, 29. II, 30.

[34] *ibid.*, III, 44. VII, 16.

[35] *ibid.*, V, 33. III, 25. VI, 19. VI, 34. XIV, 26.

[36] The *Dunciad* affords an allusion to this prolific translator (I, 154): in Cibber's library, 'the groaning shelves Philemon bends.'

[37] Spence, 320 (1743-4).

[38] E-C, VI, 70, 363. *Observations*, V, 29.

[39] *Dunciad*, IV, 484-6.

[40] E-C, II, 273.

[41] *ibid.*, 354, 520, notes.

[42] Spence, 142.

[43] E-C, VII, 350.

[44] *ibid.*, VI, 394.

moved to the free expansion of a part of the great fifth 'ode.'[45]
But Pope did note Catullus' power to 'write agreeably on trifles'—
indeed, he regarded the Roman poet and the French Voiture as the
only masters of the art:[46] a considerable tribute from the creator
of *The Rape of the Lock*.[47]

Ovid was an early favorite of Pope's. After reading Ogilby's
Homer in 'that great edition with pictures' at eight or thereabouts,
he next came to Sandys' Ovid, which he 'liked extremely.'[48] The
epic *Alcander*, begun at the age of twelve, imitated in some places
the style of Ovid. It was in his adolescence that Pope made his
translations from the *Metamorphoses* and the *Heroides*.[49] The
period was propitious to the task. Literary genres have their day;
and translation was, throughout the Augustan Age, a 'genteel'
genre, to which my Lord Roscommon had given his sanction by
the *Essay on Translated Verse*. Warton tells us that about the time
of Pope's versions of Ovid, 'it became fashionable among the wits
at Button's, the mob of gentlemen that wrote with ease, to translate Ovid.'[50] The Rev. Dr. Trapp, later professor of Poetry at
Oxford, essayed some versions of Ovid, upon the merit of which
Pope's early correspondent Cromwell requested the poet's verdict.
A brief 'character' of Ovid emerges in the answer from the midst
of an emphasis upon grasping the proper and especial quality of
each author one translates:[51] 'I think he [Trapp] has nothing of
the main characteristic of his author, a graceful easiness.[52] For let
the sense be never so exactly rendered, unless an author looks like
himself in his air, habit, and manner, it is a disguise and not a

---

[45] *Volpone*, Act III, Scene 6.   [46] E-C, VI, 125.

[47] Of course the 'trifles' of Catullus—the sparrow, the yacht, the white
teeth, etc.—are worlds apart in mood and treatment from the elegant
artificialities of Voiture and Pope.

[48] Spence, 276.

[49] *The Fable of Dryope. Vertumnus and Pomona. Sappho to Phaon.*

[50] *Genius of Pope*, II, 25. The 'united performances' of these gentlemen
were got into form and published by Garth, with a Preface 'written in a
flowing and lively style, but full of strange opinions. He declares that
none of the classic poets had the talent of expressing himself with more
force and perspicuity than Ovid. . . .' There were two of these collections:
'*Ovid's Metamorphoses, in Fifteen Books, translated by the Most Eminent
Hands*.' J. Tonson, 1717 (for list of contributors see Griffith, 71), to
which Pope's contribution was the Fable of Dryope; and '*Ovid's Epistles,
Translated by Several Hands*'. The 8th edition (1712) was the first to
contain Pope's *Sappho to Phaon*.

[51] Dryden similarly held that the translator must maintain 'the character
of an author which distinguishes him from all others and makes him appear that individual poet whom you would interpret.'

[52] Cf. Dryden's 'sweet gracefulness of youth' in his Preface to the translations from Ovid's Epistles.

translation.'[53] Cromwell himself was trying his hand at some translations the same year (1710); and Pope thanks him[54] for a version of Ovid's elegy: 'It is very much an image of that author's writing, who has an agreeableness that charms us without correctness,[55] like a mistress whose faults we see, but love her with them all.' He has his favorites among the elegies: 'I could be glad to know if you have translated the 11th elegy of *Lib.* II, *Ad Amicam Navigantem*, the 8th of Book III, or the 11th of Book III, which are above all others my particular favorites, especially the last of these.'[56] Upon another occasion he praised the elegies for their evidence of 'method.'[57]

This early fondness lingered on into a period when the taste for Ovid seemed old-fashioned and the former estimate of him exaggerated. Spence, with all his veneration for Pope, is obliged to confess that the latter had always, on its account, 'perhaps a little more regard for Ovid's *Metamorphoses* than he might otherwise have had.'[58] What seemed to Spence 'mistaken taste' was to Warton, or by Warton's time, 'bad taste.'[59]

The Maronolatry of the Renaissance—of Vida and Scaliger—was beginning to wane, but it was only beginning. To match the Invention and Nature of Homer, there were always the Judgment and Art of Virgil. There is every reason to suppose that our poet was quite as devoted to Virgil as to Homer, though as Dryden had already made 'the Mantuan' speak in English numbers and prefixed his translation with a lengthy and learned discourse, it was left Pope to pay, by a corresponding service, his especial honor to the poet of Nature. The Preface allows the balances, at any rate for the time, to swing somewhat in Homer's favor; but even in the Preface there is cautious safeguard that 'what has been said of Virgil' in contrasting him with Homer has 'no way derogated from his character.' Each great author has his 'principal character and distinguishing excellence;' 'No author or man ever excelled all the world in more than one faculty, and as Homer has done this in *Invention*, Virgil has in *Judgment*,'[60] 'Homer was the greater genius, Virgil the better artist.' One who has at all caught the tone of English Augustanism will know that 'better artist' is no slight praise; and that though its panegyric went out to Genius, its esteem went to Art.

[53] E-C, VI, 112.
[54] *ibid.*, VI, 98.
[55] Ovid, it seems, had not been to school to Mr. Waller.
[56] E-C, VI, 99.
[57] Spence, 1.
[58] *ibid.*, 274.
[59] *Genius of Pope*, II, 25.
[60] Durham, 335.

In his *Temple of Fame*, Pope has been far more successful with
his 'character' of Virgil than with that of Homer. The latter is
vague and generalized, the former very precisely and happily expressive of Virgil's finished technic, his 'judgment,' and his dependence upon Homer:

> a shrine of gold was reared;
> Finished the whole, and labored every part,
> With patient touches of unwearied art:
> The Mantuan there in sober triumph sate,
> Composed his posture, and his looks sedate;
> On Homer still he fixed a reverent eye,
> Great without pride, in modest majesty.[61]

It has well been said that 'It was the "patient touches of unwearied
art" which admitted him to Pope's Temple of Fame.'[62]

Virgil's *Eclogues* Pope thought the 'sweetest poems in the
world';[63] and of their 'correctness,' he told Spence, "Tis difficult to
find out any fault in Virgil's *Eclogues* or *Georgics*—He could not
bear to have any appear in his *Aeneid*, and therefore ordered it to
be burned.'[64] The comparison of Theocritus and Virgil as pastoral
poets is made, on the whole, to favor the latter: 'Virgil, who copies
Theocritus, refines upon his original; and in all points where
judgment is principally concerned, he is much superior to his
master. Though some of his subjects are not pastoral in themselves
but only seem to be such,[65] they have a wonderful variety in
them which the Greek was a stranger to. He exceeds him in regularity and brevity, and falls short of him in nothing but simplicity
and propriety of style; the first of which was the fault of his age,
and the last of his language.'[66] No doubt this censure for lack of
simplicity is derivative rather than personal; for Pope himself followed Virgil in representing an idealized and conventionalized
country life. In 'the last days' there had arisen persons like Ambrose
Philips who ventured to question this convention, and who gave
examples of another, more rustic and indigenous, sort of pastoral

---

[61] ll. 196-202.

[62] Nitchie, 148.

[63] Spence, 24. He was distinguishing between softness and sweetness in
versification. Ovid and Dryden are softer, Virgil and Waller sweeter.

[64] Spence, 215.

[65] i.e., the pastoralism is sometimes simply a convention.

[66] *Discourse on Pastoral Poetry*, E-C, I, 262. Dryden says that it was impossible for Virgil to imitate the sweet rusticity of Theocritus' dialect
'because the severity of the Roman language denied him that advantage'
(Preface to the *Sylvae*). Critics of the period were as fond as we of impres-
sionistic generalizations upon the relative merits of the various 'polite'
languages.

writing. In the satirical essay which Pope wrote for the *Guardian* ironically attacking his own poems, it was necessary to attack, on the same premises, his model: 'As simplicity is the distinguishing characteristic of Pastoral,[67] Virgil hath been thought guilty of too courtly a style; his language is perfectly pure, and he often forgets he is among peasants. I have frequently wondered that, since he was so conversant in the writings of Ennius, he had not imitated the rusticity of the Doric as well by the help of the old obsolete Roman language as Philips hath by the antiquated English. For example, might he not have said *quoi* instead of *cui*, *quoijum* for *cujum*, *volt* for *vult*, etc. . . . ?'[68] And again, 'Mr. Pope hath fallen into the same error with Virgil. His clowns do not converse in all the simplicity proper to the country. . . . He introduces Daphnis, Alexis, and Thyrsis on British plains, as Virgil had done before him on the Mantuan; whereas Philips, who hath the strictest regard for propriety, makes choice of names peculiar to the country, such as Hobbinol, Lobbin, Cuddy and Colin Clout.'[69] Although Pope later praises the *Shepherd's Calendar*, it is not for its language; and he might very well feel that Philips, in imitating that, was copying not the strength but the weakness of Spenser.

The Pope-Philips controversy, whatever the immediate motives, had a deeper underlying significance. It was the conflict between classicism,—or if you choose, neo-classicism,—and an incipient romanticism, the cult of 'local color.' According to the theory of Virgil and Pope and the Italian and French pastoralists who came between them, the pastoral did not pretend to be a realistic study of rural life. As Fontenelle says,[70] we are not interested in the miseries of country life nor its coarsenesses: what pleases us in it is the tranquillity and leisure which may attend it and afford opportunity for the diversions which conventionally form the themes of the pastoral. The pastoral, according to this conception, paints not peasants but men; it is an 'imitation' of universal human life under the accidental form of shepherds and shepherdesses.

In Pope's own *Pastorals*, with the versification of which he took great pains,[71] he professes to follow Theocritus, Virgil, and Spenser. There is good evidence, however, that Virgil was more in

---

[67] 'The true character of the Eclogue is simplicity and modesty.' Rapin, II, 226.

[68] Neo-classical taste was against the introduction of antiquated words. See *Essay on Criticism*, II, 325-36: 'Some by old words to fame have made pretense,' etc. See also the remarks on Miltonic imitators in the Postscript to the *Odyssey*.

[69] E-C, X, 508. Philips' shepherds are endowed with Spenserian names.

[70] *Oeuvres*, V, 9-10.

[71] Spence, 312.

his mind than his English or his Greek model.'[72] Mr. Bowyer, the learned printer,[73] identified for Warton's edition the passages in the *Pastorals* imitated from the classics. With some few exceptions, all these 'imitations' were from Virgil, and, says a special student of the subject, 'a careful search will reveal more that Mr. Bowyer failed to find or Pope did not care to note.'[74] Not to press details, the *Spring* opens with lines from the sixth eclogue and is in form an imitation of the third and seventh, especially the third, 'a song contest'; *Summer* is a combination of the second and the tenth of the *Eclogues*; *Autumn*, as Bowyer pointed out, 'consists of two parts, like the eighth of Virgil.' With a full realization of his dependence upon the Latin eclogue, Pope calls upon the 'Mantuan nymphs' for their aid.[75] Both parts have refrains like those in Virgil. Finally, the fourth pastoral is in general modelled on the fifth eclogue, a lament for Daphnis; and as Virgil had made the first line of his *Eclogues*, the last of his *Georgics*, so the first line of Pope's *Pastorals* appears as the last of *Windsor Forest*.[76]

Besides these serious imitations, Pope, concurring with the fashion of the time, parodied many passages from Virgil[77] in his *Rape of the Lock* and *Dunciad*. The latter is almost a cento of incidents and phrases from the Latin classics and the English poets; but by far the greatest number of 'imitations' is Virgilian.[78]

There remain to be noted some miscellaneous references to Virgil, all of at least curious interest. The *Culex*, now thought spurious, is by Pope regarded as a kind of 'first piece or exercise of Virgil's.'[79] In Pope's day, as well as in Spenser's, it was supposed that one must follow Virgil in making one's *magnum opus* the last of a carefully gradated series of studies.[80] There were the *Eclogues* and there were the *Georgics* before there was the *Aeneid*; and even the composition of *Pastorals* required the previous apprenticeship with something yet slighter.

[72] Nitchie, 165.
[73] See E-C, IX, 521, n.
[74] Nitchie, 165.
[75] *ibid.*, 168.
[76] *ibid.*, 170.

[77] See Nitchie, 243-4 for list of seventeenth-eighteenth century parodies of Virgil.

[78] In his notes Pope acknowledged sixty-four imitations, and Wakefield thinks he has identified thirteen more. *The Publisher to the Reader*, prefixed to the first edition of the *Dunciad*, would suggest that the copious borrowings from Virgil, rather than Homer, were intended to make the reader suppose that another than Pope was author of the poem. Cf. E-C, IV, 266.

[79] E-C, VII, 23.

[80] Virgil 'raised himself by his *Eclogues* and *Georgics*, as by so many steps, to the sublime character of heroic verse.' Rapin, II, 149.

Unless I misread, there is some characteristically neo-classical background, too, in the following remarks to Spence: 'Virgil is very sparing in his commendations of other poets; and scarce ever does it unless he is forced. He hints at Theocritus[81] because he had taken so much from him and his subject led to it; and does the same by Hesiod[82] for the same reasons.' 'There are not above two or three lines in Virgil from Hesiod's works, he acknowledges imitating that poet; and would never do so, for two or three lines only.'[83] I interpret this puzzling passage to mean that, in Pope's opinion, Virgil was chary of acknowledging indebtedness to earlier poets; and that when he confesses to the borrowing of a few lines, as he does with regard to Hesiod, one is to take that as evidence that the borrowing was far more extensive than the acknowledgment. No doubt one must not lean too heavily upon this passage; certainly it was not intended as a severe condemnation of Virgil. Perhaps there was an autobiographical, half-humorous pleasure in catching a great predecessor in subterfuge. But if such is the case, of course Pope has amusingly misconceived the background of the whole. Virgil's indebtedness to Hesiod, whose *Works and Days* furnished a Greek prototype to the *Georgics*, was frank and apparent, as was that to Lucretius. A Latin poet who followed a Greek model in his genre more or less closely was not guilty of plagiarism because he did not list at the bottom of his pages, as it was fashionable to do in Pope's own day, the passages he was imitating.[84]

It is certainly exaggerating and modernizing to suppose, as Pope does, that 'the *Aeneid* was evidently a party piece: as much so as *Absalom and Achitophel*,'[85] even when one makes fullest allowance for nationalism and the desire to recommend an emperor to republicans as among the motives of Virgil.[86]

In the *Temple of Fame* where, after the neo-classical convention, each 'kind' is represented by a Greek and his analogous Roman, Horace is made the parallel to Pindar: both wrote odes. In accordance with this arrangement, the graceful lines to be quoted confine their attention to the lyric art of the Roman poet:

[81] Eclogue VI, 8.

[82] *Georgics*, II, 176.

[83] Spence, 215-16. The punctuation of the clumsy and baffling second sentence is as in the original.

[84] See also Spence, 217 on Virgil's indebtedness to earlier Roman writers.

[85] Spence, 217.

[86] See E-C, VI, 99, for an exegesis of a passage in the *Aeneid*, Book II.

Here happy Horace tuned th' Ausonian lyre
To sweeter sounds, and tempered Pindar's fire:
Pleased with Alcaeus' manly rage t' infuse
The softer spirit of the Sapphic muse.
The polished pillar different sculptures grace,
A work outlasting monumental brass.[87]
Here smiling loves and bachanals appear,
The Julian star, and great Augustus here;
The doves, that round the infant poet spread
Myrtles and bays, hung hovering o'er his head.[88]

This passage of only ten lines 'is replete with allusions to the Odes, containing in its short compass ten or more such references, and indicating already Pope's wonderful power to weld into a new and original whole material that he had gathered from many sources.'[89]

The translation of Horace has been the delight and despair of vernacular poets in all centuries. In the 'ages' of Dryden and Pope the versions were frequently very free. The *belles infidèles* of d'Ablancourt find plenty of English parallels. It was customary ingeniously to adapt a foreign original to national taste, to substitute for the topical allusions of one country those of the other. Thus the Soame-Dryden version of Boileau's *Art Poétique* supplies a running commentary on the history of English poetry and draws its examples from the English poets where the original has used French poetry and French poets. Dryden carefully distinguished three degrees of closeness in translation—metaphrase, paraphrase, and imitation. The distinctions are not inviolable; and paraphrase runs imperceptibly into imitation. Pope's versions are commonly 'imitations.' Of his two versions of the Odes (Bk. IV, 8 and 9), the latter is fragmentary and very soon substitutes for Homer, Pindar, Alcaeus, and Anacreon the native worthies, Milton, Spenser, Waller, and Cowley. The former is fairly close to the original both in letter and spirit; and the variations in the interest of topical allusion are uncommonly happy, as when Pope renders *'Non sum qualis eram bonae Sub regno Cinarae'* with

I am not now, alas, the man
As in the gentle reign of my Queen Anne.[90]

[87] *Odes*, Book III, 30: 'Exegi monumentum aere perennius.'
[88] ll. 221-36.
[89] Goad, 134.
[90] In neither of the odes does Pope attempt elaborate stanzaic forms; but, it is interesting to note, in neither does he use his 'standard' heroic couplet. One is in octosyllabic quatrains; the other in distichs, the first line octosyllabic, the last decasyllabic.

The *Satires* and *Epistles* of Horace were sure to appeal to the greatest of English satirists by their acute and detailed observation of manner and their shrewd wit and wisdom; and, Dr. Johnson to the contrary, the *Imitations* have given pleasure to common readers.[91] The reflections and judgments of Horace were, as Pope says in his Advertisement, 'seasonable to the present times.' The Epistle *To Augustus* becomes, *mutatis mutandis*, a survey of the English poets. One can read between the lines in the analysis of the original: 'Horace here pleads the cause of his contemporaries, first against the taste of the town, whose humor it was to magnify the authors of the preceding age;[92] secondly, against the court and nobility, who encouraged only the writers for the theatre,'[93] and so on. Such was, with all their differences in temper, the likeness between translator and translated[94] that one shares Spence's regret that Pope did not live to make a complete version,[95] and is surprised that Bolingbroke was required to suggest the undertaking.

Pope 'met with Statius very early, liked him much, and translated a good deal from him; and to the last he used to call him the best of all the Latin epic poets after Virgil';[96] or, as it is elsewhere more strongly put, 'He used to declare that, of the Latin poets, he preferred Statius next after Virgil.'[97] The translation of the first book of the *Thebaid* was declared by the poet to have been done at the age of fourteen, but it was not published until he was twenty-four, and Elwin suspects, no doubt justly, that it was mostly written shortly before publication.[98] Pope's taste for Statius had, like his taste for Ovid, to be apologetically attributed by Spence to an early favoritism; and the half-professed romanticist Warton falls into neo-classical temper and diction: 'It was in his childhood

[91] E-C, III, 347.

[92] The 'age' of Dryden and Congreve.

[93] E-C, III, 347.

[94] Bobertag, however, puts it rather too strongly when he says (*Englische Studien*, III, 75) 'Q. Horatius Flaccus und Alexander Pope sind geistesverwandte wie es veilleicht in der Literatur wenige gibt.'

[95] Spence, 297. 'When I was saying to him that he had already imitated a third part of Horace's Satires and Epistles, and how much it was to be wished that he would go on with them, he could not believe that he had gone near so far; but, upon computing, it appeared to be above a third. He seemed on this not disinclined to carry it further; but his last illness was then growing upon him, and robbed us of him and all hopes of that kind in a few months after.' The existent Imitations are of Satires I from Book I, and II and VI from Book II; Epistles I, VI, and VII from Book I, and I and II from Book II.

[96] Spence, 274.

[97] Ruffhead, 14, n.

[98] E-C, I, 47.

only that Pope could make choice of so injudicious a writer as
Statius to translate.'[99]

But his critics might have spared their fears. Pope himself, at
the age of twenty, fresh from the manuals of Horace and Bossu,
was perfectly able to detect the 'injudiciousness' of a poet of the
Silver Age; and he very obligingly pointed it out in several
of his adolescently learned letters to Cromwell: 'You will find, I
doubt not, upon reading, that Statius was none of the discreetest
poets, though he was the best versifier next Virgil. In the very
beginning he unluckily betrays his ignorance in the rules of
poetry (which Horace had already taught the Romans) when he
asks his Muse where to begin his *Thebaid*, and seems to doubt
whether it should not be *ab ovo Ledaeo*. When he comes to the
scene of his poem, and the prize in dispute between the brothers,
he gives us a very mean opinion of it—*Pugna est de paupere regno*:
Very different from the conduct of his master, Virgil, who at the
entrance of his poem informs his reader of the greatness of its
subject—*Tantae molis erat Romanam condere gentem*.'[100] Other
rules have been broken. 'The duration of the action of Statius'
poem may as well be excepted against, as many things besides in
him, which I wonder Bossu had not observed;[101] for instead of
confining his narration to one year, it is manifestly exceeded in the
first two books. . . . But Bossu himself is mistaken in one particular relating to the commencement of the action, saying in Book II,
cap. 8, that Statius opens it with Europa's Rape, whereas the poet
only deliberates whether he should or not. . . . Indeed, there are
numberless particulars blameworthy in our author, which I have
tried to soften in the version.'[102] This passage he finds 'most ex-
travagantly hyperbolical'; nor did he 'ever read a greater piece of
tautology than' that; and in the journey of Polynices he is
properly shocked to discover gross geographical error. Surely
Spence and Warton need not have feared the taste which could be
so 'regular' and 'judicial' with its favorite.

Of the Latin satirists other than Horace, Pope seems best to
have known Persius. Four of his verses he quoted in the days of
his eloquent apostolate to Cromwell, with the observation that 'these
four lines are as elegant and musical as any in Persius, not excepting those six or seven Mr. Dryden quotes as the only such in all

[99] E-C, I, 43.
[100] *ibid.*, VI, 74.
[101] Book II, chapter 8, of Le Bossu, entitled 'Of the Faults which Corrupt
the Unity of the Action,' is devoted to making a horrible example of the
Thebaid.
[102] E-C, VI, 79-80.

that author.'[103] Fourteen years afterward the same passage was quoted in a letter to Broome, Pope noting that there are not many lines in Persius so 'beautiful,' 'though there are many very sensible and philosophical.'[104] Sheridan sent Pope a copy of his new prose translation of Persius.[105] Presumably the poet had read his Juvenal, though the evidence is slight.[106] At least four separate passages from Martial are quoted in the letters.[107]

Tibullus is once quoted. There is a brief epistolary excerpt from one of Seneca's tragedies. To Dr. Parnell, its Augustan translator, the *Pervigilium Veneris* is praised as a masterpiece in kind.[108]

Except for Cicero, it would seem that Pope's acquaintance with Latin prose was slight. He occasionally quotes from or cites Pliny, Tacitus, Aulus Gellius, and Macrobius.[109] The passages from Cicero quoted in the letters and the notes to Homer are drawn from a considerable number of the writings—*De Legibus, De Oratoribus*, the *Tusculan Disputations*, the *Orations, De Natura Deorum*,[110] the *Rhetoric*. Of course some of these may have been borrowed from their citation in later authorities. The description of 'Tully' in *The Temple of Fame* is curiously vague, the sort of general praise which one might pay who felt no devotion but the duty of respect and homage.

We have interesting evidence that Pope did not share the worship of Cicero's prose-diction, sentence structure, rhythm—which in Ascham and some of his Continental contemporaries attained the fanatical pitch of the Maronolatry among the poets. When Warburton was negotiating for the genteel embalmment in Latin prose of the *Essay on Man*, the poet, coveting the honor, yet feared that the translator's puristic Ciceronianism might preclude the exactness of the version. 'The translation you are a much better judge of than I,' he wrote the Bishop of Gloucester, 'as your continued familiarity with the learned languages makes you infinitely more a master of them. I would only recommend that the translator's attention to Tully's Latinity may not preclude his usage of some terms which may be more precise in modern philosophy[111] than

[103] E-C, VI, 105.
[104] *ibid.*, VIII, 78.
[105] *ibid.*, VII, 136.
[106] *ibid.*, VII, 483; *Observations*, V: XXIX.
[107] *ibid.*, VI, 67, 107; VIII, 26, 273.
[108] *ibid.*, IX, 363; VI, 281; VII, 460.
[109] In the *Observations*.
[110] *Observations*, VII: XL. III: XXIX. VI: XXIII. V: XXXIV. E-C, VI, 86, 581; II, 54.
[111] Comment is later made on Pope's admiration for modern philosophy, especially Bacon, Hobbes, and Locke.

such as he could serve himself of, especially in matters meta-physical. I think this specimen close enough and clear also, *as far as the classical phrases allow*; from which yet I would rather he sometimes deviated than suffered the sense to be either dubious or clouded too much.'[112] Evidently, though the friend of the classics and 'correctness,' Pope was yet more the friend of reason.

Pope's acquaintance with ancient literature was, like that of most of the men of letters of his day, not profound; it was scanty as regards Greek. Homer was generally read, but the Greek drama-tists and Plato were neglected. With Latin literature Pope was commendably conversant. There is hardly an important author in it with which he was unfamiliar, and Ovid, Statius, Virgil, and Horace, he had made his permanent possessions. The classicism of the French and English Augustans was not Hellenism: that was yet to come; the 'Greek view of life' yet awaited its Winckelmann and Goethe to expound it. Before the balance could swing to the large sanity of the Greeks, revolt against the license of thought and emotion in the Renaissance must veer more sharply to the other extreme. In the urbanity of Horace and the disciplined art of Virgil Pope, like his contemporaries, found the inspiration nec-essary to the production in English life and literature of an 'ele-gant' and 'judicious' classicism.

[112] E-C, IX, 211-12.

CHAPTER VII

STUDIES IN CONTINENTAL AUTHORS

POPE was distinctly a man of the Renaissance and the Enlightenment.[1] His view of the Middle Ages was not informed
or meliorated by his inherited religion; a rationalist, he was
willing to credit the worst of the long centuries between the old
and the new classicism.

> Much was believed, but little understood,
> And to be dull was construed to be good;
> A second deluge learning thus o'errun
> And the monks finished what the Goths begun.[2]

According to the youthful historian, it was Erasmus who was
responsible for the end of 'the wild torrent of a barbarous age';
indeed, he is gravely asserted to have driven the 'holy vandals,'
the monks, 'off the stage,' though precisely when this personally
effected dissolution of monasticism took place one may be permitted
to wonder. Surely stronger forces than the humanism and satire of
Erasmus were at work in the Reformation. This strange passage
in the *Essay on Criticism* aroused, as might be expected, something
of a disturbance in the local Catholic society,[3] and threatenings
were heard of a storm which never broke. It was as a Churchman
who was at the same time disinterested friend of mankind and
enemy of imposture and corruption without and within ecclesiastical walls that Erasmus interested Pope. No doubt he saw a parallel between their cases: both remained in the Church, yet both
were far from bound by its dogmas (one has only to read the
Encomium Moriae to see how little positive doctrine Erasmus
held); both were men of letters and satirists; both isolated from
their fellow churchmen by their tolerance. During the worst of the
little tempest of 1711, Pope wrote his companion in the faith: 'I

---

[1] See Bobertag's *Pope's Verhältnis zu der Aufklärung des 18 j. h.* (*Englische Studien*, XXIX, 26-62).

[2] *Essay on Criticism*, III, 130-3.

[3] '. . . the zealous papists thought the monks treated with too much
contempt, and Erasmus too studiously praised.' Johnson: *Lives of the
Poets*, II, 98.

will set before me that excellent example of that great man and great saint, Erasmus, who in the midst of calumny proceeded with all the calmness of innocence and the unrevenging spirit of primitive Christianity. However, I would advise them [the shocked zealous Catholics] to suffer the mention of him [in the *Essay*] to pass unregarded, lest I should be forced to do that for his reputation which I would never do for my own—I mean to vindicate so great a light of our church from the malice of past times and the ignorance of the present, in a language which may extend farther than that in which the trifle about criticism is written.'[4] The proposed *Vita* was never written;[5] but it was certainly not loss of interest in the great humanist which put an end to the project. In one of those equally vague and bland 'affirmations' of Christian faith with which Pope was pleased to favor his friends he spoke of himself as 'of the religion of Erasmus, a Catholic.'[6]

Of the Italian poets who wrote in the vernacular, Pope's knowledge was not great. Dante he knew not at all: this ignorance was all but universal in his day.[7] A learned Italian, Dr. Cocchi, said to Spence,[8] with the condescension of a post-Petrarchan, that 'Dante wrote before we began to be at all refined; and of course his celebrated poem is a sort of Gothic work.'

Tasso and Ariosto[9] Pope read in translation[10] when in the full course of his 'great reading period.' 'I even then liked Tasso better than Ariosto,' he told Spence, 'as I do still.'[11] But after he had reached the maturity of fifteen, he passed a period in London with the express intention of learning French and Italian. According to Ruffhead,[12] he 'mastered those languages with surprising dispatch.' It is possible that Tasso at least was later re-read in the original. In the *Observations on the Iliad*, Tasso is, after Virgil and Milton,

---

[4] E-C, VI, 143.

[5] Pope was a pretty accurate judge of his own powers, and was careful to leave his Latinity to be conjectured. He is reported to have written a treatise, in Latin, on the old buildings in Rome, the material collected from the old writers in Graevius; but neither this or any other specimen of his powers in Latin prose is available. See Spence, 204.

[6] E-C, VII, 175.

[7] In the age of Johnson also; Gray is a notable exception. There is an interesting note on Dante and the English eighteenth century appended to Brown, 324.

[8] Spence, 98.

[9] Ariosto is a few times cited, e.g., *Observations on Iliad*, XIV: XXIII; and, interestingly, in one of Pope's own notes to the *Rape*, E-C, II, 179, n. 5.

[10] Ariosto, presumably, in the translation of Harrington, 1591; Tasso in that of Fairfax, 1600.

[11] Spence, 279. Ruffhead (14, n.) bears the same testimony.

[12] *Life*, 12-13.

the epic poet most frequently cited for his parallels to—or, more precisely, his imitations of—Homer. Extended passages are quoted from the *Jerusalem Delivered*—in the Italian ; and there is evident a detailed knowledge of episodes, characters, and motives in Tasso's work. Some examples may be given. Pope points out the imitation of the cestus of Venus in the magical girdle of Armida.[13] He is keen to detect similes imitated by Tasso from Homer.[14] Sarpedon and Glaucus, bravest of Trojan auxiliaries, were Greeks by birth. 'Tasso in this manner has introduced an agreeable episode which shows Clorinda the offspring of Christian parents, tho' engaged in the service of the Infidels (Cant. 12).'[15] 'This interposition of the two heralds to part the combatants on the approach of night (1. 334) is applied by Tasso in the 6th book of his *Jerusalem* to the single combat of Tancred and Argantes. The Herald's speech, and particularly that remarkable injunction to *obey the night*, are translated literally by that author.'[16] The following differentiation of the Homeric original and subsequent 'catalogues' is pointed : 'Of the moderns, those which most excel owe their beauty to the imitation of some single particular only of Homer. Thus the chief grace of Tasso's catalogue consists in the description of the heroes, without anything remarkable on the side of the countries : of the pieces of story he has interwoven, that of Tancred's amour to Clorinda is ill-placed and evidently too long for the rest.'[17] There is a touch of realism in the comment made on Tasso's imitation of the glimpse of the Grecian leaders from the walls of Troy, 'where Erminia from the walls of Jerusalem points out the chief warriors to the King' ; Pope considers 'the latter part is perhaps copied too closely and minutely, for he [Tasso] describes Godfrey to be of a port that bespeaks him a prince, the next of somewhat a lower stature,' and so on.[18]

Pope's early friend, Walsh, possessed 'a considerable knowledge of the Italian poets at a period when those delightful writers were neglected by his countrymen.'[19] He took an especial interest in pastoral comedy, and urged Pope to attempt something in that 'kind.' It was no doubt at his suggestion that the young poet read Tasso's *Aminta* and Guarini's *Pastor Fido*, the most celebrated examples of the form ; it is to Walsh that Pope sends his comment on the two. Were he to write a pastoral play he would, he says, 'certainly displease all those who are charmed with Guarini and

---

[13] *Observations*, XIV : XX.
[14] *ibid.*, VI : LV.
[15] *ibid.*, VI : X.
[16] *ibid.*, VII : XXXIV.
[17] *ibid.*, II : Preface.
[18] *ibid.*, III : XXIII ; see also *ibid.*, VII, XXXIV.
[19] Dyce, in the Aldine Pope, I, xix.

Bonarelli, and imitate Tasso, not only in the simplicity of his thoughts, but in that of the fable too.' Accordingly he praises the *Aminta* because its plot lacks complexity and there is nothing in it 'but happens by mere chance,' while 'the contrary is observable in *Pastor Fido*, where Corisca is so perfect a mistress of intrigue that the plot could not have been brought to pass without her.'[20]

There is evidence from both ends of Pope's life that he had a taste for the now too nearly forgotten Italian poets of the Renaissance '*Qui Latine scripserunt*.' Dr. Johnson speaks of them as not much explored by other English writers, contemned by Boileau, and 'too generally neglected. Pope, however, was not ashamed of their acquaintance, nor ungrateful for the advantages which he might have derived from it.'[21]

Politian he read when very young; and he marked the *Ambra* as his favorite, adding in the margin, 'Optimum hoc, ut puto, Politiani opus est.' He retained his admiration for it in later life, to the distress of Spence, who found in it too much of the manner of Claudian.[22] The same obliging scribe preserves the series of summary judgments that 'Politian is one of the first rate modern Italian poets. Molza, very good. Bembo and Sadoleto write pure Latin, but are stiff and unpoetical.'[23] Pope once obliged his early friend Cromwell with his learning to the effect that '*The Fable of the Nightingale* in Philips' *Pastorals* is taken from Famianus Strada's Latin poem on the same subject, in his *Prolusiones Academicae*; only the tomb he erects at the end is added from Virgil's conclusion of the *Culex*.' He quotes at length from the Latin; then additionally notes that Crashaw has imitated the same original (in *Music's Duel*).[24]

In 1740—that is to say, toward the close of his life—Pope brought out in a two-volume edition the Latin poems of Italian poets.[25] This work, which Saintsbury speaks of as 'that rather remarkable collection . . . of which not much notice has been taken by Pope's biographers,'[26] was a re-issue of an older collection, with

---

[20] E-C, VI; 52.
[21] *Lives of the Poets*, III, 182. Dr. Johnson himself had a 'peculiar fondness for modern Latin poetry' (See Houston, 15-16), and proposed editing Politian (Boswell, I, 90).
[22] Spence, 273-4.
[23] *ibid.*, 23.
[24] E-C, VI, 109.
[25] *Selecta Poemata Italorum. Qui Latine Scripserunt. Cura cujusdam anonymi anno 1684 congesta, iterum in lucem data, una cum aliorum Italorum operibus, Accurante A. Pope. London, J. P. Knapton, 1740.*
[26] *History of Literary Criticism*, II, 455.

some additions. It contains no preface and no notes; the only editorial labor visible consists in an appendage of corrections. The edition is still the standard—indeed, I believe, the only available —collection of the poets represented; and it still appears in modern bibliographies—chiefly as the source for citations from Vida.

Warton wrote characteristically of the undertaking, 'Pope amused himself in 1740 in republishing *Selecta Carmina Italorum*, but he took no notice of the edition from which he borrowed his collection,[27] called *Anthologia*, printed in London in 12mo., 1684, with a most judicious Preface, and one of the best pieces of modern Latinity, falsely ascribed to Atterbury; which he omitted, I think, very improperly. What he added was a very indifferent poem of Aonius Palearius, *De Immortalitate Animi*, in three books, when he might have enriched his collection by many more pieces of Vida, Ant. Flaminius, Cotta, Sannazarius, Politianus,[28] Molza, and the Strozzi. . . .'[29]

It may be useful—since the volumes are somewhat rare—to include here a list of the poets who appear in the collection. Volume One is divided into three parts. The first consists of the eclogues of Sannazarius, Amaltheus, and Vida; the second, of the curious long poems of Fracastorius on Syphilis, or '*Morbus Gallicus*,'[30] and *Alcon*, or *de cura canum venaticorum*. Part three adds to Vida's long poems, *Bombycum*, *Poeticorum*, and *Scacchia*,[31] the three books of Palearius on the immortality of the soul. Volume Two, again in three parts, contains elegies by Sannazarius, Janus Etruscus, Titus Stroza of Ferrara, Hercules Stroza, Molza, Naugerius, Pontanus, Politianus, Areostus (Ariosto); odes by Flaminius, Augurellius, Sannazarius, Pontanus, Naugerius, Areostus, Crinitus, Archius, Politianus, Amaltheus, J. Cotta, G. Buchananus (the celebrated Scotch scholar, George Buchanan), Vaxis, Fascitellius, Parlistaneus, and Amaltheus; finally, *Sylvae* by Politianus (*Nutricia, Rusticus, Manto, Ambra*), Sadoletus, Bembo, Fracastoro, Castilionius (Castiglione, author of *Il Cortegiano*), and Amaltheus.

[27] This is a curious assertion. The title-page says, '*cura cujusdam anonymi anno 1684 congesta.*'

[28] Sannazaro; Politian.

[29] Warton, *Works of Pope*, I, lxi-ii.

[30] This poem was greatly admired by scholars. For interesting list of didactic poems of sixteenth-eighteenth centuries see Warton, *Genius of Pope*, II, 54-5. Rapin called it 'the most excellent poem in Latin verse that these latter ages has [*sic*] produced in Italy. . . .' *Works*, II, 148 (tr. by Kennett).

[31] Vida's game of chess is the original of the game of *ombre* in the *Rape*.

Notice has already been taken of Pope's study of the modern languages (i.e., French and Italian) in London. Ruffhead speaks of this as a thorough discipline: 'He readily submitted himself to the fatigue and drudgery of perpetually recurring to grammars and dictionaries,' and 'insensibly made himself master' of the languages. But doubts have been cast upon this mastery. Voltaire, in particular, who was several times Pope's guest, said he 'could hardly read' French and 'spoke not one syllable of the language.'[32] He doubted that Pope had written the letter in French which was addressed under his name to Racine the younger,[33] in the reply to the latter's attack on the orthodoxy of *The Essay on Man*. 'Pope, to his knowledge had not skill enough in the French language to have been able to have written this letter to Racine; and, if he really wrote it, he must suddenly have been blest with a gift of tongues as a reward for writing so admirable a work as the *Essay on Man*!'[34] Pope himself spoke modestly of his attainments in this as in the 'learned' languages. He prefaced the *critique* of Voltaire's *Henriade* which Lord Bolingbroke requested of him with the apology, 'I cannot pretend to judge with any exactness of the beauties of a foreign language which I understand but imperfectly.'[35] Nevertheless, there is ground for thinking that though he may not have been able to converse in French or perhaps to write in it, yet he was able to read it with fair fluency. De Quincey, commenting on Voltaire's comments, observes sensibly that 'Pope in his [Voltaire's] presence would decline to speak or read a language of which the pronunciation was confessedly beyond him.'[36] Or if he did, the impression left would be still worse.

[32] *Oeuvres*, XXII, 178. Pope 'pouvait à peine lire de français, . . . il ne parlait pas un mot de notre langue. . . .'

[33] Louis Racine, (1692-1763) son of the celebrated tragic poet; himself a Jansensist, and poet of *La Grace* and *Religion*.

[34] Warton, *Works of Pope*, I, xlvii. There is an elaborate note on this letter in Hill's ed. of *Lives of the Poets*, III, 215, n. Voltaire claimed that Ramsay was responsible for the 'sentiments' of the letter (not wishing it thought that Pope had retracted his deism). Elwin thinks Ramsay merely translated. E-C, II, 291.

[35] E-C, VII, 401.

[36] The British have never been famous for their mastery of French pronunciation. We need not recall Chaucer's prioress who spoke French 'after the scole of Stratford atte Bowe'; but it is interesting to know that the 'Eminent Augustans' had studied at the same school. 'Johnson, though thoroughly versed in that language and a professed admirer of Boileau and LaBruyere, did not understand its pronunciation'; and Edmund Burke, who was another devoted Bolevian, read his French 'not only with the English accent, but exactly as if the two nations had one pronunciation in common of the alphabet.' (These contemporary accounts are quoted in Clark, 55 and 79.)

In fact, no man ever will pronounce or talk a language which he does not use for some part of every day in the real intercourse of life. But that Pope read French of an ordinary cast with fluency enough is evident from the extensive use which he made of Madame Dacier's labors on the *Iliad*, and still more of La Valterie's prose translation of the *Iliad*.'[37] In Pope's 1718 correspondence with the Duke of Buckingham over the La Motte-Dacier controversy Pope showed 'accurate acquaintance' with the French authors concerned. 'In particular, he characterized the excellent notes upon Horace of M. Dacier the husband in very just terms as distinguished from those of his conceited and half-learned wife.'[38] Dacier's nine-volume edition of Horace was not yet in English. Pope 'read critically' the French translations of his own *Essay on Man, on Criticism*, and *the Rape*; and 'spoke of them as a critic.'[39] De Quincey may be considered to make his case.

As one would expect, his acquaintance with French literature was largely confined to the seventeenth century. The great sixteenth century prose classics, Rabelais and Montaigne, he seems to have read, but without marked appreciation. He once speaks of reading the letters of Montaigne in the edition of Coste;[40] and at least twice quotes or cites from the moralist.[41] Once the autobiographical candor of the moralist prompts a comparison: 'I love to pour out all myself as plain . . . as old Montaigne.'[42]

Swift had a great fondness for Rabelais, and at his recommendation Pope attempted to read, but without ardor. He told Spence, 'Dr. Swift was a great reader and admirer of Rabelais; and used sometimes to scold me for not liking him enough. Indeed, there were so many things in his works in which I could not see any manner of meaning driven at that I could never read him over with any patience.'[43] Upon another occasion he gave the following account of Rabelais' procedure: He 'had written some sensible pieces which the world did not regard at all.—"I will write something (says he) that they shall take notice of"; and so sat down to writing nonsense. Everybody allows that there are several things without any manner of meaning in his *Pantagruel*. Dr. Swift likes

[37] *Works*, IV, 246. Pope speaks of La Valterie's as 'a very elegant prose translation'; 'so elegant that the style of it was evidently the original and model of the famous *Telemaque*.' E-C, X, 146.

[38] De Quincey, IV, 246.

[39] *ibid.*, IV, 247.

[40] E-C, VI, 380. P. Coste, who was at one time preceptor to the Earl of Shaftsbury, produced, according to Warton, the best edition of Montaigne ever published.

[41] E-C, VII, 7; VIII, 214; VI, 380.

[42] *First Satire of the Second Book of Horace*, 51-2.

[43] Spence, 141.

it much, and thinks there are more good things in it than I do. Friar John's character is maintained throughout with a great deal of spirit. His concealed characters are touched only in part, and by fits: as, for example, though the king's mistress be meant in such a particular related of Gargantua's mare, the very next thing that is said of the mare will not, perhaps, at all apply to the mistress.'[44] With these passing censures, Pope was content, without emulation, to let his friend Swift 'laugh and shake in Rabelais' easy chair.'[45]

It is impossible to say with what particularity he knew the great tragic dramatists, Corneille and Racine; but it was at any rate sufficient to enable him to indulge in the favorite pastime of contrasting them. To be sure, speaking to Spence of absurd comparisons, he cited as such Homer with Virgil, and Corneille with Racine, with the just comment, 'These are *magis pares quam similes.*' Nevertheless, the eighteenth century was quite as fond of this pleasing parlor *divertissement* as the nineteenth, with its antitheses of Tennyson and Browning, Dickens and Thackeray; and Pope himself indulged:

> Exact Racine and Corneille's noble fire
> Showed us that France had something to admire.[46]

or again, slightly amplified, 'Racine's character is justness and correctness; Corneille's, passion and life: Corneille[47] stumbles oftener, and has greater excellencies.'[48] Still more amplified is the pair of eulogies with which Pope is represented as favoring Boileau in Hades, and for which Pope's devoted friend and junior, Lord Lyttleton, is the trustworthy authority.[49] Racine is praised for his sweetness and correctness, Corneille for his 'masculine strength and greatness of thought'; the one is compared to the swan, the other to the eagle. 'The *Athalia* of Racine is in my judgment equal to the sublimest plays of Corneille, and the tender passions are certainly touched by that elegant and most pathetic writer with a

[44] *Spence*, 207-8.
[45] *Dunciad*, I, 22. Pope was not the only one to notice the resemblance between the two satirists. Voltaire (*Oeuvres*, XXII, 174) says, 'M. Swift est Rabelais dans son bon sens.'
[46] *Epistle to Augustus*, 274-5.
[47] It is interesting to note that Pope rhymes Corneille with Ozell (*Dunciad*, I, 286).
[48] Spence, 10.
[49] In his *Dialogues of the Dead*. Pope called Lyttleton 'a very particular and very deserving friend, one of those whom his own merit has forced me to contract an intimacy with, after I had sworn never to love a man more. . . . I mean Mr. Lyttleton, one of the worthiest of the rising generation.' E-C, VII, 367 (written in 1738).

much finer hand. He is also by far more correct than the other, and more harmonious and noble in his versification.'[50] In the same dialogue Pope is represented as seeing the great French dramatist walking hand in hand with the great Greeks (Euripides, Sophocles, and Menander), while the English dramatists seem not so fond of classical company. 'They sometimes shove rudely by them, and give themselves airs of superiority. They slight their reprimands, and laugh at their precepts. In short, they will be tried by *their country* alone. . . .'[51]

Boileau was the French poet whom Pope best knew and most esteemed; 'the first poet of the French,' he called him, 'in the same manner as Virgil of the Latin: Malherbe, *longo intervallo*, the second.'[52] If he did not write the Letter prefixed to the *Dunciad*— and there is reason for thinking he did—Pope would have agreed with the amplified characterization there given of Boileau as 'the greatest poet and most judicious critic of his age and country, admirable for his talents, and yet perhaps even more admirable for his judgment in the proper application of them.'[53]

It was with happy propriety that Lyttleton brought the great classical poets of France and England together in the longest and best of his *Dialogues of the Dead*. Boileau recalls being told that Pope had made him his poetic model: contemporaries were, we know from other sources, fond of speaking of the 'English Boileau'[54] Pope replies, with what is a polite evasion, 'We both followed Horace.'[55] Both did indeed partly follow Horace; but, as we have already seen, Pope's following was sometimes derivative. A little later in the conversation, the English poet is pleased to draw the parallel in some detail: 'We both of us carried the beauty of our diction and the harmony of our numbers to the highest perfection that our languages would admit. Our poems were labored and polished to the utmost degree of correctness, yet without losing their fire, or the pleasing appearance of freedom and ease.'[56]

[50] Lyttleton, 120-1.
[51] *ibid.*, 120. Even Dryden asserts, in contradistinction to the 'rules of the French stage' 'which are extremely different from ours by reason of their opposite taste,' the necessity for English dramatists' following the 'opposite taste' of their public: 'Our audience will not be pleased but with variety of accidents, an underplot, and many actors . . .' (Ker., II, 17 and 7).
[52] Spence, 10.
[53] E-C, IV, 46.
[54] Voltaire himself so speaks of Pope. *Oeuvres*, XXII, 184.
[55] See Voltaire's *Parallèle d'Horace, de Boileau, et de Pope* (*Oeuvres*, XXIV, 223 ff.).
[56] Lyttleton, 115.

It is in the *Essay on Criticism*,[57] *the Rape of the Lock*, and the *Satires* that the relation between the two poets is most closely traced. 'Pope refers to the *Lutrin* in his manuscript notes on the Remarks of Dennis,[58] and certainly had it in mind when he framed the scheme of his poem.'[59] A few brief passages in *The Rape* seem 'direct echoes' of Boileau; there are more which come through the mediation of Garth's *Dispensary*. The allegorical figure Spleen seems suggested by Boileau's portraits of La Discorde and La Chicane. As Ariel appears in a dream to Belinda to warn her of approaching disaster, so in *Le Lutrin* Discord 'appears to the sleeping treasurer, warning him against the encroachment of the rebellious precentor.' The address of the gnome to the goddess of Spleen 'in its conception and construction, in the very sequence of its clauses,' seems modelled on the speech of Sidrac to Chicane. Like Pope, Boileau made a special feature of introducing into his mock-heroic poem parodies of well-known passages in the classics.[60]

'All readers of Pope's satires must also,' says De Quincey, 'recollect numerous proofs that he has read Boileau with so much feeling of his peculiar merit that he has appropriated and naturalized in English some of his best passages.'[61] These approximations have been collected by Professor Clark, and prove not nearly so 'numerous' as one might have supposed[62]—even if one considers all the amassed parallels as real imitations, instead of the similar thoughts of similar minds. Most convincing is the suggested indebtedness of the *Epistle to Dr. Arbuthnot* to Boileau's Ninth Satire, the *Address à Son Esprit*, (this Dr. Johnson had pointed out in his *Life of Pope*[63]) and his Tenth Epistle. 'Nearly all these borrowings concern passages dealing with his personality, his integrity as a satirist, his entertainment of the great, his parentage.'[64] Like Pope, Boileau had enumerated the distinguished who had praised him and urged him to write in contrast to the undiscriminating who scoffed; like him, he had given an account of his ancestry and parents; like him, he had urged the uprightness of his character.[65] Professor Clark goes so far as to think that Pope 'clothed himself

---

[57] cf. pp. 16-19, *supra*.

[58] Dennis' pamphlet against *The Rape of the Lock*. See E-C, II, 132.

[59] E-C, II, 126. Elwin works out in detail the likenesses between these two 'serio-comical' poems. Pope once cites an incident from *Le Lutrin* in his *Observations on the Iliad* (XIV, 23).

[60] The parallels given are taken from Clark, 198-203.

[61] *Works*, IV, 247.

[62] Clark, 210-14.

[63] *Lives of the Poets*, III, 177.

[64] Clark, 215.

[65] *ibid.*, 215-19.

in Boileau's personality' in this *Apologia*; that his pretended zeal for truth and morality and scorn for the base and the mean was all a pose 'suggested to him by the reading of Boileau's poems.'[66] This seems to me to plead the cause too far. If Pope's profession and his practice were not wholly consonant, it is hardly necessary to find the source of the profession in his reading. It is easy enough to interpret one's personal resentments as righteous indignation, to see in one's foe the enemy of sound learning and true virtue; and self-deception is the commonest of deceptions. Pope did not need to look at Boileau's portrait when he could find a flattering likeness of himself in the mirror vanity holds up before every man.

Chapelain, whose reputation as a poet was attacked and ruined by the great Boileau, Pope ranked at 'about the rate of our Sir W. Davenant; he has strong thoughts and no versification.'[67] It was a happy thought, thus to bring together the writers of the 'Christian epics,' *La Pucelle* and *Gondibert*.

With the great moralists of the French seventeenth century we might expect Pope to feel a very considerable affinity; and such seems to have been the case, though the relation is rather hinted than expressed by Pope himself and has become explicit only in the commentators.

Pope already knew Pascal in 1711, and quotes to his correspondent from one of the *Lettres Provinciales*.[68] In 1730-1731, when he was planning his *Moral Essays*, Caryll suggested to him the *Pensées* of Pascal as a parallel undertaking which might serve as model. Pope replied, 'Your recommendation of Pascal's *Pensées* is a good one, though I have been before hand with you in it; but he will be of little use to my design, which is rather to ridicule all men than preach to them. I fear our age is past all other correction.'[69] But if the disparity between forms and purposes was, as Pope was quite correct in thinking, too great to make the one work any guide to the construction of the other, the two moralists had more than a little in common. Both had studied themselves as well as society; both were able to penetrate subterfuge and illusion; both were conscious of the paradox of humanity: its baseness and its dignity; its shame and its glory; the animal in it and the god. Both practised the antithesis as something more than a rhetorical device: To both there was a philosophy of life in the sharp contrasts which exist in man himself as well as in the society which he has evoked. The great passage which opens the Second Epistle of the *Essay on Man* is perhaps chiefly to be attributed to Pascal. The *Adventurer* thought reflections in the lines beginning, 'Chaos of thought and passion all

[66] *ibid.*, 219.
[67] Spence, 22.
[68] E-C, VI, 154.
[69] *ibid.*, VI, 326.

confused,' were 'minutely copied from Pascal,' who wrote 'what a
chimera then is man! What a confused chaos! What a subject of
contradiction! A professed judge of all things, and yet a feeble
worm of the earth! The great depository and guardian of truth, and
yet a mere huddle of uncertainty! The glory and the scandal of the
universe!'[70] There is certainly a very considerable likeness in these
parallels; and no doubt a direct search would find many more.

Pope professed not to share La Rochefoucauld's cynicism. 'As
L'Esprit, La Rochefoucauld, and that sort of people, prove all
virtues are disguised vices, I would engage to prove all vices to be
disguised virtues. Neither, indeed, is true; but this would be a
more agreeable subject, and would overturn their whole scheme.'[71]
And, indeed, in the confused optimism of the *Essay on Man*, there
are evidences of his dallying with this 'more agreeable subject.'
He tells us that 'The surest virtues thus from passions shoot.'
There is no ultimate distinction between selfishness and altruism:
'self-love and social' are 'the same.' Mandeville was right in
thinking private vices the foundation of public benefits.

> one man's weakness grows the strength of all.
> Wants, frailties, passions, closer still ally
> The common int'rest, or endear the tie.[72]

When Pope was social satirist rather than social philosopher,
however, he was constitutionally of La Rochefoucauld's turn of
mind; and perhaps the lightly tossed off disavowal to Spence simply gives evidence of another concealment of obligation. Warton
was very willing to render proof of his own reading and insight in
discovering specific indebtedness of the English to the French
moralist. Three of these, consistent with Pope's inconsistency,
occur in the same *Essay on Man* which may be thought to attempt
the refutation of La Rochefoucauld. They are verses 157-8, 169-
70, and 272, all in the Second Epistle. The second of these citations, the thought that the love of ease is often triumphant over
what we are wont to think the stronger passions, is 'an acute observation, plainly taken from La Rochefoucauld.'[73]

There is no other reference to the writer of *La Sagesse* (1601)

---

[70] *Pensées*, Article XXII. For the *Adventurer's* identification see Warton:
Genius of Pope, II, 78.

[71] Spence, 11.

[72] *Essay on Man*: 183; III, 318; II, 252-4.

[73] Warton, *Genius of Pope*, II, 85. La Rochefoucauld wrote: 'C'est se
tromper que de croire qu'il n'y ait que les violentes passions, comme l'ambition et l'amour, qui puissent triompher des autres. La paresse, toute
languissante qu'elle est, ne laisse pas d'en être souvent la maîtresse . . .'
(Maxim 266. See also E-C, II, 308-9).

than the line in the First Epistle, 'what made, say Montaigne, or more sage Charron'; but Warton informs us 'Pope has borrowed many remarks from Charron, of which sensible writer Bolingbroke was particularly fond.'[74]

The comment on La Bruyère is good, if thin. In 1722 Pope wrote Miss Judith Cowper, the poetess, 'The book you mention, Bruyère's *Characters*, will make any one know the world, and I believe at the same time despise it; which is a sign it will make one know it thoroughly.[75] It is certainly the proof of a master-hand that can give such striking likenesses in such slight sketches and in so few strokes on each subject.'[76]

When Racine the younger accused Pope of infidelity in his *Essay on Man*, Pope sent him in reply not only the commentary on the work in which the learned Dr. Warburton, Lord Bishop of Gloucester, 'proved' its orthodoxy, but a protest in his own or another's French that 'mes sentiments sont diamétralement opposés à ceux de Spinoza et même à ceux de Leibnitz, puis qu'ils sont parfaitement conformés à ceux de M. Pascal et de M. l'Archevêque de Fénelon, et je ferois gloire d'imiter la docilité du dernier en soumettant toujours toutes mes opinions particulières aux décisions de l'Église.'[77] Methinks the gentleman doth protest too much! Had the Holy See been pleased to read this 'submission,' it must surely have been amused at the citation of Pascal, the Jansenist, and Fénelon, the Quietist, as models of orthodoxy.

It is doubtful if Pope ever read the spiritual writings of the Archbishop of Cambrai. But his *Telemachus*, that admired didactic epic in prose, was recommended to students of Homer and modern imitations: 'The conduct, turn, and disposition of the fable [in the *Odyssey*] is also what the critics allow to be the better model for epic writers to follow: accordingly we find much more of the cast of this poem than of the other [the *Iliad*] in the *Aeneid*, and (what next to that is perhaps the greatest example) in the *Telemachus*.'[78] Next after Virgil and Milton 'the Archbishop of Cambrai's *Telemachus* may give him [the student of Homer] the truest idea of the spirit and turn of our author.'[79] The *genre* was not, however, pure; the endorsement could not be complete. 'For my own part,' he told Spence, 'though I don't like that poetic kind

[74] *Genius of Pope*, II, 129.

[75] This is, of course, a favorite theme with Pope. Whether his professed aversion to the world was anything more than profession it is difficult to tell.

[76] E-C, IX, 421.

[77] Quoted in Warton, *Works of Pope*, I, xlvii.

[78] *Odyssey*, V, 269.

[79] Durham, 349.

of prose writing, yet I always read *Telemachus* with pleasure.'—
'That must be, then,' ventures the friend, 'from the good sense and
spirit of humanity that runs through the whole work?' 'Yes, it
must be that; for nothing else could make me forget my prejudices
against the style it is written in so much as I do.'[80]

While the gentlemen were taking a 'judicious' pleasure in the
'good sense and spirit of humanity' of *Telemachus*, the ladies were
passing the languorous pre-dinner hours with the delights of the
interminable French romances. 'As long as *Atalantis* shall be
read'[81] was the contemporary euphemism for 'forever.' References
in the letters which accompany the gift to the Misses Blount of
Mlle. de Scudéry's five volume *Grand Cyrus* would seem to indicate that Pope had himself read, or at any rate sampled, the book
of which he was donor.[82]

Another gift to 'the ladies,' the works of the genteel letter writer
and poet, Voiture, was accompanied by some elegant verses[83]
which began with characterization:

> In these gay thoughts the Loves and Graces shine,
> And all the writer lives in every line;
> His easy art may happy nature seem,
> Trifles themselves are elegant in him.

One must not expect the feelings moved by Voiture: 'in his letters
[he] wants sentiment: he wrote only to divert parties over their
tea.'[84] But it is eulogy enough to say, 'who beside Catullus and
Voiture can write agreeably upon trifles?'[85] Some graceful French
verses which Pope quoted without acknowledgment his correspondent, Cromwell, found in Voiture: and it was from a 'hint' in
the poems of the same author that Pope composed the 'humorous'
rondeau which he weighted with a long and pretentious history of
the *genre*.[86]

We pass now to the eighteenth century. Pope was an admirer of
Bayle and his *Dictionnaire Historique et Critique*. It was a high

---

[80] Spence, 141. *Télémaque* (1699) was a great favorite in England. It
'has, in whole or in part, been rendered into English over thirty times, and
some of these translations have seen six or even twelve editions.' Havens,
341.
[81] *Rape of the Lock*, III, 165.
[82] E-C, IX, 270.
[83] *Epistle to Mrs. Blount*, 1-4.
[84] Spence, 22.
[85] E-C, VI, 125.
[86] *ibid.*, VI, 100; VI, 97. Swift also praised Voiture in verse; see his
lines 'To Mr. Delany, Nov. 10, 1718' which begin:

> Voiture in various lights displays
> That irony which turns to praise. . . .

compliment he paid his old printer, Jacob Tonson, when he called him 'the perfect image and likeness of Bayle's Dictionary; so full of matter, secret history, and wit and spirit.'[87] And it was a high compliment he paid Bayle when, to someone who was speaking of the sceptic's 'manner in his Dictionary,' he said, 'Ay, he is the only man that ever collected with so much judgment and wrote with so much spirit at the same time.'[88]

Pope and Voltaire were personally acquainted. When the latter came upon his visit to England, he brought with him a letter of introduction to the former. He was treated to a dinner at Twickenham, during the course of which he described his malady in terms so gross that 'the poor lady [Mrs. Pope] was obliged immediately to rise from the table.' There were further unpleasantnesses. Pope alleged that Voltaire was, while he stayed in England, a spy for the court. He played a trick to test out his hypothesis: wrote a letter which was calculated to annoy the court, and found his 'secret communication' immediately imparted to the authorities. When Voltaire left England, he said to Pope, 'And now I am come to bid farewell to a man who has never treated me seriously from the first hour of my acquaintance with him to this moment.' 'Mr. Pope said the observation was just, and the reason of his conduct has been given above.'[89]

But personal differences were not allowed to disturb the professional esteem in which each held the other. Voltaire's admiration for Pope, as poet and philosopher, seems to have been almost without bounds. It was at the time of Voltaire's visit to England that Pope's chariot fell into the water with temporary injury, through the broken glass, to two of the poet's fingers; and a graceful note expressed the Frenchman's solicitude: 'Is it possible that those fingers which have written *The Rape of the Lock* and the *Criticism*, which have dressed Homer so becomingly in an English coat, should have been so barbarously treated? Let the hand of Dennis, or of your poetasters, be cut off. Yours is sacred.'[90] The *Essay on Man* he called 'le plus beau poème didactique, le plus utile, le plus sublime qu'on ait jamais fait dans aucune langue.'[91] He characterized Pope as 'le poète le plus élégant, le plus correct, et . . . le

[87] E-C, VIII, 279.

[88] Spence, 215.

[89] Ruffhead, 165. Warburton was R's authority for Pope's relations with Voltaire.

[90] Ruffhead, 164.

[91] *Oeuvres*, XXII, 177. That Voltaire's enthusiasm over the *Essay* was later considerably tempered is made clear in a recent study of the marginal comments he made in his copy. See G. R. Havens' interesting article in *Modern Language Notes*, XLIII, 429-39.

plus harmonieux qu'ait eu l'Angleterre.'[92] And, comparing and
preferring Pope to Horace and Boileau, he wrote:

> Pope *approfondit* ce qu'ils ont *effleuré*
> D'un esprit plus hardi, d'un pas plus assuré,
> Il porta le flambeau dans l'abîme de l'être;
> Et l'homme *avec lui seul* appris à se connoître.
> L'art quelquefois frivole, et quelquefois divine,
> L'art des vers est dans Pope utile au genre humain.[93]

Pope was less effusive, more judicial, in his pronouncements
upon Voltaire. *Mariamne* he read; later a presentation copy from
the author was brought him through the mediation of Caryll. Of
this he has left no opinion; but his analysis of the *Henriade* in a
letter to Lord Bolingbroke constitutes one of the longest and most
formal pieces of criticism we have from him excepting the prefaces
and the *Essay*.

'I cannot pretend to judge with any exactness of the beauties of
a foreign language which I understand but imperfectly. I can only
tell my thoughts in relation to the design and conduct of the poem,
or the sentiments. I think the forming of the machines upon the
allegorical persons of virtues and vices very reasonable, it being
equally proper to ancient and modern subjects and to all religions
and times. Nor do we look upon them so much as heathen divinities
as natural passions. This is not the case when Jupiter, Juno, etc.
are introduced, who though sometimes considered as physical
powers,[94] yet that sort of allegory lies not open enough to the apprehension. We care not to study or anatomize a poem, but only
to read it for our entertainment. It should certainly be a sort of
machinery for the meaning of which one is not at a loss for a
moment.[95] Without something of this nature, his poem would too
much resemble Lucan or Silius, and indeed the subject being so
modern, a more violent or remote kind of fable or fiction would
not suit it. If I have anything to wish on this head, it were to have
a little more of the fictitious, I dare not say the wonderful, for the
reason just now given. Yet that would give it a greater resemblance to the ancient epic poem. He has helped it much in my

---

[92] *Oeuvres*, XXII, 176.

[93] Written after Pope's death, to Frederick of Prussia. *Oeuvres*, IX, 441.

[94] Pope in his *Observations on the Iliad* frequently 'explicates' the alleged allegorical sense. Le Bossu had said, Vol. II, Book V, chap. 1, 'toutes
ces personnes divines sont allegoriques.'

[95] According to the humanism or quasi-humanism of Pope and his
friends, 'men of a right understanding' do not stoop to the laborious
exegesis of the scholar: they 'generally see at once all that an author can
reasonably mean. . . .' *Observations on the Iliad*, I. Introduction.

opinion by throwing so much of the story into narrative, and entering at once into the middle of the subject, as well as by making
the action single,[96] namely only the siege of Paris. This brings it
nearer the model of Homer and Virgil. Yet I cannot help fancying
if the fabulous part were a little more extended[97] into descriptions
and speeches, etc., it would be of service. . . .

'As to all the parts of the work which relate to the actions or
sentiments of men, or to characters and manners, they are undoubtedly excellent, and the forte of the poem.

'His characters and sentences are not, like Lucan's,[98] too professed or formal and particularized, but full, short, and judicious,
and seem naturally to rise from an occasion either of telling what
the man was, or what he thought. It seems to me that his judgment
of mankind, and his observations of human actions in a lofty and
philosophical view is one of the principal characteristics of the
writer, who however is not less a poet for being a man of sense, as
Seneca and his nephew were. Do not smile when I add that I esteem him for that honest-principled spirit of true religion which
shines through the whole, and from whence, unknown as I am to
Mr. de Voltaire, I conclude him at once a free-thinker and a lover
of quiet; no bigot, but yet no heretic; one who honors authority
and national sanctions without prejudice to truth or charity; one
who has studied controversy less than reason, and the Fathers[99]
less than mankind. . . .'[100]

I am afraid we shall have to smile at the discovery of the 'spirit
of true religion' in the great rationalist, and acquire some of the
'mistiness' which Newman ironically called the 'mother of wisdom'
in our theology before we find him 'no bigot, but yet no heretic.'

The critical remarks constitute a part of what, carried out with
greater regularity and completeness, would comprise a satisfactor-
ily orthodox *examen* of an epic poem. Le Bossu had given, in
detail, the outline for such a properly conducted *examen*; and
Pope, like Addison in his criticism of *Paradise Lost*, follows in his
train. The language, or diction, is passed over, and the character of

[96] 'This action should have three qualifications in it. First, it should be
but one action. . . .' Addison, *Spectator*, No. 267.
[97] Vida gives directions how 'with just art to lengthen the design beyond
its native bounds' in *Ars*, II, 345-66.
[98] It was Virgil's praise that in his 'sentiments' 'Everything is just and
natural'; he has 'none of the epigrammatic turns of Lucan.' Addison,
Spectator, No. 279.
[99] In this like Pope himself, who wrote Bolingbroke, 'give me leave to
assure you that I have studied neither the Fathers nor the Councils.' E-C,
VII, 396.
[100] E-C, VII, 401-2.

the 'fable' is not treated in detail, though we are assured that it is 'one'; but the 'machines' are discussed with some pretense at exhaustiveness, the 'manners' are appraised, and there are some 'judicious' comments on the 'sentiments' or 'sentences.'[101]

The remarks on the nature of the 'machines' recall the seventeenth century controversy over the *'merveilleux païen'* in which Boileau was the chief challenger, and the chief defendants were Scudery, Perrault, and Chapelain.[102] Voltaire had discovered—and Pope praises him for discovering—the device of reviving the characters of the old moralities, dispensing with the necessity for choosing between the classical polytheism and the 'truer' modern monotheism by rejecting both and substituting personifications of the virtues and vices.

A few words of summary may prove useful. Of the Italian poets, Pope seems to have known and enjoyed Tasso most. His edition of the Latin poets of the Renaissance bore explicit testimony to a taste we might otherwise have inferred.

It seems clear that Pope was able to read, though not to speak, French; but in any case much of French literature was easily accessible in English. The Augustan Age was rich in translators and translations, and all the more important Continental books, then as now, were speedily made available to English readers.

As we might expect, it was the 'classical' literature of the seventeenth century which was strongest in its appeal to Pope. He knew Montaigne and Rabelais, but felt little in common with the robustious and physical humanism of the latter: in Boileau and La Rochefoucauld and La Bruyère he found a humanism more polished and urbane and disciplined. Of his Continental contemporaries, Voltaire was kin to him in spirit: both were *philosophes* if not, in the modern sense, philosophers; they were the chief representatives in prose and poetry respectively of what we call the Enlightenment—the reign of deistic rationalism. In both classicism was the composite result of many causes—realism, anti-mediaevalism, the conception of man as a social being.

The surprising fact is not that Pope knew his French classicists, but that it is so difficult to trace any considerable influence they exerted upon him. The dependence of English upon French classicism has so long been a commonplace of criticism that studies attempting to minimize the debt—such studies as Mr. Gosse's *From Shakespeare to Pope*—have had little success in dissipating it. Several points may profitably be made in this connection. In the first

---

[101] Some will recall that Ben Jonson listed among the 'correctnesses' of his *Sejanus* its 'fullness and frequency of sentence.'

[102] For specimen documents on both sides see Vial and Denise, I, 236-45.

place, it was French criticism rather than French literature which influenced English writers. Criticism and exposition are characteristically French forms: France, 'like ancient Greece, has always been the nursing-mother of ideas.' In the seventeenth and eighteenth, as in the nineteenth century with Taine and Sainte-Beuve, French criticism ruled the civilized world. In the next place, Pope was of the second generation of English neo-classicists: he could find his point of view in the great men of the 'Last Age'—the Restoration, in Dryden and Walsh and Buckingham and Rochester. In the third place, as we need to have repeated again and again, similar points of view may arise from similar social conditions rather than from the indebtedness of the one to the other. Analogous causes produce analogous effects.

Pope passed his formative years when the 'classical' point of view was dominant; the older friends who encouraged him, such as Walsh and Wycherley, belonged to that 'school of thought'; his own artistic and sensitive nature inclined him to appreciate form and finesse in literary expression. There was little need for specific indebtedness to a foreign literature when so many influences converged to induce an analogous temper.

CHAPTER VIII

ONE would fancy from the commonplaces still in the air that the neo-classicists' only reading was in the ancient languages—chiefly the Latin—and in the French. Undoubtedly their critical principles, so far as they were what may properly be described as neo-classical, came mediately or immediately out of the Latin-French school; but the most partisan of them were better read in the great English poets than the casual reader is apt to suppose. In particular is this true of the greater men, whose taste as well as national pride forbade them wholly to coincide in the division of our poetry by an *At Last Waller Came*.[1] Men like Dryden and Pope, while they sincerely bowed the knee in the temple of Le Bossu and company, with equal sincerity worshipped from time to time at the shrines of the great 'Gothic' poets of their people,—Chaucer and Spenser and Shakespeare. They were hard put to it to reconcile their devotions with one another: even Dryden was never able to manage it, but allowed his conscience and his enthusiasm to alternate with distressing results to those who seek to categorize his criticism.

By Dryden's time the knowledge of Middle English pronunciation had almost entirely passed away; and those who praised Chaucer for his gift at narrative were obliged to confess the imperfections of his meter. Thomas Speght, whose editions of Chaucer appeared in 1598 and 1602, was confident that the poet wrote in decasyllabic (i.e., heroic) verse; but Dryden could and did contradict him with all the assurance of a man of letters who opposes the crochet of some pedant. 'I cannot go so far as he who published the last edition of him; for he would make us believe the fault is in our ears, and that there were really ten syllables in a verse where we find but nine: but this opinion is not worth confuting; 'tis so gross and obvious an error that common sense . . . must convince the reader that equality of numbers in every verse which we call *heroic* was either not known or not always practised in Chaucer's age. It

---

[1] cf. Soame's Anglicization of Boileau's 'Enfin Malherbe vint' (*L'Art Poétique*, I, 131).

were an easy matter to produce some thousand of his verses which are lame for want of half a foot and sometimes a whole one, and which no pronunciation can make otherwise.'[2] When one considers the corruption of the texts and the ignorance of the sounded final *e*, it is perhaps more wonder that Speght saw the light than that Dryden sat in darkness.

Unfortunately, not only was Chaucer's reputation sustained wholly by his narrative power for three centuries; but there was wanting also recognition of the great variety of which he was capable as a narrator. 'From the accidental circumstance of Dryden and Pope having copied the gay and ludicrous parts of Chaucer, the common notion seems to have arisen that Chaucer's vein of poetry was chiefly turned to the light and ridiculous.'[3] Warton regards the choice as 'accidental'; but in point of fact neither Pope nor Dryden shows in his critical observations that he was aware of Chaucer's gift for sentiment and for pathos. Even the *Preface to the Fables*, with its never too much to be admired appreciation of Chaucer's *Comédie Humaine*, gives the impression that the *Tales* are largely 'merry' in the sinister sense: 'I have confined my choice to such tales of Chaucer as savour nothing of immodesty.' The 'ribaldry' is 'very gross in many of his works.'[4]

Let me illustrate these aspects of the Augustan view of Chaucer from Pope. The set 'character' of the poet given to Spence may be thought to summarize Dryden's remarks in the *Preface to the Fables*, which Pope must have known: 'I read Chaucer still with as much pleasure as almost any of our poets. He is a master of manners,[5] of description; and the first tale-teller in the true enlivened natural way.'[6]

In the *Essay on Criticism* the unintelligibility of Chaucer's speech to the Age of Anne serves as an illustration of the impermanency of all vernaculars.

[2] Preface to the *Fables* (Ker, II, 259).

[3] Warton, II, 7. There is reason to fear there was a current misconception. The youthful Addison wrote, in his *Account of the Greatest English Poets*:

> Chaucer first, a merry bard arose,
> And many a story told in rhyme and prose;
>
> . . . .
> In vain he jests in his unpolished strain
> And tries to make his readers laugh in vain.

[4] Ker, II, 263.

[5] Dryden wrote of Chaucer: 'he has taken into the compass of his *Canterbury Tales* the various manners and humors (as we now call them) of the whole English nation in his age.' Ker, II, 262.

[6] Spence, 19.

> Our sons their father's failing language see
> And such as Chaucer is, shall Dryden be.[7]

But in spite of his obscured diction, there were those who read and prized Chaucer. Dryden speaks of some who attempted to dissuade him from 'modernizing' the *Tales*; who supposed there was 'a certain veneration due to his old language, and that it would be little less than profanation and sacrilege to alter it.'[8] There were beginning to be *virtuosi* and antiquarians who prized manuscripts and black letter: who prized books for their age, not their merit. It is against this antiquarian zeal for the 'English Ennius' that Pope declaims in the lines:

> Authors, like coins, grow dear as they grow old;
> It is the rust we value, not the gold.
> Chaucer's worst ribaldry is learned by rote,
> And beastly Skelton heads of houses quote.[9]

Though 'Chaucer's worst ribaldry' is not intended to imply that there is nothing else in the poet, Pope seemed to suggest that it was at least characteristic of Chaucer by the brief 'imitation' he professed to have written in youth,[10] but did not publish until 1727. The poem combines stumbling versification (prevailingly octosyllabic, as Chaucer's was scanned at the time) with a coarseness lacking the excuse of wit—such a combination as Pope almost nowhere else perpetrates.

In undertaking what now seems the gratuitous task of 'modernizing' Chaucer, Pope had Dryden as forerunner and patron. 'Chaucer, I confess,' we read in the *Preface to the Fables*, 'is a rough diamond and must first be polished ere he shines.' '. . . I have not tied myself to a literal translation, but have often omitted what I judged unnecessary or not of dignity enough to appear in the company of better thoughts. I have presumed further, in some places, and added somewhat of my own where I thought my author was deficient and had not given his thoughts their true lustre for want of words in the beginning of our language.'[11] Pope allowed

[7] *Essay*, II, 481-2. cf. Waller's *Of English Verse*:
> Poets that lasting marble seek
> Must carve in Latin or in Greek;
> *We* write in sand; our language grows,
> And, like the tide, our work o'erflows.

[8] Ker, II, 266.

[9] *To Augustus*, 35-8. Cf. the picture of the *virtuoso* in Epistle IV, *Of the Use of Riches* (133-40):
> For Locke or Milton 'tis in vain to look;
> These shelves admit not any modern book.

[10] E-C, IV, 423.   [11] Ker, II, 265.

himself a similar freedom to add, amplify, subtract, condense, and
—harder to forgive—to point and smarten.

To be sure, there are exculpating circumstances. The paraphrases like the 'imitations,' were done in youth—'for the most
part, indeed, but a sort of exercises,' Pope wrote of them. 'Mr.
Dryden's *Fables* came out about that time, which occasioned the
translations from Chaucer.'[12] Warburton is the authority for the
statement that Pope did not intend to include this group of poems
in the final edition of his works.[13] And, finally, the poems are
pleasant enough reading by themselves: it is when we compare
them with the original that the disparity in tone and temper dis-
tresses.

This disparity has been admirably analyzed by Professor Lounsbury. Of the *Merchant's Tale* he writes: 'We look in vain in these
mechanically correct and carefully balanced lines for the absolute
naturalness of the original, its exquisite ease, and the delicate
humor which makes itself felt everywhere, and is not obtrusive
anywhere. For it is the special characteristic of Pope's modernizations that he puts into the very front what Chaucer purposely kept
in the background. Where the one suggests or insinuates, the other
asserts.'[14] In the same tale Pope has misunderstood and felt the
necessity for removing the 'delicious absurdity' of putting into
the mouths of the King and Queen of Faery a discussion of the
moral character of Solomon.

Still better put are the comments on the modernization of the
Wife of Bath's Prologue. 'But there has a good deal more been left
out than a number of lines. The humor, the wit, the keen observation of life, the undertone of melancholy which runs persistently
through the rollicking utterance that characterizes this remarkable production—these are but faintly reflected in this paraphrase.'[15] 'The purely sensual side of her nature is all that is shown
in the modernization. The poetical element is gone entirely. Nothing is seen of the half-sad and yet reckless abandon with which
she reconciles herself to the approach of that future of joylessness
which she recognizes that the inevitable hours are bringing. . . .'[16]

There seems no disguising the fact that Pope approaches Chaucer, as did Arnold more than a century later, without expecting to
find in him the 'high seriousness' both thought of as characteristic

[12] E-C, I, 39. Dryden's *Fables* 'were in the hands of every reader when
Pope was learning his art.'
[13] *Works of Pope*, ed. Warburton (London, 1751), I, v.
[14] Lounsbury, *Studies in Chaucer*, III, 180.
[15] *ibid.*, 181.
[16] *ibid.*, 182.

of the classics. Something of patronage ever mingles with the praise. It is always remembered that 'even after Chaucer there was a Spenser, a Harrington, a Fairfax, before Waller and Denham were in being; and our numbers were in their nonage till these last appeared.'[17] We should hardly, today, think it in the best taste to paraphrase lines from the *Knight's Tale* for humorous purpose, as Pope did, when, at the death of Lord Orrery's dog, he wrote: 'I doubt not how much Bounce was lamented. They might say, as the Athenians did to Arcite in Chaucer,[18]

> Ah Arcite! gentle Knight, why wouldst thou die
> When thou hadst gold enough, and Emily!

> Ah Bounce! ah gentle beast, why wouldst thou die
> When thou hadst meat enough, and Orrery.'[19]

A suggestion of Chaucer's more serious powers was given by the *Temple of Fame* (published in 1715), which 'owed its plan and its whole action, besides most of the circumstances narrated'[20] to the *House of Fame*. Pope in the 'advertisement' spoke of the 'hint' of the piece as alone taken from Chaucer. 'The design is in a manner entirely altered, the descriptions and most of the particular thoughts my own.'[21] But Elwin is correct in thinking that this underrates Pope's obligations to the original. Again, Pope professed that his indebtedness to Chaucer was confined to the Third Book; but, as both Lounsbury and Elwin have pointed out, passages from the Second Book were also modernized.[22] In 1736 the poem appeared in the form fashionable for 'imitations' of the classics, with the parallel passages from Chaucer appended at the bottom of the page.

Pope knew something of the influence exerted upon Chaucer and Gower by the French 'vision' poets, such as the authors of the *Roman de la Rose*. 'Chaucer and his contemporaries borrowed a good deal from the Provençal[23] poets, the best account of whom, in our language, is in Rymer's piece on Tragedy.'[24]

[17] Dryden (Ker, II, 259).

[18] ll. 2835-6, apparently; but the first verse is invented and the second follows Dryden's modernization more closely than the original.

[19] E-C, VIII, 518. Cf. for another inaccurate quotation, E-C, VI, 124.

[20] Lounsbury, *Studies in Chaucer*, III, 183.

[21] E-C, I, 187.

[22] *ibid.*, 187.

[23] Simply equivalent to Old French.

[24] Spence, 172, cf. Dryden: 'Chaucer (as you have formerly been told by our learned Mr. Rymer) first adorned and amplified our barren tongue from the Provençal, which was then the most polished of all the modern languages; but this subject has been copiously treated by that great critic, who deserves no little commendation from us his countrymen.' Ker, II, 249.

Probably the account in Rymer is the extent of Pope's knowledge of the 'old Provençal poets' hinted at in a recommendation to the poetess, Miss Cowper:[25] 'I could wish you tried something in the descriptive way on any subject you please, mixed with vision and moral, like pieces of the old Provençal poets, which abound with fancy and are the most amusing scenes in nature. There are three or four of this kind in Chaucer admirable: *The Flower and the Leaf* everybody has been delighted with.'[26]

Pope says nothing of Chaucer's relations to the Italians, though he must have read in Dryden's Preface to the *Fables* the extended account of this second influence.[27]

Spence received a pronouncement upon the other Middle English court poet: 'There is but little that is worth reading in Gower; he wants the spirit of poetry and the descriptiveness that are in Chaucer.'[28] No doubt Pope had but 'dipped into' Gower.

The interesting outline for a history of English poets according to its 'schools' which Pope once drew up shows knowledge of at least the names and positions of the other more important contemporaries and successors of Chaucer. The 'School of Provence' is said to comprise 'Chaucer's Visions, Romaunt of the Rose,[29] Pierce Plowman, Tales from Boccace,[30] Gower.' *Piers the Plowman* is only in slight measure a descendant of 'Provençal' poetry; but the confusion is easily attributable to the prevalence in Old French literature of the 'vision' device there employed. The 'School of Chaucer'—or, as we now say, the Imitators of Chaucer—are 'Lydgate, T. Occleve, Walt. de Mapes, Skelton.'[31]

[25] Sept. 26, 1723. E-C, I, 431.

[26] This apocryphal Chaucer was read, no doubt, in the modernization of Dryden.

[27] Ker, II, 254-5.

[28] Spence, 20.

[29] The incomplete Middle English version, I suppose, which is partly at least, the work of Chaucer.

[30] Ruffhead, 328.

[31] Of course, de Mapes, or Map, died early in the thirteenth century and has no connection with Chaucer. But Map and his writings are still enveloped in considerable mystery; hence this eighteenth century anachronism need not overly surprise. The inclusion of Skelton has some justification in the Chaucerian influence seen in *Garlands of Laurel* and *Bowge of Courte,* though Skelton seems now rather to belong to the early sixteenth century group which includes Barclay and Sackville and Gascoigne.

The quoted outline of the 'rise and progress of English poetry as it came from the Provençal poets' is given in Ruffhead's *Life,* 328. There is a curious bibliographical inscription prefixed by Pope which reads 'Rymer, 2nd Part, pp. 65, 66, 67, 77. Petrarch, 78. Catal. of Provençals.' Rymer's '2nd Part' is his *A Short View of Tragedy* (the *Tragedies of the Last Age* of fifteen years earlier was re-issued as 'Part I'). The pages cited do not,

'Skeltonics' were hardly likely to please the sensitive ear of Pope;
and 'beastly Skelton'[32] is mentioned only for purposes of denunciation: 'Skelton's poems are all low and bad: there's nothing in
them that's worth reading.'[33]

Sackville Pope had read; and he commends him, both as poet
and as dramatist. He was 'the best English poet between Chaucer's
and Spenser's time.'[34] 'The Induction in the *Mirror for Magistrates*
was written by him too, and is very good and very poetical.'[35] In
the outline of Era I of our poetry, the Induction is listed as belong-
ing to the 'School of Dante': today the influence of Chaucer and
Virgil seems clearer, though the possible influence of Dante is
allowed.

Not many people in Pope's day knew Sackville and Norton's
Gorboduc at first hand, as the following from the poet's letter
to Digby will show: 'Mr. Warton[36] forced me to take *Gorboduc*,
which has since done me great credit with several people, as it has
done Dryden and Oldham[37] some unkindness in showing there is
as much difference between their Gorboduc and this, as between
Queen Anne and King George. It is truly a scandal that men should
write with contempt of a piece which they never once saw, as those
two poets did, who were ignorant even of the sex[38] as well as the
sense of Gorboduc.'[39] Something more to the point of the play than
this righteous indignation is found in the observation to Spence
that 'Sackville's tragedy of *Gorboduc* is written in a much purer

as one expects, give the material from which the grouping of the English
poets was drawn up. Chaucer is the only English poet of the earlier period
included in Rymer's absolutely unmethodized book, and he at no length.
'Petrarch 78' seems to mean, see page 78 in Rymer for account of Petrarch; on page 78 Petrarch is named, but no more; elsewhere there is
no mention of him. Rymer does devote much space (his book is a 'view'
of a good many other things besides tragedy) to the Provençal poets;
and evidently the bibliographical note is simply intended as a reference
to the 'best account . . . in our language' of the school from which
modern English poetry took its rise.

[32] Epistle *To Augustus*, 38.
[33] Spence, 173.
[34] I believe modern taste would not dissent from this.
[35] Spence, 21.
[36] Professor of Poetry at Oxford; father of Thomas and Joseph Warton.
[37] John Oldham (1653-1683), cynical satirist and 'rugged' versifier,
whom Pope called 'a very indelicate writer: he has strong rage, but it is
too much like Billingsgate'; whom he called 'too rough and coarse'
(Spence, 19; 136).
[38] Dryden had written, in the Dedication to *Rival Ladies*,

> When Bussy d'Ambois and his fustian took,
> And men were ravished with Queen Gorboduc.

[39] E-C, IX, 67-8.

style than Shakespeare's was in several of his first plays.[40] Sackville imitates the manner of Seneca's tragedies very closely, and writes without affectation or bombast, the two great sins of our oldest tragic writers.'[41] The 'outline of poetry' lists the 'Original of good tragedy, Seneca' as the model of *Gorboduc*. The thrust at the extravagance of Elizabethan style and the praise of Senecan tragedy are alike orthodox neo-classicism.

Gorboduc was a learned play. On the other hand *Gammer Gurton's Needle* had originally been acclaimed by the people, and in Pope's time was the prey of antiquarians. The combination was hardly likely to please an eighteenth century man of letters; and accordingly we are not surprised at the note appended to the reference in the Epistle *To Augustus*, 'A piece of very low humor; one of the first printed plays in English, and therefore much valued by some antiquaries.'[42]

The 'First Era' of the outline gives us one more group, the 'School of Petrarch,'—the Earl of Surrey,[43] Sir Thomas Wyatt, Sir Philip Sidney, and 'G. Gascoyn, Translator of Aristo's Com.'[44]

We come now to Spenser. What did the eighteenth century think of him? Nineteenth century romanticists assumed that they had re-discovered Spenser as well as Milton and Shakespeare. Later, under the instigation of interesting studies by Professors Beers and Phelps, it was customary for scholars to suppose that love for Spenser—and Milton—in the eighteenth century was the possession of the romanticists only; and such romanticists they proceeded to discover in considerable abundance. But yet more recent study has shown that a love for Spenser was not confined to the pale spirits who looked before and after, and pined for what is not. 'The essential truth is that the neo-classicists had a genuine admiration for Spenser, and that they appreciated a great aspect of his genius now misunderstood through the influence of literary epicures from Leigh Hunt down to our "Art for Art's Sake" men who know not what they do. The Augustans appreciated Spenser's moral earnestness and his allegory.' They also 'knew and often named many of Spenser's qualities which we admire today; his

[40] 'In his first plays' is cautious censure.
[41] Spence, 21.
[42] E-C, III, 355 and n.
[43] See *Windsor Forest*, 291-8, for graceful tribute to Surrey, 'The Granville of a former age,' and 'Fair Geraldine, bright object of his vows.' Pope's own note upon the reference calls Surrey 'one of the first refiners of the English poetry; famous in the time of Henry VIII for his sonnets.' E-C, I, 357, n.
[44] Gascoigne's translation, *The Supposes*, was acted in 1566.

sweetness, his peculiar kind of naïve simplicity, his tenderness, his copious fancy.'[45]

Of course, as in neo-classical admiration for the other great English poets before Dryden, there was a mixture of wholesome censure. Orthodoxy agreed with the learned Rymer: 'Spenser, I think, may be reckoned the first of our heroic poets; he had a large spirit, a sharp judgment, and a genius for heroic poesie, perhaps above any that ever writ since Virgil.[46] But our misfortune is, he wanted a true idea,[47] and lost himself by following an unfaithful guide. Though besides Homer and Virgil he had read Tasso, yet he rather suffered himself to be misled by Ariosto. . . . All is fanciful and chimerical, without any uniformity, without any foundation in truth; his poem is perfect fairyland.'[48] Dryden distressed nineteenth century taste more by his first clause than he placated it by the second in the observation that 'Spenser wanted only to have read the rules of Bossu; for no man was ever born with a greater genius or had more knowledge to support it.'[49]

No doubt Pope would have admitted, if pressed, the unfortunate lack of the 'rules' in Spenser, though possibly he could have squared Spenser with orthodoxy as his friend Hughes did, by distinguishing between the rules of the classical epic and the rules of 'Gothic' poetry;[50] but he was not called upon to make an extended or official pronouncement upon this subject. He was free to read the poet for enjoyment; and this he seems to have done with surprising thoroughness. Even before Pope was twelve, his Spenser was 'a great favorite.'[51] He told Spence in 1743-1744, 'I read the *Faerie Queen* when I was about twelve with infinite delight, and I think it gave me as much when I read it over about a year or two ago.'[52]

There is plenty of evidence that this acquaintance with and fondness for Spenser was not confined to his earliest and latest years. In 1715, he wrote Hughes, the 'greatest Spenser scholar of the early eighteenth century,'[53] in appreciation of the gift of the

[45] Cory, 407-8. The vindication is developed at some length.

[46] This declaration ought to be recalled to the credit both of neo-classicism and its extremest English representative—whom Professor Saintsbury dubs one of the worst critics that ever lived.

[47] In a Platonic sense, of course: a normative model.

[48] Spingarn, II, 167-8.

[49] Ker, II, 220.

[50] This recalls the Italian controversy over the heroic poems of Ariosto and Tasso. See Spingarn's *Literary Criticism in the Renaissance*, 112-24.

[51] The other two very early favorites were—the incongruity of the three is characteristic—Waller and Dryden. Spence, 19.

[52] Spence, 296.

[53] Cory, 416.

latter's 'entertaining and judicious essays on Spenser': 'The present you make me is of the most agreeable nature imaginable, for
Spenser has been ever a favorite poet to me: he is like a mistress
whose faults[54] we see, but love her with them all.'[55] In his *Observations on The Iliad* (1715-1720) he shows by his citation of parallels and imitations a detailed knowledge of the *Faerie Queen*. For
example, he refers at length[56] to Spenser's use of the Girdle of
Venus (Book IV, Canto 5); he notices the Spenserian imitation of
the Homeric use of the phantom of a hero to delude the enemy:[57]
'Spenser in the eighth canto of the third book seems to have improved this imagination in the creation of his false Florimel, who
performs all the functions of life, and gives occasion for many
adventures.' The Homeric catalogue recalls to his mind 'Spenser's
enumeration of the British and Irish rivers in the eleventh canto of
his fourth book,'—'one of the noblest in the world if we consider
his subject was more confined [than the Homeric], and can excuse
his not observing the order or course of the country; but his variety
of description and fruitfulness of imagination are nowhere more
admirable than in that part.'[58]

There is no evidence that it was the 'moral earnestness' and the
'allegory' in Spenser—the aspects of him generally appreciated of
the Augustans, as Professor Cory rightly informs us—which attracted Pope. 'After reading a canto of Spenser two or three days
ago to an old lady between seventy and eighty years of age, she
said that I had been showing her a gallery of pictures. I don't
know how it is, but she said very right: there is something in
Spenser that pleases one as strongly in one's old age as it did in
one's youth.'[59] One must not press this comment too far, but it looks
as if this Augustan old lady and this Augustan poet relished just
that in Spenser which the average modern reader relishes: not the
ethical framework or the elaborately entangled plots, but the
pageantry, the succession of colorful incident and vignette.

Lord Lyttleton, in his longest Dialogue, represents Pope as discoursing upon Spenser to Boileau. The sentiments expressed bear

[54] Spenser's chief faults, according to Pope's friend, Spence (in his *Dissertation on the Defects of Spenser's Allegory*), were the mixing of the
fables of heathendom with the truths of Christianity (for which Boileau
censured the French epic writers) and the too close following of Ariosto.

[55] E-C, X, 120.

[56] *Observations*, XIV: XX.

[57] *ibid.*, V: XLV.

[58] *ibid.*, II, On the Catalogue. Professor Cory could have made his case
for Pope as a Spenserian still stronger had he looked into the *Observations
on the Iliad* as Professor Havens did in his Miltonic studies.

[59] Spence, 296.

the evidence of authenticity; and it is quite within the bounds of
the probable that they represent the substance of an actual pronouncement on the subject such as Pope would be apt to make to
a favorite young friend, himself a man of letters.

Boileau has seen an eminent English poet some times in the company of Homer and Virgil, but more often with Tasso, Ariosto, and
Dante.[60] Pope: 'I understand you mean Spenser. He had a great
poetical genius. There is a force and beauty in some of his images
and descriptions[61] equal to any in the best of those writers you have
seen him converse with. But he had not always the art of *shading*
his pictures. He brings the minute and disagreeable parts too much
into sight; and with many sublime and noble ideas mingles too
frequently vulgar and mean. His poem is moral and allegorical;
but the allegory, being continued throughout the whole work,
fatigues the mind;[62] and as every canto has a different fable
and a different hero, there is no passion to interest the heart as a
whole, nor any permanent object to fix the attention. Had he
chosen a subject proper for epic poetry, he seems to have had
elevation and strength in his genius sufficient to make him a great
epic poet; but now he can hardly be ranked in that class.'[63]

The series of early Imitations includes one of Spenser as well
as of Chaucer. The famous stanza is employed; there is the customary attempt at archaistic effect; there is detailed description—a
series of vivid pictures; further, there are the personifications in
which Spenser abounds. But all is burlesqued. 'He that was unacquainted with Spenser, and was to form his ideas of the turn and
manner of his genius from this piece, would undoubtedly suppose
that he abounded in filthy images and excelled in describing the
lower scenes of life.'[64] The alley by the water-side where

> on the broken pavement, here and there,
> Doth many a stinking sprat and herring lie;
> A brandy and tobacco shop is near,
> And hens, and dogs, and hogs are feeding by;
> And here a sailor's jacket hangs to dry.
> At ev'ry door are sun-burnt matrons seen,

[60] All in some sense 'Gothic' poets. But the conjunction is interesting.
[61] Notice again the emphasis on the pictorial quality of Spenser.
[62] The eighteenth century editor Hughes was an admirer of allegory, but
felt the necessity for formulating rules on the subject. Spence, in his *Dissertation*, indulged in 'an orthodox lament at the need of rules for allegory'
(Cory, 416, 418).
[63] Lyttleton, 127-8. The Fourth Edition omits the concluding clause.
[64] Warton, II, 29.

Mending old nets to catch the scaly fry;
Now singing shrill, and scolding eft between;
Scolds answer foul-mouth'd scolds; bad neighborhood,
    I ween.[65]

is admirable in kind,—a study in the genre of Hogarth or Crabbe.
But though Lyttleton makes Pope complain of Spenser that 'He
brings the minute and disagreeable parts too much into sight,'
there is surely a sharp distinction to be drawn between this comic
realism and the portentous ugliness of some of the episodes and
vignettes in the *Faerie Queen.*

The 'imitation' of Spenser has aroused considerable comment
from critics. Warton felt that Spenser had been sadly misrepresented. Professor Phelps has used the poems as instance of his
theory that Spenser was particularly the prey of Augustan burlesque.[66] But the critics have been successfully answered by other
critics. Courthope says, 'Warton's criticisms are strangely beside
the mark. This Imitation is merely so-called in the sense in which
the parodies in the *Dunciad* are imitations—it is, in fact, a broad
burlesque. Pope meant to turn the style of Spenser upside down.
. . .'[67] And Cory concludes, 'Professor Phelps makes too much of
the Spenserian burlesque . . . which Pope and Gay wrote in a
few moments of triviality. If we examine consistently all the
vulgar parodies in eighteenth century poetry and make the same in-
ferences, we are forced to conclude that the Augustans admired
nobody, ancient or modern. In France, the fountain-head of neo-
classicism, Virgil, when his divinity was at its height, was trav-
estied by Scarron.'[68]

Besides the *Faerie Queen,* Pope knew at least the *Prothalamion,*
the *Epithalamion,* and the *Shepherd's Calendar.*[69] He imitates the
refrain of the first;[70] quotes the refrain of the second;[71] imitates a
passage from the third;[72] the fourth was one of the chief models
of his *Pastorals.* There are occasional imitations throughout, but
the second pastoral is 'an ostensible imitation of Spenser's first

[65] E-C, IV, 426.
[66] *Beginnings of the English Romantic Movement,* 53.
[67] E-C, IV, 425, n.
[68] Cory, 407. Even the 'learned' and neo-classical Dennis published a
volume burlesquing the ancients. Paul, 110.
[69] E-C cites from *Colin Clout* and *Astrophel* parallel passages which do
not seem particularly convincing. (I, 281, 295.)
[70] In *Spring,* E-C, I, 266.
[71] *Summer,* E-C, I, 278. Attributed by Pope in a note. Pope mentions the
Epithalamion in a letter to Lady Mary. E-C, IX, 354.
[72] *Dunciad,* IV, 421-2. E-C, IV, 212, and n.

eclogue, which is devoted to a lover's complaint.'[73] In the prefaced
Discourse on Pastoral Poetry, Pope expressed himself at some
length on the *Shepherd's Calendar*; and these remarks are the
result of his own reading of Spenser, as comparison with the brief
passage on the subject in Dryden's *Dedication of the Pastorals*
of Virgil will show.[74] Dryden supplies merely the corroborative
authority for the assurance of the first sentence:

'Spenser's *Calendar*, in Mr. Dryden's opinion, is the most complete work of this kind which any nation has produced ever since
the time of Virgil. Not but that he may be thought imperfect in
some few points. His Eclogues are somewhat too long if we compare them with the ancients.[75] He is sometimes too allegorical, and
treats of matters of religion in an allegorical style, as the Mantuan
had done before him. He has employed the lyric measure, which
is contrary to the practice of the old poets. His stanza is not still
the same, nor always well chosen. This last may be the reason
that his expression is sometimes not concise enough; for the tetras-
tic has obliged him to extend his sense to the length of four lines,
which would have been more closely confined in the couplet.

'In the manners, thoughts, and characters, he comes near to
Theocritus himself; though, notwithstanding all the care he has
taken, he is certainly inferior in his dialect; for the Doric had its
beauty and propriety in the time of Theocritus; it was used in part
of Greece, and frequently in the mouths of many of the greatest
persons, whereas the old English and country phrases of Spenser
were either entirely obsolete, or spoken only by people of the lowest condition. As there is a difference betwixt simplicity and rusticity, so the expression of simple thoughts should be plain, but

[73] E-C, I, 276, n.

[74] I reproduce the entirety of Dryden's remarks on the *Calendar*: 'Our
own nation has produced a third poet in this kind [i.e., the pastoral], not
inferior to the two former [Theocritus and Virgil]: for the *Shepherd's
Calendar* of Spenser is not to be matched in any modern language, not even
by Tasso's *Aminta* which infinitely transcends Guarini's *Pastor Fido*. . . .

'But Spenser, being master of our Northern dialect and skilled in Chaucer's English, has so exactly imitated the Doric of Theocritus that his love
is a perfect image of that passion which God infused into both sexes
before it was corrupted with the knowledge of arts and the ceremonies of
what we call good manners.'

(*Works*, ed. Saintsbury, XIII, 324-5). Observing the foot-note reference to
Dryden at the opening of the paragraphs in Pope's *Discourse*, I was inclined to think I should find the substance of his remarks there; but the
'hint' upon which he worked was very slight.

[75] Pope had said earlier in the discourse that the Eclogue should be
brief. The authorities for this rule were Rapin and Chetwood in his
Preface to Dryden's *Pastorals*. See E-C, I, 259, and n.

not clownish.[76] The addition he had made of a calendar[77] to his Eclogues is very beautiful; since by this, besides the general moral of innocence and simplicity, which is common to other authors of pastoral, he has one peculiar to himself; he compares human life to the several seasons, and at once exposes to his readers a view of the great and little worlds, in their various changes and aspects. Yet the scrupulous division of his pastorals into months has obliged him either to repeat the same description, in other words, for three months together; or, when it was exhausted before, entirely to omit it; whence it comes to pass that some of his Eclogues (as the Sixth, Eighth, and Tenth, for example) have nothing but the titles to distinguish them. The reason is evident, because the year has not that variety in it to furnish every month with a particular description, as it may every season.'[78]

In a passage in the manuscript, omitted in the published version, Pope speaks of having taken the design of his *Pastorals* from Spenser: 'For, looking upon Spenser as the father of English pastoral, I thought myself unworthy to be esteemed even the meanest of his sons, unless I bore some resemblance to him.'[79]

Upon the basis of adduced evidence, I think we may agree with Professor Cory in calling Pope a 'warm admirer' of the great Elizabethan poet, and add that he was a student of him as well.[80] But the 'neo-classical balance' in which we are told Spenser was tried and 'found wanting in few respects' is for the most part in the background; and it is interesting to see that what chiefly struck the mature Pope in the *Faerie Queen* was the pageant of form and color with which the average modern reader is delighted.

In the 'outline' for a history of poetry,[81] Spenser inaugurates the second Era; and we told that he was 'from the School of Ariosto and Petrarch'—in reference to the *Faerie Queen*, which was planned in imitation of Ariosto, and the sonnets, which derive from the Petrarchan tradition. And then comes a group of poets and poems bracketed as 'School of Spenser, and from Italian Sonnets': 'W. Brown's Pastorals;[82] Ph. Fletcher's Purple Island, Alabaster,

[76] Fontenelle, in his *Discours sur l'Eclogue*, makes much of 'toning down' the rusticity of actual peasants when one puts them into poetry. He prefers 'la delicatesse' of Moschus and Bion to 'la grossièreté' of Theocritus. *Oeuvres*, V, 18.

[77] Referring, of course, to the arrangement of the calendar by months.

[78] E-C, I, 262-4. Hence Pope devotes a pastoral to each season.

[79] *ibid.*, I, 264, n.

[80] Cory seems to have taken into account neither the notes to Homer nor the *Discourse on the Pastorals*.

[81] Ruffhead, 329.

[82] *Britannia's Pastorals*, by William Browne (1591-1645), are patriotic poems in imitation of Spenser.

Piscatory, etc.;[83] S. Daniel; Sir Walter Raleigh; Milton's Juvenilia, Heath,[84] Habinton.'[85]

The imitators of Spenser are sometimes remarked to Spence. 'Samuel Daniel, the historian, is unpoetical; but has good sense often.'[86] 'Milton, in his first pieces, is an evident follower of Spenser, too—in his famous *Allegro* and *Penseroso*, and in a few other pieces.'[87] Drayton and Fairfax are added to the list.[88] Upon the second alignment, Pope parts company with Dryden, who speaks as if Spenser and Fairfax were co-equally the 'great masters in our language' in the reign of Elizabeth and makes them each the parent of a mighty son—Spenser, of Milton; and Fairfax, of 'our famous Waller.'[89] Drayton appears again as 'a very mediocre poet' who is 'yet taken some notice of because Selden[90] writ a few notes on one of his poems.'[91]

Pope was not a student of the drama; and the great Elizabethan theater was for him—as for most of the men of letters from the Restoration on, including Dryden—narrowed to the works of Shakespeare, Ben Jonson, and Beaumont and Fletcher. The 'grand style' in dramatic verse had passed out of vogue: it was now suggestive of rant and bombast. The 'way of Chapman, Massinger, and all the tragic writers of those days' was to 'stiffen' their style with 'high words and metaphors': they 'mistook it for a sign of greatness.'[92] It was 'mighty simple in Rowe,' Spence was told, 'to write a play now, professedly in Shakespeare's style,—that is,

---

[83] Phineas Fletcher (1582-1650) wrote *The Purple Island* and *Piscatory Eclogues* but no *Alabaster*. Pope has evidently interspersed not another title by Fletcher, but the name of the Latin poet, William Alabaster (1567-1640), who is praised in Spenser's *Colin Clout's Come Home Again* (ll. 400-1).

[84] Evidently Robert Heath, *floruit* 1650; author of *Clarastella*, a series of love poems (*D.N.B.*, XXV, 349).

[85] William Habington (1605-1654) was the author of *Castara*, a collection of love poems.

[86] Spence, 22. The 'historian' is in recognition of his *History of the Civil Wars* of York and Lancaster, in seven books of verse.

[87] Dryden wrote in his *Preface to the Fables*, 'Milton was the poetical son of Spenser. . . . Milton has acknowledged to me that Spenser was his original. . . .' Ker, II, 247.

[88] Spence, 21. Drayton imitated the *Shepherd's Calendar* in his *Shepherd's Garland* (1606). Edward, Lord Fairfax, was the Elizabethan translator of *Jerusalem Delivered* (1600).

[89] Preface to the *Fables* (Ker, II, 247).

[90] In 1612, at the request of Drayton, then poet-laureate, John Selden (1584-1654) wrote notes on the first eighteen cantos of the *Polyolbion*. *D.N.B.*, LI, 213.

[91] E-C, IX, 225.

[92] Spence, 173-4.

professedly in the style of a bad age.'⁹³ Many of the Elizabethan
dramatists had become mere names; otherwise Pope would not
have been able to deliver himself casually of such an indiscrim-
inate grouping of types and ranks as 'Webster, Marston, Goff,
Kyd, and Massinger were the persons he instanced as tolerable
writers of tragedy in Ben Jonson's time.'⁹⁴ Even the great four had
become prey of the kind of conventionalized characterization
which is the lot of unread classics:

In all debates where critics bear a part,
Not one but nods and talks of Jonson's art,
Of Shakespeare's nature and of Cowley's wit:
How Beaumont's judgment checked what Fletcher writ.⁹⁵

One would expect Pope to find much to please him in Ben Jonson, critic and dramatist. Here was a genuine English classicist
who preached and, though not pedantically, practised the 'rules of
Aristotle.' One wonders that Dryden and Pope, both patriotic, did
not trace their descent as classicists from Jonson and the Sidney
of the *Apology* rather than from the French. Pope was not unaware
of Jonson's critical position; he takes express note of his 'correctness' in the Preface to Shakespeare, where he tells us that 'not only
the common audience had no notion of the rules of writing, but
few even of the better sort piqued themselves upon any great
degree of knowledge or nicety that way, till Ben Jonson, getting
possession of the stage, brought critical learning into vogue. And
that this was not done without difficulty may appear from those
frequent lessons (and, indeed, almost declamations) which he was
forced to prefix to his first plays⁹⁶ and put into the mouth of his
actors, the *Grex*, *Chorus*, etc., to remove the prejudices and inform
the judgment of his hearers.'⁹⁷ In the same Preface Pope gives a
just account, for which he had the authority of Betterton,⁹⁸ of the
relations between Jonson and his great contemporary. He 'cannot
help thinking these two great poets were friends and lived on
amicable terms, and in offices of society with each other';⁹⁹ he

⁹³ *ibid.*, 174. Mr. Singer, Spence's editor, thinks that 'It would have been
as well for Pope's reputation as a critic if it had never been recorded'
(*Anecdotes*, 174). But the point of view comes out elsewhere as well and
was by no means peculiar to Pope. Dryden wrote of 'Bussy d'Ambois and
his fustian.'
⁹⁴ Spence, 21.
⁹⁵ *To Augustus*, 81-4.
⁹⁶ Jonson, like Dryden and Shaw, was given to prefaces.
⁹⁷ E-C, X, 537.
⁹⁸ Spence, 5.
⁹⁹ E-C, X, 541.

cannot agree with Dryden that there is anything 'invidious' or 'sparing' in Jonson's celebrated verses *To the Memory of his Beloved Mr. William Shakespeare.* He expressly mentions Jonson's *Discoveries* and its estimate of Shakespeare.[100]

Jonson's plays were still well known in Pope's youth. In the Epistle *To Augustus* we hear of 'each true Briton' as loyal to 'Ben'; and 'What boy but hears the sayings of old Ben?'[101] Of course the 'humor' characters were what one would most naturally recall of Jonson: it is interesting to find Pope referring, in widely scattered places, to Fungoso, in *Every Man out of his Humor,* Morose, in *Epicene,* and Abel Drugger, in *The Alchemist.*[102] He reprinted in the *Grub Street Journal* of December 6, 1733, a scene from *The Poetaster* 'which he considered applicable to the slanderous charges brought against him by Lord Hervey.'[103] Of the tragedies, he knew at least *Catiline.*[104] Jonson's dramatic powers waned of course in his later years; and a footnote of Pope's identifies with his 'last fruits'—what Dryden used to call 'the dotages'—the reference to

> Ben, old and poor, as little seemed to heed
> The life to come in every poet's creed.[105]

It must have been the memory of these over many 'dotages' which prompted Pope's unfortunate remark about the 'trash' of Jonson's works 'taken altogether,'[106] for he included Jonson in a list he drew up of the best English comic dramatists[107] which included besides him only Shakespeare, Fletcher, Wycherley, Congreve, Etheredge, and Vanbrugh—surely the highest honor which could be paid.

That accomplished prelate and man of letters, Bishop Hall, came very near the honor of having his satires after the manner of Juvenal 'versified' by Pope. Singer, who edited Hall's *Satires* as well as the *Anecdotes* of Spence, is the authority for the statement that 'when these satires were shown to Pope at a late period of his poetical career, he was so sensible of their merit as to wish he had seen them sooner.'[108] The regret was, no doubt, genuine. Here was an earliest of English satirists in Pope's own medium, the heroic

---

[100] E-C, X, 542.
[101] ll. 41 and 80.
[102] E-C, II, 53; Spence, 9; E-C, IX, 390.
[103] *ibid.,* V, 263.
[104] *ibid.,* X, 540.
[105] *To Augustus,* 73-4.
[106] Spence, 9.
[107] *ibid.,* 46.
[108] Preface to Hall's *Satires,* Chiswick Press, London, 1824.

couplet—a satirist, too, who 'imitated' one of the most reputable of ancient models,[109] and was capable of versification far smoother than Donne's. Warburton gives us Pope's estimate of Hall and the project for honoring him with Augustan dress: 'He [Pope] intended to have given two or three of Bishop Hall's [satires] likewise, whose force and classical elegance he much admired; but as Hall was a better versifier, and, as a mere academic, had not his vein vitiated, like Donne's, by the fantastic language of courts, Mr. Pope's purpose was only to correct a little and smooth the versification. In the first edition of Hall's *Satires*, which was in Mr. Pope's library, we find that long satire called the First of the Sixth Book corrected throughout and the versification mended for his use.'[110]

Of Elizabethan prose writers Pope knew at least Ascham, whose famous strictures upon the Italianate Englishmen he recalls,[110] and Bacon, the first of the great line of English empiricists. He is 'known to have been remarkably fond' of the essays of Bacon,[111] though he rarely quotes from them. The *Essay on Man* cites Verulam as a notable instance of the highest mental powers joined to a reprehensible character:

> If parts allure thee, think how Bacon shined,
> The wisest, brightest, meanest of mankind.[112]

The estimate given Spence is similarly a total impression, not a judgment of literary powers alone. One can hardly hope to temper with comment the eulogy that 'Lord Bacon was the greatest genius that England (or perhaps any country) ever produced,'[113] particularly when its pronouncer had shortly before proclaimed, 'You know, I don't deal much in hyperboles'; but one may remark that such an estimate proceeds from a humanism which desires for man development and balance of powers rather than the exploitation of the literary talent alone.

We come now to the 'next age' and Milton. Upon the subject of the eighteenth century and the great epic poet of Puritanism and the Renaissance a flood of light has been cast in recent years. Critics began by finding in Milton (as in Spenser) a source for the sentiment of romanticism. But more recent studies—and preeminently, of course, Dr. Havens' masterly work—have shown that

---

[109] E-C, III, 423. Pope wrote *Optima Satira* as the head of the satire selected for 'correction.' In his *Apology for Smectymnuus* Milton denounced Hall's 'hobbling distich.' One wonders if he would have preferred it polished by Mr. Pope.

[110] Spence, 176.

[111] Warton, ed. Pope's *Works*, I, 129.

[112] Epistle IV, 281-2; E-C, II, 449.

[113] Spence, 169.

a fondness for Milton was not confined in the eighteenth century to any class of persons. He was a national glory;[114] and if romanticists (of whom there were few consciously such) read him for the 'magnificently wild' character of *Paradise Lost* or the musing melancholy of *Il Penseroso*, the Puritan middle classes placed his epic near the Bible, Foxe, and Bunyan, and thence learned their theology;[115] and the classicists, thanks to Addison's extended series of *Spectator* papers,[116] studied the poet with the assurance that he had been examined 'by the rules of epic poetry' and found conformable.[117] Nowadays, when the necessity for obeying the 'laws of poetry' seems not so apparent, the neo-classical Milton may amuse as well as surprise. But it is by no means so certain that Milton would not have welcomed examination in the light of the practice of Homer and Virgil, and the theory of Aristotle and Horace. He was himself a student of the Italian criticism of the Renaissance and could discourse with entire seriousness of 'what the laws are of a true epic poem, what of a dramatic, what of a lyric, what decorum is, what are the great masterpieces to observe.'[118] He was a learned poet who knew his classics and could 'imitate' their architecture and their 'beauties.' Dr. Havens need not, I think, invoke the *Zeitgeist* in apology for the point of view of the 'maligned Augustans': 'If a critic of our time says that *Paradise Lost* is equal to the *Iliad* or the *Aeneïd*, the comment indicates little more than enthusiasm; but if a contemporary of Dryden or Johnson made the same remark it meant that the English epic had stood the test of being measured by the highest possible standard,—indeed by the only standard for great poetry.'[119] All this is quite true; but it is just that sort of critical parallel, an *examen* in the light of just those models, which Milton would desire; and we should perhaps blush rather for current nescience than for old-fashioned classicism.

We are nowhere told that Milton was an especial favorite of Pope's, but there is abundant evidence that he was known early and *in toto*; and the specific criticisms proffered show balance and intelligent judgment.

[114] Even Dr. Johnson, whose *Life of Milton* was attacked by the Miltonians as unjust, wrote in it: 'What Englishman can take pleasure in transcribing passages which, if they lessen the reputation of Milton, diminish in some degree the honor of our country' (*Lives of the Poets*, I, 181). See also Hamelius, 87-94.

[115] Havens, 33-6, deals with Milton's audience of the religious.

[116] Nos. 267-370 (Saturdays only).

[117] See particularly *Spectator* no. 267.

[118] *Treatise of Education* (*The Works of Milton*, London, 1851, IV, 389).

[119] Havens, 20.

Even in his *Alcander*, written when he was twelve or thirteen, Pope imitated the style of Milton in one part.[120] In 1705, he sent to his friend Trumbull a book containing the Minor Poems, then very little known, with his commendation.[121] In 1712, he includes a passage from *Paradise Lost* in a collection of 'winter pieces' from the great poets—Homer and Virgil being the others—characterizing the writers as 'some of the greatest geniuses for description which the world ever bred.'[122] And in 1732, when Dr. Bentley's celebrated edition of Milton appeared amid storms of protest from the friends of the 'emended' poet, Pope read through the edition with care, and annotated in the margin with *recte, bene, pulchre*, at the appropriate places.[123]

These are external evidences of life-long interest in Milton. A more impressive exhibit is made by the tables drawn up by Wakefield, Leather,[124] and Havens of passages imitated or referred to in annotation; on the strength of which Dr. Havens is prepared to say that Pope 'appears to have been more widely acquainted with the complete body of Milton's poems than any other man of his time,'[125] and that 'many a person who has prided himself on his enjoyment of *Paradise Lost* and thought that Pope had no conception of what true poetry is has not possessed a tithe of the scorned bard's knowledge of Milton.'[126] Phrases and lines from Milton appear thirty times in the *Dunciad*, fifty-six times in the translations of the *Iliad*: in all, there are over a hundred and ninety.[127] Nor are Pope's borrowings 'crowded into a few pieces.' They are dispersed through at least twenty-five of his poems, and it is 'significant that, while practically all the earlier pilferers from Milton made use of his epic only (few persons at the time having any appreciation of the minor poems), yet Pope used the

[120] Spence, 277.

[121] E-C, VI, 2. It was through the Wartons' father that Pope came to know Milton's Minor Poems. Thomas Warton, in the Preface to his edition of Milton, says of Pope: 'We find him soon afterwards sprinkling his *Eloisa and Abelard* with epithets and phrases pilfered from *Comus* and the *Penseroso*' (quoted in Hill's edition of *Lives of the Poets*, III, 236, n). Havens defends Pope against the charge of borrowing without acknowledgment (115).

[122] E-C, VI, 176.

[123] VIII, 294. For the Bentley edition see Havens, 29, and the fuller account in Hamelius, 14-7.

[124] Gilbert Wakefield's edition of Pope's Homer; Mary Leather's 'Pope as a Student of Milton,' in *Englische Studien*, XXV, 398-410.

[125] Havens, 15.

[126] *ibid.*, 113.

[127] For list of 'Parallel Passages Showing Expressions Probably Borrowed from Milton' see Appendix A, 573-83, in Havens.

shorter pieces in his earlier and later work, and except in the *Dunciad* and the Homer borrowed from them quite as much as he did from the epic. Lines or phrases from nearly all of them appear in his verse,—from *Allegro*, *Penseroso*, *Comus* (there are nineteen from *Comus*), *Lycidas*, the *Nativity*, from three of the sonnets, and even from *Arcades* and the *Vacation Exercise*.'[128] Levy was also laid upon *Paradise Regained*[129] and *Samson*; and 'every book of *Paradise Lost* yielded one or more contributions to his work.'[130]

Thorough acquaintance with Milton is also shown—is perhaps most conspicuous—in the *Observations on the Iliad*, where *Paradise Lost* is not only, as Dr. Havens says, 'either quoted from or referred to thirty-nine times,'[131] but, more significantly, is used, along with Virgil, to furnish parallel passages and 'imitations,' and occupies, in this connection, a place second only to Virgil and very much above Tasso. The comparisons are frequently at some length, and throw an illumination upon the extent to which Milton was, as Pope calls him, an 'admirer and imitator' of Homer. I cite a few instances. Upon Bk. II, v. 552, it is remarked, 'The lowness of this image in comparison with those which precede it will naturally shock a modern critic, and would scarcely be forgiven in a poet of these times.

'Milton, who was a close imitator of our author, has often copied him in these humble comparisons. He has not scrupled to insert one in the midst of that pompous description of the rout of the rebel angels in the Sixth Book, where the Son of God in all dreadful majesty is represented pouring his vengeance upon them:—*as a herd of goats, or timorous flocks together*,' etc.

Commenting upon Homer's device of repetition, Pope recalls his *Paradise Lost*: 'Milton was so great an admirer and imitator of our author as not to have scrupled even at this kind of repetition. The passage is at the end of his Tenth Book, where, Adam having declared he would prostrate himself before God in certain particular acts of humiliation, those acts are immediately after described by the poet in the same words.'[132]

In at least one case, Milton's treatment of a particular theme is preferred to that by the sacrosanct Homer and Virgil.[133]

The explicit pronouncements on Milton all relate to *Paradise*

---

[128] Havens, 114-15.
[129] Termed by Pope in a letter to Atterbury Milton's 'worst work.' E-C, IX, 45.
[130] Havens, 115, n.
[131] *ibid.*, 114, n.
[132] *Observations*, I : XLIII.
[133] The figure : God weighing in His golden scales. *Observations*, VIII : IX.

Lost. Pope had heard of the original uncertainty as to the form the great work should assume, but found no evidence: 'Milton was a great master of the Italian poets; and I have been told that what he himself wrote in Italian[134] is in exceeding good Italian. I can't think that he ever meant to make a tragedy of his Fall of Man. At least I have Andreini's *Adamo*, and don't find that he has taken anything from it.'[135] Addison, in a paper devoted to the 'blemishes' of the epic, complains of 'an unnecessary ostentation of learning which occurs very frequently.' 'Milton seems ambitious of letting us know, by his excursions on freewill and predestination, and his many glances upon history, astronomy, geography, and the like, as well as by the terms and phrases he sometimes makes use of, that he was acquainted with the whole circle of arts and sciences.'[136] It is perhaps in echo of the *Spectator* pronouncement, which he must have read, that Pope remarked of his own early epic, 'I had flung all my learning into it, as indeed Milton has done too much in his *Paradise Lost*.'[137]

The quatrain upon Milton in the Epistle *To Augustus* has generally been thought felicitous and is frequently quoted:

> Milton's strong pinion now not heaven can bound,[138]
> Now serpent-like, in prose, he sweeps the ground;[139]
> In quibbles angel and archangel join
> And God the Father turns a school-divine.[140]

The Miltonic 'grand style' interested the most 'correct' of stylists: he experimented with its diction in his Homeric translation, and in the *Postscript* to the *Odyssey* discoursed upon the subject at some length; 'Some use has been made to this end ['to dignify and solemnize these plainer poets which hardly admit of

---

[134] Sonnets and *canzone.*

[135] Spence, 175-6.

[136] *Spectator*, no. 298.

[137] Spence, 197.

[138] Lyttleton represents Pope as saying of Milton: 'His genius was indeed so vast and sublime that his poem seems beyond the limits of criticism; as his subject is beyond the limits of nature. The bright and excessive blaze of poetical fire which shines in so many parts of his poem [*Paradise Lost*] will hardly permit one to see its faults!' (123). The quatrain to which I append this makes it evident that Pope's eye was not so dazzled after all.

[139] Dryden wrote in his *Essay on Satire* (Ker, II, 29), 'It is true, he rung into a flat of thought sometimes for a hundred lines together. . . .'

[140] According to Dixon, the modern reader 'is not merely languid in his appreciation of the theology, he is even distressed by it. The Deity argues, and unhappily argues unconvincingly . . .' (p. 204). 'It has been said, and said with perfect truth, he argues 'like a school divine' (205). The French critics have not been slow to see the ridiculous in the celestial metaphysics.

any poetical ornaments'] of the style of Milton. A just and
moderate mixture of old words may have an effect like the working old abbey stones into a building, which I have sometimes seen
to give a kind of venerable air, and yet not destroy the neatness,
elegance, and equality requisite to a new work: I mean without
rendering it too unfamiliar, or remote from that ease and smoothness[141] which ought always to accompany narrative or dialogue.
In reading a style judiciously antiquated, one finds a pleasure not
unlike that of travelling on an old Roman way; but then the road
must be as good as the way is ancient; the style must be such in
which we may evenly proceed without being put to short stops by
sudden abruptness, or puzzled by frequent turnings and transpositions.[142] No man delights in furrows and stumbling blocks;
and let our love to antiquity be ever so great, a fine ruin is one
thing, and a heap of rubbish another. The imitators of Milton,
like most other imitators, are not copies but caricatures of their
original;[143] they are a hundred times more obsolete and cramp[144]
than he, and equally so in all places: whereas it should have been
observed of Milton that he is not lavish of his exotic words and
phrases everywhere alike, but employs them more where the subject is marvellous, vast, and strange, as in the scenes of Heaven,
Hell, Chaos, etc., than where it is turned to the natural or agreeable, as in the pictures of paradise, the loves of our first parents,
the entertainment of angels, and the like.[145] In general, this unusual style better serves to awaken our ideas in the descriptive
and in the imaging and picturesque parts than it agrees with the
lower sort of narrations, the character of which is simplicity and
purity. Milton has several of the latter, where we find not an antiquated, affected, or uncouth word[146] for some hundred lines to-

[141] Here we have a compact exhibit of neo-classical *desiderata* in style:
neatness, elegance, equality (i.e., regularity), ease, and smoothness.

[142] Pope's objection to Miltonic inversion is more directly stated below.

[143] Milton was termed in a letter to Atterbury an author 'whom you so
justly prefer to all his followers' (E-C, IX, 45). 'Though his [Milton's]
formal style may fit the higher parts of his own poem, it does very ill for
others who write on natural and pastoral subjects' (Spence, 174). He had
in mind John Philips (1676-1708), who turned out several didactic and
mock-heroic poems in blank verse, the best-known of which is *Cyder*.

[144] Milton's conciseness produces often a stiffness.

[145] *Paradise Lost*, like the *Aeneid*, combined the subjects of the Homeric
epics. It has its battles, but it has, too, its idyllic scenes and its vistas of
history. No other critic has distinguished in Milton the two manners corresponding to the two 'matters.'

[146] Of course the Miltonic diction was a subject for eighteenth century
comment. Addison thought we must allow that Milton's style is 'often too
much labored, and sometimes obscured by old words, transpositions, and

gether; as in his fifth book, the latter part of the eighth, the former of the tenth and eleventh books, and in the narration of Michael in the twelfth. I wonder indeed that he, who ventured (contrary to the practice of all other epic poets) to imitate Homer's lowness in the narrative, should not also have copied his plainness and perspicuity in the dramatic parts: since in his speeches (where clearness above all is necessary) there is frequently such transposition and forced construction that the very sense is not to be discovered without a second or third reading: and in this certainly he ought to be no example.'[147]

There remains to be noted an interesting proposed connection between Pope and Milton which was never effected. In 1722, the Bishop of Rochester (Dr. Atterbury), friend of the Augustan poet, and avowed admirer of the Puritan, urged the revision of *Samson Agonistes*: 'I shall not press you as to time, but, some time or other, I wish you would review and polish that piece. If upon a new perusal of it (which I desire you to make) you think as I do that it is written in the very spirit of the ancients, it deserves your care, and is capable of being improved, with little trouble, into a perfect model and standard of tragic poetry. . . .'[148] The proposal was not one to amaze. 'Polished' versions of the older poets and the poets of freer versification were *de rigeur*. Pope himself had modernized Donne and Chaucer. To neo-classical ears, the blank verse of Milton was no doubt distressingly irregular, with its abundance of 'overflow,' its varied caesuras, its frequent departures from iambic norm in stress, its occasional catalectic lines. Bentley, whose famous edition of Milton appeared in 1732, was sure that the accepted text had been falsified and was full of gross errors; and undertook the most daring sort of emendation to 'restore' what

foreign idioms.' But he thinks the poet required 'recourse to these foreign assistances. Our language sunk under him, and was unequal to that greatness of soul which furnished him with such glorious conceptions' (*Spectator*, no. 297). Dr. Johnson is not so disposed to justify: 'But the truth is, that, both in prose and verse, he had formed his style by a perverse and pedantic principle. He was desirous to use English words with a foreign idiom.' 'Of him, at last, may be said what Jonson says of Spenser, that he *wrote no language*, but has formed what Butler calls a *Babylonish Dialect*, in itself harsh and barbarous . . .' (*Lives of the Poets*, I, 190-1). It should be observed that Milton's diction probably does not seem as antiquated to us as it did to the Augustans. See Havens, 115-16, for list of words then obsolete which have since 'come in' again.

[147] *Odyssey*, V, 278-9. See also Spence, 174, for Pope's later *résumé* of the same subject (1734-1736): 'Milton's style is not natural; it is an exotic style.'

[148] E-C, IX, 49.

he supposed was the original 'smooth' versification.[149] We may be thankful that either taste or lack of inclination prevented Pope from undertaking similarly to apply the polish.

As has just been said, the treatment denied *Samson* was bestowed upon Dr. Donne, two of whose Satires were modernized at the request of the Duke of Shrewsbury and Lord Oxford, and published in 1735.[150] Dr. Johnson, in general a very friendly critic, speaks slightingly of the poems and, after terming them a 'revival, in smoother numbers,' adverts to the probability of early composition: 'They made no great impression on the public. Pope seems to have known their imbecility and therefore suppressed them while he was yet contending to rise in reputation, but ventured them when he thought their deficiencies more likely to be imputed to Donne than to himself.'[151] Warton, on the other hand, who was inclined to be unfriendly, bestows praise in which I concur when he says, Donne 'had degraded and deformed a vast fund of sterling wit and strong sense by the most harsh and uncouth diction. Pope succeeded in giving harmony to a writer more rough and rugged than even any of his age, and who profited so little by the example Spenser had set of a musical and mellifluous versification. . . .'[152]

Even from the freer modern point of view, Donne's Satires are crabbed and jolting; and Pope has distinctly improved their readability. He has not only 'smoothed' the versification, but he has brightened and sharpened. Satire, to be read after the contemporaneity of its allusions has passed, must be spiced; must glitter with point. Neither Hall's nor Donne's does; but Pope has the secret. Once, it is true, the depth of feeling and finality of expression which characterize Donne's lyrics enter the Satires; and these qualities are entirely missing from the new version. But for the rest, the slightly expanded modernizations[153] are certainly superior.[154]

[149] For examples of the emendations see Hamelius, 95.

[150] The Second and the Fourth Satires. The Third was 'versified' by Pope's friend, Dr. Parnell.

[151] *Lives of the Poets*, III, 177.

[152] *Genius of Pope*, II, 348. Dryden said of the Donne of the *Satires*, 'were he translated into numbers and English, he would yet be wanting in the dignity of expression.' *Essay on Satire* (Ker, II, 19).

[153] The Second Satire has 112 lines in the original and 128 in Pope; the Fourth, 244 lines in Donne and 287 in Pope. Contemporary names and incidents are substituted for those in the original.

[154] For an example:

Donne : The ladies come. As pirates which do know
      That there came weak ships fraught with cochineal,
      The men board them, and praise (as they think) well
      Their beauties; they the men's wits; both are bought.

Dryden's description of Donne as 'the greatest wit, though not the best poet of our nation'[155] is recalled by Pope's pronouncement to Spence: 'Donne had no imagination, but as much wit, I think, as any writer can possibly have;'[156] in which the antithesis of imagination and wit may be interpreted to equate that of the 'true' and 'false' wit of the *Essay on Criticism*. Dr. Johnson, apropos of the 'metaphysical school,' having quoted the famous definition of 'true' wit from Pope, attempted his own account: 'But wit, abstracted from its effects upon the hearer may be more rigorously and philosophically considered as a kind of *discordia concors*; a combination of dissimilar images, or discovery of occult resemblances in things apparently unlike. Of wit, thus defined, they have more than enough.'[157] The trio of neo-classical dictators—Dryden, Pope, and Johnson—are thus seen to agree in their aversion to the poetry of intellectual passion and 'conceits'; in sharp distinction to current taste, which is ready to place Donne in the first rank of English lyric poets as well as in the first rank of English prose masters. It is only by the resolute exercise of the historical imagination that we can understand Pope's commendation of Donne's *Epistles*, *Metempsychosis*, and *Satires* as 'his best things.'[158]

The group of poets known as the 'metaphysicals'[159] were later associated with the name of Cowley; but even Dr. Johnson recognized that Cowley was not the first practitioner of the manner of Marino: it had been 'recommended by the example of Donne.'[160] But Dr. Johnson's acquaintance with seventeenth century poetry was scanty. He says of Donne and Jonson, 'when their reputation was high, they had undoubtedly more imitators than time has left behind. Their immediate successors of whom any remembrance can be said to remain were Suckling, Waller, Denham, Cowley, Cleveland, and Milton.' Pope exhibits much more acquaintance with

Pope: Painted for sight, and essenced for the smell,
(E-C, III,   Like frigates fraught with spice and cochineal,
442)   Sail in the ladies: how each pirate eyes
      So weak a vessel, and so rich a prize!
      Top-gallant he, and she in all her trim,
      He boarded her, she striking sail to him;
      'Dear Countess! You have charms all hearts to hit!'
      And 'Sweet Sir Fopling! You have so much wit!'

[155] Dedication of *Eleonora* (Saintsbury's ed., XI, 123).
[156] Spence, 136.
[157] *Lives of the Poets*, I, 20.
[158] Spence, 144.
[159] The term was not originated by Johnson. Dryden says Donne 'affects the metaphysics not only in his satires but in his amorous verses' (*Essay on Satire*, Ker, II, 19), and Pope uses both noun and adjective.
[160] *Lives of the Poets*, I, 22.

the Jacobean and Caroline poets. In his outline history of poetry already several times mentioned, he lists a 'School of Donne' which places with fair accuracy a considerable number of poets, some decidedly minor. They are: Cowley, Davenant, Drayton, Overbury, Randolph, Sir John Davis (i.e., Davies), Sir John Beaumont, Cartwright, Cleveland, Crashaw, Bishop Corbet, and Lord Falkland.[161] The more important of these come in for critical attention elsewhere; Drayton has already done so.[162] Davenant is again expressly mentioned as a 'scholar of Donne's' who 'took his sententiousness and metaphysics from him.' Pope's judgment upon *Gondibert* agrees with that of Mr. Gosse[163] in the safe assertion that it is 'not a good poem if you take it in the whole; but there are a great many good things in it.'[164]

The name of Cowley was still great in the land when Pope was beginning to read poetry; and though the two poets represented the passing and the prevailing schools of taste respectively, and though the *Essay on Criticism* gave the final order of banishment to the 'metaphysical' poetry of 'the last age,' Pope retained an affection for Cowley. He 'is a fine poet in spite of all his faults.'[165] *Windsor Forest*, when the roster of its poets is called, offers occasion for an elegiac celebration of the 'harp' of Cowley. In 1737, *To Augustus* registered the oblivion of the former favorite only to add in half-apology the expression of a lingering personal fondness:

> Who now reads Cowley? if he pleases yet,
> His moral pleases, not his pointed wit;[166]
> Forgot his epic, nay Pindaric art;
> But still I love the language of his heart.[167]

[161] Drayton does not really belong to this group at all. Sir Thomas Overbury is better known for his *Characters*. Thomas Randolph (1605-1635) is more properly a 'son of Ben.' Sir John Davies' philosophical poem *Nosce Teipsum* was published in 1602. Beaumont's dates are 1583-1627; John Cleveland's, 1613-1659. William Cartwright (1611-1643) was a gifted young scholar and preacher who imitated Donne and Jonson also. Richard Corbet (1582-1634) was Bishop of Oxford and later of Norwich.

[162] *supra*, 21-2.

[163] *Gondibert* is 'very obscure and ill-constructed. Its merit consists in the grace of some of the episodes, and in the sententious vigor of single lines' (9).

[164] Spence, 170.

[165] *ibid.*, 173.

[166] '. . . Dr. Donne and Mr. Cowley confounded metaphysics and love, and turned wit into point.' Oldmixon, vi.

[167] E-C, III, 353. His 'epic art' was displayed in the *Davideis*, of which only three books were finished. The *Pindaric Odes* set a fashion and were greatly admired in their day: they have, wrote Dr. Johnson, 'so long

Finally, the 'Imitations of English Poets' include two of Cowley—one in heroic couplets, the other, in graceful six-line stanzas of octosyllabics. The second, *Weeping*, hits off the conceits of Cowley very happily, without caricature.[168]

Crashaw was also—no doubt, because he was a son of the Roman Church—early known; though, as one would expect, the 'beauties' of this today much extolled poet were hardly of the sort to attract or influence an Augustan. Nevertheless, we are so fortunate as to have from Pope an extended analysis of Crashaw written in the days when his letters were still the vehicles for essay-like pronouncements on style and 'the poets.'

It was to his fellow-churchman Cromwell that Pope sent his copy of Crashaw, with the *examen* quotations from which are to be found in nearly all modern editions: 'having read him twice or thrice, I find him one of those whose works may just deserve reading. I take this poet to have writ like a gentleman, that is, at leisure hours, and more to keep out of idleness than to establish a reputation, so that nothing regular or just can be expected from him. All that regards design, form, fable, which is the soul of poetry,[169] all that concerns exactness, or consent of parts,[170] which is the body, will probably be lacking. Only pretty conceptions, fine metaphors, glittering expressions, and something of a neat cast of verse, which are properly the dress, gems, or loose ornaments of poetry, may be found in these verses.'

'This author formed himself upon Petrarch, or rather upon Marino.[171] His thoughts, one may observe, in the main, are pretty; but oftentimes far-fetched, and too often strained and stiffened to make them appear the greater. For men are never so apt to think a thing great as when it is odd or wonderful; and inconsiderate authors would rather be admired than understood. This ambition of surprising a reader is the true natural cause of all fustian, or bombast, in poetry. To confirm what I have said,

enjoyed the highest degree of poetical reputation that I am not willing to dismiss them with unabated censure' (*Lives*, I, 48). Modern taste agrees with Pope in preferring the language of Cowley's heart,—for example, in the beautiful tributes to Crashaw and Hervey.

[168] E-C, IV, 431-2. A foot-note gives the source of the imitation in a lyric of Cowley's of the same name. Pope has altered and improved the 'conceit.'

[169] This commonplace of neo-classical criticism goes back to Aristotle, who called the fable (or plot) the 'very soul of tragedy.' *Poetics*, Chapter VI.

[170] That is, the careful proportioning of parts to each other and to the whole.

[171] The same attribution was made to Spence, in conjunction with the remark, 'Crashaw is a worse sort of Cowley' (22).

you need but look into his first poem of the *Weeper*, where the 2nd, 4th, 6th, 14th, and 21st stanzas are as sublimely dull as the 7th, 8th, 9th, 16th, 17th, 20th, and 23rd stanzas of the same copy are soft and pleasing; and if these last want anything, it is an easier and more unaffected expression. The remaining thoughts in that poem might have been spared, being either but repetitions, or very trivial and mean. And by this example in the first, one may guess all the rest to be like this,—a mixture of tender, gentle thoughts and suitable expressions, of forced and inextricable conceits, and of needless fillers-up to the rest. From all which, it is plain this author writ fast, and set down what came uppermost.

'To speak of his numbers is a little difficult, they are so various and irregular, and mostly Pindaric.[172] It is evident his heroic verse,[173] the best example of which is his *Music's Duel*, is carelessly made up; but one may imagine from what it now is, that, had he taken more care, it had been musical and pleasing enough—not extremely majestic, but sweet:[174] and the time considered of his writing[175] he was, even as incorrect as he is, none of the worst versificators.

'I will just observe that the best pieces of this author are a paraphrase on Psalm XXIII; on Lessius; Epitaph on Mr. Ashton; *Wishes to his Supposed Mistress*; and the *Dies Irae*.'[176]

Pope had a fondness for what Professor Saintsbury calls 'comparative tickets': a series of poets are graded upon the basis of Crashaw. 'Herbert is lower than Crashaw, Sir John Beaumont higher, and Donne a good deal so.' This is the only reference to the Rector of Bemerton, whose poems Pope must have glanced into in his 'reading years.' Of course Herbert would seem 'lower than Crashaw' even to neo-classical taste which abhorred with Dryden[177]

---

[172] i.e., without set stanzaic form or rhyme-scheme.

[173] i.e., verse in heroic couplet.

[174] i.e., like Waller rather than like the 'majestic' Denham.

[175] cf. Spence, 174.

[176] E-C, VI, 116-18. Of course the selection is significant: the superb *Flaming Heart* and *Hymn to Saint Teresa* are omitted, and several minor but 'smooth' productions in octosyllabic couplets included. Pope found his reading in Crashaw useful when he came to write his *Eloisa to Abelard*. See E-C, VI, 117, n. for borrowings.

Mr. L. C. Martin, in his recent edition of Crashaw (Oxford Press, 1927, xlii) speaks of Pope's epistolary comment as 'The first piece of real and considered criticism of Crashaw. . . .'

[177]   Some peaceful province in Acrostic Land.
     There thou may'st wings display and altars raise. . . .
                              Dryden: *MacFlecknoe*: 206-7

and Addison the 'false wit' of 'whole sentences or poems cast into the figure of eggs, axes, or altars.'[178]

As to Boileau Malherbe seemed the inaugurator of the modern age in poetry, so to Dryden, Pope, and Johnson, the great age of English literature—the age when emulation of the ancients was begun, and rough versification emended, and 'conceits' displaced by 'just thoughts'—was opened by the advent of Waller and Denham. In such summary accounts of the history of English poetry as are now and then interspersed in critical writings of the period, there is a respectful pause and a bow of homage at these names. These were the persons who closed the couplet, who put an end to what Dr. Johnson calls 'the old manner of continuing the sense ungracefully from verse to verse,' and regulated the caesura, and who prepared the way for Dryden. Prior expressed the creed of orthodoxy when he said, 'Denham and Waller improved our versification, and Dryden perfected it.' 'Denham,' remarks Dr. Johnson, again in perfect orthodoxy, 'is deservedly considered as one of the fathers of English poetry.'[179] Pope's references to these great names have the occasional and casual air of standard opinion. We hear in the *Essay on Criticism* of 'Denham's strength and Waller's sweetness';[180] and the antithesis of virtues is elsewhere continued with 'majestic' and 'lofty' Denham and 'smooth' Waller.[181] Waller was imitated in two 'sweet' and 'smooth' studies in the delicate adulation of the court;[182] Denham's celebrated *Cooper's Hill*, which set a fashion for what Dr. Johnson calls 'local poetry,' was carefully studied and annotated, the additions and omissions of later corrected versions noted, the 'admirable judgment' of Denham lauded.[183] We are told in *Windsor Forest* that

> On Cooper's Hill eternal wreaths shall grow
> While lasts the mountain, or while Thames shall flow.

Waller is honored in the 'outline' of English poetry by a group of 'Models' which includes Carew 'in matter' and Sandys and

[178] Addison, *Spectator*, no. 62.

[179] Both quotations are from the Life of Denham: *Lives of the Poets*, I, 81; 75.

[180] Part II, 161.

[181] *Windsor Forest*, 271, 280. *To Augustus*, 267.

[182] E-C, IV, 429-30. Pope gracefully referred to these verses (see n.) which he wrote in youth when a 'great admirer of Waller,' as 'perhaps such imitations as the awkward country dames make after the fine and well-bred ladies of the Court.'

[183] Spence, 281-2. Spence appends, as 'a very useful lesson for a poet,' an elaborate scheme of the alterations made. The famous quatrain from *Cooper's Hill*, beginning 'O could I flow like thee,' has been happily parodied in the 'character' of Welsted, *Dunciad*, III, 169-72.

Fairfax 'in versification.'[184] Carew was 'a bad Waller,' and Granville, Lord Lansdowne, to whom Pope dedicated *Windsor Forest,* whose Essay *On Unnatural Flights in Poetry* was much admired by 'the critics,' was also of the 'school' of Waller.[185]

'Denham and Waller improved our versification, and Dryden perfected it.' Stories of the sort which would naturally arise to connect the declining and ascending luminaries of the poetic heavens, though existent, are, it seems, to be discredited. But when he was a 'very young boy' Pope 'prevailed with a friend to carry him to a coffee house which Dryden frequented,' Warburton says; and there, though 'not so happy as to know him: *Virgilium tantum vidi.*'[186] At Windsor Forest he passed from his Spenser to his Dryden: 'The works of Spenser he perused with great delight. . . . But on the first view of Dryden's works he was so struck with the excellence of a writer whose talents were congenial with his own that he abandoned the rest and studied his writings with uncommon pleasure and unremitting attention. He used to say that Dryden had improved the art of versification beyond any of the preceding poets, and that he would have been perfect in it, had he not been so often obliged to write with precipitation. His works, therefore, served as one of the models from whence our poet copied, and he even adopted the very turns of his periods,[187] just as Mr. Addison did those of Sir William Temple in prose. . . . He never spoke of him [Dryden] without a kind of rapturous veneration.'[188]

Pope's feeling toward 'that great man, whose memory I do and always have reverenced'[189] was always this side idolatry. He differs now and then from his critical judgments; he will concur in Cromwell's 'censure of the use of sea-terms in Mr. Dryden's Virgil' 'because no terms of art, or cant-words, suit with the majesty and dignity of style which epic poetry requires';[189] he laments that

> Even copious Dryden wanted, or forgot,
> The last and greatest art—the art to blot.[190]

But the 'veneration' never passed away, nor was Pope ever remiss in paying the tribute of gratitude as well as respect to his poetic

---

[184] Ruffhead, 329. 'Fairfax was acknowledged by him as his model.' *Lives of the Poets,* I, 293. For Sandys, see E-C, V, 18 and 20, and Schelling, *Ben Jonson and The Classical School,* 8 and 18.

[185] Spence, 21.

[186] E-C, VI, 15 and n. cf. also Spence, 332.

[187] See E-C foot-notes for abundant evidence of the 'adoption of turns.' Pope borrowed phrases from Dryden's translations of Virgil and others as well as from the original poems.

[188] Ruffhead, 17, 18. Ruffhead's ultimate source is Warburton.

[189] E-C, VI, 107; also 122.

[190] *To Augustus,* 280-1.

father. 'Dryden always uses proper language,—lively, natural, and fitted to the subject. It is scarce ever too high or too low; never, perhaps, except in his plays.'[191] 'I learned versification wholly from Dryden's works, who had improved it much beyond any of our former poets, and would probably have brought it to its perfection had not he been unhappily obliged to write so often in haste.'[192] This near-perfect versification was happily characterized in one of the seldom permitted triplets:

> Waller was smooth, but Dryden taught to join
> The varying verse, the full-resounding line,
> The long majestic march, and energy divine.[193]

Though Pope never made pretense to being a critic of the stage, a depreciation from Spence called forth a defense of the plays: 'I don't think Dryden so bad a dramatic writer as you seem to. There are as many things finely said in his plays as almost by any body. Besides his three best (*All for Love, Don Sebastian*, and *The Spanish Friar*) there are others that are good, as *Sir Martin Mar-All, Limberham*, and *The Conquest of Granada*. His *Wild Gallant* was written while he was a boy and is very bad.'[194] Pope was careful to say that his *Ode for Music* was not written to rival the *Alexander's Feast* of Dryden, but at Steele's request.[195]

Pope was familiar, as we should expect him to be, with Butler's great satire, *Hudibras*. Strange to say, he does not seem to have used his knowledge for purposes of imitation:[196] perhaps the subject of satire had changed too greatly: pedants had taken the place of Puritans. In 1737, he commented to Spence: 'Butler set out on too narrow a plan, and even that design is not kept up. He sinks into little true particulars about the Widow, etc.—The enthusiastic Knight and the ignorant Squire, over-religious in two different ways, and always quarreling together, is [*sic*] the chief point of view in it.'[197] The proposed history of poetry was to honor *Hudibras* by giving some account of its 'originals,' Sir John Mennis and Thomas Baynal.[198]

[191] Spence, 281.
[192] *ibid.*, 281.
[193] *To Augustus*, 267-9.
[194] Spence, 170-1.
[195] *ibid.*, 158. Pages 261-3 of the *Anecdotes* are devoted to bits of Dryden's private history and habits with which Pope regaled Spence. An amusing *dictum* asserts that 'Dryden was not a very genteel man; he was intimate with none but political men.'
[196] I do not find any of E-C's few parallels from *Hudibras* very convincing.
[197] Spence, 208.
[198] Mennis, or Mennes (1599-1671) was admiral in his Majesty's service. His verses, chiefly *vers de société*, seem to have caught the fancy of the age, and have been since described as the 'ideal of wit and mirth, but

Pope followed Dryden[199] in paying court to noble lords of literary ambition: indeed the deference in which my Lord Lansdowne, Lord Roscommon, Sheffield, Duke of Buckinghamshire, Lord Dorset, and the Earl of Rochester were held was common to great and small among the critics. They belonged to 'the wits of either Charles's days—the mob of gentlemen who wrote with ease.'[200] They were the inditers of graceful songs—the last glow of Elizabethan lyricism—and of witty enough satire. Four wrote in couplets brief critical treatises which reflected the views of neoclassical orthodoxy. Gifted amateurs, they could, without the necessity for compunction on the critic's part, be praised for their fortunate combination of elegance and wit. As Pope himself wrote:

> But let a lord once own the happy lines,
> How the wit brightens! how the style refines!
> Before his sacred name flies every fault,
> And each exalted stanza teems with thought.[201]

The indulgence which one may properly show to gifted amateurs of noble birth comes out in comment to Spence: 'Lord Dorset's things are all excellent in their way; for one should consider his pieces as a sort of epigrams: wit was his talent. He and Lord Rochester[202] should be considered as holiday writers—as gentlemen that diverted themselves now and then with poetry—rather than as poets.'[203] The preeminence of Lord Dorset was once asserted: 'Rochester is the medium between him [Oldham, who is 'too rough and coarse'] and Dorset. Lord Dorset is the best of all those writers. "What! Better than Lord Rochester?" Yes, Rochester has neither so much delicacy or exactness as Lord Dorset.'[204] Both Rochester and Dorset had the honor of inclusion in the 'Imitations of English Poets';[205] Rochester was also dignified by 'Verses Left

most of the pieces are coarse' (*D.N.B.*, XXXVII, 225). Perhaps it is his *Merry News from Epsom Wells* Pope has in mind. I am unable to identify Baynal.

[199] See the fulsome flattery of Sheffield in the *Essay on Satire*.

[200] *To Augustus*, 107-8.

[201] *Essay on Criticism*, II, 219-22. Dr. Johnson says happily, apropos of Savage's brief period of gentility: 'So powerful is genius when it is invested with the glitter of affluence! Men willingly pay to fortune that regard which they owe to merit, and are pleased when they have an opportunity at once of gratifying their vanity and practising their duty.' *Lives of the Poets*, II, 358.

[202] Lord Dorset (1637-1705). John Wilmot, Earl of Rochester (1647-1680).

[203] Spence, 281.

[204] *ibid.*, 136.

[205] Rochester's *On Nothing* was delightfully imitated in the terzains of *On Silence*. E-C, IV, 432-4. Dorset was imitated in the somewhat coarse

by Mr. Pope on his Lying in the Same Bed which Wilmot, the
Celebrated Earl of Rochester, Slept in,'[206] and Dorset by an epitaph
which celebrates 'the grace of courts, the Muses' pride, Patron of
arts, and judge of nature':

> Blest satirist! Who touched the mean so true
> And showed, vice had his hate and pity too.[207]

Lord Buckingham was one of Pope's earliest patrons—he appears
in the *Essay on Criticism* in the little band of those who 'restored
Wit's fundamental laws'—;[208] he wrote a set of verses in praise
of the translation of Homer;[209] and after his Grace's death, his
papers were, at the request of the Duchess, ordered and corrected
for the press by Pope.[210]

Restoration comedy half attracted, half repelled. It had precision and regularity, but it seemed too often to strain for effect;
to attain wit at the sacrifice of nature. Yet at its best it reproduces
the easy elegance of gentlemen's conversation. Thus we are told of
Congreve, who was a friend of Pope's as far back as the period of
Windsor Forest and the *Pastorals*, and to whom the Homer was
dedicated, that 'Mr. Pope esteemed him for the manners of a
gentleman and a man of honor, and the sagest of the poetic tribe.
He thought nothing wanting in his comedies but the simplicity
and truth of nature.'[211] And when Spence remarked of Wycherley,
also an early patron,[212] 'In spite of his good sense, I could never
read his plays with true pleasure, from the general stiffness of

'characters' *Artemisia* and *Phrynne*, E-C, IV, 435-6; in *The Challenge, A
Court Ballad*, E-C, IV, 478; and also, as Professor Case has just shown
(*M.L.N.*, XLIII, 321-2) in *To the Author of a Poem Entitled 'Successio.'*
  [206] E-C, IV, 498.
  [207] *ibid.*, IV, 381-2.
  [208] Part III, 163-4.
  [209] E-C, IV, 454 and n.
  [210] The edition was published in 1722; E-C, VIII, 191, n.
  [211] Ruffhead, 383.
  [212] Pope's *Autumn* was dedicated to Wycherley, and addresses this early
patron in somewhat heavily laid-on eulogy as

> Thou, whom the Nine with Plautus' wit inspire,
> The art of Terence, and Menander's fire;
> Whose sense instructs us, and whose humor charms,
> Whose judgment sways us, and whose spirit warms!

For the personal relations between Pope and Wycherley see E-C, V, 73-5.
The poet's 'first real introduction to town life was through Wycherley,
whom, as he told Spence, he used to follow like a dog' . . . (*ibid.*, 77).
With what was said above of Dryden's lack of 'gentility' is to be contrasted
the praise of Wycherley as 'a very genteel man; and had the nobleman look
as much as the Duke of Buckingham' just praised for looking the part
(Spence, 284).

the style,' Pope seconded: 'Ay, that was occasioned by his always studying for antitheses.'[213] But on the other hand, 'None of our writers have a freer, easier way for comedy than Etheredge and Vanbrugh.'[214] When Swift gave vent in satire to his dislike of Vanbrugh,[215] Pope defended him as 'the most easy, careless writer and companion in the world,' who 'wrote and built just as his fancy led him, or as those he built for and wrote for directed him.'[216] Yet another distinction was bestowed upon Vanbrugh. 'Prior is called the English Fontaine for his tales,' he told him; 'nothing is more unlike. But your *Fables* have the very spirit of this celebrated French poet.'[217] It was not to find blemishes but to illustrate the thesis that comedy required even 'greater labor' than tragedy as it found 'indulgence less' that Pope enjoined:

> Observe how seldom ev'n the best succeed:
> Tell me if Congreve's fools are fools indeed?
> What pert, low dialogues has Farquhar writ![218]
> How Van wants grace, who never wanted wit:[219]

Of 'Hasty' Shadwell, Jonson's successor and enemy, we have the comment: 'The virtuoso of Shadwell does not maintain his character with equal strength to the end; and this was that writer's general fault. Wycherley used to say of him that he knew how to start a fool very well,[220] but that he was never able to run him down.'[221]

The two chief tragic dramatists of the age were Otway and Rowe. Both excelled in pathos. 'Otway has written but two tragedies out of six that are pathetic. I believe he did it without much design, as Lillo has done it in his *Barnwell*. 'Tis a talent of nature, rather than an effect of judgment, to write so movingly.'[222] In *To Augustus*,[223] Otway is selected with Shakespeare as evidence that England was not dependent on France for her tragedy:

> Not but the tragic spirit was our own,
> And full in Shakespeare, fair in Otway shone.

[213] Spence, 161.
[214] *ibid.*, 46.
[215] In his *Vanbrugh's House.*
[216] Ruffhead, 384, n.
[217] *ibid.*, Vanbrugh's answer may be recorded: 'It may be so; but, I protest to you, I never read Fontaine's *Fables.*'
[218] 'Mr. Pope always used to call Farquhar a farce writer.' Spence, 67.
[219] *To Augustus*, 285-8.
[220] Shadwell abounded in 'humor' characters.
[221] Spence, 13.
[222] *ibid.*, 215.
[223] 276-7.

But unfortunately, like Shakespeare, he did not make 'correctness' his 'care.' He failed to 'polish' and 'refine.'[224]

Rowe, Pope's predecessor at the editing of Shakespeare, author of *Jane Shore* and *Lady Jane Grey*—the latter 'professedly in Shakespeare's style, that is, professedly in the style of a bad age,'[225] became a friend of the young poet in 1712 or thereabouts; paid a week's visit at Binfield in 1713. The friendship was lifelong, and Pope wrote the epilogue to *Jane Shore* and the gracious epitaph for Rowe's tomb in the Abbey:

> Thy reliques, Rowe, to this sad shrine we trust,
> And near thy Shakespeare place thy honored bust.
> Oh! next him, skilled to draw the tender tear. . . .[226]

Passing from the Restoration period to the age of Anne and George and the men of letters contemporary with our critic, we may pause to note Pope's admiration for the great English philosopher Locke, whose *Essay on the Human Understanding* appeared in 1680. He 'became delighted with that precision of thought which is the characteristic of that immortal essay.'[227] It was the day when 'Locke on the Understanding' was fashionable reading for all classes from the critic to the *beau monde*,[228] but surely no one ever paid higher tribute to this sage work than that admirer of the French and the ancients who could write: 'There is a great number of exceeding good writers among the French,' but 'they don't indeed think so closely or speak so clearly as Locke';[229] and 'How very strange and inconclusive does the reasoning of Tully and Plato often appear to us . . . there certainly is not any one of the ancients who reasons so well as our Mr. Locke or even as Hobbes.'[230] Only Descartes was ever so distinctly a national philosopher: to parallel Pope's praise we must go to Fontenelle's dismissal of ancient thought with an 'At length, Descartes came!'[231]

Of his literary contemporaries, Pope said: 'I think I have publicly praised all the best writers of my time';[232] and even an unkind critic would have difficulty in disproving his assertion. He was

[224] *ibid.*, 278.
[225] Spence, 174.
[226] E-C, IV, 384-5 and n. *To Augustus* represents Rowe as 'standard' 'for the passions' (86).
[227] Ruffhead, 13.
[228] The *Spectator*, nos. 62 and 37, bears evidence to the range.
[229] Spence, 199.
[230] *ibid.*, 199.
[231] 'Avant Descartes, on raissonnoit plus commodément; les siècles passés sont bien heureux de n'avoir pas eu cet homme-là.' *Oeuvres*, V, 290.
[232] E-C, X, 17.

the friend of all the great of the day who remain classics; and his enemies were, if not all 'dunces,' men of distinctly inferior literary —as distinguished from critical or scientific—ability. Of course, the close personal relations between the great made it easy to prefer charges of cabalism against them: each was made famous by the praise of the other; and they united their pretensions to exclude from the public favor those outside the charmed circle. One of these unfortunates who figured in the *Dunciad* wrote in this vein: 'The poets and critics of our time, for several years together, formed cabals and societies to support each other's reputation. They seemed to incorporate themselves and allowed none to deal in criticism and poetry that were not free of their company. They praised one another without measure, in public at least, and tossed the feather from one to t'other as people do at shuttlecock.'[233] Did Pope praise his friends because they were his friends? or did he choose his friends in full recognition of their greatness? The latter seems the more probable. Every classical age has had its similar 'circle' of the eminent; and no doubt in every age there have been Oldmixons to suspect the eminence.

It is true that Pope's relations with Addison, Steele, Swift, Gay, Prior, and the rest seem to have been personal rather than literary in character: at any rate, this is true as regards the correspondence. In his later period, Pope was not given to writing in a 'professional' vein: the literary criticism is very largely confined to the early letters to Walsh, Cromwell, and Caryll. It is hard to believe that in social intercourse with his friends there was not conversation of books and current composition; but in the carefully written and carefully preserved epistles, there is rather the studious assumption of the character of the man of the world, the gentleman: the poet indulges in the solemn platitudes of stoicism and the asseverations of undying friendship. Perhaps there was a cautious wisdom in all this; perhaps particular appraisals of the work of one's friends are always in danger of imperilling the friendships: safer to preserve, as one always can, the attitude of a general admiration.

These comments upon the critical 'remains' about to be presented are intended to account for the paucity of the remains and at the same time to interpret their value. Pope does not attempt such a rounded estimate of the literary work of his friends as a whole as circumstances would make inexpedient: we are to infer the estimated merit from the friendship[234] as well as the remarks.

---

[233] Oldmixon, 67. This was said apropos of the flattering reviews in the *Spectator*, and, in particular, of Addison's praise of the *Essay on Criticism*.
[234] I shall not deal in any detail with the 'personal relations' of the

Pope made the acquaintance of Addison and Steele during his brief period in London; for some time, he was a member of their 'little senate' at Button's coffee house. Addison praised the *Essay on Criticism*; Steele persuaded the poet to write his *Ode on St. Cecilia's Day*; the *Guardian* published a handful of his essays.[235] Though the friendships later cooled, and though the celebrated 'character' of 'Atticus' has survived all the more favorable comment, Pope never disparaged Addison's literary ability; and the fairly extensive remarks upon his personal habits to Spence are, though acute, not unfriendly.[236] In *To Augustus*[237] occasion was taken for a very amiable tribute to the influence of Addison's instructions in the *Spectator*:

> And in our own (excuse some courtly stains)
> No whiter page than Addison's remains.
> He from the taste obscene reclaims our youth,
> And sets the passions on the side of truth;
> Forms the soft bosom with the gentlest art,
> And pours each human virtue in the heart.

Addison is represented as having, like so many others, especially prized his lesser talent. He 'seemed to value himself more upon his poetry than upon his prose, though he wrote the latter with such particular ease, fluency, and happiness.'[238] And unfortunately, he distrusted his own judgment: 'He would show his verses to several friends; and would alter almost everything that any of them hinted at as wrong. He seemed too diffident of himself, and too much concerned about his character as a poet. . . .'[239] Of Addison's poems, Pope liked the *Letter from Italy* best—he 'used formerly to like' it 'extremely'—; 'even more than his *Campaign*.'[240]

In prose, too, he was prone to over much revision. He 'wrote very fluently, but he was sometimes very slow and scrupulous in correcting.' 'Many of his *Spectators* he wrote very fast, and sent them to the press as soon as they were written. It seems to have been best for him not to have too much time to correct.'[241]

---

men, for which see Dr. Lochner's Leipzig dissertation (1910), *Popes Literarische Beziehungen zu seinen Zeitgenossen.*

[235] E-C, V, 80-1.

[236] This, for example: 'Addison was perfect good company with intimates; and had something more charming in his conversation than I ever knew in any other man; but with any mixture of strangers, and sometimes only with one, he seemed to preserve his dignity much, with a stiff sort of silence.' Spence, 50.

[237] Written in 1737.

[238] Spence, 257.

[239] *ibid.*, 49.

[240] *ibid.*, 316 (written in 1743).

[241] *ibid.*, 49-50.

A certain disparity in judgment has been discovered between what was written of *Cato* to Caryll in 1712-1713, and what was told Spence in 1737. In the former, Pope says: 'I have had lately the entertainment of reading Mr. Addison's tragedy of Cato. The scene is in Utica, and the time the last night of his life. It drew tears from me in several parts of the fourth and fifth acts, where the beauty of virtue appears so charming that I believe if it comes on the theater we shall enjoy that which Plato thought the greatest pleasure an exalted soul could be capable of, a view of virtue itself dressed in person, color, and action. . . . I question if any play has ever conduced so immediately to morals as this.'[242]

To Spence, Pope declares: 'When Mr. Addison had finished his *Cato*, he brought it to me, desired to have my sincere opinion of it . . . I gave him my opinion sincerely, which was that I thought he had better not act it, and that he would get reputation enough by only printing it. This I said, as thinking the lines well written, but the piece not theatrical enough.'[243] Courthope accounts for this supposed disparity by supposing that 'having forgotten his early opinion of the play, he threw his more mature judgment into the form of a piquant anecdote which had no foundation in reality.'[244] But the two accounts are not contradictory: one praises the sentiments of the play; the other declares its merits literary rather than dramatic.

Addison's knowledge of the earlier English poets does not seem to have equalled Pope's; and upon one occasion the latter, with righteous superiority, had to complain of the former as having, in his *Account of the Greatest English Poets*, given the 'character of some of our best poets' only by hearsay. 'Thus his character of Chaucer is diametrically opposite to the truth: he blames him for his want of humor.[245] The character he gives of Spenser is false too; and I have heard him say that he never read Spenser till fifteen years after he wrote it.'[246]

Of all Pope's friends, Swift was at once the greatest and the closest, though the friendship, which began when the Dean was in London sending back to Stella in Ireland his accounts of notables of the kingdom and of the republic of letters, had for long years to

[242] E-C, VI, 181-2.
[243] Spence, 196.
[244] E-C, V, 84.
[245] But Pope is inexact here. Addison thinks of Chaucer as a 'merry bard' whose humor has become antiquated and crude when judged by the standards of the Age of Reason:

> In vain he jests in his unpolished strain,
> And tries to make his readers laugh in vain.

[246] Spence, 50.

sustain itself through correspondence. Pope and Swift published a
number of Miscellanies together; they collaborated in *Scriblerus*;
to Swift was dedicated the *Dunciad*, in lines which emphasize the
variety of the Dean's publications and moods:

> O thou! Whatever title please thine ear,
> Dean, Drapier, Bickerstaff, or Gulliver!
> Whether thou choose Cervantes' serious air,
> Or laugh and shake in Rabelais' easy chair,
> Or praise the Court, or magnify mankind,
> Or thy grieved country's copper chains unbind.[247]

There is no doubt of the admiration in which each held the
literary genius of the other; but particular judgments are far to
seek, and the copious correspondence between them lamentably
lacking in critical *dicta*. Even the interesting letter which Gay and
Pope wrote the Dean just after the publication of *Gulliver* reports
rather the opinions of critics in general than those of the writers:
'The politicians to a man agree that it is free from particular
reflections, but that the satire on general societies of men is too
severe'; Bolingbroke 'least approves'; 'the Duchess Dowager of
Marlborough is in raptures at it'; churchgoers think 'the design
impious'; and so on. Even the interesting and now standard
judgment that 'the flying island is the least entertaining' is attributed to 'other critics,' who agree that 'this part was not written
by the same hand.'[248] The friend was surely eminent over the
critic in such a general tribute to Swift, man and author, as Pope
sent to Lord Orrery: 'My sincere love for this valuable, indeed incomparable, man will accompany him through life and pursue his
memory were I to live a hundred lives, as many of his works will
live, which are absolutely original, unequalled, unexampled.' One's
acquaintance with comparative literature does not need to be very
profound to know that these adjectives no more apply to Swift
than to any other educated man since the Greeks. But by collabo-
rating with him in the several Miscellanies, Pope paid him the high
honor of equality with the greatest poet of the age and promised
him that honor in perpetuity: 'Our Miscellany is now quite printed.
I am prodigiously pleased with this joint volume, in which, methinks, we look like friends, side by side, serious and merry by
turns, conversing interchangeably, and walking down hand in
hand to posterity, not with stiff forms of learned authors, flattering
each other, and setting the rest of mankind at nought, but in a

---

[247] I, 19-24. The copper chains of Ireland were unbound by the *Drapier
Letters*.
[248] E-C, VII, 88-90.

free, unimportant, natural, easy manner, diverting others just as we diverted ourselves.'[249] 'At all adventures,' he wrote Swift, 'yours and my name shall stand linked as friends to posterity, both in verse and prose, and, as Tully calls it, *in consuetudine studiorum.*'[250]

Similarly lacking is any estimate of the literary worth of Gay, since 1713 one of Pope's 'poetical dependants,' who 'lived with him in close companionship for more than twenty years,'[251] who dedicated to the 'rising genius' his *Rural Sports*, who published his *Shepherd's Week* to ridicule Pope's enemy, Philips,[252] who hailed the completion of the monumental Homer with his *ottava rima Welcome from Greece.* Surely Pope must have read all Gay's graceful, witty poems with relish; but no appreciation remains: the epitaph written for Gay's tomb in the Abbey praised the man, not the poet; unless one finds a brief literary 'character' in

> With native humor tempering virtuous rage,
> Formed to delight at once and lash the age.[253]

Prior was an acquaintance[254] and an admiration: he is one of seven poets selected as 'authorities for poetical language.'[255] 'Pope's first inclination to attempt a composition of . . . [the] tender kind arose . . . from his perusal of Prior's *Nut-brown Maid.*'[256] In the Miscellany of 1727, *Eloisa to Abelard* was prefixed with some verses from *Alma*,[257] a poem which Pope greatly admired. Prior himself prized his long and labored epic *Solomon* the most of his works; but when he asked Pope how he liked it, Pope made the tactful reply, 'Your *Alma* is a masterpiece.'[258] After Prior's death, his friend had the opportunity of examining the copious literary remains—'at least half as much as all his published works. And there are nine or ten copies of verses among them which I thought much better than several things he himself published. In particular, I remember there was a dialogue . . . between Apollo and Daphne which pleased me as much as anything of his I ever read. There are also four dialogues in prose between persons of character very strongly opposed to one another which I thought very good. One of them was between Charles the Fifth and his tutor, Adrian the Sixth, to show the different turns of a

---

[249] E-C, VII, 94.
[250] *ibid.*, 123.
[251] *ibid.*, V, 255.
[252] *ibid.*, 124-5.
[253] *ibid.*, IV, 389. But see *Dunciad* (E-C, IV, 184, n).
[254] There is at least one letter from Pope to Prior extant: E-C, X, 105.
[255] Spence, 311, n.
[256] Johnson: *Lives of the Poets*, III, 105.
[257] E-C, II, 218.
[258] *ibid.*, X, 330, n.

person who had studied human nature only in his closet, and of one who had rambled all over Europe.'[259] This praise of what seems to the modern reader very charming prose hardly agrees with Pope's dictum at a later time that 'Prior, indeed, was nothing out of verse' and 'could not write in a style fit for history.'[260] The just quoted disparagement is false, at any rate.

Another friend within the so-called 'classical' circle was Dr. Parnell, a minor poet of taste,[261] also something of a wit, who contributed, at Pope's request, 'some very beautiful copies'—i.e., poems—to Tonson's *Miscellany*.[262] Pope called his *Pandora* and *Eclogue upon Health* 'two of the most beautiful things I ever read';[263] and after his friend's death, published a selection of his poems with 'a very elegant dedication to the Earl of Oxford.' Pope exercised his discretion: 'What he gave me leave to publish was but a small part of what he left behind him; but it was the best, and I will not make it worse by enlarging it.'[264] The suppressed poems, published in 1758, were valueless.

Pope's literary friendships were not confined to those of his own school. Criticism looking back may see in Thomson and his descriptive blank verse the advent of a new era; but Pope was conscious of no such alignment, nor was Thomson. 'There seems no reason to doubt the statement made by Johnson that Pope once expressed his regard for Thomson in a poetical epistle sent to him while abroad. . . .'[265] When the *Seasons* was published by subscription in 1730, Pope took three copies. He termed it in the prefatory matter of the *Dunciad* an 'elegant and philosophical poem.'[266] It was for long believed that Pope actually had a hand in the *Seasons*: that he wrote the lines in *Autumn* beginning, 'Thoughtless of beauty, she was beauty's self';[267] that his was the other hand in which important corrections are found made in 'the celebrated interleaved copy' of 1738. This agreeable fiction seems now to have gone the way of other agreeable fictions.[268] Nevertheless, the relations between the poets were decidedly friendly. As Dr. de Maar justly puts it, 'there is nothing of the rebel in Thomson, and he certainly did not choose blank verse out of a mere desire to differ from Pope and his compeers. Pope accepted the

[259] Spence, 48-9. The other dialogues are between Montaigne and Locke, Cromwell and his mad porter, and Sir Thomas More and the Vicar of Bray.
[260] Spence, 175.
[261] Certainly far from what Gray calls him, 'the dunghill of Irish Grub-street.' E-C, VIII, 28, n.
[262] *ibid.*, VII, 412.
[263] *ibid.*, VII, 464.
[264] *ibid.*, VIII, 28.
[265] G. C. Macaulay, 33.
[266] E-C, IV, 66.
[267] Perry, 386-7.
[268] Macaulay, 243. The 'other hand' is now thought to be Lord Lyttleton's.

Seasons, [and] enjoyed the poem. . . .'[269] There is no reason to doubt that Pope's sentiments are correctly expressed when his (and Thomson's) friend, Lyttleton, represents him as saying of the poet of the *Seasons*, 'He painted Nature exactly, and with great strength of pencil. His imagination was rich, extensive, sublime; but his diction was frequently obscure and affected. Nor did he know when to stop, or what to reject.'[270]

Dr. Young, author of the then admired *Night Thoughts*,[271] began as a satirist in the orthodox heroic couplets[272] and ended, with his *Conjectures on Original Composition*, (1759) in 'romantic individualism.' In the *Conjectures*, Young turned away from Pope; but during the latter's lifetime he was far from a rebel, and in the *Night Thoughts*, he took particular occasion to pay tribute to Pope and his *Essay on Man*:

> O! had he pressed his theme, pursued the track
> Which opens out of darkness into day!
> O! had he mounted on his wing of fire,
> Soared where I sink, and sung immortal man,[273]

Pope, in his turn, recognized the talents of Young. Far from envying a rival's success at his own *genre*, he praised him as 'the witty and moral satirist.'[274] To Warburton, Pope expressed what seems the just view of the Young of the *Night Thoughts*: he 'had much of a sublime genius, though without common sense; so that his genius, having no guide, was perpetually liable to degenerate into bombast.'[275]

Friendly, too, were Pope's relations with Lady Winchilsea, now regarded as of the incipient school of romanticism. The lady wrote commendatory verses which were prefixed to the gentleman's first volume of poems;[276] and he replied to her defence of 'female wits'

---

[269] *History of Modern English Romanticism*, I, 116.

[270] *Dialogues of the Dead*, 129. Pope knew Thomson's tragedies also. See E-C, V, 75.

[271] Now, as Mr. Gosse (213) makes brave to say, too much neglected.

[272] Warton prefers his *Universal Passion* to Pope's Satires.

[273] Pope's disciple, Harte, speaks of having seen the letter Dr. Young wrote Pope urging him to 'write something on the side of revelation' to supplement the *natural religion* of the *Essay on Man*. E-C, II, 269.

[274] *ibid.*, IV, 66.

[275] Ruffhead, 224. An item may be appended from the same source (225) which will illustrate at once the carelessness of Anglican churchmanship in the eighteenth century and the occasional knowledge of Roman authorities and practices exhibited by the poet. When Young decided to take orders, he applied for direction in the study of theology not to Sherlock, Atterbury, or Burnet, but to Pope, 'who, in a youthful frolic, recommended Thomas Aquinas to him.' The advice was taken!

[276] E-C, V, 173, n.

against his gentle sneer in *The Rape* with an *Impromptu* which gracefully and gallantly avoids retraction:

> Fate doomed the fall of every female wit;
> But doomed it then when first Ardelia writ.[277]

Some of the praise survives the condescension with which Pope habitually honored the ladies.

Defoe appears in the *Dunciad* 'earless on high' and 'unabashed,'[278] as he stood in the pillory for writing his *Short Way with Dissenters* and later pamphlets: 'the provocation he had given Pope was that in his *System of Magic* he had thrown out some sarcasms against 'Sylphs and Gnomes.'[279] But in 1742, he is given impartial praise which more than makes up for the passing vignette in the satire: 'The first part of *Robinson Crusoe* is very good. Defoe wrote a vast number of things, and none bad, though none are excellent except this. There is something good in all he has written.'[280]

The only contemporary poets surviving in anthologies and histories whose work Pope disparaged were the two Philipses—John, didactic poet in quasi-Miltonic blank verse, for whose famous *Cyder* Pope 'frequently expressed his total dislike,' though its author was patronized by Bolingbroke;[281] and Ambrose, or, by the offensive nickname which came to cling to him, Namby-Pamby. This minor poet had the misfortune to publish a set of Pastorals in the same volume of Tonson's *Miscellanies* with those of Pope. Though a year and a half afterward 'he agreed with the *Tatler* that we had no better eclogues in the language,'[282] subsequent and continued praise of Philips in the *Spectator* and later in the *Guardian*, culminating in the claim that this minor poet was among the four masters of the art,[283] naturally rankled with Pope; and he took the neat revenge of publishing in the *Guardian*[284] an

---

[277] *ibid.*, IV, 454. 'Ardelia' was the name under which the lady first published. 'There are certain serious lapses from this attitude of friendship,' however. Miss Reynolds believes that Phoebe Clinket, the bluestocking and 'female wit' of *Three Hours after Marriage*, was a character of Pope's devising and was intended to satirize the Countess of Winchilsea. (cf. lvii and lxiv-ix of the *Poems*.)

[278] II, 147.

[279] E-C, IV, 239. He also printed some lines against Pope signed in another name after his *Life of Campbell* (1720).

[280] Spence, 258-9.

[281] E-C, IX, 82, n.

[282] *ibid.*, I, 250.

[283] The others were Theocritus, Virgil, and Spenser. E-C, I, 251, *Guardian*, No. 32.

[284] No. 40, reprinted in E-C, X, 507, ff.

ironical treatise in which he selected for praise the worst passages from Philips, contrasting with them the best from his own. Pope, like Fontenelle, held that the manners and diction should be neither too polite nor too rustic: the design was to represent shepherds as they might have been in the Golden Age, not as they are. Accordingly he censures Theocritus' swains as 'perhaps too much inclining to rusticity.'[285] But in this mock-praise he pretends to admire Philips' reproduction of 'the antiquated English' of the country-side and to reprehend his own poems because 'His clowns do not converse in all the simplicity proper to the country;'[286] he effectively ridicules the 'beautiful rusticity'[287] of Philips, his 'simple' diction, his repetitions, and his homely proverbs.[288] But though jealousy may have been the occasion for the animosity, it is hard to suppose that Pope could have in any event esteemed the generality of Philips' work. This poet's jingling simpleness of style entirely missed the charm of Blake's *Songs of Innocence*. In the following comment, Pope no doubt had in mind such a lyric as the *To Miss Charlotte Pultney in her Mother's Arms* now sometimes included in anthologies: 'Gay is writing tales for Prince William; I suppose Philips will take this very ill, for two reasons: one, that he thinks all childish things belong to him; and the other, because he will take it ill to be taught that one may write things to a child without being childish.'[289] The comment seems substantially just.

We have already had proof of Pope's interest in English philosophy and philosophers. Of those contemporary with him we know that he read Berkeley, Shaftesbury, Mandeville, and the deist Wollaston,[290] besides his 'guide, philosopher, and friend,'[291] Bolingbroke. Pope made Berkeley's acquaintance at Steele's house in 1713.[292] The two corresponded for some years.[293] Berkeley was a frank admirer of Pope's genius: he called the translation of Homer a 'noble work,'[294] and said of the *Rape*, 'Style, painting, judgment, spirit I had already admired in other of your writings; but in this I am charmed with the magic of your invention, with all those images, allusions, and inexplicable beauties which you raise so surprisingly and at the same time so naturally out of a trifle.'[295] Pope, in turn, commended *The Minute Philosopher*,[296]

[285] E-C, I, 261.
[286] *ibid.*, X, 508.
[287] *ibid.*, 511.
[288] *ibid.*, X, 512.
[293] The letters are reprinted in E-C, IX, 1-6.
[294] *ibid.*, IX, 5.
[295] *ibid.*, IX, 1.
[296] *Alciphron. ibid.*, VII, 264.

[289] *ibid.*, VII, 67.
[290] *ibid.*, II, 285; and IX, 149.
[291] *Essay on Man*, IV, 390.
[292] E-C, IX, 1, n.

and described Berkeley—without much exaggeration—as possessing 'every virtue under heaven.'[297]

The fourth book of the *Dunciad* has its gibe at Shaftesbury and his 'enthusiasm':

> That bright image to our fancy draw,
> Which Theocles[298] in raptured vision saw,
> While through poetic scenes the Genius roves,
> Or wanders wild in Academic groves.[299]

But, as Warton remarks,[300] 'After borrowing so largely from this treatise [*The Moralists*], our author should not, methinks, have ridiculed it.' Shaftesbury was one of the important sources, directly and indirectly, of the *Essay on Man*, particularly the First Epistle. Sometimes the ideas came from Shaftesbury through Bolingbroke; sometimes the former was used rather than the latter when the two authorities differed on a point; sometimes the phrasing indicates that an idea found in both was actually taken from Shaftesbury.[301]

Without grasping its implications, Pope made considerable use of the *Fable of the Bees* in his *Essay on Man*, and his *Third Epistle*. In the former, like Mandeville, he 'founds virtue on vice. The ruling passion is evil, but reason gives it a bias towards good.'[302] In the latter, he makes use of Mandeville's paradox that private vice makes for public good. 'He starts with what is in effect an attack upon luxury and civilization . . . ; yet he afterwards asserts that the constitution of society which he has thus condemned, is ordained and prompted by heaven itself.'[303] Some passages of the *Fable* were actually paraphrased;[304] and the manuscript of the *Essay on Man* had, in place of the present line II, 240, the direct paraphrase of the sub-title of the *Fable*: 'And public good extracts from private vice.'

The partiality of friend for friend will no doubt have to be summoned in to account for Pope's admiration for his 'guide, philosopher, and friend,' whom he calls 'absolutely the best writer

---

[297] In *Epilogue to the Satires*. E-C, III, 477.

[298] Theocles is one of the persons in Shaftesbury's long dialogue, *The Moralist, A Rhapsody on Virtue*.

[299] *Dunciad*, IV, 487-90.

[300] *Genius of Pope*, II, 94, n.

[301] These points are developed with the parallels in C. A. Moore's excellent article on 'Shaftesbury and the Ethical Poets in England,' *P.M.L.A.* XXI, 264-325.

[302] E-C, II, 307.

[303] *ibid.*, III, 121.

[304] F. B. Kaye, in his recent edition of Mandeville (I, cxviii-ix and n.) thinks vs. 13-14 and 25-6 of the *Third Epistle* and *Essay on Man*, III, 193-4 'derive definitely from the *Fable*.' E-C gives a few more parallels.

of the age,' and of whom he says, 'Lord Bolingbroke will be more known to posterity as a writer and philosopher than as a states-man.'[305] Truly amazing is the conjunction in which this forgotten eminent Augustan is placed when Pope writes Swift, 'You and Lord Bolingbroke are the only men to whom I write. . . . You are indeed almost the only men I know who either can write in this age, or whose writings will reach the next.'[306] Even allowing for hyperbole, this is too much! It is doubtful if posterity will recall 'St. John' from his 'delusive turnips,' even though Matthew Arnold has ventured to raise a voice in his behalf.[307]

Nor will we be apt to sympathize with the praise of Bishop Warburton, who after a period of being Pope's enemy became his friend and literary executor and the ingenious rehabilitator of his orthodoxy,—even though there is an assisting vagueness in the description of him as 'the greatest general critic I ever knew; the most capable of seeing through all the possibilities of things.'[308] But again, let it be remembered that Warburton has found others to praise him. Dr. Johnson expressed his 'admiration of the fer-tility of Warburton's genius and of the variety of his materials,' and said to a friend, 'Warburton is perhaps the last man who has written with a mind full of reading and reflection.'[309]

In his later years there grew up a company of younger men of letters between whom and Pope there was a friendly connection. Some of the poets are now forgotten, such as Robert, Earl Nugent, to whom the great poet paid 'many poetical thanks' for his *Ode to Lord Marchmont*;[310] the Reverend Walter Harte, tutor to Lord Chesterfield's son and correspondent, whose *Essay on Reason* Pope says it would 'in no way displease' him to have ascribed to him as a part of the *Essay on Man*;[311] David Mallet, whose *Of Verbal Criticism, An Epistle to Mr. Pope Occasioned by Theobald's Shake-speare and Bentley's Milton*—the point of view easily to be sur-mised—was read 'over and over with great and just delight';[312]

---

[305] Spence, 143.

[306] VII, 345. 'This age' must refer to Pope's younger contemporaries, not to Addison, Prior, Parnell, Gay, etc.

[307] ' *"Who now reads Bolingbroke?"* [Pope's, *Who now reads Cowley?*] asked Burke scornfully. And the right answer is, so far as regards, at any rate, the historical writings, "Far too few of us; the more's the pity".'— *Mixed Essays*, 168. More recently (1923) Bolingbroke has been praised by Charles Whibley (*The Criterion*, I, 203-16, 348-62).

[308] Spence, 337.

[309] Boswell, IV, 49.

[310] E-C, VII, 378.

[311] *ibid.*, X, 87. The next Epistle of Pope on Man had been announced to have as its subject Human Reason.

[312] *ibid.*, X, 86. Mallet, like others of the time, was ambiguous between

and the Rev. Christopher Pitt, translator into heroics of the *Aeneid* and Vida's *Ars Poetica*; which latter Pope read 'with eagerness' and thought 'both a correct and a spirited translation.'[313]

The name and romantic career of Richard Savage linger on through Dr. Johnson's discursive biography. Less known, perhaps, is Pope's connection with this strange figure. At the time of the War with the Dunces, Savage published a collection of pieces defending Pope, an action which secured for him the enmity of many minor poets. 'Mr. Savage, however,' says Dr. Johnson,[314] 'set all the malice of all the pigmy writers at defiance, and thought the friendship of Mr. Pope cheaply purchased by being exposed to their censure and their hatred; nor had he any reason to repent of the preference, for he found Mr. Pope a steady and unalienable friend almost to the end of his life.' In his last period, Savage was 'chiefly supported by Mr. Pope's bounty, who procured an annual subscription for him to the amount of 50 pounds *per annum*, of which he contributed 20 pounds *per annum* himself.'[315] Pope seems to have esteemed the poet as well as the man: he praised Savage's principal poem, *The Wanderer*.[316] The now much admired *Song to David* was not published until 1763, and one can hardly hope that Pope would have taken pleasure in it; but it is interesting to know that in his earlier days Christopher Smart translated the *Ode on St. Cecilia's Day* and the *Essay on Criticism* into Latin, and was, in consequence, 'very civilly' received at the home of the great Mr. Pope.[317]

A separate paragraph must be devoted to recalling the connection between Pope and Dr. Johnson, the luminaries of successive periods in our literary history. 'Johnson's *London* was published in May, 1738; and it is remarkable that it came out on the same morning with Pope's satire entitled "*1738*," so that England had at once its Juvenal and Horace as poetical monitors.'[318] Though the new poem was greatly lauded, and 'the first buzz in the literary circles was, "Here is an unknown poet, greater even than Pope",'

classicism and romanticism so-called. The classical *Epistle* mentioned in the text was written in 1733; but already in 1724 the poet had published his ballad of *William and Margaret*, of which Mr. Gosse says that it 'in some sense inaugurated the new romantic school' (222). He was friend and admirer of Thomson as well as of Pope (with the latter he corresponded from 1729-1743).

[313] E-C, X, 129.
[314] *Lives of the Poets*, II, 363.
[315] Ruffhead, 391. Savage did not prove a very grateful or tractable pensioner. See Johnson's Life and Pope's letters of remonstrance, X, 100-2.
[316] *Lives of the Poets*, II, 364-5.
[317] E-C, X, 98, 99, and n.
[318] Boswell, I, 126.

the older poet not only exhibited no jealousy but joined in the laudation. He requested a friend to discover who the new author was, and when informed 'that his name was Johnson, and that he was some obscure man, Pope said, "He will soon be *déterré*".'[319] Later discovering that Johnson required a master's degree in order to compete for the mastership of a school, Pope attempted through his friends to have the necessary degree granted by Dublin.[320] In a note sent with the *London* to Richardson, he wrote, 'Mr. P. from the merit of this work, which was all the knowledge he had of him, endeavored to serve him without his [i.e. Johnson's] own application.' 'Who,' said Johnson, when he heard of the note, 'would not be proud to have such a man as Pope solicitous in inquiring about him?'[321] This gratuitous kindness must have done much to confirm the great 'lexicographer' in the loyalty he always manifested for the person and work of Pope.

Johnson himself reports a similar kindness of Pope's toward Akenside.[322] The latter's *Pleasures of the Imagination*, written when the poet was about twenty-two, was brought to London in 1743, the year before Pope's death, and offered to Dodsley for a hundred and twenty pounds. Before accepting, the cautious publisher took the work to Pope for his judgment; he was advised 'not to make a niggardly offer; for "this was no every day writer".' Yet the *Pleasures* is a 'romantic' poem in blank verse. Here is another example of Pope's catholicity.

The length of this chapter has perhaps surprised. Pope, a neoclassicist, whose whole gospel was comprised in the French rules, —what could he have in common with the great 'Gothic' literature of England? But the fact remains that Pope was a student and an admirer of all the greatest poets of his nation,—Chaucer, Spenser, Shakespeare, Milton; that few in his day knew them so well. The fact remains that he was ever ready to speak humbly of himself, the 'last, the meanest'[323] of the Muse's sons, and to magnify his predecessors. 'I know too well,' he wrote Caryll, 'the vast difference between those who truly deserve the name of poets and men of wit, and one who is nothing but what he owes to them; and I keep the pictures of Dryden, Milton, Shakespeare, etc., in my chamber, round about me, that the constant remembrance of them may keep me always humble.'[324]

There is no single aspect of Pope that has been more neglected than his love for the great English poets and his extensive familiarity with them and with English literature in general. In spite of

[319] Boswell, I, 129.
[320] *ibid.*, I, 132-3 and n.
[321] *ibid.*, I, 143.

[322] *Lives of the Poets*, III, 412.
[323] E-C, I, 196.
[324] *ibid.*, VI, 145.

an early utterance or two to the contrary, Pope was a devout nationalist. He found his chief inspiration not in the literature of Rome or France but in that of his own country,—in Shakespeare, Spenser, Milton, and Dryden. He does not begin a new line: he follows in their train.

CHAPTER IX

CONCLUSION

'AMONG the conventions of the day, the most conspicuous is the convention of revolt. The only really unconventional person among us is the one who is not revolting against convention.'[1] If it be granted (and must it not be?) that Professor Grandgent's neat paradox is substantially true, then the difficulty under which the average reader of Pope labors is apparent. We (and this in the main includes scholars as well as literati) admire the innovator and the radical, the novel and the amazing. The dazzling achievements of the physical sciences in the nineteenth and twentieth centuries have left even the wariest among us with the suspicion that 'progress' and 'evolution' are also to be expected in the spheres of the good, the true, and the beautiful.[2] With our vague but exhilarating conception of an eternal 'onwards and upwards' we find humanism, with its notions of unchanging human nature, of permanent 'laws' of taste and principles of conduct, difficult to attain. We must look 'Science, the false Messiah,'[3] squarely in the face, must be ready to draw some necessary distinctions between the material world and the world of values, before we can sympathetically or soundly evaluate the intellectual (and this includes the critical) position of Boileau, Pope, Dryden, Johnson. We must see the point of Addison's contention that 'It is impossible for us who live in the later ages of the world to make observations in criticism, morality . . . which have not been touched on by others,' and of Dr. Johnson's, that 'great things cannot have escaped former observation.'[4] We must school ourselves, if we require such schooling, to humility in the presence of corporate human experience, as expressed in tradition and the 'best that has been said and thought in the world.' We must, with Joubert, feel our peril when we differ in religion from the saints and in poetry from the poets.[5]

---

[1] Grandgent: *Old and New*, 5.
[2] The idea of progress led the modernists in the French *Querelle des Anciens et des Modernes* to make much the same sort of false application that is made today. cf. the discussion in the earlier pages of Chapter III.
[3] Mr. C. E. Ayres has just published a book under this title.
[4] *Spectator*, No. 253. *Lives*, I, 21.
[5] 'Il faut craindre de se tromper en poésie quand on ne pense pas comme

Pope, both as poet and as critic, felt himself the heir of the ages, the last, albeit the 'meanest,' of the Muse's sons.[6] He was not so presumptuous as to suppose that in either poetry or criticism it was for him to begin *de novo*; to write as if none had written before him. He was in a great tradition; and his task consisted of the assimilation of this tradition, and of its reproduction in forms adapted to the time and place of the poet: a substance in some real sense unchanging is given 'appearance' and 'local habitation' through the imagination and the judgment of the individual writer. True poetry and true criticism will both of necessity adopt as their substance what has oft been said: they will be far from any affectation of novelty;[7] they will prefer being true to being new. But both will make fresh application of permanent realities: abiding experience is Protean in its assumption of new forms; and art and criticism should both properly be occupied in pursuing reality through its manifold appearances. And in both there is the never-ending quest for the *mot juste*, for the perfect expression; the attempt to say with really definitive exactness what one really means. Assuredly one of the greatest triumphs of art—some will say the greatest—is to make our version of a truth or an experience the 'classic' version. Nature—unchanging human experience—may be dressed to such advantage that she is ever afterward remembered in that particular costume: even Pope, the 'last' of the Muse's sons and the last of a long line of critics, may hope to express some permanent aspects of life and art better than they have ever before been expressed.

Much of what has just been said in interpretation of Pope is also applicable, it will properly be felt, to such other seventeenth and eighteenth century humanists as Boileau, Dryden, Rapin, and Johnson. It has not been the purpose of this study to make out that Pope was really a romanticist in disguise and so to rescue him from the opprobrium of neo-classicism; but rather to do the fairer thing—assist in the rehabilitation of the maligned and misunderstood attitude.

One's estimate of Pope cannot, in the long run, be isolated from one's estimate of the tradition to which he fell heir, of the principles of art upon which he operated, of the philosophy of life to which he gave classic expression. One cannot evaluate Pope as the

les poètes, et en religion quand on ne pense pas comme les saints.' *Pensées*, Article I, No. 263.

[6] E-C, I, 195.

[7] Apropos of Christ's compiling the Lord's Prayer from the ancient euchologies of the Jews, Grotius remarks, 'Tam longe abfuit ipse Dominus Ecclesiae ab omni affectatione non necessariae novitatis.'

Augustans did without in some degree seeing substantial truth in the whole Augustan attitude.

I have spoken of rehabilitating the attitude. It should be clear in the light of previous pages that this attitude is by no means the caricature 'neo-' or 'pseudo-classicism' of the popular textbooks. The whole history of criticism is full of confusions in terminology; it is not only when we come to the distinction between *classic* and *romantic* that we have to walk warily. If by 'neo-classic' one means a literary judgment exclusively based on an appeal to the ancient classics and to the 'rules' thence derived, then there were few neo-classicists, and Pope was certainly not among those few. Pope, like Boileau, Dryden, Rapin, and Johnson, genuinely appreciated the classics and respected as canons useful in practice the codifications drawn up from these classics by the great critics. But none of these men was restricted to this. All five aimed at synthesizing the best critical thought and standards of their day. Pope, like the others, appeals to reason or common sense, to Nature, to taste, to 'inspiration,' as well as to classical precedent.[8] He can write appreciatively of Shakespeare, and differ with Homer and Madame Dacier, Homer's advocate.[9] He makes no attempt to set up a critical system more exact and uncompromising than life's. Accordingly, I must regard 'neo-classicist' literally interpreted as an inaccurate characterization of Pope and of the other Augustan synoptics. I should prefer to call them humanists or neo-humanists.[10] But 'humanist' itself is not the least ambiguous of terms; and in any case the nomenclature employed matters far less than the distinction.

Pope's eclecticism and synopticism were both abetted, no doubt, by his aversion to extremists, specialists, and virtuosi. The cultured gentleman, the man of the world (both Augustan ideals and Pope's ideals) was not a party man, not an enthusiast, much less a fanatic. He tried to 'see life steadily and see it whole'; was not to be whisked away by any particular wind of doctrine. Even his devotion to the classics must be classic, not romantic.

The aversion to pedants is, I think, to be regarded as subsumed under the aversion to specialists: pedants see things out of their proportions. Where to draw the line between profitable scholarship and pedantry is not readily apparent. Those who attack pedantry

---

[8] The evidence has been given in Chapter I.

[9] Mme. Dacier perhaps comes as near to the type neo-classicist as anyone. Cf. the *Postscript* to the *Odyssey* for Pope's differences with her.

[10] The Renaissance humanists were students of the classics, and took a classical, as contrasted to mediaeval, attitude toward life. Later so-called humanistic movements have involved opposition to naturalism on the one hand and theism on the other; have stressed reason and self-control. Pope was a humanist in almost any sense one might choose to employ.

run always the risk of attacking scholarship unawares. Pope cannot be acquitted of having attacked 'true' as well as 'false' studies; nor of exhibiting himself in the effort as a belletristic trifler. He does not emerge entirely unscathed from his combats with Bentley and Theobald; and his satire of Wanley strikes one as a little heavy. It may be with some justice that Dr. Johnson complains of 'unseasonable levity and affected gaiety' in the *Observations*, of 'too many appeals . . . to the ladies.'[11] The ease of the belletristic critic who wishes to be nothing if not literary is sometimes not unaptly to be described as 'the ease of a trifler.' Nor can Pope be acquitted of having ventured, somewhat light-heartedly from our modern point of view, upon his translating and editing. But there is much to be said on the other side. The ideal literary critic who combines the most accurate learning with the most sensitive feeling for poetry and the most acute and balanced judgment is still merely an ideal. Who shall edit a poetic classic, the scholar or the poet? If one must resort to so vicious a contrast, there are still many competent judges who will choose the poet. In the contemporary controversies between university savants and free-lance men of letters it is not always the savant who wins out. At any rate, scholarship and specialization have their grave risks; and it is useful that poets and educated general readers should disseminate the corrective emphasis upon literary values and universal truths.

One of Pope's charges against the pedant dunces is that they make no distinction between great and small, between major and minor writers.

> For me what Virgil, Pliny, may deny,
> Manilius or Solinus shall supply.
> For Attic phrase in Plato let them seek,
> I poach in Suidas for unlicensed Greek.[12]

It is fair to say that contemporary scholars are not to be exempted from magnifying those very minor authors who happen not before to have been 'edited.' And in literary Alexandrians like Mr. Carl Van Vechten one seems to discern a perverse and exotic fondness for writers who have in common their obscurity and their quality of being 'minor.' But Pope's friendships were with the greatest of his day, men like Swift and Berkeley and Atterbury; his principal reading was in the great poets, Virgil, Spenser, Milton, Dryden; he chose as subjects for his translating and editing the two greatest European poets, as they might fairly be regarded, Homer and

[11] *Lives*, III, 240.
[12] *Dunciad*, IV, 225-8.

Shakespeare. These associations seem to me significant: they point to a certain largeness of attitude, a certain catholicity in Pope to which adequate justice has never been done.

There are those who would grant the Preface to Homer this largeness, but deny it to the *Essay on Criticism*. I am not of their number. Pope's Preface and his *Observations* are 'appreciations,' not treatises. He is not attempting to legislate general canons of poetry, but to interpret sympathetically a great poet. Perhaps an 'appreciation' will always seem to some more catholic, as it is certainly more expansive, than a critical treatise. But this is, I venture to think, a distinction more specious than sound. Pope's contemporaries were conscious of no such 'progress' or 'evolution' in his critical theory, nor am I. The differences between the *Essay* and the Preface are to be accounted for by the difference between the *genres* and the general scheme of the works. The Preface is developed, in flowing and oratund fashion, from a single theme, Homer's invention; the *Essay* attempts, like the *Artes* of Horace, Vida, and Boileau, to pronounce upon a large number of particular points,—points, too, of varying importance. A stylistic contrast ensues: the *Essay* amasses detail; the detail is systematized, but in the final impression detail may be said to predominate over system: the Preface to Homer, like that to Shakespeare, effects a far more easy control of particulars. But these are differences in handling and plan, not in attitude.

If attention be called to the exaltation, in the Preface, of invention, or the creative power of the poet, the answer must be that the *Essay* also exalts creation. True, the word *invention* appears but once in the *Essay*; but its use is significant; those who write 'without invention's aid' are accused of being 'drily plain' and of having to resort to magisterial criticism, to writing 'dull receipts how poems may be made' instead of producing poetry. Nor should we be misled by the single appearance of the word: critical terminology has ever been unstable, and the literary man is not always scientifically consistent in his diction. *Invention* was not the only current name for the creative power; *wit* was a term at least as acceptable, though by Pope's time somewhat more ambiguous. In the *Essay on Criticism*, *wit* is frequently used to mean the creative power. The antithesis of invention and judgment in the Preface corresponds pretty fairly with that of wit and judgment in the *Essay*. Inspiration and discipline are both necessary to the production of great literature; and Pope never forgot this, whatever the terminology he employed to express the distinction. The *Essay* does not warrant any one in supposing that rules and recipes and models can make him a poet.

The defense of the author of the *Essay on Criticism* from the still repeated charge that the French rules composed his whole gospel[13] has certainly constituted an important part of this book. Other contentions which deserve a final recital are to the effect that Pope was no narrower than the other substantial Augustan critics, and that modern students have scarcely even yet done justice to the worth of Augustan criticism taken as a whole. An attempt has been made in this study to interpret and 'justify' the humanistic point of view,—the point of view of the *honnête homme*, the cultured gentleman who is suspicious of specialists but has a genuine love for great literature and makes an art of living. Being a humanist involves keeping one's balance between pedantry and dilettantism, confessedly a difficult and precarious position. I have not dared claim for Pope that he maintained this perfect balance. But I may claim for him that he comprehended the attitude, an attitude which is, in my opinion, inferior in dignity and value to few if any of the other possible attitudes toward life and art.

A few words in conclusion upon Pope's place among the critics. He belongs with the synoptic Augustans who sought to reconcile the criteria of particular critical schools; who felt that all the things they valued—reason, taste, Nature, the classics—must be thought of as converging. The body of Pope's critical writing is somewhat less than that of the others; but, on the other hand, it is much more considerable than is generally known: when one adds to the *Essay* and the Prefaces the lengthy, charming, almost forgotten *Observations on the Iliad*, the Epistle *To Augustus*, parts of the *Dunciad*, the relevant passages from the Letters, and the numerous dicta in Spence's *Anecdotes*, one has a pretty extensive as well as varied corpus.

It cannot fairly be claimed that Pope was, in the narrow sense of the word, a systematic critic; but, if one stops to consider, one finds few critics indeed who are. Most criticism is 'occasional.' Even Dr. Johnson's *Lives*, which, by their extent and the variety of their subjects, give their writer an appearance of superior system, constitute a piece of hack work intended to fill out a 'set' of the poets; and Dryden's critical essays, prefaces occasioned by the poems and plays he was publishing, are far from expressing any attitude of exact consistency. The *Essay on Criticism* is as systematic as the other *Artes*, and Pope as systematic as most other critics.

The meaning of *originality* has already been considered at length more than once in our argument. It will be sufficient here to say that Pope is an original critic in the only sense that a humanist

---

13 See Hamelius, 105, for the charge.

would care to be. He did not propound any new and startling theory or attempt to reverse the estimate in which the world's literary masterpieces had been held; but he did make his own honest, individual adaptation of the critical doctrine of civilization, his own synthesis of the best contemporary thought, his own application to what he read of the standards thus derived. He was not an echo of other men's opinions: he called no man, not even Dryden or Boileau or Horace, master. He is like other humanistic critics (they were in the same tradition); but he is not a copy of them.

I should not undertake to say that Pope's criticism is, all things considered, as rich, as stimulating, as important as that of Dryden or that of Johnson. But I do propose for serious consideration the thesis that Pope ranks third among English critics of the Augustan age, and that his 'third' is a nearer approach to his superiors, a closer approximation, than contemporary criticism has yet conceded.

BIBLIOGRAPHY OF WORKS CITED

ABBOTT, EDWIN. *A Concordance to the Works of Pope.* New York, 1875.

ARNOLD, MATTHEW. *Mixed Essays.* New York, 1883. *On the Study of Celtic Literature and on Translating Homer.* New York, 1883.

BALDWIN, CHARLES S. *Ancient Rhetoric and Poetic.* New York, 1924.

BOBERTAG, FELIX. 'Pope's Essay on Criticism.' *Englische Studien*, III (1880), pp. 43-91.

BOILEAU, NICOLAS. *Oeuvres Complètes*, ed. Daunou, 4 vols. Paris, 1825-1826.

BOSWELL, JAMES. *The Life of Samuel Johnson*, ed. G. B. Hill. 6 vols. Oxford, 1887.

BROWN, JOSEPH. *The Critical Opinions of Samuel Johnson*, Princeton, 1926.

BRADLEY, A. C. *Shakespearean Tragedy.* 2nd ed., London, 1905.

BRUNOT, F. *Histoire de la Langue Française des Origines.* Vol. III, Première Partie. Paris, 1905.

BURNET, THOMAS and DUCKETT, GEORGE. *Homerides.* London, 1715.

CHARLTON, H. B. *Castelvetro's Theory of Poetry.* Manchester, 1913.

CLARK, A. F. B. *Boileau and the French Classical Critics in England.* Paris, 1926.

COOPER, LANE. *The Poetics of Aristotle.* Boston, 1923.

CORY, H. E. *Edmund Spenser.* Berkeley, 1917.

DACIER, MME. *L'Iliade, Traduite en Français.* 4 vols. Paris, 1756.

DE MAAR, HARKO. *A History of Modern English Romanticism.* Vol. I. London, 1924.

DENNIS, JOHN. *Remarks upon Mr. Pope's Translation of Homer.* London, 1717. *Select Works.* 2 vols. London, 1718-1721.

DEQUINCEY, THOMAS. *Works*, ed. D. Masson. 14 vols. Edinburgh, 1889-1890.

DIXON, W. MACNEILE. *English Epic and Heroic Poetry.* London, 1912.

DRYDEN, JOHN. *Works*, ed. G. Saintsbury. 18 vols. Edinburgh, 1889-1890 (See also under Ker).

DURHAM, WILLARD H. ed. *Critical Essays of the Eighteenth Century.* New Haven, 1915.

FÉNELON, FRANÇOIS. *Lettre à l'Académie*, ed. A. Cahen. Paris, 1899.

FINSLER, G. A. *Homer in der Neuzeit, von Dante bis Goethe.* Leipzig, 1912.

FISKE, GEORGE C. *Lucilius and Horace.* Madison, Wisconsin, 1920.

FONTENELLE, B. *Oeuvres.* 8 vols. Paris, 1790-1792.

FRYE, PROSSER HALL. *Literary Reviews and Criticisms.* New York, 1908.

GAYLEY, C. M. and KURTZ, B. *Methods and Materials of Literary Criticism.* Boston, 1920.

GILDON, CHARLES. *A New Rehearsal.* London, 1714.

GOAD, CAROLINE. *Horace in the English Literature of the Eighteenth Century.* New Haven, 1918.

GOETHE, J. W. *Maxims and Reflections*, tr. by Bailey Saunders. London, 1892.

GOSSE, EDMUND. *A History of Eighteenth Century Literature.* London, 1891. *From Shakespeare to Pope.* Cambridge (England), 1885.

GRIFFITH, REGINALD. *Alexander Pope; A Bibliography.* Vol. I, Part I. Austin, Texas, 1922.

HAMELIUS, P. *Die Kritik in der Englischen Literatur des 17 und 18 Jahrhunderts.* Leipzig, 1897.

HAVENS, RAYMOND D. *The Influence of Milton in English Poetry.* Cambridge, Mass., 1922.

HILLHOUSE, JAMES T. *The Grub-street Journal.* Durham, North Carolina, 1928.

HORACE. *The Satires, Epistles, and De Arte Poetica,* ed. E. C. Wickham. Oxford, 1903.

HOUSTON, PERCY H. *Doctor Johnson: A Study in Eighteenth Century Humanism.* Cambridge, Mass., 1923.

JOHNSON, SAMUEL. *Lives of the English Poets,* ed. G. B. Hill. 3 vols. Oxford, 1905.

KER, W. P., ed. *Essays of Dryden.* 2 vols. Oxford, 1903.

LANSON, G. 'Sur l'Influence de la Philosophie Cartesienne sur la Littérature Française.' *Revue de Métaphysique et de Morale,* IV, (517-50).

LEATHER, MARY. 'Pope as a Student of Milton.' *Englische Studien,* XXV, 398-410.

LE BOSSU, ABBÉ. *Traité du Poème Épique.* 2nd ed. Paris, 1677.

LOUNSBURY, THOMAS R. *Shakespeare as a Dramatic Artist.* New York, 1901. *Studies in Chaucer.* 3 vols. New York, 1892. *The Text of Shakespeare.* New York, 1906. Unless otherwise specified, references to 'Lounsbury' are to this last work.

LYTTLETON, GEORGE. *Dialogues of the Dead.* 2nd ed., London, 1760.

MACAULAY, G. C. *James Thomson.* London, 1908.

MANDEVILLE, BERNARD. *The Fable of the Bees,* ed. F. B. Kaye. 2 vols. Oxford, 1924.

MEAD, WILLIAM E. *The Versification of Pope in its Relation to the Seventeenth Century.* Leipzig, 1889.

MOORE, CECIL A. 'Shaftesbury and the Ethical Poets in England.' *P.M.L.A.,* XXI, 264-325.

NISARD, J. M. N. D. *Histoire de la Littérature Française.* 4 vols. Paris, 1844-1861.

NITCHIE, ELIZABETH. *Vergil and the English Poets.* New York, 1919.

OLDMIXON, JOHN. *The Arts of Logic and Rhetoric.* London, 1728.

PAUL, H. G. *John Dennis.* New York, 1910.

PERRAULT, CHARLES. *Parallèle des Anciens et des Modernes.* 2 vols. Amsterdam, 1693.

PERRY, THOMAS S. *English Literature in the Eighteenth Century.* New York, 1883.

POPE, ALEXANDER. *The Iliad of Homer.* 6 vols. London, 1715-1720. *The Odyssey of Homer.* 5 vols. London, 1725-1726. *The Works of Shakespeare.* 6 vols. London, 1725. *Works of Pope,* ed. W. Elwin and W. J. Courthope. 10 vols. London, 1871-89. This, still the standard edition of Pope, is referred to as E-C. *Works of Pope,* ed. J. Warton. 9 vols. London, 1797.

RAPIN, RENE. *Whole Critical Works* (tr. by Basil Kennett; 1st ed., 1705). 2 vols. 3rd ed., London, 1731.

REYNOLDS, SIR JOSHUA. *Discourses,* ed. Burnet. London, 1842.

RIGAULT, H. *Histoire de la Querelle des Anciens et des Modernes.* Paris, 1856.

RUFFHEAD, OWEN. *Life of Alexander Pope.* London, 1769.

RYMER, THOMAS. *A Short View of Tragedy*. London, 1693.

SAINTSBURY, GEORGE. *A History of Criticism*. 3 vols. Edinburgh, 1900-1904. *Historical Manual of English Prosody*. London, 1914.

SCHELLING, FELIX. *Ben Jonson and the Classical School*. Baltimore, 1898.

SCOTT, JOHN A. *The Unity of Homer*. Berkeley, California, 1921.

SCHÜCKING, LEVIN L. *Character Problems in Shakespeare*. New York, 1922.

SELLAR, WILLIAM. *Horace and the Elegiac Poets*. 2nd ed., Oxford, 1899.

SMITH, D. NICHOL. *Eighteenth Century Essays on Shakespeare*. Glasgow, 1903.

SMITH, LOGAN PEARSALL. *Four Words*. S.P.E. Tract no. 17. Oxford, 1924.

Spectator, The, ed. G. A. Aiken. 8 vols. London, 1898.

SPENCE, JOSEPH. *Anecdotes*, ed. S. W. Singer. London, 1820.

SPINGARN, JOEL E., ed. *Critical Essays of the Seventeenth Century*. 3 vols. Oxford, 1908. *Literary Criticism in the Renaissance*. 5th impression, New York, 1925.

STAPFER, PAUL. *Shakespeare and Classical Antiquity* (tr. by E. J. Carey). London, 1880.

SWIFT, JONATHAN. *Correspondence*, ed. F. E. Ball. 6 vols. London, 1910-1914. *Prose Works*, ed. Temple Scott. 12 vols. London, 1897-1908.

TERRASSON, JEAN. *Dissertation Critique sur l'Iliade*. 2 vols. Paris, 1715.

VIAL, F. and DENISE, L. *Idées et Doctrines Littéraires du XVIIe Siècle*. 4th ed., Paris, 1925. *Idées et Doctrines Littéraires du XVIIIe Siècle*. 3rd ed., Paris, 1924.

VOLTAIRE, FRANÇOIS-MARIE. *Oeuvres Complètes*, ed. L. Moland. 52 vols. Paris, 1877-1885.

WAKEFIELD, GILBERT, ed. *The Odyssey of Homer*. Tr. by Pope. 5 vols. London, 1796.

WARTON, JOSEPH. *An Essay on the Genius and Writings of Pope*. 2 vols. 5th ed., London, 1806.

WINCHILSEA, ANNE, COUNTESS OF. *Poems*, ed. Myra Reynolds. Chicago, 1903.

INDEX

Abbott, E. A., 66.
Academy, French, 52.
Achilles' Shield, 81, 110-11.
Actors, Pope on, 143-4.
Adaptation of sound to sense, 59-61.
Addison, 3, 5, 7, 11, 54, 58, 70, 87, 96-7, 168, 178, 182-3, 184, 223, 240, 243, 244, 251, 252, 259-60, 272.
Aeschylus, 190.
Akenside, 270.
Alabaster, Wm., 236.
Alcander, Pope's epic, 68, 70, 76, 170, 192, 241.
Alexander's Feast, 60.
Alexandrine, The use of, 64.
Allatius, L., 80.
Allegory in Homer, 81, 100-2.
Anachronisms in Shakespeare, 147.
Ancients, Admiration for, 17-18, 25.
Andreini, 243.
Antony and Cleopatra, 151-2.
Aonius Palearius, 207.
Aquinas, St. Thos., 264.
Ariosto, 143, 204, 230, 232, 235.
Arbuthnot, Dr., 190.
Aristotle, 6, 30, 32, 47, 117, 142-3, 188.
Arnold, Matthew, 7, 24, 52, 61, 225, 268.
Art, Function of, 96.
Art of Sinking in Poetry, 163-71.
Ascham, R., 201, 239.
As You Like It, 156-9.
Atalantis, 216.
Athelwold, 72.
Atterbury, Bp., 51, 54, 70, 184, 245; on Shakespeare, 122, 139.
Aulus Gellius, 80, 201.
Ayres, C. E., 272.

Bacon, Francis, 54, 55, 239.
Baldwin, C. S., 2.
Barnes, Joshua, 80.
Barrow, Isaac, 54, 184.
Bathos, 163-71.

Bathurst, Lord, 187.
Batteux, Abbé, 37.
Battle of the Books, 163.
Bayle, 216-7.
Beaumont and Fletcher, 144, 237.
Beaumont, Sir J., 248, 250.
'Beauties' of Shakespeare, 149-59.
Beers, H. A., 229.
Bembo, 206.
Benson, W., 180.
Bentley, R., 76, 82, 120, 124, 178, 181-2, 241, 245, 275.
Berkeley, Bp., 191, 266-7.
Betterton, 69-70, 110.
Bible and Homer, 91-2, 106.
Blackmore, Sir R., 68, 164, 167, 170, 171, 176.
Blake, W., 266.
Blank verse, Pope and, 57-9.
Bobertag, F., 5, 7, 19, 199, 203.
Boece, H., 130.
Boileau, 2, 3, 4, 5, 7, 8, 11, 13, 16-19, 20, 26, 27, 35, 40, 211-13, 218, 220, 272, 274.
Bolingbroke, 54, 56, 120, 152, 199, 261, 267-8.
Bombast, Elizabethan, 139-40.
Booth, B., 71.
Bossu, Abbé le, 3, 22, 67, 81, 99, 100, 107, 168, 200, 218, 219, 230.
Bouhours, Père, 4.
Bradley, A. C., 136, 137, 139-40, 148.
Broome, W., 79, 116, 165, 166, 186.
Browne, W., 235.
Brunetière, 27.
Brutus, Pope's epic, 59, 68-9.
Buckinghamshire, Duke of, See Mulgrave.
Burke, Edmund, 208, 268.
Burnet, T., 77.
Butler, S. (1612-80), 54, 253.

Caesura, Position of, 62-3.
Callimachus, 188.
Caracci, The, 112.

Caravaggio, 110.
Carew, 251-2.
Cartwright, W., 248.
Case, Arthur E., 255.
Castelvetro, 47.
'Catachresis,' 167.
Catalogues (in Homer), 81.
Cato, 260.
Catullus, 191-2.
Caxton, 174.
Chapelain, 66, 213, 220.
Chapman, G., 78, 114, 139, 186, 236, 237.
Characters in *Iliad*, 103-4.
Charron, 26, 214-5.
Chaucer, 51, 222-7, 260.
Chesterfield, 184.
Cibber, C., 165, 170, 171, 179-80.
Cicero, 10, 14, 65, 185, 201, 257.
Clarendon, 54.
Clark, A. F. B., 17, 212.
Cleveland, J., 248.
Clowns, in Shakespeare, 140.
Coleridge, 7, 32, 135.
Comedy of Errors, 147, 150, 154.
Comic element, in Homer, 94, 118; in Shakespeare, 141.
Conceits, 150.
Congreve, 43, 54, 184, 238, 255-6.
Cooper, Lane, 142.
Corbet, Bp., 248.
Coriolanus, 145.
Corneille, 210.
Correggio, 112.
Cory, H. E., 231, 233, 235.
Courthope, W. J., 233, 260.
Crabbe, 156, 233.
Crashaw, 206, 249-50.
Creech, T., 12.
Cuperus, 80.
Cyder, 167.
Cymbeline, 151, 156, 159.

D'Ablancourt, 198.
Dacier, Mme., 16, 78, 79, 80, 81, 83, 84-7, 90-2, 94, 105, 107, 186, 209, 274.
Daniel, Dean, 165.
Daniel, S., 236.
Dante, 204, 232.
D'Aubignac, 30, 35.
Davenant, 68, 213, 248.
Davies, Sir J., 248.

Decorum, of style, 61-2; in Homer, 104-6; in Shakespeare, 136-7.
Defoe, 161, 165, 167, 265.
De Lyra, 174.
Denham, Sir J., 63, 226, 251-2.
Dennis, J., 4, 11, 28, 29, 30, 34, 82, 85, 135, 146, 165, 171, 190, 233.
De Pons, 85, 93.
De Quincey, 186, 208-9, 212.
Descartes, 18, 26, 35, 83, 84, 257.
Description, Homer's, 108-10.
Deucalion, 68.
Dialects, Homeric, 113.
Diction, Pope's doctrine of, 51-7.
Dictionary, Authorities for a, 53-4.
Dionysius of Halicarnassus, 13, 60, 113.
Dodsley, R., 72.
Don Quixote, 62, 85.
Dorset, Lord, 254-5.
Drake, Sir F., 132.
Drama, Pope's attitude toward, 69-73.
Drayton, 236, 248.
Dryden, 2, 4, 11, 12, 19, 20, 22-4, 25, 34, 51, 53, 54, 55, 56, 60, 64, 66, 67, 68, 76, 82, 113, 116, 130, 133, 137, 138, 139, 146, 148, 172, 184, 188, 189, 192, 194, 198, 211, 222-6, 228, 230, 234, 236, 243, 246, 247, 252-3, 270, 272, 274.
Duckett, G., 165.
Dunces, The, 161-84.
Dunciad, 171-84, 196, 241.
Duport, 107.
Durham, W. H., 17.

Elision (Pope's *caesura*), 65-6.
Eloisa to Abelard, 155.
Elwin, W., 32.
Ennius, 195.
Epic, Pope's attitude toward, 67-9.
Epithets, Homeric, 92, 112.
Erasmus, 14, 203-4.
Essay on Criticism, 1-41, 276-7.
Essay on Man, 156, 157, 191, 201, 208, 213, 214, 264, 267, 268; Voltaire on, 217.
Etheredge, 238, 258.
Euripides, 190, 211.
Eusden, 165, 166, 167.
Eustathius, 79, 80, 86, 94, 101, 115.
Expletives, Use of, 63.

DATE DUE

JUN 4			
GAYLORD			PRINTED IN U.S.A.